The Guilty Innocent

Shannon Adamcik

The Guilty Innocent

By Shannon Adamcik

Published by Shannon Adamcik

Printed in the USA.

e Book is available at online retailers.

ISBN-10: 0-9882409-1-2
ISBN-13: 978-0-9882409-1-9

For Lacey
Who said, “Do something!”
And For Sean and Jamie
Who let me

There are close to three thousand children in the United States who are sentenced to die in prison. Some were sentenced when they were just thirteen years old. They are labeled “The Worst of the Worst” by the criminal justice system, but many are first time offenders. One quarter of these children did not commit murder or intend to commit murder. But due to their age, and the sentence, they will serve the longest prison terms in American history.

The United States is the only country in the world that sentences children to Life Without Parole.

TABLE OF CONTENTS

PART FOUR: THE EVIDENCE

PART FIVE: THE VIDEOTAPE

PART SIX: THE TRIALS

Preface

I decided to write this book while I was sitting in the office of attorney Ken Lyons. As the mother of a sixteen-year-old boy sentenced to Life Without Parole for the murder of a friend and classmate, my story is not an easy one to tell. Or, as was perfectly illustrated to me in Mr. Lyons office, to understand.

Mr. Lyons was one of the attorneys my husband, Sean, and I consulted with in the aftermath of our son's arrest, trial and conviction. At the time we were being sued by the victim's family.

After one particular consultation, Mr. Lyons announced that there was something he needed to tell us. "It might not be my place," he said, "but I need to remind you both, you have two other children besides Torey." He went on to tell us that the best thing we could do was to let our now 17-year-old son go, and concentrate on our two remaining children, Jamie who was 15, and Lacey who was 19. Get them into counseling, give them all of the love and attention we could, and try to get them through this intact, because clearly they were going to have problems. He said that Torey's destiny was out of our hands, and the sooner we realized that the better off we'd all be, including Torey, who now had to make his own way.

For a second it sounded reasonable. Words are like that. Mr. Lyons meant well. He spoke with good intentions, but he did not understand. What he said was bull----.

Sean and I have three children. We love each and every one of them, and we are going to do every single thing in our power to get all three of our children through this intact. No one's getting left behind. That is not an option.

This was not the first time we'd heard that particular speech. Almost anyone who feels close enough to talk about the subject with us has mentioned it to us at one time or another. Mr. Lyons did a good job. He was honest and persuasive and presented his case to us as a skilled attorney would. I knew right then that I was going to write a book. I wanted people to understand.

Any parent willing to offer such a solution as a viable option needs to stop and consider which child they have at home they could turn lose in an emergency. It simply does not work that way. Every parent facing the loss of one of their children is going to fight for all of their children. It just doesn't always appear that way from the outside looking in. And the kindest and best support you could offer is to make it easier for them, not to let go, but to hang on.

When we hear about the murder of a child, we can barely imagine the despair and horror that the child's parents must be feeling. For a brief moment we may think, "What if this was *my* child?" but we cannot fully imagine how we would go on if it were. It is something that many parents have spent seconds contemplating, but most will never have to live through.

I had imagined it. I was one of those parents who always feared something happening to one of my children, anything from kidnapping to car accidents. But I never once considered the position that I now live in: mother of the *accused.*

My feelings of loss and devastation are real. They are valid. And in fact they are surprisingly similar to what I would have felt had Torey been killed. Because that is exactly what it feels like. The pain that I feel can only be felt by a parent who has lost a child. There is simply nothing else to compare it to.

Our love for our children is a love with no bounds, an ocean with no end, and when disaster strikes, a pain that never goes away. Everyone has been through loss. We all know grief. I have lost both of my parents, and a brother. I know about loss and grief. This is very different.

I do not know the pain of losing a child to disease, of watching an innocent baby suffer, of horrible accidents, or suicide, or war, or any number of other tragedies. Those situations are not mine. But I know my pain. I can tell you everything about it. It has to do with my child. A child who at sixteen-years-old was arrested for a murder he did not commit and sentenced to life without parole.

How do you survive watching as your baby, the child in your arms, is taken from you, denied any form of human sympathy or consideration? Locked up and told there is no hope of redemption, value, or ever again belonging to the human race? How can I survive that and why would I want to?

My pain is about my child.

In the victim impact statements we were told there was only one victim. I say that is not true. We were all victims. My son is innocent. He did not kill anyone; he did not intend to kill anyone. Would I be less of a victim if he were guilty? I don't think so. No parent raises a child to be a murderer. No parent imagines their child is capable of such violence.

Our son Torey was a wonderful child, full of laughter, a gift to our home and our lives. And his new friend Brian seemed okay too. The truth is, on the surface, neither boy should have ever been involved in something like this. Both Torey and Brian came from loving homes. They both had a religious upbringing. They both did well in school. Neither boy was involved in drugs or alcohol. To see the differences…the signs…in the boys you would have had to be willing to peel the onion…to look beneath the surface…because one of the boys, despite everything, had a serious, serious problem. And there were people who knew about it, or should have.

Cassie, a sixteen-year-old girl, was murdered. That is a tragedy that most people will never experience. My son is gone too, and I will spend the rest of my life watching him die a slow and painful death in prison because of Brian Draper. Brian killed Cassie quickly; he is killing Torey slowly. I am not sure which is worse.

We are able to visit our son in prison. My other son, my daughter, my husband and I. We go as often as we can. When Torey smiles, and holds his head up, I thank God that he is with us. But when Torey hangs his head and shows his hopelessness, his despair, I do not know how we can get him through the next ten, twenty, forty years and why? What kind of a life is this?

One night I was home alone when there was a knock at the door. I never answer unless I know who is there, so I looked out the window. Parked in front of the house was what looked like an undercover police car and my legs gave way. I could not move and I could not get up to open the door. I lay shaking on the floor thinking they were there to tell me that Torey was gone. That he'd been killed. It took several minutes before I could sit up, and by then whoever was at the door was gone. I went to the phone and I called the prison. I was told that Torey was fine.

I am grateful to have my son. I am grateful to have hope. I do experience moments of despair, when I wonder if it would have been better had Torey been killed that night as Cassie was. But really, I could never face that. When there is life there is hope, and I have to hang on to that. I am sorry for Cassie. I am so, so sorry for Cassie.

This book is about my experience, not Torey's. These are my words, not his. I will refer to specific events, times, places and people, but only as I experienced them. My memory is not perfect but I will be as accurate as possible. The names of some of the minor children involved have been changed.

PART ONE

Cassie

CHAPTER ONE

The Girl on the Video

The girl on the video was standing in front of an open locker inside of a school. She wore a green and white sweatshirt over a tank top and jeans and her straight, black hair was so long that it hung past her waist. She did not look directly at the boy who was filming her, but concentrated on arranging the items inside of her locker.

The camera read 8:28 a.m. The boy with the video camera had been making a circle of the three-story school building, moving up and down the hallways, filming students from the waist down as he walked with his camera held next to his hip.

It was a strategically located position. He wasn't trying to hide the fact that he was filming. He just liked the view the camera picked up from that angle.

When he saw the girl with the long hair he stopped. She was the reason he'd brought the camera to school that day. To capture her on film.

"Hey look. It's Cassie," he said pointing his camera at her and circling back around. "Hello Cassie. I'm, uh, getting you on tape."

The girl glanced up at him but did not respond.

"Say hi, please," he coaxed.

"Hi," she answered.

" 'k. See ya..." The boy started to walk off, but turned back around and asked, "Wait... Have you seen Torey?"

"Huh uh." She shook her head no, her long hair cascading.

"He's supposed to meet me here at seven...thirty. It's eight nineteen. He's an hour late."

The girl made no comment.

"You...You don't even care do you?" he asked.

"Not really."

"Okay," he laughed, "See ya."

She turned her head and smiled directly into the camera. "Bye," she said.

The boy continued down the hall.

Cassie Jo Stoddart was the girl on the video. Chosen not because she was a beautiful sixteen-year-old girl with long dark hair that caught reddish highlights in the sun. Not because she loved flip-flops and had just had her bellybutton pierced. But because fate simply placed her in his hands.

Cassie lived with her mother, Anna, her mother's boyfriend of nine years, Victor Price, and her younger brother Andrew. She had an older sister, Kristi, but Kristi had already moved out and on with her life.

Cassie and her brother Andrew had lived with their maternal grandparents, Paul and Josephina Cisneros for most of their childhood, but they always maintained a good relationship with their mother. Anna hadn't had an easy life, but she loved her children and she wanted them back with her. Cassie and Andrew had been living with Anna for the past two years and things were going well.

Cassie was quiet at school, rather shy, but she had good friends who cared about her, people she could be herself around. Cassie was not into drugs, and she considered smoking a waste of time. She was a good student with goals. She wanted to be an attorney someday.

Cassie had a *Myspace* account where she wrote about her likes and dislikes. There were only a couple of things that Cassie disliked: judgmental people and drama queens. But there was a whole page full of things that she loved. Penguins and turtles, Hershey bars and Skittles, permanent markers, hemp bracelets, purple monkeys, water, snow, hail, snakes, summertime. Warm blankets right out of the dryer and deep thoughts. She liked her name, but she did not like the fact that it was a "blonde, cheerleader-type name." Cassie was Hispanic and proud of it.

Cassie had a boyfriend. Matt Beckham. Matt, like Cassie, was sixteen-years-old and a junior at Pocatello High School. Cassie and Matt had known each other since junior high, but they had only begun dating within the last five months or so, spending most of their time together after school at Cassie's house.

Sometimes Cassie and Matt quarreled. Matt smoked pot and Cassie wanted him to stop, but it was the only thing they argued about. Other than that they got along fine.

The weekend of September 22, 2006, Cassie was going to house-sit for her aunt and uncle at their home located in the north end of Pocatello. Cassie's uncle, Frank Contreras worked for a construction company in Jackpot, Nevada. His wife Allison and their kids were going to meet him in Jackpot for the weekend before traveling back to Pocatello together Sunday afternoon. Cassie had house-sat for the couple before and she was looking forward to doing it again. She would be taking care of the family's three cats and two dogs, a responsibility that she took seriously.

Cassie liked her aunt's house. Although on a public street, it was relatively isolated in a rural area of the city, and it was large and spacious. Cassie was going to add the money she earned this weekend, around sixty dollars, to what she had already saved for a car. Drivers' training was almost over and Cassie was looking forward to getting her driver's license.

On Friday afternoon Cassie's mother drove Cassie and Matt to the house on Whispering Cliffs and dropped them off, alone together. Anna had allowed Matt to house-sit with Cassie before and judging by what she later told the detectives, she expected him to stay this weekend as well. On the way there she lectured the two children. They were not to invite anyone over and there was to be no partying. Anna watched as Cassie unlocked the front door of the house and stepped inside before pulling her white Jeep Cherokee out of the driveway and heading home.

It was the last time Anna Stoddart ever saw her daughter alive.

Later that evening, Anna called to check on Cassie but there was no answer. She waited a few minutes and called back. This time Cassie picked up the phone. She told her mother that Matt was still with her and that everything was fine. Cassie said she had not answered the phone previously because she'd not heard it ringing. She indicated that she was having problems with the phone, or at least one of the phones in the house, and it seemed to be true. Anna called Cassie all day the next day, Saturday, but she never received an answer.

Anna had two coupons from the casino in Fort Hall, near Pocatello. One coupon was for ten dollars, the other for fifteen. Anna and Victor drove to Fort Hall Saturday morning and redeemed the coupons for beer and cigarettes. Anna also spent time with her mother that afternoon digging potatoes, but for some reason she did not check on Cassie when she could not reach her by phone.

Perhaps Anna thought that Matt was with Cassie. That is what she told Deputy Karen Hatch, the first officer to respond to the scene after Cassie was discovered. But by Saturday night Anna knew that Matt wasn't with Cassie, and that he too was having problems reaching her.

On Friday night Matt's mother picked him up at eleven p.m. and took him home. Matt tried to call Cassie numerous times on

Saturday, but like Anna, he could not get through. Finally he tried calling Cassie at home on Saturday night. Anna answered the phone when he called. Matt told Anna that he was looking for Cassie and that he had been trying unsuccessfully to reach her all day. Anna said she was having the same problem, but she did not seem overly concerned. Anna was outside with friends, smoking on her back patio when she talked to Matt. The phone beeped a couple of times, indicating a call on the other line, but Anna did not check to see who it was.

Sunday morning, Anna again attempted to call her daughter, with no luck. She cooked a late breakfast for herself and Victor. Her son Andrew had spent the night at a friend's house and hadn't returned home yet. After breakfast Victor went next door to the neighbor's house to watch NASCAR. When he came home for a beer Anna said it was time they went to check on Cassie. She was worried. The Contreras's usually arrived home around 10:30 a.m. They should have heard something by now.

Victor went next door to retrieve his cigarettes and they headed to the Contreras's home. It was approximately 1:30 p.m.

At the same time that Anna and Victor where leaving, the Contreras's were pulling into their driveway. Frank and Allison Contreras had their two teenage daughters, Kelsey and Brittany and their five-year-old son Cyrus with them, as well as one of their daughter's friends, Sadie Atkinson.

Frank parked his Dodge Durango in front of the garage and Kelsey, his eldest stepdaughter, got out of the vehicle and grabbed her bags from the back of the truck. Kelsey tried to enter the two-story house through the south basement door but it was locked, so Frank manually opened the overhead garage door for her. Inside the garage there were four interior doors and Frank noticed that they were all opened and some were partially unhinged, but for some reason this did not seem to concern him. Two of the doors led to the residence and Frank allowed Kelsey to enter the house through the door that led to the stairwell going up.

Cyrus had stuck a jawbreaker up his nose in the car. Allison immediately carried him through the other entrance into the home, which led to the downstairs bathroom to help him remove it, while Frank started unloading the car in the garage.

When Kelsey entered the house she noticed broken pieces of glass at the bottom of the stairs. Her immediate thought was that one of the dogs must have knocked something over. She carefully stepped around the glass and went upstairs to her room where she placed her bags.

While she was in her room, Kelsey noticed that the television set in the upstairs living room was on. She thought that perhaps Cassie was still in the house and that they could hang out together. Kelsey entered the hallway and headed toward the living room looking for Cassie.

That is where she found her. Cassie was lying on her back on the living room floor covered with blood. Her long hair was fanned out behind her and her face was tilted to one side. Cassie's arms were slightly raised above her head and her elbows were bent.

Kelsey stood, staring down at her cousin in disbelief. She turned and ran down the stairs. Frank was still in the garage unloading the vehicle. Kelsey flew out of the downstairs door and yelled to her father to go look upstairs. She thought that Cassie was dead.

Frank took one look at his stepdaughter and ran into the house. As soon as he opened the door his dog MoJo came rushing out. Frank grabbed him by the collar and pushed him back in, not understanding why the dog was not secured in his kennel in the backyard. He was yelling for Allison to call 911. Allison headed up the stairs not sure what was going on. Frank let the dog out of the back door at the top of the stairs and quickly kenneled him. Allison grabbed the phone and entered the living room where Frank joined her.

Cassie was lying on their living room floor, dead. She had obviously been stabbed multiple times. There was blood on one of her legs, on her chest, and blood flowing from one of her wounds had pooled around her neck. She looked swollen.

Allison dialed 911. She told the operator there was a body. They'd been gone for the weekend. They just found the body in their living room. The operator asked Allison to check for breathing and a pulse. Allison said that she was not breathing. It was her niece and she was covered in blood and there was a lot of blood around her! Allison reached out a hand and felt Cassie's shoulder. She told the operator that the body was cold to the touch and the stomach was bloated.

In a stunned, hysterical voice Allison said that she believed one of Cassie's fingers might have been severed. The operator told her to exit the house and wait for the police to arrive.

Still on the phone with the 911 dispatcher, Allison ran out of the house through the front door and onto the deck overlooking the front yard. Kelsey had told the other children what she found inside the house and they were all gathered together on the front lawn. Allison told them to stay there.

That's when Anna and Victor arrived. Anna noticed the kids on the lawn when they pulled into the driveway. The Stoddart's had their windows down and Frank yelled over at them, "Something's wrong with Cassie, I think she's dead."

Victor screamed and ran toward the house with Anna following him. As Victor opened the door to the house someone yelled that Cassie was in the living room. When Victor got there, he saw Cassie lying on the floor covered in blood. He heard Anna coming up behind him so he turned around and pushed her into the kitchen where he restrained her. Anna was screaming to see her daughter, pulling away from him, but Victor could not let Anna see Cassie like that. No.

Victor pulled Anna out of the house. She was hysterical, screaming, "My baby is dead! My baby is dead!" over and over again. Someone tried to give her a cigarette to calm her down, but she pushed it aside and crumpled to the ground in shock and disbelief. They were told the police were on their way.

Anna and Victor went back to their jeep. Anna took Frank's cell phone and called Matt. When he answered the phone she screamed at him, "What the F--- did you do to my daughter?" Victor took the phone from Anna and told Matt that Cassie was dead. Matt did not respond and Victor dropped the phone.

Deputy Karen Hatch was the closest officer on duty when the call came through. A tiny, serious woman, she was the first to arrive on the scene, but was followed closely by two Pocatello EMS Paramedics.

Deputy Karen Hatch asked the family how they entered the residence, and she and the two paramedics followed the same route that Kelsey and Frank had taken into the home. At the bottom of the stairs, just inside the door, they observed a large amount of broken glass on the floor. They turned to the right and went up the stairs. At the top of the stairs the kitchen was to their left and an outside exit was directly in front of them. They turned to the right and down a hallway that ran parallel to the stairs and entered the living room.

Rod Anderson, one of the paramedics, reached out and touched Cassie's left shoulder. He stated the body was livid. They exited the residence the same way they entered it and contac… Deputy Coroner Kim Quick.

Next to arrive were two Idaho State Police officers, Rausch and Barnes. Officer Barnes was posted near the front door where he remained until Detective Toni Vollmer arrived from the Bannock County Sheriff's Department and took charge of the investigation. She released him to help with traffic control. Deputy Hatch and Officer Rausch conducted a quick and careful search of the perimeter of the residence.

Deputy Hatch then collected written statements from Frank, Allison and Kelsey Contreras. Allison told Deputy Hatch that she thought that Matt Beckham, Cassie's boyfriend, was supposed to be staying with Cassie for the weekend.

Anna confirmed the information. She described how she dropped Cassie and Matt off at the residence at approximately five p.m. on Friday afternoon; spoke with Cassie on the phone around nine p.m. Friday night; Cassie told her at that time that Matt was with her and everything was fine, and she hadn't heard from Cassie since.

Anna said that she did not know of anyone else, besides Matt, who would have been at the residence, and she was unsure of how or when Matt left because he did not have a vehicle.

Allison called Anna's parents, the Cisneros, who notified the rest of the family. Soon Paul and Josephina Cisneros, and Andrew and Kristi Stoddart, arrived at the scene, as did Anna's brother, Paul Cisneros Jr., his wife Sandra, and Anna's Grandparents, the Alverez's.

Anna was experiencing a gamut of emotions. She cried, she screamed, she lay on the ground pounding her fists. Victor was also visibly upset. Anna's family tried to comfort her, and each other, but there was really nothing that anyone could do.

Numerous police personnel, members of the prosecutor's office, forensic specialist, and EMT paramedics arrived throughout the day. A Catholic priest was called.The residence and surrounding yard was cordoned off and a critical information log started. Cassie's family was moved across the street, to a neighbor's where they remained, waiting until the evening.

At 3:45 p.m., Detective Toni Vollmer called for a briefing of the scene and handed out assignments. She assigned a thickset detective named Andy Thomas as Case Agent, directly beneath her, and selected the crime scene team, which would conduct the walk through. It consisted of Detectives Andy Thomas, off, Bill Collins, Tom Sellers and Alex Hamilton.

e preliminary walk-through took place at 4:20 p.m. The s entered the residence, single file, through the interior garage door where the previous entries had been made. They began their observation on the bottom level of the home. It consisted of a master bedroom, a child's bedroom, and a bathroom.

Upon entry the detectives immediately noticed the pieces of broken glass at the bottom of the stairs. In the master bedroom, they also found broken pieces of cork at the foot of the bed. But they found no other noticeable evidence downstairs.

As the detectives climbed the stairs they noticed bloodstains on the carpet. They took out placards and placed them over the bloodstains as they located each one. There were a total of three bloodstains on the stairs.

When they reached the top of the stairs, they noticed that if they continued walking forward they would walk out of the back door of the residence, which was just inside of a small landing where the washer and dryer were kept. There was a hallway to the right that ran parallel to the stairs, and to their left was the kitchen, dining room area. They first walked through the kitchen, dining room and then headed down the hall.

In the hallway they once again observed bloodstains in the carpeting. These they marked with placards as they had the previous ones. Halfway down the hall they approached a T in the hallway with another hallway running to the east and the hallway they were on continuing south. The southern hallway appeared to lead to the living room. They turned east and toward the rest of the house.

Behind the first door they came to was a bathroom. They found a condom in the toilet bowl and some unidentifiable stains in the sink. They continued down the hall and opened the next door, which was a child's bedroom. A small dog ran out of the room, which they immediately captured and removed.

Opposite that door was another, opening into what appeared to be a teenager's bedroom, and next to it was another bathroom. After observing these two rooms the detectives went back to the hallway. There was one final door left. It was a room where the owners appeared to keep their animals. It contained a lot of pet hair and a bed frame on the floor, but no mattress. The detectives reentered the hallway and headed toward the living room.

There they found Cassie, on her back, in front of the

television set. As they approached her they noticed more blood on the carpet and marked the stains with placards so that investigators working the scene later would not damage the bloodstain evidence.

The detectives noticed that: Cassie was wearing yellow pajama bottoms patterned with stars, moons and suns and a white spaghetti strap shirt. Her right foot and leg were entangled in a cord that came from the back of a Sony Play Station that was plugged into the front of the television set. Her legs were slightly apart and her arms were off to the side with her elbows bent and her hands pointed upward toward her head. Her head was slightly turned toward her right arm and the pinky finger of her left hand was nearly severed. There was a visible knife wound in Cassie's left leg that had blood pooling around it and another one in the center of her chest. There were several other wounds on Cassie's upper body.

Detective Alex Hamilton noticed that there was a cordless phone lying next to Cassie's side, just two feet away.

The men went back downstairs the way they entered and exited through the garage. In observing the blood stain patterns inside the residence, on the floor, going from the body to the last bloodstain toward the bottom of the stairs, Don Wyckoff from the Idaho State Forensic lab, stated that the blood was dropping off as it was moving away from the body and down the stairs.
It indicated a single blood trail leading from Cassie's body to the outside entrance.

The detectives continued their investigation in the garage. In the northeast corner, they located through one of the four interior doors a room that the family referred to as "the club house." Inside there was a small table, some chairs, a couch and a television. On the table was a board apparatus with incense burning materials on it. They retrieved a white box with marijuana and drug paraphernalia inside. There was also a panel box where the breaker switches to the home were located. The breaker box was opened.

Another door led to the furnace area, another to the water heater and storage room, and the other to the residence through the downstairs bathroom.

The initial walkthrough concluded at 5:57 p.m. It had taken an hour and thirty-seven minutes. Detective Alex Hamilton, a meticulous man, was then given the assignment to photograph and log the evidence. He started outside of the residence and worked his way back into the home. He marked and measured at least 48 different pieces of evidence that day, most of it blood stains from the room Cassie was found in and on the walls and flooring of the hallways and the stairwell, on the inside of the entry hall door frame, on a throw rug, and the blood stains previously marked with placards on the floor.

There were bloodstains on the television set in front of where Cassie was found, but she had been attacked so violently that there were bloodstains both behind the television set as well as under the window. This had been a violent and horrendous crime.

While Detective Hamilton was photographing the evidence, Case Agent Andy Thomas, and Idaho State Police Detective John Ganske were sent to interview Matt Beckham, Cassie's boyfriend and the last known person to see Cassie alive.

The detectives needed to know what had happened from the time that Cassie and Matt were dropped off until Cassie was found murdered two days later. They were hoping to get some answers from Matt.

Matt lived with his mother, Sherry Beckham, and his younger sister in an apartment complex in north Pocatello. His father had just recently rejoined the family after a stay in rehab. Matt and Sherry met with the two detectives at the Pocatello Police Department for the interview.

Matt told the detectives that on Friday, September 22, at approximately 5:30 p.m. Cassie's mother had dropped him and Cassie off at the residence on Whispering Cliffs. Cassie was going to stay the weekend in the house caring for the property owner's animals while they were out of town. He was going to stay with Cassie Friday evening while she was house-sitting.

At around 8:20 p.m. their friends, Brian Draper and Torey Adamcik, arrived at the house. At school on Thursday he and Cassie had told Torey and Brian that they were going to be house-sitting over the weekend. They had talked about having a party, but only Torey and Brian showed up. The two boys arrived in Torey's red Geo Prism.

Matt told the detectives that when Brian and Torey first arrived they'd looked through the entire house. Matt said that Cassie and he followed them because Brian was very immature, he acted like a two-year-old most of the time, and they wanted to make sure that he did not break anything. They went through every room and eventually ended up downstairs in the garage where they played with a universal weight machine.

When they were tired of playing on the weights they decided

to watch a movie. They looked through the homeowner's movie collection and Torey selected the movie *Kill Bill Volume Two*. They carried the DVD upstairs to the living room to watch.

While they were watching the movie they ate Popsicles, which they had taken from a freezer in the basement. Matt said that he used a black handled utility knife from the kitchen to open the Popsicle box. The knife was in a protective sheath and he had shown Brian how to release the knife from the sheath when he used it.

Matt told the detectives that just before 9:30 p.m. Brian said that he needed to be home, and Brian and Torey got ready to leave. Before they left Matt asked Torey if he could spend the night at Torey's house that night and wanted Torey to come back later and pick him up. Torey said that he could probably do that. Matt said that he would check with his mother and get permission first.

Between 9:45 and ten o'clock Torey and Brian left. Matt did not see them again that night. After they left, Matt called his mother and she told him that he could not spend the night at Torey's house. She was going to pick him up because she had a surprise for him. Matt called Torey and told him that he could not spend the night.

Sometime after this, Matt said, he and Cassie had been sitting in the living room watching television when the power went off. He and Cassie had gone around the upstairs of the house trying the light switches to see if any worked, but none did. They left a few switches in the "on" position so that they would know when the power came back on. Approximately 15 to 20 minutes later, the hall light came on as well as an outlet in the kitchen that powered the cordless phone, but they were unable to get any of the other lights, or the television, to work.

During the time that the lights were off it was very dark inside the house. Matt said that he felt somewhat scared and did not want to leave the living room, so he and Cassie stayed in there. Matt noticed the Contreras's dog acting strangely. It would go into the kitchen area at the top of the stairs and bark a few times down the stairs and then go back into the living room. The dog did this several times and Matt got the feeling that someone besides he and Cassie were in the residence.

At approximately 11:00 p.m. Matt called his mother and told her that the lights were out. She said that she would pick him up soon. Matt asked his mother if Cassie could come home with them but Cassie said no, she needed to stay there to take care of the dogs. Matt's mother, Sherry Beckham, confirmed that she overheard

Cassie telling Matt that through the phone.

Matt said it was approximately 11:30 p.m. when his mother picked him up. His father was with her, which was the surprise. His father had been in rehab and Matt had not been expecting him to get out at that time.

The detectives asked Matt if Cassie was alive when he left her. Matt said that when he left the residence Cassie was alive. The power was off and she was alone.

When Matt and his parents arrived home his father read a book to the family about his recent experience in the rehab center. They watched the movie *The Rookie* together and started *The Green Mile*. Between 3:00 and 3:30 a.m. Matt went to sleep in his bedroom. When he got up in the morning he found that his father had stayed up on the couch the entire night.

Matt told the detectives that he had tried to contact Cassie several times by phone on Saturday, but he never got through to her. On Saturday night, between 7:00 and 8:00 p.m. Torey arrived at Matt's house and picked him up. Matt spent Saturday night at Torey's house. Matt said that he was still worried about Cassie and asked Torey to drive him over to the house to check on her, but Torey told him that he did not have enough gas to drive out there, that the gas in his car had to last him the entire week.

Matt told the detectives that he went home Sunday morning. He did not know that Cassie had been murdered until Anna called him on the phone Sunday afternoon and asked him what he had done to her daughter.

The detectives asked Matt what he thought about Brian and Torey. Matt told them that he thought both of them had crushes on Cassie, as they would sometimes flirt with her. After finishing the interview with Matt the two detectives headed over to Torey Adamcik's house.

Meanwhile, it was starting to get dark outside. Cassie's family was still gathered across the street from the Contreras's home. Sheriff Lorin Nielson made arrangements for the Contreras's to stay at the Ameritel while their home, which was now a crime scene, was investigated. At approximately 8:00 p.m. they were transported to the hotel where they would remain for the next several days. Neither family was allowed to remove their vehicles from the driveway.

Detective Toni Vollmer drove Anna and Victor home. The detective asked to search Cassie's room for any information that might help them with their investigation. She collected a journal and a cell phone.

While Detective Vollmer was in the home, Anna began to receive calls from people who had heard of Cassie's death. One of the Contreras's daughters had been calling people and informing them of what happened. This was very upsetting to Anna. Detective Toni Vollmer contacted Allison at the hotel. She told Allison that her daughter had been calling people and telling them what happened. Allison said that her daughter had gone to stay with friends, but that she would call her daughter and tell her not to let anyone else know what was going on.

Finally, at 10:35 p.m., approximately nine hours after she was first discovered, Cassie was removed from the house on Whispering Cliffs. At 1:23 a.m. all investigators cleared the scene. The crime scene was secured and possession maintained by the Bannock County Sheriff's Office. All evidence taken up until that point was transported to the Sheriff's Office and Detectives Mark Ballard and Toni Vollmer began labeling and sealing what they could.

Sunday was a terrible day and I did not even know it. I was blissfully unaware that our entire lives had changed. I had no idea that the hours that I was breathing through were golden and precious and slipping away. That they were going to be the last good moments that I would ever have, if not forever, at least for a long, long, time…

PART TWO

Before

CHAPTER TWO

Home

I grew up in Pocatello Idaho, a small town similar to thousands of others that dot the United States. It is a faith-based community known for its large Latter Day Saint population, but as home to a State University it offers some cultural diversity.

Pocatello primarily consists of hard working people enjoying a relatively safe place to work and raise a family. It is a growing community with a modest mall and a new Costco. There are the popular chain food restaurants to choose from, and the cost of housing is among the lowest in the state. You can live relatively well for a lot less than you can live almost anywhere. There is a popular ski lift twenty minutes from town, and with its green valleys and rolling mountains it is an outdoor paradise.

That was my home. The place I grew up. And the unlikely setting for the tragedy that hit us.

I was the youngest child in my family, the only girl, with five older brothers. My parents were LDS and deeply religious. When I was young I thought everybody lived the same way that we did. Everyone I knew had two parents. They owned the house they lived in, and every house had a swing set in the back yard. Life was pleasant.

And ever since I was a little girl, all I ever wanted to be was a mother. I wanted a husband that I loved, a cozy little home, and children. That's all. And for so long I had it all. My husband Sean and I have been happily married for 19 years. We have three beautiful children. Lacey, Torey and Jamie.

Sean is a mechanic. He has worked at the local Nissan dealership for the past 10 years, a job he enjoys. I work as a customer service representative at the local newspaper, which means if you subscribe to the Idaho State Journal, and you call in to complain because you missed your newspaper delivery, it might have been me who answered your call.

Our three children have been our joy. Lacey is hard working and studious, yet still manages to maintain an active social life. She has many friends that keep her busy. Torey is artistic and he can build anything with or without a blueprint. He was going to be an architect until he got his first video camera. After that Torey wanted to be a director. He loves movies, both making them and watching them. Jamie, our youngest, is smart--though not as studious as he could be. He enjoys team sports and plays football and lacrosse. He loves video games and talks about going to school to design them.

Sean and I lived in a comfortable home. We had stable jobs. Our children were happy and healthy. The whole future lay ahead of us. Life was good and normal and what it should be. And then suddenly, without warning, it was over.

CHAPTER THREE

Friday, September 22, 2006

Our children were settling back into the fall routine. Lacey was starting her first semester of college. Torey was a junior at Pocatello High School, and Jamie was a freshman. Torey had earned his driver's license the week before school started and he was driving Jamie and himself to school every day.

That afternoon I arrived home from work at a quarter to five. When I came in the house Torey was in the family room at the computer desk working on his I-pod, and Jamie was in his bedroom playing X-box. I checked on both of them and fixed myself a cup of coffee. When I carried my coffee back downstairs to the family room, Torey asked if he could go to his friend Cassie Stoddart's house later that night. Her boyfriend Matt Beckham was also going to be there.

This was a change of plans that had been made earlier. Adam Dykman, Torey's best friend, had previously invited Torey to go to the Pocatello High School football game with him and his girlfriend Amber Phillips. I'd liked that idea because Jamie was also going to the game and they would be there together. But Adam had not yet called and Torey was uncertain if he was still going to the game or not.

We had recently moved into a new house. We'd lived in the old house since Jamie was in kindergarten and Torey in the second grade. Because I was usually home by the time school let out, our children's friends often gathered at our house after school, and a typical weekend was a group of neighborhood kids spending the night.

But since we'd moved, our house was no longer the center of the neighborhood. In fact we did not even live in the neighborhood anymore, and our children wanted to hang out with their friends at their homes more often. This was hard for me to get used to. I was used to the kids being under our roof where I could do the supervising.

I told Torey, "I'm not comfortable with you going to Cassie's house." She was a friend of his from school, they had gone to a movie together, but I did not know Cassie, or her parents; and I had never even heard of Matt Beckham.

Torey was still sitting at the computer desk and I was across from him on the couch. Torey said, "I'll give you Cassie's address." He offered to write it down for me. He started looking through the desk drawers for some notepaper, but he couldn't find any. Instead he wrote the address on a roll of masking tape he found inside of one of the drawers with a black sharpie: ----*Whispering Cliffs*.

I had no idea where that was. Torey said, "It's down Hiline off of 2 ½ Mile Road." I knew where that was; it was not far from where we lived. When I was growing up it had been a remote area on the outskirts of town, but there had been a lot of new construction. Whispering Cliffs must have been one of the new streets developed.

Cassie's phone number was programmed into Torey's cell phone and I had a copy of all of his numbers. I could call him on that. Of course, he would have his cell phone with him the entire time and I could always reach him directly on it as well. There was really no reason to worry; besides I trusted Torey. I had no reason not to. He had never been in any trouble.

Brian Draper, a recent friend of Torey's, was also going to Cassie's house that night. Torey had spoken with Brian earlier and Brian had received permission from his parents to spend the night at our house if that was okay with Dad and I. Torey asked if Matt could spend the night as well. I said I preferred Brian only. We had made arrangements to attend the university's homecoming game the following afternoon with Brian and his Grandfather. "Matt can spend Saturday night," I said. I wanted to meet Matt, but I did not want to interrupt the plans we'd already made.

I decided it would be all right if I let Torey go. He just needed to call me as soon as he arrived.

Torey said he was going to pick up Brian, but that didn't make sense to me. "If Whispering Cliffs is off 2 ½ Mile Road, that's by our house." I reasoned. "Brian lives on the south end of town. Why drive clear over there to pick him up? He should drive over here."

Torey explained, "Brian doesn't have any money. His parents aren't going to pay for his gas." That sounded reasonable. Brian's parents had money, but from what I understood, they did not spend a lot of it on Brian.

I will remember this forever. Torey and I were standing in the hallway by the door to the garage. Torey was ready to go. He was so happy, just like he always was. He was smiling at me. He said, "Don't worry Mom, you will get to know Matt and you're going to like him." Torey's sweet face and reassuring words...everything was going to be all right. He reached over and gave me a kiss on the cheek.

I stood in the garage door and watched Torey pull out, completely unaware that our life, as we knew it, was about to end.

Sean worked a half a shift one Friday of every month. That day happened to be his half Friday. He could have been home as early as two o'clock, but he chose to stay at work. This is one of the hundreds of "what if's" that plagues us. If Sean had been home would he have let Torey go? We'll never know.

I dropped Jamie off with his friends at the football game, and when I returned Sean was home. We sat downstairs together, watching television, waiting for Torey to call. When Torey had not called in what I considered a reasonable amount of time, I called him on his cell phone. There was no answer so I called Pam Draper, Brian's mother. Pam said, "Torey was here, he and Brian went to see a movie."

This was the first time that I heard the two boys were going to a *movie*. Shortly after I hung up with Pam, Torey called. He said, "I'm sorry I missed your call. I'm at Cassie's house with Matt and Brian. Everything's fine."

I asked, "Are you going to stay at Cassie's house or go to a movie? Brian's mother told me that you two were going to the movies."

"Brian's talking about going to a movie," Torey said, "but I'm not sure if we'll go or not."

"You and Brian need to be home around 11:00 p.m." I said, "If you go to the nine o'clock show it'll be getting out around that time and I want you to come straight home. If you go anywhere else besides a movie you need to call me." Torey said that he would and we hung up.

Lacey was working the late shift at Dillard's, a local department store in the mall. She was going to go out with her boyfriend, Jeff, when she got off work at nine p.m. We had spoken with her earlier that night and she would be home around midnight. We expected Torey to be home around 11:00 p.m; and we were just waiting for Jamie to call when he was ready to be picked up.

While we waited, I went upstairs to read in bed, and Sean stayed downstairs watching television. At a quarter to eleven, Sean came up to the bedroom where I was reading and we called Jamie.

He did not answer. We have had this problem with Jamie before; it is usually so loud in the arena during the games that Jamie cannot hear his cell phone ringing. While we waited to call him back we called Lacey and checked in with her. She was fine.

We discussed calling Torey, but decided if he was in a movie we did not want to disturb him. We would give him time to get out of the movie and drive home.

We knew approximately what time the game would be over, and after another failed attempt to get a hold of Jamie, Sean decided that he would just drive to the Holt Arena and wait for him there. I stayed in bed reading David Copperfield. I was almost done with the book and I wanted to finish it.

Torey arrived home fifteen to twenty minutes after Sean left. He ran up the stairs to my bedroom. I knew right away that something was amiss because he looked scared, like he thought he was in trouble, and he had not taken his shoes off. That was a rule in our house, and one that everybody, friends and family alike, obeyed. No shoes.

But there was nothing in Torey's physical appearance that alarmed me. He was wearing the same clothes that he'd left in. They were not dirty, or torn or wet. He had no cuts or marks or abrasions on him. I simply assumed Torey was scared because he thought he was in trouble for being late.

Earlier in the summer, Torey had been grounded for two weeks when he came home late from a concert in the park at ISU. Torey knew the reasons why it was important for us to know where he was and whom he was with at all times. The night of the concert was the only time that Torey had ever been late and not checked in with us. I had been so worried about him that night that I'd called the police, a fact that mortified and embarrassed him.

But when Torey came running into my room I saw how upset he was. I immediately felt bad and reassured him that it was okay, he was home safe and that was all that mattered. I asked Torey where Brian was.

"He's downstairs using Lacey's bathroom," Torey said.

While Torey was in my room the garage door opened. You can hear it through the house, going up and then down. At the sound of the door, Torey kissed me goodnight on the cheek and went back downstairs. I did not see Brian that night.

Sean and Jamie arrived home minutes after Torey and Brian. While Torey was going back down the stairs after kissing me good night, Jamie came into the house. It was he and Sean who had opened the garage door.

We lived in a split entry home. When you enter the house from the front door there is a stairway that leads upstairs and one that leads down. If you enter the house from the garage, as Jamie did that night, you have to go up both flights of stairs to get to the upper level.

From the garage entrance there was a tiled entryway. Lacey's bedroom is to the right, and there is a laundry room, a bathroom, and a large open family room on the left. The stairs are next to the doorway.

When Jamie came in, Torey was coming down the bottom stairs. Brian was still in the bathroom. Jamie went into the family room and Torey followed him. Jamie had planned on watching television with Torey and Brian, but a few minutes later Brian came out of the bathroom. Brian was acting unusually hyper. This made Jamie feel uncomfortable, and he went upstairs to bed, leaving Torey and Brian alone.

With Torey and Jamie home, Sean and I went to bed. Lacey was still out but we knew that she would be home soon, and in fact we heard the garage door opening as we were drifting off to sleep.

CHAPTER FOUR

Saturday, September 23, 2006

The next morning I got up to fix the kids breakfast and discovered that Torey and Brian were gone. That upset me. Torey had just begun driving and I did not want him coming and going without asking. I asked Sean if he knew where the boys were.

"Torey asked if he could take Brian home. I let him," Sean said. He did not see Brian before they left and in fact neither Sean nor I saw Brian Friday night or Saturday morning. The first time we saw him was at the football game later that afternoon.

When Torey arrived back home, after dropping Brian off, he announced that he did not want to go to the football game anymore. That wasn't surprising. Torey has never really cared for football. That was another reason why I hadn't questioned him further about his change of plans from the night before. But I wanted to go to the game. We'd already made plans to meet Brian and his grandfather there. I told Torey I wanted him to go.

When we got to the Holt Arena we found Brian and his grandfather seated near the top row of the bleachers. I was concerned because Brian's grandfather was obviously handicapped and the seating arrangements, at the top of the narrow, concrete steps did not appear safe to me.

It was the first time that I met Brian's grandfather, but he remembered Sean from a job that Sean and his father had done for him about 20 years earlier. Sean's father was a glazier and he had replaced some windows in the grandfather's home. Evidentially, Sean had helped with the job. Brian's grandfather asked Sean if he remembered him. Sean said he did.

But neither Torey nor Brian were interested in the game. Brian sat still with hands between his knees and had a look that was like an audible sigh on his face. That was unusual for Brian who, as far as I had observed, never sat still. Brian always had a goofy walk, like a character from a silent film with the reel skipping, and he was always drumming his fingers on something. Now he sat motionless and quiet. A dark, brooding figure.

Torey was also quiet. He sat with his arms folded leaning into me and away from Brian. Neither boy was speaking to the other. Torey looked very uncomfortable and I wondered if he and Brian had had a fight. Trying to lighten the mood, I teased them. I said,

“You boys must have stayed up too late last night,” but neither one responded.

Sean said we should go home. Torey obviously wasn’t enjoying the game. But I felt we should at least try to have a good time. Even Brian’s grandfather was pleasantly smiling and trying to engage the boys. But nothing worked.

Sean gave Torey some money and told him to go get something to eat. Torey had not eaten anything since the day before. Torey said he was not hungry but he took the money and left. He came back with some nachos, which he handed to me. I offered them to Brian but he wasn’t interested.

Finally Brian and his grandfather left. We stayed a little longer but left in the middle of the fourth quarter. It was Jeff’s birthday and we’d planned to take him and Lacey out to dinner. But Torey still wasn’t hungry. He asked if he and I could go home. I said, “No. We all need to celebrate Jeff’s Birthday.” We picked up Jamie and met Lacey and Jeff at Wingers.

We sat in a booth in the front corner near the door. I had my camera with me so that I could take pictures, which I do for every birthday. Torey was worried about Matt spending the night. He was not sure if he still wanted him to. I reminded Torey, “You promised that I was going to get to meet Matt.” Jamie asked if the cousins could spend the night as well. They had called while we were at the game. I said, “Of course they can.”

The cousins are how we refer to my brother Rick’s three older children. They are Jacob, Andrew and Nathan Nelson. They are about the same age as Torey and Jamie, and they are all very close. Almost every weekend the cousins either spent the night at our house, or our boys spent the night at theirs.

Torey ordered dinner, but he would not eat. I couldn’t understand why he wasn’t hungry. I was worried about him. Torey has never been a big eater but this was unlike him. He kept saying that he had no appetite. Jeff said it was okay, he would take Torey’s dinner to his mother, Tamara, and she could have it. We ate asphalt pie and cookies and cream, and after everyone coaxed him, Torey reluctantly took one bite.

It was Jeff’s birthday, but it was also the one-year anniversary of the date our house, which we’d had custom built, was finished and we’d moved in. I took pictures of everyone around the table, happily celebrating the two anniversaries simultaneously.

When we left the restaurant, Torey took his car and picked up Matt. Nathan and Andrew also spent the night. The kids watched movies and Sean and I went to bed early.

The only thing I remember about Matt is that he and Torey were in the kitchen while I was doing the dishes the next morning, and I recall thinking what a nice kid Matt seemed to be. He had brown hair, brown eyes and he looked serious and well mannered. I thought he might be a nice friend for Torey, and I looked forward to getting to know him, but I would never get the chance.

CHAPTER FIVE

Sunday, September 24, 2006

After Matt went home Sunday morning, Sean and Torey went to Wal-Mart to do some grocery shopping, while I ran an errand at the mall and cleaned the house. Sean bought Torey some flavored water bottles, (which ended up staying in the fridge for months afterwards; no one could drink them) and some breakfast bars.

When they returned home, Sean decided to wash our car and Torey cleaned his too. Torey vacuumed out his car and wiped the windows. This did not seem strange to us at the time because we are naturally very clean and orderly people. Our house, garage, vehicles, closets; everything is kept clean and organized.

Torey is very particular about his things. Everything in his room is kept in place and in mint condition. I have no doubt that Torey cleaned his car because he was terrified of the trouble he was in, but it was not something that would cause us to question him. Torey was and is a very clean person.

At the time it seemed nice, Torey spending all this time with us, going to the football game and grocery shopping. We did not know that Torey was clinging to us out of fear and desperation. We had no idea. We were just enjoying our time with him.

That afternoon we got a call about an ad we were running in the newspaper for a dirt bike that we were trying to sell. The motorcycle ran well but it was beat-up and we wanted something newer. Sean and Torey went out to the garage to get the bike ready to sell. The person that looked at it bought it.

After dinner, Torey did his homework in the family room. He was reclining on the chaise lounge, typing on his laptop. I sat next to him. Torey had recently purchased the laptop computer from his friend, Adam. It was broken when he bought it, but he and Sean had spent hours together fixing it. Now it worked perfectly and Torey was thrilled to have it.

A couple of weeks earlier, Torey had to write an essay about 9/11 and how it affected him. After he'd written it he read it aloud to me. He asked me if I remembered that day and what I was doing. "Yes I do," I told him.

"At school the teachers brought television sets into the classrooms," he said. "The teachers tried to talk to us students about what was happening and reassure us, but it was useless because you could tell that they were scared too."

Watching Torey tapping the keys on his computer, reminded me of that night, and I smiled over at him.

Torey's face is so clear to me. The line of his chin. His eyes. I can see every detail about him. Every look. Every comment he made. I have been over it and over it in my head so many times that it's like a movie. We have the conversation about going to Cassie's house again and again. We are sitting in Wingers, Torey on my left. He is on the couch doing his homework. He is *there.* I cannot tell you exactly what Lacey or Jamie were doing that weekend, but I have every detail of Torey permanently etched in my mind.

CHAPTER SIX

A Knock at the Door

I was in bed, reading. The kids were downstairs, watching television, when the doorbell rang. I heard it and I wondered if it was someone from the church. I did not know who it could be this late on a Sunday night. I called to Sean to tell him that I was in bed, could he get the door? I did not want to talk to anyone. I was already in my pajamas.

I wondered if Sean heard me because the doorbell rang again, but he must have because I heard him answer the door. I went back to my book.

A few minutes later I realized that whoever was at the door had moved upstairs and they were now in the dining room talking with Sean. Through the door I could hear a deep voice, very serious, that I did not recognize. But Torey seemed to have joined the conversation. I put my book down and waited a moment to see if I could hear what was going on, or if they would leave. When the talking continued, I put on my robe, and went down the hall.

The kitchen and dining room are actually one room, separated by a granite island in the middle. Across from the kitchen is the living room. The lights in the living room were off, casting it in shadows. From the hall I could see Torey's back and I realized that he was sitting at the dining room table. I entered the room not knowing what was going on.

Torey was at the head of the table, his back to the hall, facing the sliding glass doors on the wall opposite. They are the entrance into the backyard and after dark the dining room is reflected in their glass like a mirror.

Sean was sitting next to Torey, on his right. Across from Sean sat two men, one dark and heavy, one light. The lighter one was on Torey's left, directly across from Sean. One seat up from him was the heavier man.

I was confused. I did not know these men, but they seemed to be talking to Torey, which did not make sense. My first thought was that maybe they were young men leaders from the church, but that could not be right. They were far too grave for that, and I had certainly never seen them before.

They were still talking when I entered the room. I stood next to Torey between him and Sean. There was a baker's rack standing against the wall and I leaned on it for support instead of drawing up a chair. I introduced myself…or Sean did. The two men nodded at me. They said they were detectives here to question Torey.

I could not believe it. I thought, question Torey about what? The situation did not make sense, but I reacted like any parent would who has never had any experience with the legal system. I was shocked, certainly, but I did not immediately distrust the detectives.

Detective Ganske introduced himself. He was the tall, blond man sitting next to Torey. He was from the Idaho State Police. He nodded toward the heavier man on his left and introduced him as Detective Andy Thomas from the Bannock County Sheriff's Office.

What those two men were bringing into our house was serious. You felt that right away. It was immediately apparent that they were in charge, they were going to question Torey, and there was nothing that Sean or I could do about it.

Detective Thomas was the first that I remember speaking. It was his voice that I had heard from the bedroom. He drew a breath and slowly exhaled. Leaning toward us across the table he said, "We were just explaining to your husband and Torey here that there has been a murder. Torey's friend Cassie was brutally murdered while she was house-sitting this weekend. We know that Torey was at the house on Friday night and we need to ask him some questions."

There are no words to describe what it was like to hear those words. Shocked, horrified, only begin to capture the feeling.

Sean was looking at the detectives. So was Torey, who was very pale. He must have been terrified, fearing for his life.

"Oh my God...How?" I asked.

Sean wanted to know what we could do to help.

Detective Thomas said, "Cassie was found this afternoon. It appears she was killed sometime Friday night. We know that her boyfriend, Matt Beckham, was with her that night, and that Torey and Brian Draper came over later. So, ahh…Matt, Torey and Brian are the last people we know of to have seen Cassie alive."

Sean said, "And the person who did this."

"Right. And the person who did this. That's what we're trying to figure out. That's what we're here to talk to Torey about."

I asked, "What are you saying?"

Ganske said, "Listen, we know this is hard. But we need to ask Torey some questions. Torey, do you know who would want to hurt Cassie?"

Torey shook his head. "No…No."

Sean interrupted, "Uhmm...if Torey was one of the last people to see her…what does that mean? This is serious."

I said to Detective Thomas, "Torey told us where he was going Friday night. He gave me the address and I called him while he was there."

Detective Thomas said, "That was smart."

I had to ask, "Is Torey a suspect? Do you really think he could have had anything to do with this? He's a kid, he's never been in any trouble! He spent the weekend with us. He came home on time! He went to the ISU football game! How could he have done something like that and not told us? He would have to be a *psychopath* to be capable of something like that."

We made so many mistakes over the next few days that helped seal Torey's fate. *That* was definitely one of them. Now that I have been educated about shock and the way kids react, I know that many kids when faced with problems commonly react in the very same way that Torey did. They are terrified of what is going to happen to them, they are in shock, and they *say nothing*. But I did not know that at the time, and I said, in front of my son, that to react the way that he did, he would have to be a psychopath. I was wrong and I will never forgive myself for saying that. Never.

Thomas said, "We are here to find out if anyone knows what happened to Cassie, or if they saw anything that might help us. We are not accusing Torey right now."

Ganske took over the questioning, again he asked, "Torey do you know anyone who would want to hurt Cassie?"

"No. No one."

"What about her boyfriend."

"No."

"They have any trouble? Fighting?"

"No."

"How did you end up going to Cassie's that night?"

"Well, Cassie said she was going to house-sit for her aunt, which she had done before, and there was going to be a party. Kids from school knew about it."

I suddenly realized that Cassie had been left alone for the weekend. I had thought that she *lived* at the house on Whispering Cliffs. I had no idea that the house was actually her aunt's and that there had been no adult supervision while Torey and Brian were there.

"Who knew about it? Could you give us any names?" one of

the detectives asked, referring to the party.

"Just some kids at school."

"Do you know of anyone else who went over there that night, who was planning on going over that night?"

"Just Brian and me. Matt was already there with Cassie when we got there. I don't know who was going to come over. Just some people knew about it so they might have come up. "

"Had you ever been to the house before?"

"No."

"How did you know how to find it?"

"Cassie told me."

"So Cassie told you."

"She invited me and Brian."

"So what did you do when you got to the house?"

"Nothing really…we just watched some movies."

"Okay...so when we start looking for fingerprints where are we going to find your fingerprints?"

"Well…we looked through the house when we first got there. Matt showed us the house. And we lifted weights downstairs in the garage. So you would find them there."

"You go through the whole house?"

"Mmm…yeah. It's a pretty big house," Torey said, nodding.

"What about in the kitchen? What about on the knives in the kitchen?"

"Well, we did look for something to eat. There will be fingerprints in the kitchen. Maybe on the drawers. We ate Popsicles."

"Okay, so you ate Popsicles and watched movies, what else did you do?"

"Nothing really. Brian got bored, he wanted to go to a movie so we left."

"Okay, what time did you leave?"

"Umm…around 8:30, somewhere around there."

I cut in and said that I had spoken with Torey on the phone while he was at Cassie's and at that time he told me that Brian was thinking of going to a movie.

Ganske asked, "You had a cell phone with you?"

Torey said, "Yes."

Detective Thomas asked, "Before we get to the movie, let me ask you this, was there anything weird happening with the lights before you left?"

"No."

"The lights were not going off and on?"

"No."

"Okay, so we would not find your fingerprints on the circuit breaker?"

"What?" Torey said. "No."

"Because what if I told you it looks like someone had been into the circuit breaker?"

"I don't know. After we left, Matt tried to scare Cassie a little bit because we called and the lights were out, and he was messing around with her, scaring her a little."

"So you called Matt and Cassie after you left?"

"Yes."

"And the lights were off when you were talking to them?"

"Yeah...Matt said the lights were out."

"And he was messing around, kinda scaring Cassie?"

"Yeah."

"Do you know about what time this was?"

"I'm not sure, before eleven. I had to be home at eleven."

"Matt's mother picked him up at the house around eleven p.m," one of the detectives stated. "They both say Cassie was alive at that time."

"So we know it was after eleven." I said.

Neither detective replied.

"If Matt's mother picked him up and Cassie was there..." I said.

"Matt's mother did not see Cassie," the detective said. "She honked her horn and waited for Matt to come out, which he did."

The statement and its implications hung in the air.

I said, "But Matt's mother picked him up, she would have noticed..."

"Like we said, they both say that Cassie was alive when they left her," Ganske said.

"We might need those phone records though. Mom, Dad," Detective Thomas said looking at us, "do you think there is any way you could get us a copy?"

Sean said, "It's T-mobile. I think I can go downstairs and print you off the last couple days. I think I can do that." He started to get up but sat back down, "This is serious. This is...What about an attorney? Are you sure we don't need an attorney? I mean we want to help you and all... but this is.... you could be looking at Torey just because he was there that night."

Ganske said, "We need to eliminate Torey so that we can move on to finding the person who did this. There is a time element we are working with here. It's like a puzzle, like a giant puzzle and we just need to get the pieces of the puzzle so we can put it all together."

"Okay. So we need to look at those phone records," Thomas said.

Sean went downstairs to see if he could print them off.

I asked, "So are we done? Is Torey eliminated? He was out of the house before Matt's mother picked him up."

"Well, we still need to ask Torey some more questions," Ganske said.

Detective Thomas said, "Okay, so you looked around the house, you watched some TV, you went downstairs. When you were downstairs where were you? Did you notice a bedroom down there?"

"There was a room, it was a smoking room," Torey replied. "Matt said the people who live there smoke pot in that room."

Detective Tomas asked, "What room downstairs? Off the master bedroom?"

"No," Torey said. "Off the garage. The people there had drugs. Maybe there was someone who did drugs? I don't know. They had drug paraphernalia there."

Detective Thomas asked, "What room off the garage?" But then he nodded his head and said, "Oh. I know what room you're talking about...yeah...That is a different kind of a room isn't it? I am not talking about that room. I mean *inside* the house. In the master bedroom."

Torey shook his head. "I don't know."

Detective Ganske took over. "So what about the movie? When did you decide to go to the movie?"

Torey said, "We were watching a movie, *Kill Bill*, and Brian was bored. He just wanted to leave. Then he said, 'Lets go to a movie.' So we left."

About this time Sean came back up with the phone records, which he handed over to the detectives, then sat back down.

"Did you see anything when you left?" one of the detectives asked Torey.

"There was a white truck driving by," Torey answered.

"Is that all you saw?"

"Just the white truck."

Sean asked him, "Do you remember any details about the truck, Tor?"

Torey shook his head.

"And when you left Cassie and Matt were just..." Ganske started to say.

"Yeah," Torey interrupted.

"They were okay, they weren't fighting or anything?"

"No."

"Okay," Ganske nodded. "So, which theater did you go to?"

"The one by K-Mart. The Carmike."

"Where did you park?"

"In the back, by the dumpsters."

"Okay, so if we go looking through the surveillance tape we are going to find your car there?" Ganske asked.

Torey paused for a second. "Yeah."

"Okay, so what about the movie? What movie did you see?"

"It was the sequel to *White Noise*, *Pulse*."

"And you watched that movie and then what did you do?"

"We came back here."

"You did not go back up to Whispering Cliffs to see Cassie and Matt?"

"No."

"Because it appears Cassie was killed right around the time you say you went to the movies."

The implication in the air was palpable. No one said a thing.

Thomas broke the silence. "So you can see why it would be important if you saw anything on your way out of the house?"

Torey nodded. "Yeah."

"So what did you see?"

"I saw the white truck. I know the people who live there do drugs because Cassie told us. They smoke pot. Maybe someone came for…some drugs...I don't know... " By now Torey was visibly struggling to maintain his composure. You could see it becoming more and more difficult for him. His voice was getting higher.

"Torey do you know anyone who would want to hurt Cassie? Anyone…anyone who could do something like this to her?" Ganske asked him again.

"No. No one would want to hurt Cassie. Cassie was not like that," Torey said.

The detectives sat back.

Ganske said, "Alright. We need you to write down

everything you told us tonight, Torey, and we need you to sign it, and we are going to need to get a couple of pictures, and then we can get out of your way. We'll need to take some pictures of your hands and then we will need to look at the car and get some pictures of the car."

Sitting at the dining room table Torey slowly wrote out what he had told the detectives. I asked again, "Are we done? Is Torey cleared now?"

Ganske said, "We are going to have to look at the phone records and that will verify where he was and if he was telling the truth."

"What does that mean?" I asked.

"We will check which towers the calls came across on."

I still did not understand.

Sean said, "Cell phones get their reception from the closest tower to them, so it is like a GPS. They can look at the towers the calls come on and know where you were when you made, or accepted, a call."

"So you are going to use that to verify his story?" I asked.

"Part of it," Ganske said.

I asked, "Why can't you just ask him about the movie now, what it was about? Then you will know he was there."

They did not respond.

Ganske took the paper Torey had written his account of the night on. We did not know it at the time but it was actually a statement that could be used in a court of law against him…And it was.

We knew absolutely nothing about the legal system. I am not even sure to this day if it was a legal interview because we were never told of Torey's rights. We were never told that he did not have to answer any questions. Or that anything he said that night could, and would be used against him.

Ganske asked Torey, "Do you have any cuts or scratches on your hands or arms?"

"No."

"Okay. I need to take pictures of your hands and arms."

Torey stood up and held out his hands front and backwards. Ganske examined Torey closely and noticed a small scratch, less than a quarter inch on his inside wrist. He asked Torey what it was from, and Torey said weight class earlier in the week. Ganske said it looked old, almost healed over. He took the pictures and asked to go outside and look at the car. Sean went with him.

While Sean and Detective Ganske were outside I asked Detective Thomas how long he had been a detective. He said something like 20 years, I can't remember exactly. I was trying to determine if he knew my brother David who had been with the Pocatello Police Department for 15 years before he had taken a job in Challis Idaho as the Chief of Police in 1992. Detective Thomas said he did remember Dave.

Torey sat back down in his chair at the table. Thomas hadn't moved. I went to where Detective Ganske had been sitting and stood between Thomas and Torey. I asked if we needed to be worried about Torey. Should we let him go to school the next day? Somebody might know that he was there Friday night and think that he knew something. He might be in danger. Thomas said he should be fine.

Torey, sitting at the head of the table, was wrecked. I could see that he was physically and emotionally drained.

Ganske and Sean came back into the house.

Detective Ganske gave me his card. They were going to go over to Brian's house and question him. It was now after 10:30 p.m. The detectives told us not to call the Drapers and tell them they were coming. They needed to be the ones who told them what was going on, not us.

I walked the two detectives to the front door, relieved that they were finally leaving. As soon as I shut the door behind them and turned around, Lacey's boyfriend Jeff was right in front of me, right in my face. I almost jumped.

He said, "You can't let Torey talk to the police like that! You need to call a lawyer!" He was very emphatic and upset. I realized he and Lacey had probably been listening from the downstairs stairwell. "What if his alibi doesn't come through?" Jeff asked, "You need to call an attorney right now!"

Surprised, I said, "Jeff, it's okay. It's okay. Torey couldn't have anything to do with this. Don't worry. They'll figure it out." I smiled at him, trying to reassure him.

Jeff said, "I hope so, because they have some kids that were *right there*." He turned and went back down the stairs.

Jeff was right. He was absolutely right. We should have called an attorney that night. I saw the position that Torey was in and recognized the fact that he could, at the very least, be stigmatized by the fact that he was there. But I did not know any better.

The bottom line is that Sean and I trusted the police, that they would do their job and find out what happened. We only saw one possibility. That someone else had broken into the house after the boys left and attacked Cassie. Someone who knew that she was going to be alone. We believed it was just a matter of time before the detectives proved it.

But it was hard to wait, and the next couple of days were difficult. I could not accept Torey as a suspect, even temporarily. I wanted to be told that he was cleared and I could not relax until I heard those words.

Back upstairs I said, "We need to call Brian's parents."

Torey said no. He would not call Brian or his parents. He looked like he was going to be sick. He went into the downstairs bathroom.

Sean said, "We're not going to call the Drapers. The detectives told us they needed to be the ones to break the news." He kept saying, "The poor girl. The poor girl," over and over again, and he too looked sick.

I felt that we should call the Drapers. This was awful. We had an obligation to let them know. I would want them to call me!

Sean put an end to it. He said, "We can't call them and we're not going to."

Torey came out of the bathroom and went into his bedroom. He lay down on his bed, lying on his side, facing the wall. I went in and laid down next to him. Torey was sobbing, his upper body racked with the force of his grief. I put my arms around him and held him. We lay like that for a long time until his crying gradually subsided and he was hiccupping the way you do after a long, hard cry.

I kept saying, "It's okay, it's okay Torey. She's okay now. She's okay."

Torey tried to talk but he could not stop crying long enough to get the words out. I rubbed his head and shushed him.

Finally he cried out, "What kind of a person can do something like that? What kind of a person, what kind of a person?"

I said I didn't know.

He kept saying it and then he said, "She must have been so scared. How could he do this, how could he do this?"

The statement scared me. I thought if I don't stop this he is going to continue down this line of thought and it seemed like he was starting to visualize what happened. I did not want that. God No! At the same time Torey was having a physiological response that was different from the sobbing. It was happening right in front of my eyes and it terrified me. Torey's skin was clammy, his face was purple, and his checks were giant splotches of bruised, purple spider veins. I could see the veins in his temples throbbing. Torey squeezed his eyes shut and drove the knuckles of his index fingers into them as if he were trying to block something out. He could only speak in fragments.

I did not know what to say or do. It was awful. I had to calm him down. I asked Torey to tell me about Cassie, what kind of a girl she was.

After awhile Torey said, "Cassie was so good. She was nice to everyone."

"Was she like Amber?" I asked, referring to his friend Adam's girlfriend.

"No, not at all. Cassie was quiet. She kept to herself. She would never hurt anyone."

I told Torey that it sounded like he had a good friend in Cassie, and that he needed to remember her that way. I lay with him for a while longer, rubbing his forehead. After awhile his breathing improved, and although he was not yet asleep, I thought he had calmed down enough that I could leave him.

Sean was in bed waiting for me when I entered the bedroom. Neither one of us knew what to say to the other.

Poor Cassie.

Sean said we should send her family flowers.

CHAPTER SEVEN

Monday, September 25, 2006

I called my brother David early Monday morning. He had been in law enforcement for 25 years but was now working for the school district. I wanted his advice. I asked him if he had heard about the girl that had been killed Friday night. The media would have just begun reporting it.

I told Dave that her name was Cassie Stoddart and she was a friend of Torey's. I told him that Torey had been over to her house Friday night, along with his friend Brian Draper, and her boyfriend Matt Beckham. The police had questioned Torey because he and his friends were the last known people to see her alive. She had been killed later that night.

"You're kidding," Dave said.

"No, I'm not."

"Geese," he drew out the word.

"Yeah…would you be worried if it was one of your boys?"

He paused, "If it was one of my boys…yeah, I'd be worried."

"You would?"

"Yeah. It's not a good position to be in."

Of course it wasn't, I knew that. "But do you really think they could consider Torey a suspect? That he could have something to do with this?"

"I don't know," Dave said. "If he was there, they have to question him…They have to find out what he knows, if he knows anything. Uhmm…"

"But they said they're trying to eliminate him as a suspect," I explained.

"That makes sense," Dave said.

"So until they tell me that they've cleared him…Until then he is a suspect right?"

"I don't know what they're thinking," he said.

"But they questioned him…"

"If he is a suspect, you don't want him talking to them. Wait 'til they clear him."

"So what do I do?"

"Just wait. It'll be okay. Don't worry. He just needs to tell them the truth."

It is difficult to be honest about the choices that I made. Torey did not want to go to school that morning. He wanted me to stay home with him. But I told him that I had to go to work and that he should go to school. There was nothing we could do. We had to go on.

I let my son down when he needed me the most. I did not give Torey the time he needed to tell me what had happened. Over the next two and a half days Torey tried to tell me, but I did not give him the opportunity. As far as I was concerned, he was not involved, and I did not want to talk to him, or anyone else, about what happened to Cassie.

I work in the circulation department of the local newspaper. When I went into work that morning the whole office was buzzing with the news of the murder. Ian Fennel, the editor, was speaking to my manager. He wanted to get the student's reactions from the high school Cassie attended, and he knew some of us in circulation had kids that went to school with her. He wanted to know whose kids knew Cassie the best, and who would be willing to give an interview.

I put my things down on my desk and sat with my back toward him.

Kay Tilley, the office manager and my immediate boss, arranged for her daughter Kiara to come in and do the interview, although Kiara and Cassie were acquaintances at best.

Kiara, who was two years older than Cassie, had actually graduated the year before. I remember thinking it was strange that they would use Kiara to do the interview. But it was the talk of the office, just like I am sure it was the talk everywhere across town that day, and Kay was just trying to be helpful.

Office personnel were questioning why Cassie was not found until Sunday. If they hadn't heard from one of their children for a few *hours* they would be driving over to check on them, let alone *days*. It was also known that some high school students were with her before she was killed, but their identities were still unknown. There was speculation about who they were, though no one seemed to think that a couple of kids could be responsible for something like this.

One of the representatives in the classified department, whose desk was across the aisle from mine, was giving out details about the kids that were at the house that night. I wondered where she was getting her information, especially since it was erroneous. She described a scene of drinking and partying.

I was watching her. She speculated that after the kids left, someone else must have entered the house and attacked Cassie, someone who knew that she was going to be alone. As she was talking she noticed that I was watching her. She turned her attention back to her work.

It was not long before I realized that coming to work, and sending Torey to school, was a mistake. It was emotionally difficult for me to listen to everyone talk about what happened, I could not imagine how much more difficult it had to be for Torey. I hoped that the school would try to keep the talk to a minimum.

But I was not thinking correctly. I thought that we could keep Matt, Torey and Brian's identities private. I did not even want to tell the school officials that Torey had been one of the boys who had been at the house that night because I saw less benefit in doing so than in shielding him, and all three boys, from the attention such knowledge would bring. I thought that even if their identities did eventually become known, it wouldn't be until much later. I honestly believed we could keep it private for some time.

I should have realized right away that everyone would know that Matt was one of the boys who had been at the house, simply because he was Cassie's boyfriend, and that it would only be a matter of time before Matt would tell who the other boys were. But, like I said, I was not thinking correctly. Or I simply was not thinking at all.

I did not want people that I worked with to know that Torey was one of the boys who had been with Cassie on the night that she was killed. I did not want to have to explain a situation I still could not believe we were involved in. And I definitely did not want to listen to the speculation going on around me any longer.

I thought if I could tell Dave Maple, the Circulation Director, what was happening, maybe he would let me leave, pick up Torey, and go home. I decided that was what I was going to do.

I knocked on his door. He was getting ready for a meeting but I asked him if he had a minute. "Just a minute, but sure, come on in," he said.

I entered his office nervously. I shut the door behind me and took the nearest chair across from his desk and sat down.

Dave was a large man with blond hair and a ready smile. He always had a "Isn't this great?" kind of attitude. I'd never seen him angry or upset. He was approachable and he seemed to care about his coworkers. That is why I thought I could speak with him.

Still I was struggling with how to begin.

I was simply going to explain the situation and ask if I could leave, but for some reason I found that impossible. I did not know how to say, "I'm worried. The police questioned my son. I want to take him home until things calm down."

Instead I heard myself say, "The girl that was killed... Cassie... Torey was one of the kids that was with her that night."

"Oh," he said. "I'm sorry."

I meant to say, "So you can see that he is obviously upset and I need to go home." But I did not say that. I just sat there for a moment hoping that Dave would understand and say it for me, but he didn't.

Finally I said, "I don't want anyone to know. I don't want Ian, (the editor) talking to him, I don't want anyone talking to him."

"Okay," Dave said.

"I don't want him in the news, and I'm worried because I work here." The fact that Ian had been in our department and that reporters had been coming and going all morning legitimized the fear.

"Don't worry about it, no one will know," Dave assured me. "Just because you work here doesn't mean you don't have the right to privacy. I understand. I'm a parent. I won't say anything and you don't need to say anything either."

"What about Kay?" I asked referring to my boss.

"Why would you need to tell Kay?" Dave asked.

"I just…I don't know." Again I wanted to say, "Because I will not be able to focus on my work, and she will notice, and I need to go home." But I just couldn't say it. It is a problem I've always had and it is the reason I went to work that day and sent Torey to school. I have a problem with confrontation. I knew if I called in to work sick or needing a personal day off that I would have to do some explaining and I could not face it.

"No. Don't say anything to anyone. Just go back to work. It will be alright," Dave said.

But it wasn't.

Torey called me at work. He was going to his friend Adam's house for lunch. I was glad that Adam was with Torey, glad that he was leaving school. I told Torey that if he did not feel like returning to school that day he didn't have to.

Torey stayed with Adam that day and even stayed for dinner

at his house that night. Torey did not come home until around seven p.m. I'd not had a chance to talk with him since that morning and I asked him how he was doing.

"I don't know."

"How was it at school?"

"I don't know. Terrible."

"Did anyone say anything to you?"

"Yeah, everyone wanted to know what happened."

"Who is everyone?"

"Everyone."

"What! They know you were there?" I asked, upset.

"Of course they know. Matt was there, Brian was there. I was there. Everyone knows."

"Oh my God! I did not even think of that!"

"How did you not know?" He looked surprised.

"I'm...I'm just...dumb...I just...didn't think...I'm sorry. "

"It's okay...I just want to go to bed. I don't feel good."

"Okay, but what did they say to you?"

"Everyone is just asking what happened and saying all this stuff about Cassie that isn't true. They don't know Cassie."

"Like what kind of stuff?" I asked.

"They're just saying stuff about her, about her family. About what happened to her. Things they don't know about."

"Like what?" I pushed. "What could they be saying?"

"I don't know. I don't want to talk about it."

"What about Adam?"

"What about him?"

"Is he helping you?"

"Yeah. Adam's helping."

That night Sean and I had a discussion about the detectives. Would they call us when Torey was eliminated as a suspect, or would they be too busy with their investigation? I was concerned that we hadn't heard from them that day. Sean took it as a good sign, but I was not so sure. I told Sean that I'd called my brother that morning and he had said not to let them question Torey while he was under investigation, but to wait until he was cleared.

Sean said, "Really!"

"Yeah."

"I wonder if we really do need a lawyer?" Sean asked.

"If I don't hear from him by noon tomorrow I'll call

Detective Ganske," I said. "Let's wait until then to decide. If Torey's not cleared I'll call you at work and let you know." I felt we did not need to spend money on an attorney if Torey was cleared, but if he wasn't…We knew nothing about the legal system, what our rights were, how to protect Torey. We would need someone to help us.

"Alright. I am going to take the number to Huntley Park with me just in case we need it," Sean said. Huntley Park was the prepaid legal service that Sean participated in through his work at Robert Allen Auto. They would eventually be the ones who would recommend the attorneys we would retain for Torey's legal defense.

"Do you think we should call Mom?" I asked Sean referring to his mother, Barbara.

"She's busy. I don't think there's a reason to worry her. We'll tell her when it's over." Sean said.

CHAPTER EIGHT

Tuesday, September 26, 2006

Torey went to school that morning. I did not expect him to make it through the day. I told him that he could come home anytime he wanted to, or he could go to Adam's house until I came home from work. Torey said that he needed to talk to me later that night.

I was having a hard time concentrating at work with the office talk still centering on Cassie. I decided I needed to confide in Kay, and let her know what was going on. I asked her if I could speak to her alone shortly after I arrived at work that morning.

"Sure," she said.

We went to a small, private office in the back of the building. "What's up?" she asked when we were seated.

"Oh God, Kay, I don't know how to say this..."

"What?"

"Torey was with Cassie the night she was killed."

"Oh my God!"

"Yeah. I'm really upset about it."

"I would be too."

"The police have been to our house."

"You're kidding," she said.

"No. And I have to call them today because they're eliminating Torey as a suspect so they can find who did this."

"They questioned Torey?" She asked in disbelief.

"Yes. On Sunday night."

"Oh my God," she said slowly.

"I know. That's why I am so upset. I needed to tell you I'm not doing good."

"No, you're doing fine, I didn't even know."

"No. I'm not really. I'm not fine," I said.

"Well, it will be okay. You know that. We'll just go back out and you do the best that you can. I understand."

I nodded my head.

"How's Torey doing?" she asked.

"Not good. He said he hates the way people are talking about Cassie, the things they're saying at school."

"I know, people can be cruel, can't they? It'll get better," she promised, nodding her head. "Let me know what I can do to help."

When we got back to our desks I whispered, "You know

Torey didn't do this, right? That's not why I told you. I just wanted you to know."

"Oh no! I know he didn't do it, I wouldn't think that," Kay assured me.

I waited until noon for one of the detectives to call me on my cell phone. When they didn't I called them. There was every chance they were finished with Torey and we just didn't know it. I stepped over to Kay's phone, she was at lunch, her desk was vacant, and took the card that Detective Ganske had given me out of my purse and dialed the number.

Detective Ganske identified himself when he answered the phone. I told him it was Shannon Adamcik calling. Torey's mom.

He said that he had been planning to call me.

I said, "I was just wondering if you had a chance to go through the phone records yet?"

"We're still working on them. As a matter of fact, the FBI is working on them," he said.

"The FBI!" I cried, shocked.

"Yeah."

"How long is *that* going to take?"

"Well, I really don't know because there are some other things in Torey's story that just aren't adding up," he said. "We're going to have to talk with him again. In fact, I was going to call you to have him come in for a polygraph."

"A polygraph! What for?" I could not believe it.

"It's just another means we use to eliminate suspects."

"Is that what you're using it for? To *eliminate* him as a suspect?" I asked, distressed.

"You know…do you really think that he was being totally honest when we talked with him the other night?" he asked.

"I'm not sure, I don't know what you mean," I said, getting more and more upset.

"Parts of his story just don't ring true," he answered.

"What parts? I don't know what you're talking about."

"I think he needs to come in and tell us the truth, because I don't feel like he was telling us the whole truth."

"What do you mean the *whole* truth? Are you saying you think he knows something or what? What could he be lying about that would make him guilty of something like *this*?"

"I just said we need to have him come in and talk to us again.

Matt and Brian have already agreed to a polygraph, and we need Torey to take one too. That's it."

"I'm going to talk to my husband, because I don't know," I said, wondering how this could be happening.

"Call your husband because we need to get Torey in as soon as possible."

"Like when?"

"We'd like him to come in sometime today."

"Not until we get those phone records back," I said. "You said when you verified his story you would eliminate him. I'll talk to you then."

"Listen," he raised his voice, "call your husband. Torey has to come in and talk to us. If he takes the polygraph and it clears him…we can move on."

After I hung up with Detective Ganske I called Sean. "We need to talk to Torey," I said. "I called Detective Ganske and they want Torey to take a polygraph. He said some of Torey's story was not checking out."

"I'm calling an attorney." Sean immediately said.

"If he has to go in, I don't know what to do." There was no way I wanted Torey questioned until he was cleared.

"We have the prepaid legal, I am going to call them and I will call you right back," Sean said.

"Hurry."

I sat at my desk stupefied. How could this be happening? We had not heard a word from the detectives all day yesterday and yet they were looking at Torey this whole time! Torey!!! Who had never been in any trouble! It was unbelievable.

When Kay returned from lunch, Dave Maple came over to her desk. Occasionally the Journal publishes pictures of its staff in the newspaper as a publicity stunt. They were going to photograph everyone in the circulation department for an upcoming issue. He wanted us to take turns going back to the photography room to get our individual pictures taken.

I had been sitting at my desk, waiting for Sean to call back, trying to maintain control. I couldn't do it any longer. I said, "I'm not getting my picture taken."

Dave thought I was teasing. "Come on," he said with a persuasive smile, "you have to."

"I'm not!" I said. I started to cry. Immediately Dave looked uncomfortable.

I was sitting at my desk, unable to move, falling apart. Dave did not know what to say, he looked around searching for help.

Kay, in her desk, next to mine, jumped up. "She just needs to take a break. Come on, let's go outside," she said, taking me by the arm.

People from all over the Journal were watching us. Katie Foster, the promotions manager, wanted to know what was going on. She went outside with us.

Once we were outside I told them about my phone call with Detective Ganske and that Sean was calling an attorney. "I'm going home," I said.

Torey was already at home when I got there. As soon as I walked through the door I said, "We have to talk, Torey."

"I want to talk to you too, Mom," he said.

Sean was still at work but he'd called me on the cell phone as I was driving home. He had talked with someone from Huntley-Park, our prepaid legal service, and they were going to have an attorney call us. I wanted to talk with Torey first.

We were in the dining room. I was sitting down on the chair at the end of the table closest to the sliding glass doors, and Torey was standing in front of them. His face was pale in the light. I looked closely at him; he had dark circles under his eyes. "How *are* you?" I asked.

"I don't know," he said.

"Are you okay?" I could tell by looking at him that he wasn't.

"I don't know."

I said, " Torey...Son...I'm worried. I talked to the detective today and he said your story's not checking out…all the way."

Torey did not say anything. I'd said I was worried and I was, but Torey *looked* worried. In fact he looked *terrified*.

"Torey, I don't want to say this, but I have to ask...Do you *know* what happened to Cassie?"

The extreme discomfort in Torey's body and the look of anguish on his face made it clear to me that whatever Torey was feeling, it was definitely painful. He was clearly having a hard time with it. He did not say anything. He looked at me and I could tell that he was going to fall apart right there in front of me. I could not take it.

"I *know* that you did not have anything to do with this Torey!

I know that! That is not what I meant." I was trying to take back what I'd said, to clarify what I'd meant. "But I just need to know if you know anything, okay, because I have to know...It's...It's something I *have to know*."

I have deep regrets about certain aspects of my parenting. I was a strict parent. I expected things to go my way, and I really tolerated very little questioning or independence in my children. I was not good at the unconditional love that this has since taught me.

I am not saying that I did not love my children. I love my children more than anything in this world. But I was caught up in things that do not matter, trivial things that I attached great significance to, such as grades and appearances. Things that I used to feel good about myself and let people around me know that I was a GOOD parent.

I told my children every day that I loved them, but no matter how many times I told my children that I loved them, the truth is I was unapproachable. I was not accepting of any standards but my own. I was critical and quick to judge and I had a sharp tongue. All sins of great parental magnitude easily cloaked under, "I just want what's best for you."

Torey and I are close. But Torey was dependent on me, controlled by me, and he was scared of me. And because of that fear, he could not open up to me.

I don't know who Torey could have opened up to. The only one I can think of would have been his friend Adam. Torey had his cousins, his brother and sister. But his best chance was probably Adam, and that would have been too hard on both of them.

"No! Nooo! Please, no," Torey cried.

I had to tell Torey about the attorney, carefully, because I did not want to give him the impression that we'd called an attorney because we thought that he might have had something to do with this, especially after the question I'd just asked. I had to make him understand that it was a precaution only.

"Torey, I'm going to tell you something and I want you to listen to me very carefully," I said. "You did not do anything. I know that. I know you better than anyone else in this world. But Dad and I want to be safe and we want to talk to an attorney. Dad's going to call an attorney today and they will be calling here. We just need to ask them some questions, okay. This does not mean that we think anything, Torey. We're just trying to do the right thing and play it safe."

I took a deep breath waiting for his reaction. Torey said, "Matt's getting an attorney. He told us at school today that his parents are getting him one."

"They're probably taking a precaution, like us." I said.

"The police are going to make him take a polygraph."

"Torey, sit down," I said, pointing to the chair next to me. He was still standing by the sliding glass door and I wanted to talk to him face to face.

Torey sat down. I told him, "A polygraph is not reliable. I don't know why they want Matt to take one."

I had been thinking about this since the detectives left Sunday night. I knew that Torey was incapable of harming someone. Torey and Brian had been to Cassie's house together and they had left together. That is why I never suspected Brian.

After Torey and Brian left, Matt was alone in the house with Cassie before his mother picked him up. But I did not think that they were alone long enough for Matt to attack Cassie, and have time to clean himself up afterwards. If Matt did this he would have had something on him when his mother picked him up.

I believed it had to be someone who came into the house after the boys were gone.

But the lights troubled me. The detectives said that Matt told them the lights went off while he was alone with Cassie. If something was happening with the lights, and Cassie was scared, why leave her alone? That made no sense. I could not imagine Matt or his mother leaving Cassie alone in the house in the dark. Why hadn't they taken her with them, or at least called her mother? Cassie was only 16 years old; she should have never been left alone.

"He said they're making him take it," Torey told me.

"Detective Ganske wants you to take one too," I said.

"Am I going to?"

"I don't know...I'm asking the lawyer what he recommends."

Though I really did not see how it could be possible, I asked Torey if he thought that Matt could have had something to do with what happened to Cassie.

"No," he said.

"What about the lights?" I asked him. "Isn't it weird that he'd leave her alone in the dark? How could he do that?"

Torey said something that, at the time, I missed. He said, "If I didn't know what was going to happen to Cassie, how would Matt know?"

I thought he meant no one expected what happened to Cassie to happen. But since then I've thought about it a lot. I think Torey might have meant what he said: that neither Torey nor Matt knew what was going to happen to Cassie, and more; that perhaps Matt knew someone was in the house and who it was, when he left Cassie alone that night.

"If you killed someone you would have something on you," Torey said.

"Yes. You would have something on you and you would leave something on the person you killed. Something like maybe a hair. And they can identify people now by the tiniest little particle. Less than a hair or a skin cell," I said.

"So can you frame someone for killing somebody if they didn't do it?" Torey asked.

"I don't know. What do you mean?"

"If someone *didn't* do it, couldn't you tell that by the DNA like you can tell if someone did do it?"

"Yeah. There are people who are cleared by DNA evidence. Sure," I said.

"I feel like I'm being framed." Torey looked at me, serious and scared.

"Ohh, Torey, no. No. They just think you might know something. Something that you don't even know that you know. No one thinks you did this," I told him, shaking my head.

Despite my objections to the police questioning Torey, what I was saying to reassure him, is what I believed was the truth.

"I'll just give them a DNA test. That will show them," Torey said.

"It's not going to come to that, Torey. This will be over long before that happens."

When the attorney from Huntley Park finally called, she spoke to Torey. The situation pertained to him and her advice was for him. She told Torey not to go the police station without representation under any circumstance. She was not a retainable attorney, because she simply contracted with Huntley-Park to give free legal advice by phone to their members who called in, but if he needed an attorney, Huntley Park would recommend one. If the police insisted on speaking with him, Torey could agree to let them question him at home, provided that he had absolutely nothing to do with the crime, and no knowledge of it. She recommended that he not take a polygraph.

"Did you tell her everything that you know?" I asked him when he hung up.

"Yeah."

"Okay."

Torey went over to Adam's house again that night but came home early. Sean and I discussed the attorney's recommendations. We decided to take her advice and not allow Torey to give a polygraph or speak with the detectives at the police station. We hoped that would be enough to protect Torey, but wondered if it was going to be necessary to retain an attorney as well. We decided that Sean would call Huntley Park in the morning and get a referral, just in case we needed it.

CHAPTER NINE

Wednesday, September 27, 2006.

It took me a long time to realize that September 27, 2006, wasn't the worst day of my life. It was the day my life ended. But the real anniversary was September 22nd.

Torey had gotten up that morning and driven himself and Jamie to school. But he called me while I was at work to say that he 'd dropped Jamie off at school and went back home. I told Torey that I had a short errand to run after work and that I would be there as soon as I was finished, at about 1:30. (I only worked a half a day on Wednesdays.)

During my shift that morning I talked with Katie Foster, the promotions manager. She wanted to know how things were going. I told her that we were in the process of retaining an attorney for Torey to help us deal with the police until he was cleared.

"How much is that going to cost you?" she asked.

"I don't know, too much I would guess," I said.

Before I left work for the day, either Detective Ganske called me, or I called him. I cannot remember which.

Detective Ganske said, "You have to bring Torey in for questioning. He was not at school today."

"I know he wasn't." I said, wondering why he had that information. "Have the phone records come back yet?"

"Yes they have. That is one of the things that we need to discuss."

"What did they say?"

"We need to talk about that in person. We need you to come in."

"Why?" I asked. "What did they say?"

"They just brought up some questions that we need answered. That's all."

"What kind of questions?"

"I think Torey can answer that the best," he said.

"This has been terrible for Torey and I'm not taking him to the police station. I think it will be much easier on him if you came to our house." I was trying to follow the advice the attorney had given Torey.

"We can't do that," Ganske said. "He needs to come down to

the station. We need him to take a polygraph and we need to take his fingerprints, all these things we have to do from here."

"It sounds like you think Torey might have had something to do with this!" I said.

"We've already talked about this. We need to fingerprint him to compare his prints to what we found in the house."

"Sean has to work today and Jamie has a football game tonight so I don't know when I'd be able to bring him in…It's just a bad night." I said. "Have you cleared him yet?"

"We can't clear him until we talk to him."

"And you need a polygraph to do that? I already told you that I do not want you talking to Torey until he's cleared!" I was emphatic and upset.

"We *cannot* clear him until we talk to him," Ganske said, upset too.

"I don't know what to say then. Give me until tomorrow. We just have too much going on right now," I said, trying to think.

Maybe if we waited long enough it would just go away. That's what I'd been hoping. But now I knew it was too late. We needed an attorney right away and I needed to stall the detectives long enough to get one.

"Listen," Ganske stated, "we are going to talk with Torey today. Not tomorrow. Today. We will give you until five o'clock tonight. But Torey is coming in tonight. There is no more messing around here."

Detective Ganske wanted me to commit to the time, and I listed a number of reasons why I could not. Jamie's football game was the most valid reason that I could come up with. I remember telling Ganske that I needed to drop Jamie off at his game first but that perhaps I could bring Torey over to the police station afterwards. I remember telling Detective Ganske that I would try to do that.

But the real problem was that I wasn't sure we could get Torey an attorney by five p.m. I finally said, "Let me call Sean, I'll have to call you back."

"It better be quick," Detective Ganske said.

I hung up and phoned Sean at work.

Sean had already spoken with Huntley Park and he was expecting to hear back from them at any moment. As soon as he received the recommendation for a local attorney he would contact the attorney and request an immediate appointment. Sean felt certain they would work us in under the conditions, but there was nothing either one of us could do but wait.

When I left work I stopped by Home Depot and exchanged two large flowerpots that I had bought for the backyard. This was the errand I told Torey I needed to run.

I remember thinking that I was being crazy, that I should go straight home and be with my son. But I kept telling myself that it was okay, I could do normal things. Just because the police wanted to question Torey did not mean anything bad was going to happen. I could shop for a minute. It was an internal war in my head that I can still remember to this day.

Sean and Torey were both at home when I got there. Sean told me that Huntley Park had recommended that we meet with Aaron Thompson, an attorney with Dial, May and Rammell to discuss Torey's legal rights. Sean had called to set up an appointment with Mr. Thompson, but he was out of the office. He spoke with Mr. Thompson's partners, Greg May and Bron Rammell, and had set up an appointment to meet with them at five p.m.

I told Sean that was when we were supposed to be at the police station. He said we could go to the station afterwards if we still needed to, or the attorneys could accompany us. That was fine with me because I had not committed to the actual time. I'd told Ganske that Sean works until 5:30 and we did have Jamie's football game to contend with as well.

Torey had been listening. He said he had something to tell us.

"What?" I asked him.

"I…lied to the police," he said.

Sean was standing at the kitchen counter eating his lunch. Torey and I were at the table. Sean came over and sat down by us.

"About what?" I asked.

"The movies. We never went to the movies," he said nervously.

"You never went to the movies! Why in the hell would you lie about the movies?" I asked.

Torey did not answer.

Sean said, "Why Torey? Tell us."

"I'm scared I'm in trouble."

"Yes you're in trouble! I told you yesterday the detectives said something was wrong with your story. Is this it?" I was very upset.

"Yeah."

"Well...Tell us!"

"Brian and I were going through cars."

"What do you mean, going through cars?" I asked.

"We were looking for change in cars."

"Are you kidding me?" I yelled at him.

"No," he said, "I'm sorry."

"You're sorry! That's a felony! Where were you?"

Sean told me to calm down. "We need to handle this one step at a time," he said. "Torey where were you?"

"We were up by Cassie's house."

"Holy crap, Torey! That puts you *right there*!" I screamed. This was awful.

Sean turned to me and said very quietly. "You either need to calm down or you need to leave the room."

"How can I calm down?" I asked.

"Because you're going to," Sean said.

He turned to Torey who was stricken with fear. "Now, we have to tell the detectives the truth. You should have done it the first night, but I can see why you didn't. After what happened to your friend, I can't believe you did this." Sean was referring to a friend of Torey's who had been caught going through cars with some other kids. The friend ended up taking the blame for everyone involved, was fined, put on probation, and grounded for months.

"The problem is, now that you've lied, it's going to be harder to make the detectives believe you. But there is a good side," Sean said.

"A good side to him being right there!" I was nearly hysterical. Torey was slumping into the table.

"Yes there is a good side!" Sean yelled at me. He turned around and faced Torey. "Torey…You might have seen something. You need to think about it. You might have noticed something that you don't even recognize."

"Like what?"

"Like a car, or a sound, or something that wasn't right. The police aren't going to care about the cars. You're not going to be in trouble for that right now. So everybody just calm down." Sean glared at me.

Actually what Sean said made sense. This might not be that bad. The detectives needed to know why Torey's phone was still in the area and that was why they were demanding to speak with us.

Sean had to go back to work. He left Torey and I alone. He

would meet us at the Attorney's office at five o'clock. He gave me the directions. Before he left Sean told Torey that it was going to be okay.

I could not help myself. Despite the fact that Torey looked so miserable, so frightened, I said, "Torey, this is exactly why I always need to know where you're at! This is why there always has to be an adult. You don't know what can happen."

"I know!" Torey cried. "I wish I wouldn't have gone!"

I'd thought to myself, even as I said it, "This is no way to learn a lesson. Things like this don't really happen." But I'd said it anyway.

Torey got up from the table and went downstairs. I followed him. He sat on the couch and pulled his books out of his backpack. I did not know what to say. I could see that Torey could not take any more. He arranged his schoolwork and I went upstairs and did what I always do when I'm worried or anxious. I cleaned the house.

At 3:20 p.m. I left to pick Jamie up from school. He was excited about the football game that night. When we got home, Torey had a bag of chips and he was sitting on the couch downstairs eating them and watching television while he did his homework. It was only a bag of chips, but it was the first time that I'd seen Torey eat in days. I smiled at him and he smiled back.

Earlier in the week Sean and I had discussed calling his mother, Barbara, and letting her know what was happening with Torey. I felt we should and I have always wondered if things would have been different if we had. She could have insisted that we get Torey an attorney right away. But Sean did not want to worry her. However, I have always relied on Barbara's advice. I decided to call her and tell Sean later.

I took the phone downstairs into Lacey's bedroom. I shut the door so that Torey would not hear me and called her. I told Barbara that Torey had been at Cassie's house the night that she was killed, and that the police had questioned him. For a moment, she did not know what to say.

"We've got an appointment with an attorney at five o'clock tonight," I said.

She agreed that was a good idea and asked that we keep her posted.

We met with the attorneys sooner than expected. At approximately four-thirty, Sean called. He said I needed to bring

Torey to the attorney's office right away.

"I thought we were going at five o'clock," I said. "I was going to drop Jamie off at his football practice on the way."

"You don't have time. I'm here now. You need to leave right away," Sean said, emphatically.

"Why?"

"I'll explain when you get here."

"What's going on?"

"Some detectives showed up at my work looking for Torey, that's what's going on!" he said. "I told them we had a meeting with an attorney and they drove me here in their car. They wouldn't let me call you."

"Oh my God, are you kidding me? We've been here all day! Ganske's not even called!" I said.

(What neither Sean nor I knew was that Brian Draper had just gone to the Bannock County Sheriff's Office and blamed Torey for Cassie's death. A task force was immediately dispatched to locate Torey. As officers arrived at Sean's work, others were on their way to our house.)

"Would you get over here now, please?" Sean said with extreme irritation.

I told Torey and Jamie that we needed to leave right away. Dad was at the attorney's office waiting for us. I quickly jotted down a note for Lacey telling her where we were. She would be coming home from school soon and getting ready for her shift at Dillard's.

"I don't have to be there yet," Jamie said referring to his game.

"I know, but I've got this appointment and I won't have time to come back and get you."

"This sucks. Why can't Lacey take me?" he asked.

"She's got work tonight," I said.

Jamie was grumbling, but he hurried and gathered up his gear. I was rushing him as Torey sat on the bottom step of the stairs putting on his shoes, a pair of black converse high-top sneakers. After years of wearing slip-on skate shoes it seemed to take Torey forever to put on a regular pair of tennis shoes. As we headed to the car I remember trying to lighten the mood. I made a little joke and put my hand on Torey's arm. He smiled at me.

Jamie was so upset about having to go with us that I did not even get a chance to talk with Torey on the ride to the attorney's office. Jamie complained the whole way. He asked how long this meeting was going to take. I told him if we were lucky I could drop him off at practice and we might finish before the game even started, but I wasn't sure. When Jamie realized we might miss his game he was shocked. That had never happened.

Minutes after the boys and I left, Jeff came over to the house to pick up some movies that he and Lacey had rented. He was driving Lacey's Honda Civic, which had an automatic garage door opener in it. As soon as Jeff pulled into the garage and exited the car, two Pocatello Police Officers came up behind him. They told him they were looking for Torey and asked to search the vehicle. Jeff let them. He watched as they ransacked everything inside the car. When they were done, he asked if he could go inside the house and retrieve the movies.

The officers asked Jeff if he knew who was inside the residence. He said that he did not. He had just arrived and had not yet been inside the house, as they well knew. The officers let Jeff enter the house, retrieve the movies, and leave.

At the same time, Adam Dykman was pulled over by a Pocatello police officer as he drove his Ford Escort down Yellowstone Highway. "What can I do for you officer?" Adam asked when the officer approached his window.

"We're looking for Torey Adamcik. I'm going to need to search your vehicle," the officer told him. Adam complied. He also told the officer that he had not seen Torey that day because Torey had not been in school.

"Is there any way he could be hiding at your house?" the officer asked him.

"No. He is not at my house," Adam said.

The officer told Adam that he needed to go to the police station for questioning. Adam called his parents and they met him there.

Dial, May and Rammell is located in old town Pocatello. It is on the top floor of the Pocatello Railroad Credit Union next to the bus depot and in front of the railroad tracks. It is not an attractive location for an attorney's office. It's surrounded by gravel and parking lots.

Sean had been standing outside of the building with the two detectives that escorted him there, waiting for me to arrive. As soon as I pulled into the parking lot the two detectives got into their separate vehicles and watched as Torey, Jamie and I joined Sean in front of the building. I did not see nor notice them.

We entered the building through the side door and climbed two flights of stairs to a dingy office space above.

At a quarter after four, Sean had been parking a car outside the garage of the dealership where he worked. As he was walking back into the shop two detectives met him in front of the garage doors and identified themselves. One was from the Pocatello Police Department. The other, Detective Anderson, was from the Bannock County Sheriff's Department.

They told Sean they were looking for Torey and they needed to find him right away. "He was not in school today," Detective Anderson said.

"We had him stay home from school," Sean said, not realizing the danger Torey was in. "He's at home now, with my wife."

"We need him at the station now."

Sean asked which station, the sheriff's office or the Pocatello Police Department?

Detective Anderson said, "It doesn't matter. He just needs to be detained. He needs to answer some questions."

Sean said, "We're in the process of retaining an attorney. We have an appointment at five o'clock tonight."

One of the detectives asked, "Will Torey be there?"

"Yes."

"Who's the attorney?"

Sean said, "Dial, May... It's just a minute from here, by the bus station."

The detective said, "I know where that is. We'll take you there."

Sean said, "Well...first I need to tell my boss I'm leaving."

Detective Anderson said, "No phone calls. We don't want you calling anyone."

Sean went inside the garage door and told his supervisor that he had finished his work for the day and was leaving.

When Sean returned, Detective Anderson pointed toward his vehicle, a gray truck, which was parked just outside the garage door. Opening the door for Sean he said, "Get in."

Sean sat in the front seat while Detective Anderson drove him to the attorney's office with the Pocatello police officer following behind them in a separate vehicle.

Detective Anderson answered a status call on the radio while they were in route. He said, "I have Mr. Adamcik. We are heading to their lawyer's office. Torey will be there. Cancel the ATL (Attempt To Locate). The plans have changed."

Once they arrived at the attorney's office, the detectives waited in the parking lot with Sean for me to arrive. Defying orders, Sean called me while they were waiting.

All that I knew was what Sean had told me over the phone.

I did not know that officers were attempting to detain Torey, nor that two detectives were sitting in the parking lot watching us, waiting to follow us when we left. I did not know any of that. And none of us knew that we had left home mere minutes before officers arrived to arrest Torey. Or that Adam was at that very moment being questioned by two detectives at the Pocatello Police Department along with his girlfriend Amber.

Inside the attorney's waiting room Sean joked about his unexpected ride in a police car, making light of the situation so that Torey would not worry. Unfortunately it put me at ease as well. I did not realize what had happened and the severity of the situation.

We sat on the couches in the reception area and waited for the attorney together. I never considered the possibility that Torey might need to speak to the attorney alone. I never considered there could be something that Torey could not say to us or in front of us. I *never* expected Torey to have any real information about what happened to Cassie.

I was worried that because of Torey's presence inside of the residence on the night that Cassie was killed, some people might consider him a suspect, and if the detectives could not find the person responsible for Cassie's murder, Torey could be stigmatized by the fact that he was there. I did not know how far the police would go to incriminate or clear him.

An older gentleman came out to greet us. He introduced himself as Greg May. We stood in a semicircle around him. Sean said, "I'm Sean, this is my wife Shannon and this is Jamie and Torey."

"Nice to meet you," Greg said, shaking our hands as we were introduced.

"And I understand we want to talk to…?" He looked from Torey to Jamie.

"Torey," Sean said, placing his hand on Torey's shoulder.

"Okay. Like I told you earlier, Sean, Aaron's out of town right now, in trial, but we could go down to the conference room and I can help you tonight."

I asked, "Should Jamie come with us?"

"He can wait here," Greg said. "I'll have someone get him a drink." Greg caught the eye of the girl behind the reception desk and nodded in Jamie's direction.

As Greg began to escort us down the hallway a tall, blond man joined us. Greg introduced him. His name was Brian Chaney. Greg told us that Brian was new to the firm and would be joining us as an observer only.

At the end of the hall, through the last doorway on the right, was a library. The room was lined, floor to ceiling, with bookshelves filled to overflowing, and even more law books were scattered on the floor, and piled on chairs. A large, rectangular table stood in the center of the room. A small computer desk was at the end opposite the door. Greg motioned us inside.

Greg sat at the head of the table. Sean took the chair to his right. Torey sat next to Sean and I sat across from Sean on Greg's left. Brian Chaney was next to me, across from Torey.

Torey was looking at me. He looked visibly worried, but I thought that he would be all right when we were finished.

"Jamie has a football game and I need to drop him off, so I might need to leave for a few minutes," I told Greg as soon as we were seated.

"Not a problem," he said. "So what's going on? What can we do for you today?" He leaned back in his chair, as if to include everyone.

Sean hesitated a moment, "Well, like I was telling you on the phone…You know about the girl that was killed?"

"Yes?"

"Torey was there that night…"

Greg slowly nodded his head. He sat up and leaned forward.

"And the police have been questioning him."

"So the police have talked to you?" Greg asked Torey, leaning in toward him, elbows on the table.

Sean answered for him, "Yes."

Greg turned to Sean. "And what did they question him about?"

"Well they came over Sunday night...told us that they had found Cassie...and they needed to talk to Torey because he and his friends were the last people to see Cassie alive."

"They needed to know if Torey knew anything that would help them," I added.

"They photographed Torey's car, his hands, and had him write down where he was Friday night." Sean continued.

Greg looked at Torey and asked, "Do you know anything about what happened to her Torey? Do you know anything at all?"

Everyone's eyes turned to Torey. He quietly said, "No," and shook his head.

"Because Torey," Greg said, still looking directly at him, "if you know anything at all, if you know anything...if you were there and something happened...in the eyes of the law you are as guilty of what happened as whoever did it. Do you understand what I am saying?"

Brian Chaney, next to me, was nodding his head.

Torey just looked at Greg. I looked at him too, but I was thinking he was missing the point. We were not there because Torey had any information. We were there because the police thought he might.

There was a knock at the door; it was opened a crack and a large man with glasses and a balding head poked through. "Sorry I'm late," he said. "Just got tied up for a minute with…" he mentioned a name to Greg. "Took longer than I thought."

"You get it taken care of?" Greg asked him.

The man shook his head, "Ehhh," and motioned with his hand so-so.

Greg told us, "This is my partner, Bron Rammell. Bron, this is Sean and Shannon Adamcik. Their son Torey." He nodded to each of us as Bron came in and closed the door.

I said, "I need to drop Jamie off or he'll be late. I'll be right back." I did not want to miss the consultation but I had to go.

"We'll just fill Bron in while you're gone," Greg said.

Jamie wanted to know how much longer until the meeting was over. I told him, "We're almost done. I just don't want you to be late."

"I can be late to practice," Jamie said.

"But then you might not be able to play in the game."

"You think you might miss the game?"

"I don't think so. I hope not. "

It was less than a mile to Jamie's practice. I was back in ten minutes.

When I returned, Bron was seated at the table. He had been telling everyone about the unreliability of polygraph testing, and explaining the reasons why Torey should refuse the test.

Torey's poor face was so drawn and tired, I looked at him and thought, "Where is my boy?" He did not look like himself.

Bron mentioned one of his previous cases. He was sure that we had heard of it, but we hadn't.

"Are you sure?" he asked us, surprised.

Sean and I shook our heads no. "We really don't follow the news that closely," I apologized.

Bron said it was a very difficult case of attempted murder. He let us know he won it. That was the kind of experience he had. He'd never lost a jury trial. Not one. He was letting us know what his record was. Both he and Greg had years of experience. They were one of the most respected law firms in the area. If we needed a defense we could not do better than Dial, May and Rammell. He guaranteed it.

Bron said, "That trial cost a little over a hundred thousand dollars to defend. And that was a few years ago. If we took a case like that to trial today, it would be more. You'd have to mortgage your house, come up with the money somewhere, before we could take it."

I did not understand what Bron was talking about. What did this have to do with Torey? I was not thinking about attempted murder or first-degree murder defenses. We were there to get help with the police interview and to protect our son.

Sean asked, "What about Torey? What about the police interview?"

Bron said, "Don't go. It's not going to be a good idea even if Torey doesn't know anything. You have to understand this police department. They're in trouble. They cannot afford to appear any more incompetent than they already do. Look at Nori Jones. They simply can't afford another case like that."

(Nori Jones was the victim of an unsolved homicide investigation.)

"But we have an appointment! They've wanted us to bring Torey in for three days now! It was the police who brought me here!" Sean said.

Bron repeated himself, "This police department… You have to understand. They are going to be working under community pressure to get this case solved and, like you said, Torey was right there. They will try to get him to say something they can use against him later if they need to. Who knows what they are going to make out of this? Don't go."

"Well then, what do you suggest we do?" Sean asked. "They said they were going to detain Torey! Obviously we have no choice but to go."

I asked, "Why can't he be questioned at home like the attorney on the phone said? Or why can't you go?" I did not understand the advice that they were giving us. It was not advice at all, because it was impossible to do what they were saying. The detectives were waiting for Torey at that very moment! Didn't they understand that?

Before Bron could answer Sean's cell phone rang. It was Detective Ganske.

Sean put his hand over the phone and said, "It's the detective. What should I tell him?"

Greg and Bron looked at each other. Neither said anything.

Sean spoke into the phone, desperately locking eyes with Greg. "We're still meeting with the attorneys. We will be there....shortly."

Ganske replied to Sean, and Sean again covered the mouthpiece and told us, "Ganske says we're already late. He wants to know when we're going to be there. What do I tell him?"

Again neither Greg nor Bron said anything.

When Sean saw that he was not going to get any help from the attorneys he finally said, "We're finishing up here."

Ganske told him, "I will see you in thirty minute then."

Sean said, "Okay."

"They're waiting for us," Sean told us, as he hung up.

Greg and Bron both looked grave. Greg leaned in across the table and looked directly at Torey. He said, "Son if you had anything to do with this, if you *know* anything about what happened, do not talk to the police. You can get an attorney. Even if Aaron does not take the case they have public defenders that you can talk to."

Bron was shaking his head. He had a look of grave concern on his face. "I would not recommend a public defender in this situation," he said. "But if you are going to need one, your best bet would be Dave Martinez. He's the only one that's any good."

I asked, "What's a public defender?"

"They are free, court appointed attorneys. But if it comes to that, remember you get what you pay for. If you need a defense, I guarantee you, you won't get the defense from them that you would get from us."

Sean asked, "Well, are you going with us tonight or not?"

And Greg spoke the words that I will remember for the rest of my life. "We are not prepared to go tonight," he said.

I would like to know why. Why couldn't they have gone with us? A couple of years have passed. We have been through the trial together; the pretrial motions, and Aaron's bitter fight to suppress the taped interview that would have *never* taken place if they would have just gone to the police station with us that night. And I want to know *why*. So far I have never received an answer to that question.

At the very least Greg should have called the detectives and told them that Torey was seeking representation and would not be giving an interview that night. But neither he nor Bron did that.

Bron said, "Just tell them that you were told that it's not a good idea to talk to them right now. You're in the process of retaining an attorney. Aaron will be available tomorrow. We can't do anything without him."

Greg said, "But look, you've gotten some good advice. You've had three good attorneys," he gestured toward Bron, Brian Chaney and himself. "We will only charge two-hundred dollars for this visit. Bron himself is a hundred and sixty-five dollars an hour so you can see what a good deal you're getting."

I could not see that at all. In fact, I could not see that they had done anything for us. And I've often wondered what they thought they did for us that night. They have never expressed any regrets, never admitted they made a mistake.

To this day I wonder why Greg and Bron allowed Sean and I into their consultation with Torey. As experienced attorneys, they should have known that if Torey had something to say about the crime, it would have been easier for him to talk to them without his parents present. And what if Torey had talked? What about his attorney-client privilege? They should have at least been mindful of that and met with him alone. They knew the gravity of the situation. We didn't. I feel it was bad attorney practice to allow us into that consultation.

And I also believe that it was unethical of Bron and Greg to allow us to go to the police station alone. They knew that detectives were attempting to force Torey into an interrogation and that Torey needed an attorney. Yet despite the fact that they obviously felt that a murder charge was likely going to be filed on a minor child, they refused to go with us. There is no doubt in my mind that they were motivated by greed. They charged us two hundred dollars for the time they spent with us that night knowing that it was of no benefit to us whatsoever.

We stood up. It was approximately 6:45 p.m.

Sean, Torey and I left.

When we got to the car, Torey climbed in the back seat. He'd hardly said a word in the attorney's office. Now he said, "I don't want to go to the police station."

Sean was upset. He said, "Are you kidding me, Torey? We were there for an hour and you said not one word, and now you're saying you don't want to go!"

"I want to go back to the attorneys," Torey said.

"Torey, you should have told them what you wanted while we were there," I said. "Now we have to explain to Detective Ganske that we'll talk to him tomorrow."

"I don't want to. I don't want to go..." Torey pleaded.

"Dad and I will talk to them Torey. We will explain everything the attorneys told us," I assured him.

"Are you going to be there the whole time?" Torey asked.

"The whole time," I promised.

"I don't want to go..."

When we arrived at the police station, Sean and I turned around in our seats and faced Torey. "It's going to be okay, son," Sean told him.

We walked into the building together. It was after hours but an officer was waiting for us at the main desk. On the left hand side, around the corner from the desk, there was a hallway with a door at the end. The officer escorted us down the hall and through the door.

As soon as we passed through it, we were confronted by a large man with a booming voice. It was like being met by a Rottweiler. Terrifying. The officer who had escorted us from the reception area blocked our way from behind. The large man pinned us in from the front. We were in a tight corridor with nowhere to turn. I asked where Detectives Ganske and Thomas were.

"They're on their way. I'm Detective Marchand," the rottweiler said. "I need to speak with you in my office." He gestured toward a doorway. Torey was looking from Sean to me.

"He can wait out here, we want to speak to you alone," Marchand said. There were two metal chairs set up against the wall across from his office. He showed Torey to one of them.

I asked, "Is Torey going to be alone? Is anyone going to talk to him?"

"No one will talk to him until we're done," Marchand said.

Sean and I followed Marchand into his office and he shut the door. We'd been separated from Torey before we even knew what was happening.

Marchand sat down at his desk, Sean and I across from him. When we first entered it felt like Sean was beside me, but the longer I talked with Marchand the more distant Sean felt. It was like I was searching for my husband through a tunnel. He was clear across the room. Marchand terrified me.

"We need to talk," the detective said in a deep, threatening voice. I remember thinking I would hate to be one of his kids when he was angry. I would hate to be *anyone* when he was angry. Marchand was beyond intimidating; he was downright frightening. There was nothing soft in Marchand. He was a man who would get his own way. Always.

He got right to the point. "We need to interview your son. Right now."

Sean said, "Yeah. You know we just met with an attorney..."

Marchand interrupted him, "I know you did. Your son needs to come clean and talk to us. Not some attorney that's going to charge you a bunch of money for nothing. I bet he charged you plenty, didn't he?"

Sean tried to make light of the situation. "Yeah...like two hundred dollars to tell us not to talk to you." He shrugged his shoulders as if to say, "so you see...I'm sorry but what can we do?"

"Well, that's what they do. They give people bad advice, and they get rich doing it. The only way we can figure out if your son's innocent or not *is* to talk to us."

He said, "So there are some inconsistencies in your son's story and we need to get them taken care of. We're not messing around with you anymore." Marchand looked like he chewed tobacco and had a lip full.

Sean's approach had not worked. I was more direct. "Torey is not going to say anything to you tonight that can be used against him. If you want to talk to him you can wait until tomorrow when he'll have an attorney."

Instantly Marchand erupted. He angrily shouted, "*We're not waiting until tomorrow! You have jerked us around long enough and we are going to find out RIGHT NOW if Torey's in this or out of this! We are not waiting until tomorrow*!"

"I'll tell you right now, he's out of it!" I said.

"How can I know if he's out of it or not when you've been running around to these attorneys, refusing to cooperate!" Marchand's voice boomed.

"How could he be in it?" I said, horrified. Oh my God! Was he serious?

"I'm telling you, your son is either involved, or he's not. That's it. There's no alternative. *And if he does not cooperate with us right now, we're going to arrest him.*"

Detectives Thomas and Ganske entered the office. Ganske leaned on the wall to the left of Marchand, and Detective Thomas stood by the door behind us. We were surrounded, but next to Marchand these detectives were my best friends. Hopefully I could appeal to them.

"We met with an attorney and he told us not to speak with you. He said that you're dealing with too many unsolved cases," I tried to explain to all of them, while focusing on Ganske. "You're going to want to solve this case. You know.... you don't want another Nori Jones on your hands. You have to understand...I don't want Torey to say anything that you could end up using against him later...He just wants to talk to his attorney."

That was a mistake. All three detectives took my plea as a personal accusation. They wanted to know what unsolved cases I was talking about. They had an outstanding record solving crime. The case I was referring to was a special circumstance. Something I could not understand. Not their fault.

"I haven't been doing this for twenty years, I haven't invested myself into this job just to throw it all away!" Thomas stated. Trying to be reasonable I changed tactics. "Our younger son is at a football game. We just can't do this tonight." Oh please, oh please, oh please I prayed, let us go. "We have to pick him up."

"Listen," Marchand said, "everybody has cooperated except for you. Matt, Brian…everyone. The time has now come for you to do the right thing. Torey is not going anywhere until we talk to him."

"What about Matt?" I asked. If they suspected one of the boys surely it would have to be Matt. He was the last one with Cassie.

"Matt's been here today, we're done with him," Marchand

said.

"You're done with him?" What did that mean?

"Did he have an attorney?" I asked, "I heard that he was going to get an attorney."

"He did not have an attorney."

"Are you sure?" I was so confused.

"Yes we're sure. Matt did not have an attorney."

"Matt's been cleared by polygraph," Thomas said.

"If Matt's cleared what about Brian?" I asked.

"Brian has already been here."

"Brian and Torey were together the whole time!" I said. "If you're done with Brian, why do you need to talk to Torey? Have you arrested Brian?" I asked.

Ganske or Thomas, one of them said, "Brian has not been detained." We did not know it at the time, but this was a lie. Brian was currently in custody.

Thomas said, "Brian's parents have been very helpful. We have talked to them and they just want the truth. They have *fully* cooperated with us."

"These are parents...who no matter what...want to help find who did this," Marchand said, implying that we did not.

"We want to help too…" I said.

I really did. But I did not feel good about allowing an interview in circumstances an attorney had told us were not in Torey's best interest. Who knew where it could lead?

Ganske said, "We are not here to trick Torey into saying anything. We just want the truth."

All I wanted was an attorney, someone to help, because I was unsure of the situation, what I should do. I just wanted someone to explain to us what was going on, to be there with Torey, on his side, and level the playing field for us, because I felt that we were in way over our heads.

I tried to explain that to the detectives, but all they cared about was getting their interview. They insisted on it. We were at a standstill for the better part of an hour.

"Can't you interview Torey at our house?" I asked. "Please...we have Jamie...you have to understand...can't we do that tonight, or wait until tomorrow when Torey will have an attorney?"

Marchand had had enough. It was now time for him to get his way. "You're out of time," he thundered. "Do you understand what you're involved in here? We're going to get this over with right here, right now." He was large, shaking his head, pointing his finger in my face. I could just picture him throwing his chair back and ripping out a pair of handcuffs. "Torey's not going anywhere tonight!" He bellowed.

I felt like a smudge on the wall beside him, but Marchand was the last person on earth I would let talk to Torey. He would have to kill me first.

From the side of the room Ganske took a different approach. "We think it would be best if we were allowed to interview Torey alone. We have found that kids tend to open up and be more honest when their parents are not sitting with them," he said. "We need to do that here. We are not interviewing Torey at your home." He shook his head.

I said, " We were told to wait for our attorney..."

Marchand said, "He is not leaving here tonight. I will arrest your son if he does not cooperate."

Sean said, "Torey wants to cooperate. He never said he did not want to cooperate."

I looked from Sean back to Thomas and Ganske. It was clear what was going to happen. They were not going to let us leave. Sean knew that. We could either let them question Torey, or watch as they arrested him. It was as simple as that.

"If you have to interview Torey, Sean and I are going to be there the whole time," I said, beaten and defeated.

Ganske said, "We can do that."

"Can we end it at anytime?" I asked.

Both Ganske and Thomas said that we could, but I didn't believe them. If it was true, I would have ended it before it even began.

Ganske again said that it would be best if they interviewed Torey alone. But I ignored the request.

Torey was still sitting in the same chair outside of the door that we'd left him in. It had been close to an hour, maybe more, since we entered Marchand's office. Torey had no idea what we'd been talking about. Before we could say anything to him the detectives whisked Torey into a small interview room where Sean and I followed.

There was a table. Torey was sat down at the closed end of the table next to the wall. Ganske sat beside Torey, and Thomas sat across from him. He was surrounded. I looked for an opportunity to tell Torey that I was sorry, that I had tried to ask for an attorney, but there was none.

The detectives had control of Torey from the time they opened the door of Marchand's office until after they had him seated and were starting the interview. We never had a chance to say a word. Not even two minutes had passed since we left Marchand's office and the interview had begun.

CHAPTER TEN

The Interrogation

Ganske was the lead questioner. He started by telling Torey they were there to "clarify some things." I thought that meant the movie, which we now knew Torey had never attended. I was thinking: Tell the truth. Get the hell out of here. Get an attorney.

The prosecution later claimed that Ganske had read Torey his Miranda Rights near the beginning of the interview. Technically I suppose he did, but I was in the room and I certainly never knew that Torey was being Mirandized. Sean didn't either. Ganske did not actually say the very familiar words you hear on TV.

Ganske said, (sic) "Anytime you are interviewed by the police for the most part and you're coming down to the station or the interview room here, people sometimes get the impression they are in custody...are not free to leave so, it's a good time to give you your rights so you understand it, you know that your rights are per Miranda."

Torey had no Rights per Miranda. Everyone in the room knew that we were not free to leave, and we certainly weren't permitted to wait for an attorney.

Ganske rummaged through a day planner that was at least two inches thick. He pulled out a document, which he quickly read. He called it a "formality," he played down its importance, and he told Torey to sign it. The whole process took a minute and 35 seconds. That was Torey's "Miranda" warning.

For an hour and fifteen minutes Detective Ganske questioned Torey about his whereabouts on September 22, 2006. Torey told the detectives the same version of events that he had given them Sunday night when they first questioned him until he got to the point where he had claimed he'd left with Brian to see a movie. Torey admitted that was a lie.

Torey said the truth was that he and Brian had actually left the house to burglarize cars that were parked in the neighborhood. Torey explained that he had been scared to tell the truth because he had a friend that was on probation for burglarizing cars and he did not want to get into trouble. Torey gave a detailed description of the cars that were burglarized and what had been taken.

As Detective Ganske questioned Torey, he referred to the log of phone calls that had been made and received on Torey's cell phone. There had been numerous calls from and to Cassie's house. Each call was meticulously examined. As Torey was relaying his story, Ganske kept telling him that they were there to help him, that they just needed the truth and that if he told the truth, the truth would "set him free."

Someone needed to pick Jamie up from his football game. I wanted to ask Sean if we could call his mother to get him, but I was scared to interrupt. The interview seemed to be almost over. They had covered the night up until the boys came home.

Ganske said, "We're going to kick it up a notch." I wondered what that meant.

He asked Torey, "Did you leave the house again, at anytime that night?"

Torey said, "No."

Ganske asked, "Are you sure? What if we have a clerk at Common Cents saying you were there later that night?"

Torey said, "The Common Cents down by our house? Yeah. We went to get Brian a soda."

I did not panic. Whenever someone spends the night at our house the kids usually end up going down the street to the convenience store. Common Cents is very close. It wasn't unusual. What was unusual is that they hadn't told me they were going. That surprised me.

I could see how it could appear incriminating to the detectives though, especially at first sight. The fact that the boys were in the neighborhood where Cassie was found, that they were driving around at night. It did not look good, but it *was* understandable. Nothing that could not be explained.

But I was getting scared. Something did not feel right…something in the room, in Torey, and the detectives. I was starting to feel like I was watching something unfold in front of me and I was uncertain of what it was. I needed it to stop for a minute. I needed to think.

Jamie's game had to be over. What would he do if he came out of the locker room and no one was there?

Ganske asked, "Why did you need to get Brian a soda?"

Torey said, "Brian didn't like what we had in the refrigerator."

"Okay…" Ganske nodded his head.

I *had* to go. I kept telling myself that it was almost over, but now I was out of time. I had to get Jamie. I said, "I need to pick up

Jamie." I also needed a chance to think, and I wanted the questions to end.

There was a sigh in the room, an exhale. Everyone shifted positions in their seats. I thought, "Everyone's ready for a break. We're all feeling the tension."

Thomas and Ganske said no problem. I could go.

Sean asked if they would let me back in. They said they would. When I left I truly believed that the questions would stop. I truly believed that they would wait for me to return before questioning Torey any further. It was my first experience with law enforcement officers, and in spite of everything, I still trusted them.

I had to pick up Jamie and get back to the interview quickly. My heart raced as I drove. I knew that Torey had nothing to do with Cassie's murder. I *knew* it...but something definitely did not feel right, and I could not figure out what it was. Brian and Torey had been together...Brian and Torey had been together...That kept distracting me as I was trying to work it out in my mind. Torey could not have done it. He was with Brian, so Brian could not have done it either. It *never* occurred to me that Brian could have done this in front of Torey. *Never.*

Until I suddenly *knew* it! And it was like a brilliant flash, a thunderbolt from heaven that illuminated everything. It was not like a small ah-ha moment, the kind that we all get from time to time. It was like the opening of the universe and a revelation from God. It was huge! But that was not to come until later that night.

I arrived at the football game just as it ended. As I waited for Jamie to get out of the locker room I spoke with Candy Lindley. Her son Jordan was one of Jamie's best friends.

I tried to behave as normal as possible because I did not want Candy to know that anything unusual was going on. I certainly did not want her to know that Torey had been at Cassie's house the night that she was killed and was at that very moment being questioned by the police. I still thought we'd take Torey home that night and only our closest friends and family would know what we'd been through.

Jamie was happy. He was excited about his night and the game and was telling me about it in the car. I told him that Dad and Torey were still at the police station and that we needed to pick them up. He could not believe it. Though I was in a hurry, I decided that it would be better if I quickly dropped Jamie off at home. There was a possibility that the interview might last longer than I thought, and I did not want to subject him to a long wait in the police station.

Our house was at the top of a hill. As I approached it I could not understand what I was seeing. There were cars everywhere. For a moment I wondered if the neighbors were having a party. But the cars were in our driveway and around our house and there seemed to be people everywhere. I could not pull into the driveway and a man got out of his truck and came up to my window.

I thought, *What's going on*? He waved for me to unroll the window and I looked up at him. He held up a badge. He said that Torey had been arrested. Charged with murder. For a second he disappeared and I could not see anything. I opened my eyes and he was there. I could hear Jamie crying next to me. I asked about my husband, he was with Torey. How was Sean with Torey if Torey was arrested? How could they arrest Torey? They said they wouldn't arrest him if we allowed the interview. How could this be happening?

He said they had search warrants and they were going to search our house. It was going to take some time. He said we had to leave. I told him that my daughter was coming home from work and *they* could not be here. The whole house was lit up and there were people everywhere.

I have a memory of driving to Dillard's where Lacey was about to get off work, and meeting her in the parking lot where I told her that she could not go home, though that is absolutely not what happened.

What happened was Sean called Lacey on her cell phone and told her that she needed to come down to the police station. Her boyfriend Jeff had her car and she called him to pick her up at work, which he did, and they drove to the police station together.

I do not remember anything about arriving at the police station or how I got there. Lacey has told me that she and Jeff arrived at the station first, that Jamie and I arrived a few minutes later, and that after he and I arrived the three of them, Lacey, Jeff and Jamie, waited together in the front corridor of the police station while I went into the back with a detective. I believe that would have been Marchand because the next thing I remember was sitting in his office.

We were back in Marchand's office, the office where we had asked for the interview to be postponed. Sean was there. And Marchand, Thomas and Ganske. They were talking but I could not hear what they were saying. It was like my head was underwater. I tried to clear my head but I could not hear and I could not see. I was in a dark tunnel. I had to hear what they were saying. In slow motion I heard that…Torey...had killed…Cassie...that Brian…had told them… everything.

NO! NO! NO! NO!

Sean was saying you don't know Torey...and Detective Thomas said a life sentence, probably 25 years...We're sorry...Sorry....and then someone said something about it's not the end of the world...and I was trying to comprehend that, because clearly it *was* the end of the world...

And…suddenly in a flash, it hit me!!

Brian! Brian! Brian! BRIAN! BRIAN! BRIAN! Everything came to me like a tidal wave. Brian Draper!

CHAPTER ELEVEN

Brian Draper

The first time I heard Brian Draper's name was the year before, shortly after we'd moved into our new house. Torey had just started the 10th grade. He mentioned Brian's name in a passing conversation.

Torey had many interests, but his primary interest was movies, both making them, which he did with his friends on an old video camera, and collecting them.

Torey loved all movie genres: comedy, drama, action adventure, horror and suspense. He began his movie collection in middle school with seasons of The Simpson's, Adam Sandler movies, and other teen marketed films, but he had recently started adding R-rated movies to his collection, and to this I objected. Vigorously.

But Sean did not feel the same as I did, and though he encouraged Torey to make good movie choices, he did not restrict him to certain ratings or topics. It was a sore spot in our marriage. Sean defended his position by pointing out that most of the movies Torey purchased were fine. He minimized the negative, while he claimed I accentuated it.

One afternoon, Torey was in his bedroom rearranging his movie collection. I watched as he put them away. While he did we had a discussion about what each of us liked and appreciated in different kinds of movies and why I disapproved so strongly of others. While we were talking Torey asked me what I had against horror films. I told him that violence, as entertainment, simply did not appeal to me.

Torey said he could understand that. It was the reason he did not collect the modern graphic and violent horror movies that are popular today, like *Ghost Ship.* He liked the older classics from the 70's and 80's such as *Nightmare on Elm Street* and *Halloween.* They did not have a lot of profanity and they were scary.

Torey then went on to tell me about this "really sick kid" named Brian Draper. Brian *loved* really gross horror movies. The ones that you can't even buy in stores. Most people that watch horror movies don't turn into serial killers, but if someone was going to turn into a killer, Torey said, it would be Brian Draper.

I told Torey I hope you're staying away from that kid! And

Torey said of course he was. He did not like Brian *at all.* Torey finished putting away his movies and I went about my day.

Torey did not speak about Brian again and it was not long before the conversation faded from my memory.

Nine months later, it was mid-July 2006. There was a knock at the door. When I answered it there was a boy I'd never seen before, standing on the doorstep, asking for Torey. He was tall and dark, with thin black hair. He appeared nervous, unable to stand still. I immediately felt uncomfortable, like I should shut the door. Tell him Torey wasn't home and send him away.

Maybe it was just his physical appearance. There was an air of neglect about him. He was wearing a blue City of Pocatello work shirt, jeans and an old pair of Converse tennis shoes. He was not clean, or did not appear to be, and he was excessively thin.

I called Torey to the door and he and the boy went upstairs to Torey's room together for about five minutes and then the boy left. After he left I asked Torey who that was.

"His name is Brian. He's just a kid from school," Torey told me. Torey said that he and Brian were planning to write a movie script together. Torey hadn't made a movie since we'd moved into our new house, and I was glad that he had met someone who apparently shared his interest.

Over the next several weeks Torey and Brian made plans to work on their movie script together, but something always seemed to come up. Brian appeared to be more talk than action. He never came over when he said he was going to. Still Brian and Torey's friendship was developing. They went to a movie with friends in late July but I did not see Brian again until August. By then I'd heard Torey talk about Brian, I knew who he was, and I did not feel so uncomfortable with the developing friendship.

Brian, it turned out, was not the neglected boy that I'd first perceived. His parents were well off, or at last appeared to be. Their home was located in Johnny Creek in the southern foothills above the city, one of the most affluent subdivisions in the area. They drove a Lexus and a Mercedes.

Torey was awed by Brian's wealth. Supposedly Brian had a couch and a coffee table in his bedroom and the whole downstairs of his parent's spacious home to himself. One afternoon Brian took Torey to Fred Myers, a local shopping center. Brian could have gone to Fred Myers alone but he wanted to show Torey what he was about to do, which was to buy four hundred dollars worth of movies at one time.

Brian, impressed with Torey's movie collection, had to have a better one for himself. (We later learned that was a pattern of Brian's: Jealousy.) But Torey, not realizing Brian's motivation, was simply astonished that Brian could spend money like that.

I'd heard conflicting stories about the Draper family. Some people said that they spent a lot of money on their son and daughter, giving them anything they wanted. Others said that the family was deeply in debt and could not afford to give their children much at all. The truth was probably a combination of the two. They lived a lavish lifestyle, but were deeply in debt.

As the start of the school year drew nearer we saw more of Brian. Torey introduced him to his friend Adam, who at first disliked Brian and even discouraged Torey from hanging out with him, but later change his mind. Adam told me that Brian just kind of grew on him once he got to know him and I could see how that could happen. Brian was smart and funny and a bit of a clown, probably fun to be around. Before we knew it all three boys were hanging out together.

And in some ways Brian grew on me too, in the short time that I got to know him. He had a quirky little personality and he got along well with Torey. They made each other laugh. Plus, Brian appeared to come from a good home, he was supervised, not involved in drugs or alcohol, and by those criteria's he seemed fine.

But sometimes I still felt uneasy around Brian. I told myself that there was nothing tangible, nothing concrete that I could put my finger on.

But that wasn't *entirely* true...

There was a particular incident that took place two weeks before Cassie was killed that I will never forget. Brian and Torey had gone to El' Heradero's and returned with a bag of spicy pork burritos. They carried the bag of burritos into Torey's room and shut the door to watch a movie. Sometime later I went to Torey's room to rehang his curtains, which I had previously washed. I knocked on the door and Torey let me in. The blinds were down, the room dark.

I crossed over to Torey's bed, which was under the window, and climbed onto it, glancing over my shoulder to see what they were watching. I was trying to be quiet as I hung the curtains, but what I saw on the screen disturbed me. It seemed to be filled with zombies and I could tell that this was a movie that I did not want Torey to see.

I immediately assumed it was Brian's. This wasn't the first

movie that Brian brought over to our house that I disapproved off, and I wondered if every movie that Brian had purchased with his four-hundred-dollars was a horror movie. Even Torey had begun purchasing horror movies, and I blamed Brian's influence.

I climbed off the bed and told Brian and Torey that I did not allow these types of movies in my home. Torey said the movie wasn't bad, I just happened to walk in at the wrong time. Brian cheerfully said, "You're just like my mom." He turned toward Torey and told him, "You see Torey I told you, she's just like my mom." Brian smiled at me conspiratorially. "My mom hates these movies too."

I could not believe it. Brian was trying to manipulate me! I said, "I'm going to call your mother and let her know what kind of movies you're bringing over here." I went into the kitchen and got the phone. When I returned Brian freaked out. He begged me not to call his mother, "P-p-please don't do that, my m-m-mom is not as n-n-nice as you are. I'll be in s-s-so much t-t-trouble. P-p-please!" Brian was so upset that he could hardly speak.

Torey had recently begun stuttering when he talked, an annoying habit that bothered both Sean and I. Now I realized what Torey had been doing. Mimicking Brian!

Unsure of what to do, I put the phone down. Torey had a movie case, like a bookcase, that stood on the floor by his window. I stood in front of it and looked at Torey's movies. I said, "I don't like these horror movies, Torey. You've gotten five or six more in the short time you and Brian have been friends." I looked at him sharply, wondering what kind of an influence Brian really was.

"This movie's r-r-really… not t-t-that bad," Brian said, referring to the movie on the screen. "I saw it for the first time when I was in the s-s-seventh grade and it totally…messed me up." He nodded his head enthusiastically, "Yeah…It's awes-s-some."

Something triggered inside of me as Brian spoke. I grabbed Torey by the arm and pulled him out of his room and into my bedroom. I backed Torey into the corner between my bed and the wall. "I do not want these movies in my house," I screamed. "This is my home!" I wanted to know what Brian meant, totally messed up, and what was Torey doing with him! I felt sick to my stomach. Torey didn't respond. He just stared at me. Sean came running into the bedroom wanting to know what was going on. I still had Torey backed in the corner.

Sean told me that I had to calm down, and leave Torey alone.

I was so angry I was shaking. Sean held me by my shoulders and pulled me away from Torey. Torey never said one word to me; he just looked at me with what felt like cold hatred and walked past me and back into his bedroom with Brian.

Sean said, "What's the matter with you? You had your own son cowering in the corner!" Disgustedly he said, "You need help." He walked out of the bedroom and slammed the door behind him.

I fell on my bed and cried. I did not know what was wrong with me...maybe I *was* crazy, but something in the way Brian looked at me scared me.

I wish Brian had left that day. I wish that would have been the end of Brian and Torey's friendship. But Brian did not leave and it was not the end of their friendship. Brian stopped bringing horror movies over to the house and Torey started watching the *First Season of Lost*. So I thought, at least my "tantrum" made a difference. Hopefully the inappropriate movies, (and my bad feelings) were something we could put behind us.

But the incident stuck in my mind.

A few days later, Torey was doing his homework at the dining room table while I was cleaning up after dinner. Torey regularly did his homework in the kitchen while I cooked dinner or cleaned up afterwards and I enjoyed having him in there with me. He was pleasant company.

Out of the blue, Torey asked me about the Columbine High School massacre. He wanted to know if I had ever heard of it.

Surprised, I asked why he wanted to know.

"Oh no reason. It was just something that Brian was talking about."

"Well, Columbine was a terrible thing." I said. "I don't think you or Brian should be talking about it." I put a quick end to the conversation, bothered by the topic.

Still I was troubled. As I finished washing the dishes it sat on my mind. Why Columbine? As far as I knew, Torey had never even heard of Columbine. He would have been in grade school when it happened, probably no more than seven or eight years old. Why would Brian talk about something so distant... so irrelevant?

Suddenly it connected in my mind with the horror movies that Brian had brought over. Up to my elbows in dishwater I remembered something that Torey had said. I did not panic because I did not see a reason to. It was absurd. I dried my hands with a dishtowel and looked at Torey.

Torey had gone back to his homework, silently busy. I looked at him across the granite countertop to the table where he was sitting and asked, "Is Brian the kid you told me about last year?"

"What kid?" Torey asked.

"The kid that could grow up to be a serial killer," I said.

At first Torey looked at me with a blank expression on his face and then I saw his face change as he remembered what he had said. "Yeah, I did say that, didn't I?" He looked reflective.

"That was BRIAN!" I yelled.

"Well, I hated him last year, remember? I only said that to make him sound bad."

"How bad did you need to make him sound? You said he could be a serial killer!"

It was not a Eureka moment. It was not a moment where I began to question if perhaps Brian was dangerous. In fact it never once crossed my mind that Brian could be dangerous. He was a kid for Christ's sake! He might get into a car accident because he drove like a wild teenager; who knows, he might secretly smoke pot, or talk nasty; but he could not be a serial killer! It wasn't possible.

It was just a connection; one that I did not take seriously. And because I did not take the connection seriously, because I did not look deeper, and question Brian further, it cost my son his freedom and Cassie her life.

Now I had to make another connection, in Marchand's office on September 27, 2006. And that one, I had to take seriously.

CHAPTER TWELVE

Torey

I needed to see my son. I asked to see Torey, and Sean and I were led back to the room where he had been interviewed. There he was. My baby! Alone. Scared. Terrified. I felt like a piece of glass that had just been shattered. I was just waiting to fall into a million pieces. But I had to stay strong for my son and let him know that he was going to be okay. Get that message through to him. We were going to get an attorney. He was going to be okay.

Just make it through tonight. That is what I thought. Just make it through tonight.

Detectives took Torey away. He turned to me as he passed, his small face floating by in front of me. He said, "Don't get an attorney, Mom. We can't afford one." And he was gone.

And in that moment I died. The person that I was was no more.

We had two children sitting down the hall, not knowing what was happening.... but how could we go on, when our lives had just ended?

We stood in the empty corridor, Thomas and Ganske, Sean and I. The detectives told us what was going to happen next. Torey was going to be taken to the Bannock County Jail.

I said, "I don't know where that is."

They said that Torey would be alone that night and not mixed with other prisoners. He would be safe. They gave us a name. Lieutenant Peterson. She could answer all of our questions and they gave us her phone number. They recommended that we call her in the morning. There would be an arraignment. Neither Sean nor I knew what that was, but it did not matter. What mattered was that Torey was gone...Torey was gone… and we had to get him back.

Ganske said we needed to get a lawyer. If it were his son he would hire an attorney, not use a public defender; but if he had to use a public defender it would be Dave Martinez. *That name again.*

Marchand was walking us down the hall, back to our other children. Jamie in his mud flaked football uniform; Lacey crying, her face tear streaked. Jeff was there and he was doing his best to comfort them both.

I kept saying, "Brian...its Brian... Brian..."

Thomas said, "Torey likes those horror movies."

Brian brought them over. I would not let them watch them. "Brian likes the horror movies...that's Brian. Brian..." They had the boys mixed up. How? How had they mixed the boys up?

PART THREE

After

CHAPTER THIRTEEN

Searching For Help

There is pain that can never be prepared for, so powerful that it is beyond words or expression. That pain is the loss of your child. It is the kind of pain that you never knew existed and that changes your life forever. It is a thousand times worse than anything you imagine it to be.

I believe it is even more devastating if you've lost your child to a senseless act of violence that no matter how hard you try, you can never understand. You wonder how you are capable of surviving the deep loss of someone you love so very much and the never to be answered question, *why*?

I know that Cassie's family lives with that pain. We do too.

When Torey was arrested our world fell apart. Looking back, I cannot believe we survived it. It was that bad. Like surviving a plane crash, something you should not be able to do.

Everyone reacts differently to a tragedy. People have an idea about how they believe they would react in a given circumstance, but it seldom works that way. You do not know how your mind or body is going to react to the shock until you've actually gone through it, because when the death or loss of a child hits you, you are immediately plunged into an abyss unlike anything you could ever imagine. What you do in that abyss is anyone's guess. You could cry, or scream, or faint, or crumble, or just sit in silent, shocked disbelief, but whatever you do, it is nothing but an unconscious physical response, like breathing, because you're certainly not thinking. You're not planning. Your mind is disconnected from your body, and you're in a state of unreality and disbelief that it is utterly overwhelming.

Reality is slow to sink in. My first response was denial. I could not believe what was happening was real, and that it was happening to *us*. I did not break down. I did not cry or wail or throw myself on the ground, but my life ended just the same as if I had.

I went into shock. For days I could not eat or sleep. The lack of appetite was easy to ignore, but the lack of sleep was more problematic. After a few days I literally could not see straight. I would doze wherever I sat but as soon as I closed my eyes I would have the most unspeakable nightmares.

I knew that Torey did not hurt Cassie, but I had no idea what happened to her, and it tormented me. I dreamt of Cassie over and over again. She was with me every second and I would cry, "Why didn't Brian kill me! If Brian had to do this to someone, why not me?" I could not live with this and I did not want to. I felt obligated to go on for my children, but not one single part of *me* wanted to. I wanted to die.

I was consumed with Torey. For over a year and a half I dreamt of him every single night. He filled my dreams. I would try to save him from everything imaginable, from car accidents to wild animals. Torey was always in danger and I could never get to him in time.

My heart started aching and it feels as if it has been pierced with a knife. It is a constant pain. I had never paid attention to my heart before, never noticed its beating. Now it pains me every day.

Everything is hard; holidays, graduations, weddings and birthdays. There is always someone missing. Someone who should be there and isn't. We will never have closure; it will never be okay. One of our children is in pain and there is absolutely nothing we can do about it. It is impossible to make peace with that.

At the end of the police interview, after Torey had been arrested, Detective Thomas said to Sean, "I'm sorry...I cannot even imagine." And Sean said it best when he answered, "Neither can I."

We could not imagine. This was beyond imagining.

Torey was arrested and we needed help. There was only one person we could turn to, Sean's mother, Barbara. How we got there or what we told her I do not know, but I remember her opening her front door and suddenly she was holding Lacey and Jamie and we were sobbing, all of us, right there in her open doorway.

Mom kept asking us over and over again how this happened, but we didn't know. It was too much for Jamie. He let go of the arms around him and went downstairs by himself.

Somehow Barbara managed to pull herself together. Though racked with grief, she stayed strong. She said, "We'll get an attorney first thing in the morning." This was not something where we could take a chance with a public defender. We needed the best attorney we could find, and she was going to make sure that we got one.

Sean sat shaking his head, as if saying, "No, No," enough times was going to change anything. I kept thinking it was all a mistake. Soon the detectives would find out who Torey was, what kind of a boy he was, and they would give him back to us. We just had to reason with them. But Mom recognized right away what we were involved in. She knew that this was going to be a fight for Torey's *life*. We had to give it all we had. She focused her attention on what needed to be done.

Lacey was sitting on the couch next to Jeff. She said, "Mom, you better check on Jamie," I nodded and went downstairs. Jamie was laying on the couch in his football pants and jersey. He had tears running down his checks, dripping off his nose and chin, wetting the pillow his head lay on. He turned his face away from me when I knelt beside him and I did not know what to say. I touched his back and told him that I loved him. I did not know the thoughts racing through his head, but I could imagine. The next few weeks and months would be the worst living nightmare I could ever imagine. This was the beginning.

Mom wanted us to spend the night, but I had to go home. We waited for the police to call and tell us they were done searching the house, but they never did. Around 1:30 a.m. we returned home to see if they had finished.

As we drove up the street I could see that the cars that had surrounded the house were gone. It was dark and the house looked vacant. We went inside. The closet door under the stairs stood ajar and the closet light was on. We went upstairs to the kitchen where some of the cabinet doors hung open, but aside from Torey's room, those were the only visible signs that the house had been searched that night.

You would think that someone going through every single thing you own would be disturbing. But I felt nothing about it then and I feel nothing about it now. The detectives took Torey's car, the computers from our home, cameras, some clothing, and miscellaneous items from the garage. On the kitchen table they left us four yellow-copied pages of numbered items that they had taken from our home, but all of it was meaningless junk. How could I care about any of that? My *son* was gone.

What you have to understand is that when you lose a child nothing else matters. Literally. You're numb, your empty, your void. There is only one thing that can fill that void. Getting the child back.

What happened? Suddenly we were in a nightmare. There was no preparation, no clue. We were going along fine in life when suddenly BAM!! It was over. Everything we had ever believed in and worked for *gone*.

In the blackness of the night I lay sobbing on the bathroom

floor. I crawled through the hall to Torey's bedroom where I buried my face in his pillow and wept. I could hear Sean's agonized cries coming to me from the other room but he was far, far away.

Early the next morning Lacey came racing upstairs with her cell phone. She said that Torey tried to call and we had missed the call! I thought, "Torey can't call. We will never talk to Torey again. They've taken him away." But there *was* a message and it *was* from Torey.

I suddenly remembered that when you're arrested you're allowed a phone call. We had missed the one and only phone call that Torey was going to be allowed to make! I screamed and ran for Sean.

Sean was sitting on the edge of the bed, waiting for his mother to call with any attorney recommendations that she might have received before we went back to Bron Rammell and Greg May. We ourselves did not know what to do or whom to call. But no matter what Sean wanted to be at the office of Dial, May and Rammell before their doors opened at 9 a.m. They were the attorneys Huntley Park recommended. In our naiveté that was the best we had to go on.

I told Sean, "Torey called! His phone call, we missed it!"

We searched the house for the phone number the detectives had given us the night before, but we couldn't find it. After a few moments of intense panic we realized that we did not need it. We could call the jail directly. We looked up the number and I dialed. When the phone was answered I asked to speak with Lieutenant Peterson. The call was transferred. When she answered I tried to remain calm. I introduced myself and explained that our son had been arrested and that we'd missed a call from him.

Lieutenant Peterson was aware of our situation. She told me that she would allow Torey to call us back shortly. She also told me that she would be available later to answer any questions that we may have. She was professional, but kind. I thanked her and we hung up.

Within minutes Torey called. I cried when I heard his voice. Torey wanted to know what was going on. We told him that we were getting an attorney. He said that he had been trying to call us collect but the cell phone would not accept the charges. He was worried because he was locked in a cell and they only let him out for a few minutes to call us and had taken him back to the cell when he could not get through.

Lacey, Jamie, Sean and I were gathered around the phone together. We tried to make Torey understand that we were there for him, and that we would take care of him. Lacey was sobbing. She had tears running down her face and chin. "I love you Torey," she said, encouraging him to stay strong. Jamie was crying just as hard. He had spent most of his life at his brother's side. He could barely talk but he managed to tell Torey that he loved him too.

After the phone call ended Jamie went back to his room and shut the door. Lacey went downstairs to Jeff, howling loudly as she made her way. Jeff had stayed the night comforting Lacey while Sean and I were upstairs, too locked in our grief to help anyone.

Sean and I immediately called Mom. She had been researching attorneys and had contacted Kelly Kumm. She knew that we needed to get someone out to see Torey right away and she had been working on that all morning. But we did not have time to discuss Kelly's law firm. By now it was almost nine a.m. and Sean was anxious to leave. He asked his mother to meet us at the office of Dial, May and Rammell as soon as possible. She said she would.

Sean stood at the foot of the stairs urging me to hurry.

I was in Torey's bedroom looking for something. What, I did not know. But I needed to take something to the attorneys that would show them right away that Torey was just a *child*.

"Hurry up! Were late," Sean shouted.

In a panic I scanned the room. I looked at everything, Torey's bed, his posters, his movie case. I stood in Torey's closet and my eyes fell on the school notebooks sitting on his shelf. I grabbed them and hugged them to my chest.

"I'm ready!" I said, running down the steps.

Sean and I met Mom in the parking lot of the attorney's office. Bron was standing in the reception area when we entered, and as soon as he saw us he knew that Torey had been arrested. Before we could say a word we were quickly ushered into his office along with Brian Chaney and Greg May. The door was closed.

In the front section of Bron's office there was a small consultation area. Two couches faced each other with a coffee table in between. Greg and Mom sat on one couch, Sean and I across from them on the other. Bron pulled up two chairs, one for Brian Chaney the other for himself.

As soon as everyone was seated Sean and Mom began to sob

uncontrollably. Brian Chaney was quick with two boxes of tissue. Greg said that I was in shock and I remember thinking, "No, I'm not. I'm here. I'm not in a hospital somewhere." Which is what I imagined something like this would do to a person.

But Greg was right. He asked, "They arrested him?"

Sean said, "Yeah...Last night."

Greg and Bron were gravely nodding their heads.

When Sean and Barbara were back under control, Bron told us what we could expect to happen. He said that there would be an arraignment that afternoon. Greg and Bron discussed the possibility of Torey being in the courtroom for the arraignment, or if he would be on a monitor. I did not know what they were talking about, but before I could ask, Bron brought up the possibility that we could ask for bail, which initiated a whole other discussion between the two attorneys.

It was too much for me. I could not comprehend the reality of the situation. The only thing that mattered was that Torey was gone and I wanted them to tell me how they were going to get him back.

I focused on Greg. "We discussed this after you left last night," he said. "This is going to be a big case, and we had to talk to Aaron before we could agree to take it."

Oh my God, I hadn't thought of that! What if they were unwilling to take it? What if no one was willing to take it?

Greg said, "I don't litigate much anymore, that will be up to Bron and Aaron. But they've agreed to take the case and I'm going to help. We all are." He looked at Brian Channey, who nodded. "I wish Aaron was here." Greg added. "He's young, talented. I wish you could meet him. We're proud to have him with us. He'll do a good job."

Bron leaned in toward us sympathetically. "But like we told you last night, it's going to be a considerable amount of money. You need to contact your mortgage company right away. You need to take out money anywhere you can get it."

"I don't know how..." I started.

"I'm sure you both have jobs, a house. It'll be alright," Bron said about our future, as if we still had one.

Sean brought up Huntley Park. "We have benefits with prepaid legal," he said.

Greg said, "Good. Aaron contracts with them, and so do I. That's a savings of twenty-five percent for each of us. Bron…?"

Bron was shaking his head apologetically. "No. I can't do

that."

Greg stated, "Well, it will be like we told you, at least $100,000. That's *the least.* It could go as high as $125. Maybe more."

"What if it's more than a hundred and twenty-five?" I asked as if I had that kind of money.

"When we start getting up there we can make payment arrangements, but it shouldn't go much beyond that. $125-30 should be about what it will be."

"Is that with the benefit from Huntley Park?" Sean asked.

Before Greg could answer, Mom, who had been sitting quietly, cut him off. "The money's not the issue right now. It doesn't matter how much it's going to cost. I will find the money somewhere. *This is my Grandson.*" She was shaking and her voice was full of emotion.

Sean said, "Mom..."

"Sean, look, maybe I will have to live with you someday. You can take care of me in my old age. I don't know. But you will pay me back somehow." She nodded her head at her son reassuringly. "I just can't talk about money right now."

Her expression changed as she looked at Bron and Greg. "What matters right now is a sixteen-year-old boy…who doesn't have a clue what's going on. He's alone...He's terrified." Tears streamed down her face and her voice broke, and for a minute she could not go on. She looked so alone sitting on the end of the couch with no one to lean on, no one to hold her. We were silent as she struggled to regain control. But she got her point across. We were there to talk about Torey.

After a few moments she took a deep breath, "I contacted Kelly Kumm's office this morning and they are sending someone over to speak with Torey." She finished what she needed to say.

Greg said, "You're right. Someone *does* need to go out and speak with Torey. Kelly is a good man, is he going himself?"

"He's sending a woman from his office," Mom answered.

One of them said, "Okay, that would be Naomi."

Bron said, "Good. Like I was telling you before, there will be an arraignment today at one o'clock. They will make sure that Torey's prepared for it."

"What is an arraignment?" I finally asked.

Bron explained, "When someone is arrested, there is a hearing where they are told what they are being arrested for. At that time they plead guilty or not guilty to the charges. That is an arraignment. It does not matter if it is a murder charge or a drunk driving charge," he added in what turned out to be the perfect example. There was only one other individual who was arraigned with Torey and Brian that day, and that was exactly what he was charged with.

Mom said, "Someone needs to tell Torey that he needs to plead Not Guilty!"

Greg said, "Kelly will tell him."

I asked, "How do you know that? How do you know what Kelly will tell him to say?"

"You always plead Not Guilty at an arraignment. We don't have to worry about that," Greg said.

I was confused. How can you always plead not guilty? What if you're guilty?

Mom's emotions did not prevent her from thinking clearly. She was not going to take their word for it. "Torey is a sixteen-year-old child," she said. "He's not going to know what to do for Christ Sake! I want someone to go out there and tell him exactly what he needs to say!"

Bron said, "I understand. I will go out and talk to him as soon as we decide that is what you want. Like I told you," he looked at Sean and me, "I've done this before. I'm not saying that we have more experience than anyone else, but I am telling you that you will not find anyone who will fight harder for your son than we will."

Greg was even clearer. He let us know exactly what our choices were. He said, "Kelly started out here with us. Who do you think trained him? Kelly learned everything he knows *from us*. Kelly is a good attorney. But it's up to you. You can either have the teacher or you can have the student."

I did not care. There was only one thing that mattered to me. Getting my son back. "I want my son back. Torey could…not…do...this… I…want him to have a...a...a...chance... He's just a k-iidd. He won't…know what to do." I was trying to say the most important words of my life, but I'd lost all use of language. "Look…" I pushed the school notebooks that I had taken from Torey's bedroom out to Bron, who took them from me, but did not open them.

Instead he looked at me, directly at me, and said, "I understand. I understand what you're trying to say."

Greg said, "We can take this case. Look at Bron--he's ready

to go. We can get over to Torey, make sure that he understands."

What else could we do? We needed help and they seemed to be the best option we had.

"Can I send a note to Torey with you?" I asked Bron.

"Absolutely," he said. And then considering the situation added, "You know it might be the only way you can communicate with Torey for awhile. Let me get you some paper." He stepped to his desk around the corner from where we were sitting and brought back a notepad. I sat for a minute wondering what to write. I decided just a note telling Torey how much I loved him would have to suffice.

Greg said, "There's a contract you'll need to sign. I'll get it." He went out the door.

Sean told Bron, "Torey told me something last night that you need to know."

"When?" Bron asked.

"At the police station, during the interview. I talked to him alone before they arrested him," Sean said.

"After the interview?"

"Yeah, after they said they were going to arrest him."

"Were the detectives present?"

"No, they were in the interview room, they let me talk to Torey alone for a minute in an office across the hall."

"We're going to need to step outside to talk about this," Bron said.

I hadn't heard any of this and I started to get up to go with them when Bron stopped me. "It's confidential information," he said. "I can't let you hear it."

"This is my son!" I cried, not understanding why I could not hear what was said. No one was closer to Torey than I was.

"I'm sorry," Bron said, shaking his head. He handed me Torey's notebooks and left the room with Sean. Mom and I waited alone with Brian Cheney.

Alone with Bron, Sean told the attorney what he had not told me. That Torey told him that Brian killed Cassie. Torey had said he hadn't actually seen the murder but he'd *heard* it.

Greg came back into the office, and I signed the contract. Minutes later Sean and Bron returned.

"We'll need at least a seven thousand dollar retainer to get started," Greg said.

"Will you take a personal check?" Mom asked.

"Certainly." Greg's tone was compassionate, it said I hate to take your money…but what else can I do?

Mom made out the check while Sean signed the contract.

Bron immediately went into action. He said that he would go directly to the jail and tell Torey exactly what he needed to say at the arraignment. Brian Chaney would call Naomi on her cell phone, and someone from the office would contact Kelly Kumm and let him know that his services were no longer required.

On the way out of the office, Mom turned to Greg, "You have to get these kids some help," she said referring to Sean and I. "They've got to be able to hold it together for the other two children, and for Torey."

Greg glanced at Sean and said, "We will. Do they have a bishop, someone in the church they can talk with?"

Mom said, "Just get them some help."

CHAPTER FOURTEEN

The Arraignment

We were told to be at the courthouse at twelve o'clock and that Greg or Bron would meet us there. Sean, Mom and I drove to Quiznos, a sandwich shop directly across the street from the courthouse and waited. None of us had eaten and Mom asked if we wanted to order off the menu. We shook our heads no. "I didn't think so," she said.

We sat in the back under the picture windows watching the courthouse and the traffic going by. We were quietly discussing if Torey would be in the courtroom and if we would be able to see him when my cell phone rang. The sound startled me and I jumped. It was my brother David. He hadn't heard from us since Monday morning, and was calling to see how we were doing.

I told David that Torey had been arrested and charged with murder. It was the first time I said the words out loud and I could not believe they were coming out of my mouth. They sounded so incredible. I told David we were across the street from the courthouse, and that there was going to be an arraignment in just a matter of minutes.

"You're kidding," David said, shocked.

"No."

When Torey was arrested I felt like we'd been plunged into a world alone, a world where no one else existed. It was just Sean, and the kids and I. The only other people that existed were the people that we let in, first Mom, and then the attorneys, David was my first contact outside of that small, small world but it was not enough to reconnect me to the outside.

I was not thinking about our family. Our work. School. Nothing. All of that had ceased to exist. It was gone. It never occurred to me that we had friends and family who were about to hear through the news, that Torey had been arrested and charged with First Degree Murder. But David knew what was about to happen. He hung up the phone and began calling everyone that he could reach.

When it was time to go, Sean, Mom and I, crossed the street and entered the courthouse. We looked for the courtroom where the arraignment was to take place, but when we found it the doors were closed and the benches in front were lined with people waiting to get in. We were not sure where to go. We walked down the hall and around the corner to an open bench where we sat down to wait.

There was a door to the side of us and a young couple, apparently just married, came out into the hallway. They were cheerful, dressed in jeans and dress shirts. Down the hall from us sat a man and a woman. They were about our age. He had red hair; she was brunette. The man had his arm around his wife's shoulder. They both looked disoriented and devastated. I thought, "That must be Cassie's family, oh my God! That's Cassie's family!"

It was actually *Brian's* mom and dad. Sean had met Brian's mother once when she picked Brian up from our house, but I had never seen them before. Brian is Hispanic and I thought his parents would be too, but unbeknownst to me, Brian was adopted.

The new husband, looking at everyone around him, made a comment about the gloom in the atmosphere spoiling his wedding day. Mom said something underneath her breath and the couple left.

Suddenly Bron appeared, a reassuring presence that we were not alone. He sat down next to us and told us what was happening. He had a copy of the charges against Torey and Brian with him. He explained that the boys were being charged together and would be appearing together at the arraignment. I was not sure what that meant.

Bron said, "The prosecutor had the option of either charging the boys jointly, or each one individually. That's all that means. We will talk more about that later."

Bron gave the copy of the charges to Sean, who quickly read them and passed them to me. These were the first legal papers that I had ever seen, and I was not sure what to make of them. The first page was not grandiose, not emblazoned in scarlet as I imagined such a paper would be, but was rather generic.

Then I looked at the second page. One glance at it was enough to know that I was not reading it. Not then anyway. I gave the papers back to Bron, not realizing that the judge was about to seal the record, and that it would be months before I would have another opportunity to read the complaint again.

It was fortunate that the judge sealed the record because it eliminated the press access to the case, but it also caused Sean and me a lot of pain. Once the record was sealed we had no way of knowing what happened, or what was being alleged to have happened, to Cassie. The attorneys represented Torey. They took the position that to protect their client they would tell us nothing. That decision caused us to suffer through months of unanswered questions and greatly delayed our ability to aid in Torey's defense.

When it was time to enter the courtroom, Bron said to follow him closely. There would be press and we might need to pass through them. He had mentioned the press earlier, but I did not understand what he meant.

Mom, Sean and I sat together on the inside front row. The courtroom was full of people, but I was so focused on Torey that I was unaware of them. In fact, I had the same sensation that I'd had the night before in Marchand's office. My hearing and vision constricted, this time thankfully so.

When my vision finally cleared, I saw that the judge was speaking with a man on a television screen in front of him. They were discussing a drunken driving charge. My first thought was, "We must be in the wrong place!" But then I remembered what Bron had said earlier.

There were two tables in front of us. Bron was at one and another attorney, large, fair skinned and bald headed, was at the other. The tables were separated from the seats in the courtroom by a half wall. The judge was in front of the tables on a high bench facing everyone.

I know that Mark Hiedeman or Vic Pearson, prosecutors for the State, had to be there, but I do not remember them at all.

The man on the television screen disappeared. The screen flashed and Torey appeared. He was standing in a concrete room in front of a round, metal table. He was wearing scrubs, like a doctor wears, only they were yellow. His hair was unkempt and he looked disoriented, as if he had either just woken up, or had been up all night.

Torey could not see us. All that he could see was the judge. From the very beginning Torey was alone in an adult court where he was unable to defend himself.

Brian was with Torey, and he was wearing the same yellow scrubs that Torey had on. The judge spoke to them, and Torey, who had a microphone in his hand, looked confused. It was very tense in the room. I cannot remember what the judge was saying. I was listening for Torey's response. But Torey looked scared and passed the microphone to Brian, who took it easily and spoke clearly.

I heard Brian say, "Not Guilty." He held the microphone for Torey who repeated the same. Brian's calm demeanor surprised me. He seemed remarkably relaxed, especially in comparison to Torey.

Later I found out why.

Brian had gone to the police station with his parents the day before and blamed the entire thing on Torey. He had even taken detectives to the evidence, hoping to further incriminate Torey. Brian thought that he would simply tell the detectives that Torey was responsible for Cassie's murder and they would believe him. That they would arrest Torey, and he himself would go free.

Brian was still expecting to go home.

The judge accepted the pleas and ordered a preliminary hearing to be held in district court. Brian's attorney requested bail and the judge set it at a million dollars. Brian's attorney leapt to his feet, outraged. He said a million dollars was unconscionable. Brian was a sixteen-year-old kid, not a flight risk, how was he supposed to come up with money like that?

I did not understand why Bron wasn't saying anything. Didn't he want to fight for Torey? But Bron later told us that he knew bail was a losing battle, and he did not choose to participate.

Brian's attorney turned out to be Dave Martinez, the attorney that both Greg and the detectives recommended we use, if we used a public defender. He and his boss, Chief Public Defender Randy Schulthies, represented Brian together.

The bail was set at a million dollars. Before I even realized the hearing was over, Bron was motioning for us to follow him. He led us down one hallway and then another. He said, "Move fast, we don't want to talk to the press." We passed through two glass doors at the foot of the building and were outside.

Just outside the door stood a group of reporters. Bron was already gone and Sean and Mom were hurriedly cutting across the grass to the car, avoiding the sidewalk and the people on it. I followed after them. A reporter from my work, Jimmy Hancock, saw us and broke away from the crowd.

"Excuse me," Jimmy said, and I turned and looked at him, surprised to see him there. He said, "I'm sorry. Any comment?" I slowly shook my head and turned and ran down the street to our car, wondering, where do we go from here?

The arraignment was broadcast live on the local news channels and word immediately spread through the shocked community that two sixteen-year-old classmates of Cassie had been arrested and charged with her murder. Brian and Torey's names and pictures were released through the press. Headlines blared: "*Kids*

Killing Kids" and rumors of national news coverage quickly began circulating. It was just the beginning of a media nightmare.

As soon as we arrived home, Sean and I went into the bedroom to lie down. We were in a sea of despair with nothing to ease the pain, wondering what was happening to our son. What was he thinking? What was he feeling? I wondered how we could go on. We had lost our lives. It was not like a fire, or a flood, something that we could rebuild from. Our very life was gone. It was over and we knew it.

As we were lying on the bed the phone rang. Mere minutes after the news was released Tom Romriell called. He was one of the service writers from Sean's work, and a friend. Lying on the bed next to Sean I could hear Tom's voice coming through the phone, worried, concerned. He told Sean to take as much time as he needed. His job was safe. Everyone was just so sorry...so sad for us. Was there anything they could do?

Sean thanked him and hung up. He rolled into my shoulder and cried. Later that day Robert Allen, Sean's boss, sent us flowers. The first of many we received in the following days and weeks.

Katie Foster called. The message was the same. She told me that she personally removed my home phone number from the employee listing and off of my desk telephone to make sure that no one at the Journal, meaning reporters, would be tempted to call. She said that I was to take as much time off as I needed before returning to work.

Bill Kunerth, the publisher at the Journal, called a meeting immediately after they found out who had been arrested. He made it clear that my job was safe and that the reporters were not to question me at work. In fact, Bill outlined a strategy for when I returned to work and no one was to discuss the case in front of me at all.

The paper that I worked for ultimately provided the bulk of the press coverage. But Bill was mindful of my feelings, and for this I am grateful. I was terrified of going back to work where my son's arrest was the biggest story. Every day was difficult for me, but Bill did what he could to make it easier.

My brother, David, tried to reach our family before the news did. My brothers Bob, Rick, David, and Mike rallied around us with their families, as did Sean's sisters Ann and Cyndi. Over the next several days and weeks they made sure that we were never alone. Mom brought over enough food to feed everyone. So did my sister-in-laws, Pam and Mary.

The first night Mom said that she hated to leave us, but that she would be back again in the morning. All we could do, Lacey and Jamie, Sean and I, was cry and cry and cry. But our family kept us going. Others showed up to help. Friends offered cards, and flowers, and food and prayers and helped our family carry us on.

My chronological memory of those first days is gone, but certain images stand out with the clarity of a snapshot. Our family gathered around the dining room table. My brothers and their wives, Cyndi and Ann, and of course Mom. I kept saying, "I don't know what happened. I don't know what happened," over and over again.

Everything was dreamlike and surreal. Sean was falling apart.

One morning I woke up alone in bed. It was light outside and I went looking for Sean. I found him in his bathrobe sitting on the swing on the back patio, sobbing. I watched him through the sliding glass door, afraid to open it. When I finally did he was crying, "my son...my son...my son…" I did not know what to do. I did not know how we could carry on if Sean fell apart, and I was terrified. When I went to him he clung to me, and he was soft and wet and I wanted to quickly turn the tables on him but I couldn't. I could not do that to him.

The nightmare that I was living in was so unbelievable that it played with my mind. Sometimes I would open my eyes in the morning and for one brief glorious second I would think, "It was all a dream!!! *All a dream!*" Because I had dreamt about it so vividly it *had* to be a dream, it could not be real, and I would almost laugh with relief.

But then I would realize it was not a dream, and Torey was gone. I could almost feel my mind snap as the jarring reality settled in once more.

I tried to escape. I locked myself in my bedroom, and I lay on my bed. For months afterwards I had to keep my bedroom door closed, because if I caught an *accidental* glimpse inside that room, my heart would stop. Every nook and cranny of it reminded me of the pain that I was in. It was a heartbroken, wretched place. That place of attempted escape.

There was no escape because you cannot sleep, you cannot dream when your child has been arrested for murder. There are no dreams left. Only nightmares.

CHAPTER FIFTEEN

The Lives We Lost

I met Sean when I was eighteen and he was twenty-one. We connected immediately, emotionally more than physically. We were best friends before we ever fell in love, and we are still best friends today. If there really is such a thing as a soul mate, Sean is mine. Together we built a wonderful life.

Sean and I wanted children and we started our family early. Sean was a patient father and I was an involved mother. We loved our children more than anything in the world and our time with them was precious. I did not work until the children started school, and after they started school I volunteered in their classrooms. Every year we planned a family vacation together. We went to *Disneyland, Knott's Berry Farm*, *Yellowstone Park*, and a cruise through *Mexico*.

Lacey was two years older than Torey, and Torey was two years older than Jamie. The children were all close, but the two boys were exceptionally so. I could never think of one without the other. All of our children were sociable and had friends in school, but they also enjoyed a close extended family. Some of their cousins were friends as well as relatives.

When Torey was eight we built a house next door to my mother. Our children grew up on the same street that I grew up on, a rural, cul-de-sac with a park and two schools at the end of it. The homes and property on the street were known by the names of the families who lived in them. The Greens, the Nelsons, the McDaniels…

Wilcox Elementary bordered the park at the end of the street, and across the park was Hawthorne Junior High. It was a good, stable neighborhood and our children loved living next door to their grandmother. They built strong friendships with good kids in the neighborhood and the parents in the neighborhood knew each other from the mutual school, sports, and church activities their children shared.

We probably would have stayed in that house, but my mother developed cancer and passed away. It was a loss we felt every day. A couple of years later, a young woman who lived around the corner from us was attacked and murdered in her home. The street we lived on was quiet, but it was right off a main highway. It did not feel safe anymore, and we began to think about moving.

We finally made the decision in 2005. By then a manufactured home had gone between my mother's house and ours. Once that happened moving was inevitable. We built a new house in a more secluded neighborhood and moved into it on September 23, 2005, when Torey was fifteen years old.

We liked our old house so much that we had the same floor plan built again. It was not a large home, but it was comfortable. There were four bedrooms and three baths. And we were fortunate. Our house was new and nearly paid off. We put in the yard and planted a garden.

But the move was not as easy as we hoped. We missed the old neighborhood and the children missed their friends, still we adjusted. Lacey started college and Torey earned his driver's license. Jamie discovered Lacrosse, which had recently made its debut in Pocatello, and was playing middie. Football season was ahead and so was bowling. Torey was on the high school league.

Our life was full and pleasantly predictable. Sean's job was stable as was mine. Everyone was healthy. There was no clue that something was on the horizon that could change everything.

The only inkling of a problem was that Torey's new friend Brian was bringing over movies that I did not approve of. But that was more of a reflection of my values than a clue that something was dreadfully wrong.

No. Our life was perfect, or as nearly perfect as could be expected, and Sean and I knew it. We counted our blessings and were grateful, but we never expected them to end.

Sean and I might have been unprepared for the tragedy that befell us, but it was Torey, who had spent his entire life in the center of a loving family, who was devastated, who truly lost everything.

Torey was a small baby, but from the beginning he was loaded with personality. He was active, and imaginative, and mischievous, but so happy and good-natured that he was easy to raise.

Torey was anemic when he was born and he had to receive blood transfusions before we could take him home. It was painful to see his small body hooked to tubes and wires, and once I got him in my arms I did not want to put him down again. That was fine with Torey. He was a cuddly baby.

During Torey's six-week checkup his pediatrician told us that Torey was never going to be the tallest kid on the block. When I asked what that meant he said, "Torey is within normal limits, but he's on the smaller end of the scale. Torey is never going to be tall."

But that was okay. We thought he was perfect just the way he was.

Shortly after Torey's birth my brother Robert sold Sean and I a manufactured home that he'd been using as a rental property. It was small and cozy and served as our home for the first two years of Torey's life, until Jamie came along and we simply outgrew it.

Our next home was a small house we purchased on Holman Street. Sean worked at Courtesy Ford during the day as a mechanic and attended night school. I opened a home day care center so that I could stay home with our three children and help with the finances. My nephews Jacob, Andrew and Nathan, were the same ages as Lacey, Torey and Jamie. They were in my day care, so the cousins grew up together.

As a toddler, Torey could be mischievous. When he was three years old he disappeared. In a panic I searched the house and yard for him. A neighbor came over to help me search. When we could not find him I frantically dialed 911, but right before the officers arrived we found Torey hiding under the next-door neighbor's camping trailer smiling from ear to ear, thoroughly enjoying the excitement he'd caused.

During another incident Torey locked himself in my car. I stood outside in a parking lot, knocking on the window, pleading with my three-year-old to unlock the door while he watched me through the glass, smiling mightily.

When Torey started first grade, his teacher suggested we put him in speech pathology because he lisped. Torey had trouble with his S's, which he dropped. He'd say 'nake for snake, or 'nack for snack. Torey did well in speech pathology and his lisp quickly improved and disappeared.

The same teacher told us that Torey might have a learning disability. She said that Torey knew his letter sounds well enough, but that he was having difficulty putting them together. It was the first indication we had that Torey might have a reading problem. But Torey was very young and he was smart. I thought he would outgrow it, which he has, but it took a long time. (Torey took adaptive reading classes from elementary school through the tenth grade.) But no matter how hard Torey struggled in school, he never failed a class. He did the best that he could, I helped him, his teachers encouraged him, and he did well. You would never know that Torey had a problem unless you looked at his IEP, (Individualized Education Program).

Torey always had a magnitude of interests, and one of his earliest interests was building. Before he started kindergarten, Torey could build working structures with tinker toys. By the time he was in the third grade, Torey was building the large Knex roller coasters by himself, and in the fifth grade he built the Knex Ball Factory. That was quite an achievement because the ball factory is over five feet tall with hundreds of small, intricate pieces. Even at that young age Torey could follow a blueprint, or make up his own designs.

In 1998, when Torey was seven years old, Sean and I sold our house on Holman Street. My mother, whom I've always been very close to, offered us the vacant lot next to her house so that we could build on it. It was a wonderful opportunity for us and we moved in with her while our new house was under construction.

But right before the contractor excavated I made a decision that I believe affected our entire lives. The lot Mom offered us was a quarter acre. We originally planned to build in the center of the property, but when we had the land surveyed I told her that we would only accept the first seventy-five feet of it. That would leave a vacant lot between Mom's house and ours. I knew mom valued her privacy, and I did not want to take that away from her.

Later, after my mother passed away, the undeveloped lot was sold. I had not considered that possibility when I made the decision. When a manufactured home went in we decided to move. And moving from that home, and away from our children's friends, may have set us on the course that ended in disaster.

But we had no intention of moving when the house was built. We were thrilled to live next door to my mother. My father had passed away before the children were old enough to remember him, but their grandmother had been actively involved in their lives every day since their births. Unfortunately my mother was diagnosed with cancer and passed away on August 3, 2000. Her death was a painful loss.

After mother's passing, my brother David and his wife Pam purchased Mom's house. It is their home now. Their three boys, Riley, Ty and Brady, lived next door to us until we moved in the summer of 2005. Our children loved having their grandmother and cousins next door. They grew up part of a large, extended family.

Just as his pediatrician predicted, Torey was always one of the shorter boys in his class. One day in the third grade, Torey came home from school very excited. He told me that he had met someone who was, "just my size." That was Max McClure, and he and Torey shared a close friendship. Max may have been short, but he, like Torey, was loaded with personality.

Max collected Poke'mon cards and once he introduced Torey to the wonders of card collection, Torey was hooked. Torey had his heart set on collecting every last Poke'mon card, especially Charmeleon. And Torey did his best to collect them all. Hours of chores and daily reading resulted in hundreds of Poke'mon cards, but never, unfortunately, a Charmeleon.

Torey rarely handled his Poke'mon cards. They were much too valuable to him. But it was not just his Poke'mon cards that Torey took care of. Torey treated everything he owned with respect. He played with his toys, but he did not damage them. And collecting was a passion he retained.

When Torey was in the fifth grade he met David Luras. David, like Torey, was small for his age, but he was very quick and limber. He could do black flips and ride a unicycle while juggling. Torey admired David's skills, but their friendship was balanced. They both had quiet, easygoing personalities.

David wasn't the only friend that Torey had. There was KC Miller, Brian Silvia and Adam Dykman. Combined with Jamie and Lacey's friends, we always had a house full.

And the children were active. There was a ski resort less than thirty minutes from Pocatello. Torey and Jamie snowboarded every winter with their friends, and during the summer we regularly went camping, hiking and dirt bike riding together.

But there was another activity that the kids participated in that was a direct reflection of Torey's interest. Filming movies. Torey has been interested in movies for as long as I can remember.

It was no secret that he wanted to be a director.

Sean began filming home movies when Lacey was born. Not just birthdays and holidays, but everything. The kids constantly had a video camera on them. While they ate dinner, slept, rode their bikes, or played at the park.

When Torey was in the sixth grade he started filming home movies himself. Adding commentary, he would improvise commercials. Soon Torey began filming short stories with his brother and sister. Eventually he began making movies with his friends.

David Luras, Brian Silvia, Jake Smith and some of Jamie's friends, as well as Lacey and the cousins, spent hours filming movies with Torey. It was fun and I saw no problem with it.

Torey wanted to film all the time, but eventually his friends grew tired of it. They went from making movies every day, to making them once in awhile, to not making them at all.

Torey was extremely disappointed. He still wanted to make movies; he just didn't have anyone to do it with, until the end of Tenth grade when he met *Brian Draper*.

Brian loved the idea of making a movie, but even he couldn't have predicted where this was going to lead.

CHAPTER SIXTEEN

A New Reality

Torey...Oh my *God*...*Torey*...

We had to find out what was happening to him. Sean and I called Lieutenant Peterson. The first thing that she told us was that Torey was not completely gone from our lives. He was still with us and we could still help him. In my desperation I thought that the Lieutenant was trying to give us hope. And she could have been. But she was also telling us about our new reality.

As a minor child in an adult jail, Torey was not going to be allowed contact with other inmates. He was placed in isolation and denied any form of human contact whatsoever. Lieutenant Peterson called this *Protective Custody*. Torey would remain locked in a cell for twenty-three hours a day, every day, and would be let out of his cell for only one hour each day to shower, use the phone, or watch television.

While Torey was out of his cell the other inmates would have to be placed in theirs. Torey's hour out of his cell would be up to the discretion of the guards, so it would vary from day to day.

I asked about Torey's cell. Lieutenant Peterson said that it was a cinderblock room about the size of a small bathroom. The only view outside of the cell was a long, narrow window in the metal door. But the window's intention was to give the guards a view into the cell, not the inmate a view out.

There was a sink and a toilet inside the cell and a metal bed secured to the floor. The mattress was actually a thin pad that sat on top of the metal frame. Torey was allowed two blankets and two sheets, but no pillow.

Lieutenant Peterson told us that Torey could have three paperback books in his cell, a Bible, sheets of notepaper, and a golf pencil, no eraser, for writing. She told us that Torey could purchase a small amount of snack food, if he had money, from a list that she called "commissary," but that was it. That was all he would be allowed.

I tried to comprehend such a barren existence, but was unable to. Sean and I were in shock, but Torey's life was decimated. Sean and I were reeling from the loss of our son, but our son was living through the very real loss of his *life*. I suddenly knew there was no comparison.

After the Lieutenant finished horrifying us with the details of Torey's living conditions, she told us three things that what we could do to help him. We could set up a phone account where Torey could call us collect during the hour out of his cell each day. (My brother, Michael, anxious to help, immediately paid for a landline to be installed in our home for that very purpose.) We could put money on the commissary account so that Torey could purchase necessary items, and we could *visit* him.

Until we spoke with Lieutenant Peterson I thought that Torey had been taken from us, and that we would never see him again. At the time I did not know that you could visit people in jail or prison. But she told us that we could visit Torey for half an hour on Wednesdays and Sundays during visitation hours, which the jail made available to everyone.

What these visits meant was…*life*. It is not easy to see your son in prison. We've seen our son as no parent should ever have to, handcuffed and shackled, morose and helpless, behind glass, and out of reach.

But we could *see* Torey. We could lay our eyes on him, and he could see us. We could not touch, we could not feel, but we could see, and we could talk, and that was enough. It kept us going.

What these visits meant to Torey, a 16-year-old child, locked in a jail cell the size of a small bathroom for 23 hours a day, with no human contact, no one to talk to, no sensory stimulation, or recreation or exercise for eleven long months, I cannot say. I do not know how he survived it. By the grace of God, he did.

While I was speaking to Lieutenant Peterson, Sean realized that Torey had been in the jail for almost twenty-four hours with no money. What if he needed something? (*As if commissary could help.*) He panicked.

Sean began pulling open drawers and cabinet doors looking for cash. He found his wallet and told me that he was going to the jail. I told Lieutenant Peterson that Sean was driving out there that very minute with some cash for Torey. Even though it was after hours, she let him in so that he could put money on our son's account.

By the time Sean arrived at the jail he was crying so hard he couldn't speak. Lieutenant Peterson asked him if he'd had a chance to speak with Torey yet, and Sean could not respond. Maybe she would have allowed Sean to see Torey that night, I don't know. But she was trying to be sympathetic, and Sean was in no physical condition to carry on a conversation. She took the money for Torey's account and went back inside. Sean did the best that he could to collect himself and drove back home.

There was only one way that Torey was going to make it through the circumstances that had become his life; with a lot of help, and the support of the people that he loved. Torey had to know that the people he loved still cared about him. Thankfully they came to us before we even knew we needed them.

As soon as he learned of Torey's arrest, Adam Dykman wanted to visit him. Adam came to our house and asked permission; but at the time, Sean, locked in denial, refused to admit that the situation was not on the verge of correcting itself. He made up a story and tried to send Adam home. But thankfully, Adam saw through Sean's position and persisted.

Adam contacted the jail himself, and with his mother's help received permission to visit Torey. I, for one, was grateful. I knew how much Torey needed Adam.

When Sean and I, Lacey and Jamie, visited Torey he was withdrawn and depressed. A doctor had already diagnosed him with *Post Traumatic Stress Syndrome* and I could see the effects. Sometimes during our visits with him, Torey would sit on the other side of the glass, motionless and disinterested. He would run his finger along the bottom pane of the glass, not saying a word, just tracking the progress of his finger with his eyes, seemingly unaware that we were with him. I could not imagine the state Torey must have been in when he was alone. The fact that he was surviving seemed to be a miracle.

But when Torey saw Adam, it was like he woke up. For the first time since his arrest he showed signs of life, perhaps not quite hope, but *life*. He sat up straight, he talked, he smiled. For the first time I began to think that possibly we could get Torey through this.

After his initial visit, Adam kept coming back. He saw how much Torey needed him, and he wasn't about to let him down. Adam, it turned out, was the only one who could reach Torey in his deepest despair and give him a reason to go on.

For months, Adam and his mother, and often his father, sat with our family at the jail, waiting hours to spend a few minutes with Torey. With no way to repay them, they gave unselfishly of their time and their money and their love, never asking for anything in return.

That was a powerful lesson to me. I'd always been so consumed with my own children's welfare that I sheltered them, or perhaps a better word would be *secluded* them from anyone I felt might be questionable. Suddenly I was the mother of a child arrested for *Murder*. How could anyone stand by me, or Torey? But Lori and David Dykman did stand by us, and in so doing, provided me an example of love and compassion that I will never forget.

But Adam's position was a difficult one. He knew we truly needed him, and in fact I do not believe we could have gotten Torey through this without him. But it was a heavy burden for a young man to carry, and it cost him. The hopelessness of the situation sent Adam into a deep depression.

For a while we were scared. We did not know what was going to happen. But Adam is a strong kid, with a loving, supportive family behind him and he pulled out of it okay. Adam Dykman is going to be just fine. Adam is an amazing person.

You never know who is going to show up in your time of need. Rusty Adamson was Torey's seventh grade English teacher. She taught all three of our children, and I had always known and respected her as a teacher, but I was completely surprised when I opened my door and found her, standing on the other side, asking to help.

Rusty heard of Torey's arrest on the radio. Immediately she knew that we needed her. She searched for our home address and once she found us she announced right away that she was there to help, that she knew the truth, and that she would not be leaving us until this was over. She meant it. The entire time that Torey was incarcerated at the Bannock County Jail, Rusty never missed a weekly visit with him.

To understand the significance of Rusty's dedication you have to understand the visiting conditions at the jail. Visitation is on a first come basis with all the other inmates. Because Torey had to be kept segregated, he had to be visited in an isolated booth. That booth was shared by other segregated inmates. On visitation day each segregated inmate had to be escorted down the hallways separately, visited separately for their half an hour, and escorted back to their cell separately, before the next inmate could be brought out. In the mists of these *special movements*, there was also the *movement* of the "general population" inmates to work around.

It was a long and tedious process.

We would try to arrive at the jail before five p.m. when the doors opened. If we were lucky we were able to visit Torey by seven; but more often than not our visits were after eight and we seldom left the jail before eight-thirty. Rusty would wait these three hours, after a long day at work, in a crowded waiting room, to see Torey for the first *five minutes* of his visit.

Rusty refused to take any more time than that because she wanted us to have the precious time allowed with our son, but she felt strongly that he should know that she was there for him. She did this voluntarily every Wednesday night for almost a year, never once complaining about the wait or the inconvenience.

When Rusty first started coming to the visits I did not let her into the booth to see Torey. She would wait the entire time in the visiting hall just for me to tell Torey that she was there. Torey would ask me to let her in, but at the time we wanted every single second that we could get with our son. But when Rusty came back week after week, and I could see that Torey really wanted to see her, I asked Rusty if she would like to go in and see him. With tears in her eyes Rusty said, "Oh Shannon, I've been waiting for this."

Rusty, along with Torey's best friend Adam, his parents Lori and David Dykman, our entire family, Sean's Mom, my sister Mary, who has written to Torey every single day since his arrest, David, Pat and Alaina Luras, and of course Torey's brother and sister are the wonderful support group that carried Torey and us through to the trial and directly afterwards. They are still with us today, and I have no doubt that it is thanks to God, and to these wonderful people, that Torey is still with us too.

For days after Torey and Brian's arrest detectives interviewed some of the students at Pocatello High School, attempting to gain more evidence. During one of the interviews, a student told the detectives that Torey had a secret hiding place in his room. This prompted a second search of our home.

Lacey and I were home alone when detectives knocked on our door with a search warrant. There were six detectives on my doorstep demanding entrance into the house. Overwhelmed, I told them that I needed to call my attorneys before I could let them in. They said they'd already tried to get a hold of our attorneys and their office was closed. I really had no choice. I had to let them in.

Later I told the attorneys what happened. They said their office had been open and the receptionists were taking calls. It was highly unlikely that no one answered one of the lines. It was more likely that they had never been called in the first place.

This time the warrant was specifically for Torey's bedroom. Five officers went into Torey's room to search through his belongings while the remaining detective sat with Lacey and I in the kitchen.

Torey's room had his full sized bed in it, a bookcase designed for movies, which was full of movies and CD's, and an entertainment center with a TV, Play Station, X-box and stereo in it. Torey did not have a dresser or a nightstand. He had a large closet with closet organizers and shelves, and that is where his clothes were kept.

Torey's room was very clean and organized. There was no place to hide anything that I wouldn't have known about. His closet was sparsely filled with only three pairs of pants, five t-shirts, a sweatshirt, church clothes and pajama bottoms hanging in it. His socks and underwear, belts and shoes were on shelves in the closet that ran from floor to ceiling. On the shelves that branch out on either side were three stacks of books; Torey's yearbooks, his collection of Calvin and Hobs, and his school notebooks, which I had taken to the attorneys office when we first met with them after Torey's arrest.

The attorneys hadn't even bothered to look at Torey's notebooks, and after our meeting with them, I brought them back home and returned them to the shelf where they belonged.

I asked the detective sitting with Lacey and I what they were looking for.

"We were told Torey hides things down his heater vent," he said.

"That's not possible," I told him. "I vacuum Torey's room and make his bed every day. I have to move his bed out from the wall to make it. The back wheel snags on his heater vent every time. I would notice if something was down there."

"I believe you would," he said. "I was at the original search. Most of us were commenting on how clean your house is."

He asked if we'd just moved in. I shook my head no. "We've been here a year."

One of the detectives searching Torey's room came out to the kitchen and asked me for a hand mirror so that they could search further down the vent than they could reach. I went into the bathroom and found one. I watched the detectives search until they realized that nothing was down the heater vent. They had also been told that Torey hid things in his dresser, but since he did not own a dresser that would have been impossible. The detectives began rummaging through everything in Torey's room.

I went back to the kitchen. Lacey asked the detective, "Do you think we're going to get our computers back?"

"Yes, eventually," he said. He asked her why she asked.

"I had my homework on mine."

"Oh. You might be able to get that one returned sooner. I don't think anyone is saying, 'That Lacey, I wonder what kind of racy stuff is on her computer!'" His voice had a teasing tone.

Lacey shook her head, "No. Just school work."

"Well, you should be getting it back shortly," he reiterated, attempting to reassure her.

I walked down the hall and peered into Torey's room. A detective was sitting on the edge of Torey's bed carefully going through Torey's notebooks one page at a time. I went back to the kitchen. A few moments later the detectives came out. One of them said, "We're taking these notebooks."

"What?" I asked, horrified. I could not believe it. Taking the notebooks was like taking a piece of Torey! It was personal.

"Please, don't do that," I begged. I tried to explain, but they just handed me a receipt, as if that was all they needed to do, and left me crying.

I kept thinking why hadn't Bron kept these! I gave them to him! They were right in his hands and he did not even look at them!

But the police did. The police searched them thoroughly. They found a list on a page inside one of the notebooks entitled ***Ideas for the Movie*** that had the word Supplies written across the top of it. It was the list of props for the movie that Torey and Brian had been planning, but the prosecution submitted it as evidence of a murder conspiracy along with similar lists found in another notebook.

I cannot help feeling that I hand delivered the prosecution part of its erroneous case. Material that they could represent anyway they wanted. If only I had left the notebooks with the attorneys…

The attorneys called us in for a briefing. It was days after Torey's arrest and they wanted to prepare us for what lay ahead. Before the meeting, Greg introduced us to Aaron Thompson, the actual attorney recommended by Huntley Park, and the only attorney we had yet to meet.

Aaron was young, maybe early thirties, but he looked even younger than that. He was small, but muscular with short clipped hair and wire-rimmed glasses. When Greg introduced us, Aaron briskly shook our hands and seated himself at the conference table without a word. When the meeting concluded he commented that, "The meeting was not a complete waste of time, we accomplished something," and was gone.

The impression Aaron left me with was that he was important and that we had better warrant the use of his time. He also struck me as someone who was not going to get personally involved. But it was a mistaken impression. Aaron *was* personally involved and his briskness was a reflection of the level of responsibility he assumed for the case.

One of the items we discussed during the meeting was the preliminary hearing, where the prosecutor's burden would be to convince the judge that he had enough evidence against Torey to warrant his arrest and bind him over for trial.

After the arraignment, the prosecutor, Mark Hiedeman, announced to the press that there was a videotape involved in the crime. The attorneys told us that with the videotaped evidence, Torey and Brian *would* be bound over. But the preliminary hearing would also create an opportunity for us to view the prosecutor's case and to see the evidence against Torey.

Some defense attorneys waive the preliminary hearing. It's expensive, kind of like a mini trial, and they know they are going to get the evidence later anyway. They may also want to keep the media out of the case as long as possible. We discussed all of these issues and decided to go ahead with the preliminary hearing on the advice of our attorneys. They were certain we would lose, but they wanted to create as extensive a paper trail as possible for future appeals, if an appeal became necessary.

Another issue we faced was the fact that Torey was still being charged along with Brian, which created problems on a number of levels. Brian and Torey were adversarial. Each blamed the other for what happened to Cassie, but because they were co-defendants, in some respects, they had to work together.

Both boys had the right to disqualify one judge without cause, and each set of attorneys might differ on which judge they wanted to disqualify. That was just one issue of many. The bottom line was, one boy's attorneys could very well affect both boys' defenses, and they needed to be separated. Our attorneys felt that eventually they would be, but they wanted it done as soon as possible.

We agreed to file the motions they presented to us, and to schedule the preliminary hearing. Thus began our inadvertent education in the legal system.

I am not sure how Lacey and Jamie survived the first few days. We clung together, but there was really nothing that we could do for each other. At the time we were all going through our own personal hell.

Lacey took time off work, but she only missed two days of school before she had to go back. She's never spoken with me about what that was like for her, but I know that it was hard. I heard her crying to Jeff day after day.

Jeff practically moved into our house. Lacey needed him and he was determined to be there for her. He adamantly defended Torey, and he supported Lacey when she needed him the most. For that I am thankful. I will love Jeff forever.

Jamie withdrew. He spent hours alone in his room, especially during the first few days when there was a houseful of people. As long as there were people in the house talking about Torey, Jamie refused to come out. Only after everyone left, and the house was quiet, would he come out of his room and sit with me.

It was hard for us to know what to say to one another. I would get Mancala, a game we could play alone together, and we would play a few rounds. I did not know how to be there for Jamie in any other way besides physically. He was not talking about his loss, and I did not know how to make him feel comfortable enough to open up.

Torey and Jamie were so close. I could never picture one without the other. Jamie lost his only brother, his best friend, and I did not know how to get him through that. But it was even more complicated.

Lacey was going to ISU. She had a level of anonymity. But Jamie attended Pocatello High School, the school reeling from the loss of one of its students, and the belief that his brother was one of the people responsible. How could I send him back there?

But the school was Jamie's life. His teachers were there, his friends. Jamie wasn't leaving the house, but he was receiving dozens of calls of support every day. Jamie was scared, but he wanted to go back to the school where his friends were, to the support group that he needed.

But I couldn't let him. I kept him home day after day after day, scared to let him leave the house. He finally started asking if he could go to football practice. His friends were inviting him and he wanted to go. I reluctantly agreed. I decided if the kids accepted him at practice, I would try to get him back into school.

I drove Jamie to the practice field and parked where I could watch him. Allowing him to enter into a group of people where he could be hurt was one of the hardest things I had to do, but I did it, and Jamie was welcomed back to the team with open arms. No one said a word to him about what happened.

That was the first step. Afterwards I called the school counselor and together we arranged a plan. Jamie would go back to school, but under protective measures. We minimized Jamie's expose to the students by allowing him to go to school late and picking him up early. He would leave campus for lunch, either with friends or family.

Jamie went back to school on Monday, the ninth of October, twelve days after Torey's arrest. As I drove him to school I told him that if he needed me I would be there for him. His counselor offered to meet him inside the building, but he did not want to do that. Jamie wanted to enter the building, as if nothing had happened, and resume his life.

But he was frightened. Jamie sat in the car for a few minutes willing himself to get out. I asked him if he'd like me to go in with him and he said no. It was not easy, but Jamie opened the door and walked across the schoolyard and into the building, one of the bravest things I had ever seen him do.

I knew how he felt. Even driving in my car, I felt the eyes of everyone in the community on me. During the months after Torey's arrest, I sheltered myself at home and at work, rarely venturing beyond those confines.

I could not imagine walking into the large, enclosed school building.

The first day of school was really hard for Jamie, and the second, and the third, but Jamie went every day with determination until it got easier. By the end of the semester he was doing all right.

It turned out that we did not need to make the special arrangements. Most of the students at the school were understanding, and when they did question Jamie, it was usually just to ask how

Torey was doing.

Jamie missed enough school that he had to drop his honor classes, but he was *in* school, getting good grades, and with friends who cared about him. That's all I cared about. I was grateful for that.

I went to Aaron's office. He and Greg were there. I wanted to know if Torey had told them what happened yet, and they said that he had. They would not tell me what happened, but I asked them if they believed Torey had told them the truth.

"Yes," Aaron said, "I believe he did."

Greg said, "We all believe him, but it is a difficult story to believe. Given the circumstances."

"So what does that mean?" I asked.

"Well...we don't think he stabbed Cassie, we don't believe he did that, but we have an uphill battle in front of us, to prove that he didn't. The videotape is a nasty thing."

"How uphill?" I asked.

Greg held his hand out level and tilted it upwards until his fingers were pointing to what would be between the one o'clock and two o'clock position on a clock.

"So does he even have a chance?" I gasped.

"Yes, he has a chance."

"How much of a chance?"

"You like to put me on the spot, don't you?" Greg said. "I can't answer that right now. We're going to have to wait and see."

"See what?"

"What develops with the physical evidence, what judge we end up with, what kind of jury we'll have. There's a lot of work ahead of us."

I was not worried about the physical evidence.

"I need my son to come home." I told him.

"I know it."

I started saying things to myself, things that I could repeat to people when they asked me. "We have hope." Hope. It became a theme. A way to keep going. A justification for survival.

We clung desperately to whatever anyone could give us. All week we went through the motions, waiting for the two days that we could visit our son, leaving one visit looking forward to the next. We spent hours and hours at the jail and the hours in between waiting to go back. Back to our son, to see our son like no one ever should have to.

How had this happened? I had to know.

Unbelievably, most of the information I had came from the press, who despite a constant barrage of reporting--did not have access to the kind of details I was looking for.

The jist of the matter was well known. A young girl was killed, two of her classmates were arrested for the crime, and there was a videotape that allegedly proved their guilt. It sounded like a closed case. But I knew my son, what he was capable of, and what he was not. I knew there was much more to the story than what was being told.

PART FOUR

The Evidence

CHAPTER SEVENTEEN

Videotaped Evidence

I cannot remember when I was first told that a videotape existed. It may have been the night of Torey's arrest; I don't know. What I do know is that as soon as I comprehended what was being alleged, that the videotape was linked to Cassie's murder, and that it proved that Torey and Brian were both responsible, I had to see the tape. I remember driving to the attorney's office with Sean.

When we arrived, Brian Chaney was the only attorney present. Knowing why we were there, Brian was hesitant to speak with us. He asked us to schedule an appointment with Aaron or Bron, but when he saw how upset we were, and that we weren't leaving, he finally relented.

Brian escorted us into Bron's office and closed the door. I asked, "Have you seen the videotape?"

"I have," Brian said. I could tell by his demeanor that whatever was on the tape, it was bad--really bad. Brian looked like a physician delivering a death prognosis. I could picture him in a white coat and stethoscope; sadly shaking his head, saying, "I'm sorry--there's nothing I can do."

"We've discussed it," Brian said, "and, uhmm…you're not going to see the tape."

"We have to see the tape. This is our son," I said.

"You're going to have to talk to Aaron and Bron, but we're pretty adamant."

"What about Torey?" I asked. "Has he seen the tape? Isn't this his decision?"

"Yes. Aaron and Bron watched the tape with Torey. We're recommending to him, that you not be allowed to view the tape. You have to understand. You have to take our word for this. You do not want to see this tape."

I remember Brian saying something about maybe using an insanity defense. I did not understand. I knew my son wasn't crazy, and I knew that he was incapable of hurting someone. What was Brian talking about? What could possibly be on a videotape that could have led to *anything* like this?

"Do you think Torey killed Cassie?" I asked Brian directly. He did not answer, but his eyes told me that he did.

"It's going to be a difficult defense," he said.

I did not care what was on that videotape. Brian Chaney was an attorney in the firm. He had *access* to Torey. He should have waited until he spoke *with* Torey before reaching a conclusion. Otherwise he would be just the same as the prosecutor, judging the evidence alone, never caring about the people involved, what their thoughts and motivations were, and how everything fit together.

I was grateful that Brian Chaney was not our attorney. He would have been fired on the spot.

Brian believed we were the parents of a child who had committed a heinous crime. He was sympathetic, and I can appreciate that. But I knew that my son was innocent. I did not need sympathy. I needed someone who was willing to spend enough time with Torey that they would get to know him. I needed someone who could recognize that they had an *innocent* boy's life in their hands, and I needed somebody who was really going to care about that. Who would take it personally, and fight for Torey as if they were fighting for their own son. *That*'s what I needed.

The conversation with Brian was the beginning of a long struggle that Sean and I had with our attorneys. They refused to allow us to watch the videotape, and no amount of reasoning would change their minds. For me, it was the worst period of this entire ordeal, the not knowing.

It was admitted early on that the murder itself was not on the tape, thank God. But I could not imagine why the tape was so damning. What could the tape have to do with *this*? Did it lead up to and leave off at...Cassie's death...Did she say something that *seemed to* incriminate my son?

The *only* thing I could think of was that the kids were making a movie, and Brian got carried away. But all the movies Torey made were spoofs. How could you get carried away in a spoof? Had they been making a real life horror movie? It did not make sense.

I suffered from the most terrible nightmares. I thought they would last forever. I thought I would dream these terrible dreams for the rest of my life. Actually nightmares do not describe them. Night terrors would be a better description. I prayed to God before I slept each night to give me nothing, nothing but a black, dreamless sleep. But He never did. Not in the beginning, not for a long, long time.

What was on the video? I tortured myself with it.

Sean, listening to the attorneys, thought it *might* be too difficult for me to watch. He wanted to see it first and then decide if I should view it or not. But it was consuming me. Every day that passed I became more and more haggard. I lost weight. I couldn't eat. I couldn't sleep.

When I was a child I saw an episode on a television program that terrified me. Jim Rockford, from *The Rockford Files*, broke into a house and rescued a man who was tied to a chair right before he was beaten and stabbed. I had always been scared of the dark, but I had nightmares for months after seeing that.

That program came back to me in my dreams. I saw Cassie tied to a chair in a dark house. I saw Torey and Brian filming a horror movie and Cassie was in it. I saw Brian pretend to stab Cassie; only it turned out to be for real. I cannot, even to this day, remember that dream without being physically sick to my stomach. Every part of my body screamed *NO! NO! NO!* It was sick and terrible and awful in every way. I knew *Brian*. He had been in my home. And *Cassie,* a beautiful young girl!

How could I survive seeing these terrible scenes night after night after night? No amount of medication or sleeping pills would stop them. I *had* to know what had happened.

In the end, our attorneys had no choice. Mark Hiedeman, the prosecutor, threatened to play the videotape during the preliminary hearing. Our attorneys felt it was a ploy designed to intimidate Torey and Brian into waiving their rights to the hearing, but since neither set of defense attorneys were willing to succumb to the threat, they had to take it seriously.

Realizing the cruelty of allowing Sean and I, to view the video for the first time, unprepared, in a courtroom full of people, our attorneys finally decided to let us watch it. They called us into their office on October 31, 2006, three days before the preliminary hearing. They asked us to meet with them after their office closed, because they did not want anyone to know what we were doing. When we arrived the building was dark and locked. Aaron met us at the door and let us in. He led us down the hall to the conference room where Bron was waiting. It was just the four of us, Bron, Aaron, Sean and I.

Bron and Aaron were nervous, they were worried about our reaction to the tape, but they were also concerned that people would find out that we had viewed it. They made us promise that we'd tell no one, and in fact we never did tell anyone, except for Torey, that we had.

We were in the conference room at the end of the hall, in the room where we began with these attorneys on the day of Torey's arrest. At the end of the long conference table was a desk with a computer monitor on it. Bron sat down at the table while Sean and I huddled around the computer screen next to Aaron. Aaron loaded the DVD that the prosecution's office had copied from the video.

"Ready?" he asked.

Sean and I nodded. Aaron pressed PLAY.

I could tell right away that Torey did not make this video. Torey makes *movies*. They have a story line. There's a beginning, middle, and an end. They're planned. They make sense. They're full of humor, thought, and subtle props. The atmosphere is bright, the mood light.

This was different. Brian controlled the camera during the entire tape, and it was dark and chaotic and unlike anything that Torey had ever been involved in. It was not a movie or a story. I am not sure what Brian was doing. One of the rumors circulating was that the video was a documentary-- like a documentary of two teen-aged serial killers.

I did not know it at the time, but Brian had been obsessed for years with the Columbine killers. He downloaded clips made by Dylan Klebold and Eric Harris onto his computer at home. This was possibly a mimic of one of their clips. I don't know. I never saw those clips. But I do know that I wish my son, Torey, had never had a chance to sit in a classroom with Brian Lee Draper at Pocatello High School. I wish that with all my heart.

What the video gave me was an insight into all of the unexplained feelings that I'd had concerning Brian. Suddenly Brian was exposed and I could see what I had been sensing; only it was worse than anything I could have ever imagined. It was an insight into a deeply disturbed individual that had *nothing* to do with Torey, a direct insight into Brian Draper, a 16-year-old kid with an *evil* obsession.

Others had felt it too. In one of Anna's interviews with the police she stated that she did not like Brian, not due to facts, but just a feeling that she had. Brian had problems.

It was obvious to me that Torey was acting for the videotape. His tone of voice and facial expressions were recognizable as such. I also recognized that Torey was quoting movie lines. (Detective Alex Hamilton also recognized this and he demonstrated some examples during his testimony at trial, though it did not lead him to believe that Torey was acting.)

While we were viewing the video, Aaron explained to us what we were seeing. The tape is not recorded in chronological order, which makes it difficult to follow. You have to watch it several times, paying attention to the time stamp, to piece the different scenes together in the correct sequence. Aaron walked us through it, one sequence at a time, explaining to us what day and time we were watching as we went through it.

The film begins with a flash of color, a brief few seconds of students in a hallway in a school and all the noise associated with that, but before you can even register what you're seeing--it's gone, replaced with a scene where Torey and Brian are sitting in Torey's car.

It's dark outside. The boys are shadowed inside the vehicle. There's music in the background. They have a conversation about going into the house where their two friends are alone, and killing them. Their tone of voice is light and sarcastic. Torey says, "We're listening to the greatest rock band ever, Pink Floyd."

Brian said they checked out the whole house. He's unlocked the back doors.

Brian said, "We've waited for this for a long time." He nodded his head at the camera and repeated himself, "A long time. But you know, we're ready."

Torey said, " We're going to commit the ultimate crime of *muurder*." I'd heard that before...but before I could think about it, or tell Aaron, the video went off and came back on again, to a different scene.

I heard Brian on the camera. His tone of voice was different. Before he'd been dark and sarcastic. Now he was hyper. I was unsure of what I was seeing at first and Aaron paused the video and asked me, "Did you get that?" I looked at him and shook my head.

Aaron had to point it out to me. He said, "Let me rewind that, it's right after..." and I thought *AFTER*???

I know this is going to be hard to understand, but please try. I need to be honest. I had lost my son. He had been torn from my life in a sudden and violent way. Granted not the same kind of violence as Cassie, but violent still.

Torey was gone. That is what I was consumed with. The loss of my son was, and still is, a gaping hole in my life that can never be filled. It is like the loss of my heart, my lungs...I could only see and feel that. I was not yet feeling the loss of Cassie. She was not yet real to me. What was real to me was the very real loss of my son. The very real loss of everything in my world that had sense and meaning.

It hit me. Someone was dead. I heard Brian say, "Just killed Cassie. We just left her house. This is not a f---ing joke!"

Torey said, " I'm *sh-shaking...*"

Brian continued, "I stabbed her in…in the throat...a-and I saw her lifeless body just...uh...disappear. Dude I...just killed Cassie."

Torey said, "...oh my God!"

Brian finished, "Oh! Oh f---! That felt like it wasn't even real! *O-oh*, I mean…it went by so fast."

And then Torey said the most damning thing he says on the entire tape. "Shut the f---up! We gotta get our act straight!"

I knew at that moment someone was gone. *Gone*. I heard Brian say it, and Aaron rewound the tape, and I heard him again. We watched the tape through, intensely listening to every word, and then we rewound it. We watched the scene again, and I heard Brian in the moments after Cassie's death, describe to Torey what he had done, and I *knew* that Brian killed Cassie.

When Brian attacked Cassie, Torey instinctively reacted. He was in shock. Terrified. He ran. Some people blame Torey for that. But no one can say how they would react in the same situation, at barely sixteen years old, unless they were there. Only when you find yourself in such an unbelievable nightmare can you truly know how you would react.

For me, the tape confirmed what we knew all along. Brian killed Cassie. Torey didn't. Torey panicked. Torey ran. But Torey was innocent. There was nothing on that tape that pointed to Torey stabbing Cassie, and there was a clear confession from Brian that he had.

I told Aaron and Bron that it was okay.

Bron was shocked at my reaction. "My God!" he said, "there is the power of a mother's love! The problem is how are you going to explain something like this? This tape just hits you in the face like a furnace! It's awful."

I could see that Bron saw what was on the tape, but not what was missing.

I looked up at him and said, "Brian did it. Nowhere on that tape does Torey say that he killed Cassie. And nowhere on that tape does Brian say that Torey killed Cassie. This tape proves Brian did it. Brian makes a *clear* confession."

Bron was speechless.

Greg and Aaron had already assured me that they believed in Torey's innocence. They did not believe he stabbed Cassie. But I could see that Bron wavered. He asked me, "Even if Torey didn't stab Cassie, don't you think, after watching this, that he might have at least suspected that Brian was going to?"

"No." I did not think that.

There was nothing in Torey's behavior that indicated he was taking Brian seriously. Torey was not a risk taker. If he had been taking Brian seriously, he would have been scared. Nervous. There would have been *some* indication of those feelings on the tape. The fact that there were none, combined with the way that Torey was speaking and acting, convinced me that Torey was just playing along with Brian, following his lead.

But I did not have the words to articulate that to Bron.

Bron could not grasp the fact that Torey could be so naive as to completely trust Brian. I knew then that it would be very difficult for Bron to see this from Torey's point of view, and if he couldn't do that, he could never defend Torey. I hoped that Bron had it in him, but I believed that even if he did not, *Aaron did*.

Aaron was smart. He was not ceilinged in a black and white mentality. He could see beyond the evidence, into what lay behind the evidence. But most importantly, Aaron could understand his client; something Bron seemed incapable of doing.

From that day forward I clung to Aaron as if my life depended on him, because it did.

When we left, Sean and I finally had some understanding. The videotape was damning, but it was also part of the defense.

CHAPTER EIGHTEEN

The Preliminary Hearing

In an arrest it is the State's responsibility to prove that reasonable evidence exists that a crime occurred and that a trial is justified. A preliminary hearing, sometimes called an evidentiary hearing, is one means the State has of meeting that obligation. It is often the first opportunity one has to view at least part of the evidence involved in a case. Due to community interest, and the press, the hearing was going to be a huge event.

Sean and I explained to Lacey and Jamie what the preliminary hearing was and allowed them to decide for themselves if they were going to attend it or not. Lacey did, Jamie did not. Jamie did not go to the preliminary hearing, or any other hearing where he would be in the public's eye. Jamie held on to the hope that Torey was coming home, and that eventually life would go back to normal. He was just waiting for that day to arrive.

Unlike Jamie, Lacey knew exactly what was happening. Her pain was in front of us every day. She never put it away. She never pretended things were okay. Lacey attended every hearing that she was able to, seldom missing a court date, and her presence was a tremendous source of comfort to me, as well as Torey.

I faced the approaching hearing with a mixture of emotions. I never questioned Torey's innocence, but I questioned what happened, and why. I was hoping to finally get some answers. Still, the thought of facing whatever was revealed, in a crowded courtroom, in front of the press, was frightening. On the morning of the hearing, I was literally sick to my stomach.

Sean and I originally planned to drop Jamie off at school on the way to the courthouse, but as we were getting ready to leave, my sister-in-law, Mary, called and told us that that was not going to be possible. She was at the courthouse, which was full of people, who had been lining up for hours to get into the hearing. She needed us there to make sure that our family was let in before their seats were taken.

I'd never considered that. I'd assumed the attorneys had arranged seating for our family. But Mary said the attorneys were nowhere in sight and there was a line of people in front of the courtroom doors that stretched the length of the hallway and past the prosecutor's office. As soon as the doors opened there would be no hope for those who were not in front of the line to enter.

Sean and I immediately left for the courthouse. Our entire family planned to attend the hearing and we needed to make sure that they were allowed to do so. Lacey took Jamie to school in her car and then headed to the courthouse alone.

When Sean and I arrived there was nowhere to park. We had to park several blocks away on a residential street. I told Sean that I was worried about Lacey. I wanted to call her on her cell phone and meet her in front of the building so that she would not have to enter alone, but Sean said there wasn't time.

He pulled me by the hand as he rushed toward the courthouse while I struggled to keep up. When we finally arrived, there was a line of people at the door and we stood and waited as each person entered the building single-file through a security device that had been set up after the Timothy McVeigh bombing. As I waited in line every nerve in my body stood on end.

Sean and I entered through the license and registration entrance at the foot of the building and headed for the nearest stairs. The courtroom was on the third floor of the three-story building and the stairwell leading up was lined with people. Mary was correct. There were hundreds of people trying to get into the hearing, but I could not quite grasp the fact that that was what they were there for. There was space cordoned off at the side of the line to allow attorneys and family members room to pass. As Sean pulled me up the stairs, past the people waiting, I saw some familiar faces, but for the life of me I could not place any of them.

The third floor landing was separated from the stairwell by a glass wall, and as we headed toward the glass doors at the top of the stairs I could see what appeared to be a sea of people in the lobby ahead. Sean opened the door and we went through.

There were groups of people standing together against the walls and sitting on benches whispering and talking amongst themselves. Many people were wearing pins with pictures of Cassie on them. There was a line, two or three people wide, which stretched down the hall, around the corner, and continued farther down the adjoining hallway.

Bob and Mary saw us and ushered us near the front of the line where some of our family members were already gathered. I was grateful they were there. I could not imagine going through this alone. There were reporters and camera crews in front of us, and some kind of a security device. I noticed Adam and his family in the stairwell behind us and motioned for them to join us.

Mary was worried. There were still members of the family that we'd not yet located who were farther back in the line. She wanted to organize a search and bring everyone together.

I was so horrified about what was happening, that all I could think about was how we were going to make it through the day. The hearing was scheduled for the largest courtroom in the courthouse, but I was thoroughly unprepared for such an enormous crowd. I focused my attention on my family around me and tried to block everything else out.

Mary's fears turned out to be justified. Aaron appeared and motioned for us to follow him into a room off the corridor where Bron was already waiting. The courtroom staff had been organizing the seating for the three families, but they had a problem when it came time to seat ours.

Aaron and Bron were supposed to have coordinated with the bailiffs ahead of time, but they'd failed to do so. They never asked us how many people we were bringing, and they never told us to limit the number of people we brought, and so when it came time to seat our family there was not enough seating space available for everyone.

The attorneys did a quick head count of those of us in the room and asked if that was everyone. I said, "No. We're still missing four or five people."

Bron shook his head, "There's not going to be room."

Aaron looked at Adam's family, "Only immediate family members are going to be allowed in."

"They *are* family," I said.

Bron turned to me with exasperation. "They don't have to let any of you in." But I knew how much the Dykman's presence meant to Torey and I refused to back down. Aaron asked me again, "Are you sure?"

"Yes."

Aaron said, " Okay." We went back out to the hallway and he escorted those of us waiting together, my brother David and his wife Pam, my brother Mike who had come from Utah, Bob and Mary, my nephew Nathan, (whose dad was still trying to find a parking spot) and David, Lori and Adam Dykman, along with Sean and I, to the front of the line.

I grabbed Aaron's sleeve. "Lacey's coming."

"I'll get her in," he promised.

Lacey arrived at the last minute. She was the last family member allowed into the courtroom until after the morning recess, when my brother Rick, Sean's sister Ann, and Cyndi were all three ushered forward and allowed in together.

Out in the hall there were friends and supporters from all three families, waiting to get in. They never made it. Rusty Adamson, Torey's teacher, was one of them.

Due to some anonymous death threats made against Torey and Brian, which the sheriff's office took seriously, security was tight. We entered the courtroom single file after first passing through a metal detector and a wand check. As each person completed the security check they were ushered into the courtroom where they were met by a bailiff who showed them to their seat. We were told that if we left the room for any reason, we would not be allowed back in.

The courtroom was large. It was dived into two halves with the judge's pulpit in the center. Our family sat in the aisle on the right. The press was on the front row and our family was directly behind them on the second and part of the third row. Brian's mother and father were behind me with their family on the third and fourth row. Cameramen from different news stations lined the back wall.

Across the aisle, the first row was filled with law enforcement. Cassie's family sat in the rows behind them, and behind Cassie's family were the seats reserved for the public. Don Cotant, the principal of Pocatello High School was there as well as students who had been friends of all three children. I recognized some of them and wondered who they were there to support.

I saw David Luras and Jake Smith, both good friends of Torey since elementary school. I knew what it meant for them to be there. The lines they had waited in for hours and how hard it must be for them to sit where they were, surrounded by Cassie's family and friends, and I was touched by their presence.

Mary saw Rick Hearns, a local attorney. I did not know who he was, but Mary immediately recognized him and wondered if he was there to scout out the possibility of a lawsuit since she had heard the bailiffs say that the victim's mother's attorney was coming and they needed to find a seat for him. Later he did sue us on behalf of the Stoddart family.

Torey and Brian had been transported to the courthouse in separate vehicles, but they entered the courtroom together. Each boy was accompanied by two officers, one on each elbow. They each wore a black, bulletproof vest over their yellow jail issued prison garb. Their ankles were shackled together and they wore a knee brace, which had to be unlocked before they sat down. There was a chain around their waist that clipped to the handcuffs around their wrists, which locked their arms to their body, and made it impossible for them to move their arms other than a slight up and down movement of their wrists.

I had been praying that Torey would be allowed a haircut and a shower before such an important hearing, but it wouldn't have made a difference. Not with the way he was brought in. Torey was told not to make eye contact with his family. He had to walk into the courtroom and sit down with his back toward us. In seconds he was ushered in and sat down. Both boys were left shackled, but I think their handcuffs were removed, or at least one hand was freed for writing. Bron and Aaron had a water pitcher on the table in front of them and I remember hoping that Torey would be given such a simple thing as a drink of cold, fresh water.

Later that night Torey called and asked me why my brother Michael wasn't at the hearing. I told him that Mike had been there the whole time, seated with Brian's family on the third row. I was surprised at how quickly Torey had been able to take in who was there and who wasn't. He had not been able to spot everyone, but he had done remarkably well in the short time that he had.

Lori Dykman, who was sitting next to me, pointed out Cassie's grandfather. I had seen him once before on the news, but I hadn't seen Cassie's mother or father. I looked through the rows of people, searching for them, but I did not know who they were and I turned my eyes away and back to my son.

Torey was seated directly in front of us, with Bron and Aaron. He was unbelievably close, yet…so far away. His blond hair was ruffled and he looked so small, so young. I hoped for a glimpse of his face, but all I could see was his profile as he looked to his attorneys.

Our family had been fasting and praying since the day before, and I could feel the spirit of their love surrounding us. I hoped it was strong enough to reach Torey. I could not believe we had to watch him, our sixteen-year-old son, our baby, sit alone through this. How would he do it?

We had tried to prepare Torey for this day, but how can you really prepare someone for something like this? None of us knew what the day would bring. I prayed for God's spirit and trusted that he would get Torey through. It took all of our faith and every family member we had with us, along with our dear friends. Their presence, seated a few feet behind Torey, and enveloping us, sustained us, and with their support, and our faith in God--Torey survived. Torey survived…But not unscathed.

Finally the doors to the courtroom closed and Judge Naftz entered. Bannock County's Chief Prosecuting Attorney, Mark Hiedeman, and his assistant Vic Pearson were at a table to the left of Brian's counsel. Mark Hiedeman was tall and lean, but his most distinctive feature was his silver hair. He wore glasses, which he took off periodically to chew on, a habit he maintained throughout the trials.

Our attorneys told us that Mark Hiedeman was smart, but they did not hold the same opinion of Vic Pearson, who was young, ambitious and incredibly arrogant. Vic Pearson did most of the questioning that day, and I heard at least one person comment on his performance. They said he liked to play the peacock. But it was Mark Hiedeman who struck me. He was obviously the attorney in charge. It may have been Vic Pearson asking the questions, but it was Mark Hiedeman calling the shots.

The day before the hearing the defense attorneys filed multiple motions. Brian's attorneys wanted Judge Naftz dismissed for bias. His wife was a teacher at Pocatello High School and although she had not taught the three children involved, she had to have been affected by the atmosphere in the school. Judge Naftz denied the motion; stating that he had not discussed the case with his wife.

Brian's attorneys then filed for a continuance. Defense counsel had not been provided with much of the evidence that was to be presented at the hearing, and they had no way to cross-examine regarding evidence they did not possess. Judge Naftz agreed. He denied the motion to continue, but he promised that information defense counsel did not possess would not be allowed into the hearing.

But he did not keep his word. Throughout the morning, both sets of defense attorneys objected to testimony taken from reports, cell phone records, drawings, pictures and timelines that they did not possess, and with each objection they were overruled.

Brian's attorneys and ours filed a last minute motion to sever the boys. It had been an ongoing battle ever since their arrest, which continued up to and throughout the preliminary hearing. If the boys had been severed, each would have had their own preliminary hearing. As it was they were charged together and evidence against one could be used as evidence against both, if not in the courtroom, at least in the press. It was a distinct advantage for Mark Hiedeman, and he knew it. He fought the motion and won.

The hearing was the first real opportunity we had to see the attorneys in action, and of all the attorneys that day Dave Martinez stood out. He had remarkable verbal skill and was quick and focused. Unlike the partnership between Mark Hiedeman and Vic Pearson, Dave Martinez and Randy Schulthies were an evenly matched team.

Aaron was eager. This was undoubtedly his biggest case, likely the biggest case he would ever have, and he was determined to do his best. So was Bron. They both came to the courtroom prepared to do battle, but Bron had a serious problem. We had noticed during our consultations with him that he was exceptionally wordy and his verbose style followed him into the courtroom. Soon, Dave Martinez began to openly show his contempt for Bron's communicative abilities.

I was scared. What I saw did not install confidence. But I thought Bron and Aaron would still give us a better defense than the public defender's office could offer. We intended to test the DNA evidence, and have Torey psychologically examined. Bron told us that would never happen if the State were paying the expense.

Another consideration was the money already invested. At the end of the preliminary hearing the bill for Dial, May and Rammell exceeded $36,000 dollars. It had only been 37 days since Torey's arrest, and we were already so heavily invested with these attorneys, that we did not see how we could start over with new ones.

Besides, Bron had assured us that there was no other firm in the area with more experience than his. And I had hope for Aaron. During the hearing Aaron gave me a scare. He jumped the gun during an important objection, but I knew he had the ability to be a good attorney, and over time his verbal skills improved to the point where he not only equaled Dave Martinez, he surpassed him. Aaron dedicated himself to learning everything he could about this case, inside and out, and he truly believed in Torey. And that was worth something.

The hearing began with the prosecution. Mark Hiedeman set out to show that a crime was committed: a young girl murdered. He quickly established the chain of events that led to the questioning of Torey and Brian. Allison Contreras was called to the stand. It was the first time that I'd heard her name, or saw her. Allison was in her thirties; she had ash blonde hair that hung natural, and she wore a free flowing skirt and blouse.

Mark Hiedeman asked Allison to explain how she knew Cassie.

"She was my niece, by marriage," Allison stated.

The prosecutor asked, "Had Cassie ever house-sat for you before?"

"Yes. My husband, Frank, worked in Jackpot, Nevada. Sometimes the kids and I would visit him there. When we did, Cassie would watch the house for us while we were gone."

"Had you ever had problems with Cassie house-sitting before?"

"No. Cassie was a responsible girl. We never had any problems with her."

"What about Matt Beckham, Cassie's boyfriend? Did he ever house-sit with Cassie?"

"Yes, he did," Allison stated.

The prosecutor asked, "And you were okay with that?"

"Yes. I did not see a problem with that." Allison looked offended by the question.

Allison relayed the events that transpired after they returned home the weekend of September 22, 2006. Allison explained that her five-year-old son stuck a jawbreaker in his nostril during the latter part of the drive and when they arrived home she carried him into the downstairs bathroom to help him remove it. Frank had yelled to her, while she was in the bathroom, to call 911. She grabbed the cordless phone and headed up the stairs with Frank, not sure what was happening.

Next Mark Hiedeman asked that the 911 call Allison placed, be played for the Court. We listened as Allison told the operator, in an obviously shaken voice, that there was a body in her living room covered in blood. Allison told the operator that it was her niece, and her stomach was bloated and she did not appear to be breathing. When the operator told Allison to check for a pulse Allison responded that the body was cold to the touch.

Next, Mark Hiedeman called Deputy Karen Hatch to the

stand. She had been the first officer to respond to the scene. Deputy Hatch was a tiny woman, maybe in her early thirties, but her size did not detract from her character. She radiated competent professionalism.

Deputy Hatch confirmed that Cassie was deceased when she arrived at the scene. She further stated that Cassie appeared to have suffered multiple stab wounds. After first securing the scene, Deputy Hatch questioned the family. She learned that Matt Beckham, Cassie's boyfriend, had been with Cassie when she was dropped off at the house on Friday afternoon.

Matt Beckham was called to testify next. He was dressed in a white shirt and tie, but he also wore the large black skater shoes of a typical teen. His hair was dark and thin, and his face pasty. He looked nervous and uncomfortable.

Mark Hiedeman questioned Matt about his relationship with Cassie.

"We'd been dating for about five or six months," Matt stated.

"How much time did you and Cassie typically spend together?" the prosecutor asked.

"We saw each other pretty much every day, during that time period," Matt said.

"How well did you get along with Cassie's parents? Her mother and stepfather?"

"Alright," Matt said, though under questioning he admitted that he had, on one occasion, yelled at Anna, calling her and Cassie a couple of F------ Bit----.

Matt confirmed previous testimony concerning the weekend in question. Cassie planned to house-sit for her aunt and uncle, which she had done before. Matt admitted that he had spent the weekend with Cassie at the Contreras's house on at least one of the previous occasions that Cassie had house-sat for them in the past.

The prosecutor asked Matt what happened after they arrived at the house.

"We watched some television," Matt said.

"And, did you do anything else?"

"Yes."

"Did you have sex with Cassie?"

Matt looked uncomfortable. "Yes," he said. He used a condom, but it broke and he threw it in the wastebasket in the upstairs bathroom.

Later, Matt testified, he and Cassie called their friends, Torey

Adamcik and Brian Draper, and asked if they were coming over. Matt told the prosecutor that he and Cassie had told Torey and Brian previously that they were going to be house-sitting over the weekend, and had invited them to come over Friday evening.

Around eight p.m. Torey called Cassie from his cell phone, and told her that he and Brian were on their way, but they were lost, and needed directions. Matt said that he and Cassie both gave Torey and Brian directions, and sometime after that the two boys arrived at the house.

Matt testified that when they arrived, Brian and Torey looked through the entire house, while he and Cassie followed them.

"Why did you follow them?" Mark Hiedeman asked.

"Brian had a habit of acting like a two-year-old, and Cassie wanted to make sure that he didn't break anything," Matt said.

Matt testified that the four of them went downstairs to the garage, and everyone ended up playing on the universal weight machine. They found a box of Popsicles in the freezer and carried it upstairs. Matt opened the box with a knife he found in the kitchen. The knife had a special sheath, and Matt showed Brian how the knife worked while he opened the box. Everyone had a Popsicle, except for Brian, who did not like them.

Torey selected the movie *Kill Bill Volume Two* from the collection of video's in the house and everyone sat in the living room to watch it. While they were watching the movie, Brian disappeared downstairs toward the garage. After a few minutes, Cassie got up to find him. Approximately ten minutes later, when they hadn't returned, Matt went to check on them. After Matt went downstairs, all three came back up to the living room together, where they rejoined Torey, who was still watching the movie.

Shortly after that, Brian said he needed to go home. Brian and Torey got ready to leave. Matt said that he asked Torey if he could spend the night at his house that night and Torey said that he would come back later and pick him up if he needed a ride. Torey and Brian then left. It was approximately 9:30 p.m.

The prosecutor asked, "Did anything happen after Torey and Brian left?"

Matt said, "Yes. The power went out."

"What happened after the power went out?"

"Cassie and I walked through the upstairs of the house, testing the light switches to see if any of them worked, but they didn't. We set them to the "on" position so that we'd know when the power came back on." Matt testified that after awhile the hall light came on, and the outlet in the kitchen that powered the cordless phone, but nothing else.

Sometime after this, Matt's mother called and told him that she was coming to pick him up. She had a surprise for him; his father had just been released from rehab. Matt told his mother the power was off at Cassie's house, and asked if Cassie could come home with them, but Cassie said she couldn't leave. She had to let the animals out early in the morning. Matt's mother said that she would be there shortly. Matt called Torey and told him his mother was picking him up, and that he could not spend the night at his house.

When Matt's mother arrived, he left. "That was the last time I saw Cassie," Matt said.

"Did you try to contact Cassie after that?" the prosecutor asked.

"I tried. I called her all weekend, but I never got a response."

"When did you find out what happened?"

"Sunday afternoon. When Anna called and asked, 'What in the f--- did you do to my daughter?' That's when Victor told me that Cassie had been killed."

During cross-examination Bron asked Matt to describe the interior layout of the house, and where the living room sat in relation to the other rooms. Matt said there were two entrances into the living room, one from the hallway, and one from the stairs. The stairs led directly to the exterior door and outside, while the hallway entrance lead to another hallway where all the bedrooms were located, the kitchen and the stairway that lead downstairs to the master bedroom, and the garage.

Bron asked Matt specifically which direction Brian had gone, when he disappeared while everyone was upstairs watching the movie. Matt said that Brian went through the hallway and downstairs toward the garage, where he remained alone for several minutes, until Cassie followed after him.

(Brian admitted to detectives that he had gone downstairs alone and unlocked the door leading from the garage to the house, but Matt did not know that. Bron used Matt's testimony to corroborate Brian's statement.)

Next Bron asked Matt if he believed Torey killed Cassie.

Matt said, "Yes."

Bron asked, "When did you make up your mind about this?"

"The day that I heard they did it."

"Who told you they did it?"

"My father."

"What information does your father have, that leads him to believe that Torey is responsible?"

"He said that Torey and Brian did it just because he heard..."

"I object!" Randy Schulthies interrupted. "That's based on hearsay for foundation, and he, (Matt's father) is not subject to cross-examination, or I don't believe he's on the witness list."

Bron told the judge, "I'm just trying to demonstrate through Matt's testimony, the prejudice and preconceived notions that are prevalent in the community. There's already concern for the jury pool. Matt's testimony can establish the depth of that."

Judge Naftz sustained the objection, and Matt was released from the stand.

Next, Detective Andy Thomas was called to the stand. He was the lead investigator in Cassie's death, and had been present for the interrogations of Brian, Torey and Matt. Vic Pearson performed Detective Thomas's direct examination, which was by far the longest testimony of the day. And for Torey--the most damaging.

Vic Pearson began his examination of Detective Thomas by going over the detective's interviews with Brian Draper. Through Thomas's testimony we learned that Brian had given five separate interviews with the detectives, including the one he gave Sunday night in his home, the only interview we had known about previously.

Pearson walked Detective Thomas through his interviews with Brian Draper one at a time. He began with the first, which had taken place in Brian's home. Brian told the detectives that he and Torey visited Cassie and Matt at Cassie's house Friday evening, but left to see a movie around 9:30 p.m. The same story Torey had told. When the interview concluded, the two detectives told Brian they needed him to come to the police station later in the week to confirm his story, and he agreed that he would do so.

The following Tuesday afternoon, Brian was contacted to come into the station as requested. Brian's parents, Kerry and Pamela Draper, brought Brian to the Pocatello police station, where they allowed him to be interviewed alone. Initially, Brian relayed the same information that he had previously given. But unbeknownst to Brian, the detectives already knew that he was lying. They knew that he and Torey hadn't gone to the movies Friday night.

The detectives gave Brian plenty of rope to hang himself.

They asked him about the movie, and Brian gave them a long and detailed description, not of the movie, but of people he had seen in the movie theater with him. Finally the detectives confronted Brian. They had reviewed surveillance tape from the theater, and neither he, nor Torey, were on it. Furthermore, they had interviewed employees at the theater, and no one had seen them. And it was obvious that Brian had not seen the movie he claimed to have seen.

At first Brian denied lying. He tried to salvage his alibi, but eventually he broke down and confessed: they were right. He and Torey hadn't gone to the movies. They'd actually been burglarizing cars. Brian told the detectives he'd lied to them because he was scared of being charged with a felony.

Detective Thomas said, "That's a really stupid thing to do. How much trouble do you think you're going to be in for lying to the police during a homicide investigation? I guarantee you--it's a lot more trouble than you'd be in for car burglary!"

After questioning Brian extensively about the burglaries, Thomas asked him if he had anything to do with Cassie's murder. Brian flatly denied any knowledge of what happened to Cassie. Thomas told Brian, "You need to think about this. We're not resting until we get to the truth. If you know anything--we're going to find out."

At the beginning of the interview, Brian had been calm and relaxed. He even took his wallet out of his pants pocket and counted his money. Now he was defensive, and nervous. "How can you even think I had anything to do with this?" he asked. "That's...that's...crazy."

Detective Thomas told Brian that he needed to take a polygraph examination. Brian agreed to do so. One was scheduled for the following afternoon at the Bannock County Sheriff's Department.

This left Brian with a serious problem. He found himself scheduled for a polygraph examination that he had no hope of passing, and no way to get out of. Brian went home, where he spent a long and restless night...Thinking...Planning...Dreaming.

CHAPTER NINETEEN

Brian Blames Torey

Brian's attorneys like to portray a portrait of Brian--guilt ridden and desperate to do the right thing, running to the police to tell them the truth about what happened to Cassie. But the truth is, Brian panicked. He knew his story was falling apart, and he did the only thing he could do to try and save himself. He ran to the police and blamed the whole thing on Torey.

Brian's third interview took place on Wednesday, September 27, 2006 at approximately 2:30 p.m. It is called "The Confession Interview" because Brian confessed to being present when Cassie was killed. He also provided evidence previously undiscovered. Now, thirty-four days later, Detective Thomas, under the guidance of Vic Pearson, described that interview to the packed courtroom.

Brian, it turned out, did not take the polygraph examination that he was scheduled for. He found a way out if it after all. Brian's mother told the story, during his sentencing hearing.

Apparently on the morning of the 27th, Brian woke up very upset. Still in his pajamas, Brian ran upstairs asking for the newspaper, which he took from his mother and began to desperately search through, page after page. When Pam asked Brian what he was doing, he told her that God had appeared to him in a dream, and spoke to him through a newspaper article. God told Brian he needed to do the right thing; he was checking to see if it was real.

Pam said that Brian was extremely distraught and crying. He told her, and Kerry, that he needed to go to the police station because he knew who killed Cassie. Torey killed Cassie and he'd seen him do it.

But when compared with the known events of the day, Pam's story does not make sense. If what she said had happened--if Brian ran upstairs early in the morning, and told her and Kerry that he knew who killed Cassie, then they had information that the police needed right away. But they did not go to the police station until approximately 2:30 that afternoon.

Furthermore, Brian supposedly went to school that day. I know he left his house because he called Torey on his cell phone and asked Torey to meet him at Country Corner, a convenience store and gas station, before school started, and Torey did meet Brian there.

Brian's attorneys admit Torey met Brian at the convenience

store, though they say the conversation that took place is entirely different from the one that actually occurred. They claim Brian told Torey he wanted to confess to the detectives, tell them the truth, and that Torey threatened Brian's life if he did so. But the actual conversation was about the police interviews.

Brian explained to Torey that he had met with detectives the night before (Tuesday), and that the detectives knew that they hadn't gone to the movies Friday night, as they had claimed. Brian told the detectives that he and Torey had actually been burglarizing cars instead, and Brian told Torey that he needed to tell them the same thing. Torey agreed to do so. Brian said if they weren't careful, they'd both be going to prison. Brian informed Torey that he had another interview scheduled that afternoon with the police and that he was supposed to take a polygraph.

Torey told Brian that the detectives wanted to interview him too. Neither boy knew what to do. They were both scared. Brian had stabbed Cassie, but Torey believed he was in just as much trouble as Brian. He knew that Brian would never admit the truth, and go down alone.

After the meeting Torey came back home. I am not sure what Brian did. If he went to school, he came home early.

I believe Brian woke up distraught, as Pam testified. I am sure he was scared after his interview with the detectives the night before, and he probably had a nightmare. He was possibly searching the newspaper to see if he'd been found out.

But I do not believe Brian told his parents what he claimed to have seen until later. I believe Brian approached his parents shortly before he was scheduled for his polygraph examination with a story they could not ignore. I believe his parents took him to the police station as soon as they found out that Brian did in fact have information about the murder.

Torey knew that Brian had blamed him for stabbing Cassie, but he was shocked to hear Detective Andy Thomas describe Brian Draper's version of events in a narrative fashion, as if he himself had been there, and was visually painting a picture of what had actually occurred.

Torey blamed himself for not stopping Brian from killing Cassie even though by the time he realized what was happening, there was nothing he could do. But to hear Brian say that he, Torey, had actually *stabbed* Cassie, was more than Torey could bear. It is hard to convince someone that they do not need to worry about what other people think when their life depends upon it, but it is even harder when their heart does. Brian's lies broke Torey's heart.

Detective Thomas described the interview. Brian, along with his parents, arrived at the Bannock County Sheriff's Department shortly before they were scheduled to come in for the polygraph. Brian and his father were both visibly upset. They asked to speak to the detectives Brian had met with the night before. Detective Ganske was available, but Detective Thomas had to be called in. Thomas arrived within minutes after the call and they immediately took Brian and his parents into a taped interview room where Brian, in a very distraught manner, told them that he was now ready to talk.

Brian lunged directly into a story about how he had witnessed Torey kill Cassie. He graphically described the sights and sounds of a brutal murder preformed right in front of his eyes, gesturing with his hands as he did so. Brian said he was so surprised by what he saw that he did not believe it was real until he heard Cassie scream..."A terrible, blood curdling scream, that I will never forget for as long as I live."

Thomas and Ganske were in the interview room with Brian, but there were other detectives watching from the other side of the one-way glass, listening to Brian's story as well. As Thomas and Ganske questioned Brian, some of those detectives entered the room with questions of their own.

The story was backtracked and Brian was asked for a reenactment of the events, from the time that Torey picked him up, until the time that Cassie was murdered. Brian told the detectives that he and Torey visited Cassie and Matt, as he'd already said, but that after they left they reentered the house with a plan to scare them. Brian told the detectives that the whole thing was suppose to be a joke. Brian himself had unlocked the doors to the house while they were visiting earlier, and after they left, they'd snuck back in.

He repeated that they were just going to scare Cassie and Matt, that was the plan; but after Matt left, Brian said something came over Torey. Torey attacked and killed Cassie before Brian even knew what was happening. Brian said he was so surprised by Torey's actions that he thought that Torey and Cassie must have been playing a joke on him.

(We later learned those had been Torey's very words to Brian. After Brian attacked Cassie, Torey told Brian that he thought he and Cassie were playing a joke on him. Brian took Torey's words right out of his mouth and went to the detectives with them; only he

changed the roles between himself and Torey.)

Still on tape, Brian continued his description. He described how he'd attempted to help cover up the crime, with Torey, by burying the evidence in Blackrock Canyon. Brian offered to take the detectives to the site so that he could prove to them that what he was saying was true.

Brian looked earnest. He was nodding his head, as if he truly wanted to do the right thing. He wanted them to believe him. He had been crying throughout the whole account, gesturing wildly with his hands. His father, in the room with him, wept silently as he listened to his son. Periodically, Kerry reached over and laid his hand on Brian's shoulder. When Brian finished his story he sighed, as if it had been hard to tell, and he was relieved that it was over. He placed his hands over his face and closed his eyes. Kerry looked devastated.

It was a shocking story, and the detectives listening to it were visibly affected. Immediately a task force was formed to locate Torey and bring him into custody. The Bannock County Prosecutor's office secured a warrant for his arrest.

At approximately 4:15 p.m., two detectives arrived at Sean's work and drove him to the attorney's office. Minutes later detectives were with Jeff in our garage searching Lacey's car, while Torey's friend Adam Dykman was pulled over on Yellowstone Highway.

The interview concluded with Brian and his father being accompanied by Andy Thomas, Toni Vollmer and assorted Bannock County Sheriff Detectives to Blackrock Canyon, where Brian showed them the location of the buried evidence.

It took a while to locate the hole, but it was not deep. It was quickly excavated. Inside was a garbage bag, filled with the evidence of the crime. From the bag detectives removed a videotape, and Brian Draper probably had a near coronary. He had forgotten that the tape was buried with everything else. He asked to speak alone with Detective Toni Vollmer when they returned to the station.

Brian told Detective Vollmer that the tape had nothing to do with what happened to Cassie. He tried to get it back, but that wasn't going to happen. The tape was immediately taken for cleaning and played. That is how Brian Draper ended up giving his true confession that day, Wednesday the 27th of September 2006. Not in person. Not on purpose. But on a videotape that he'd made himself and delivered right into the detectives' hands.

Brian Draper did not go home after framing Torey as he had hoped. He too was arrested and charged with First Degree Murder.

I think God might have had something to do with Brian's confession, after all.

During Detective Thomas's rendition of Brian's statements, our attorneys vigorously objected to his testimony. It is our Sixth Amendment right to confront our accusers. Brian had accused Torey of killing Cassie, but Torey could not confront Brian, because it was not Brian on the stand; it was Detective Thomas testifying to what Brian had said. But no matter how many times our attorneys objected, Judge Naftz continually overruled them.

To introduce Brian's statements through Thomas allowed Brian's accusation against Torey, no matter how untrue, to be used against him. Torey was not allowed to confront his accuser, and Thomas's testimony *was* a violation of Torey's rights and extremely prejudicial. Judge Naftz finally recognized this, but too late. He tried to rectify the situation by saying that he would not take Brian's statements into account in his ruling against Torey. But Thomas's testimony was not only prejudicial in the courtroom, it was prejudicial in the press, and there was nothing that Judge Naftz could do to rectify that.

The press had been anxiously awaiting details of the crime. This was the first version of events they had been given. The fact that Torey denied it, or that it was factually incorrect, did not deter them from reporting it. Brian's version of events dominated the news that night and was reported the next day. Many people read it as if it were true, and made up their minds before they even had a chance to hear Torey's side of the story.

But it not only hurt Torey, it affected our other children as well. Candy, Jamie's friend Jordan's mother, had picked Jamie up from school, and offered to let him spend the night at her house. She knew that Sean and I were going to need time alone after the hearing, and we gratefully accepted her offer.

But the next morning, Candy read the newspaper. She went to the bedroom where Jamie was sleeping, and woke him up. She told him that his brother was going to prison. Jamie was stunned. He had trusted Candy and her family to care for him. Instantly, Candy took that feeling away from him.

It was not Candy's place to say anything to Jamie, and certainly not in such a callous manner. Jamie's whole life had changed in ways that he was too young to comprehend. He did not know what had been lost, and where this would end. All that he knew was that he was scared, and that he needed compassion and understanding to get through this.

Candy later apologized, but it was a lesson in the power of the press; and in who had the conviction to support us, and who did not.

It was hard to listen as Detective Thomas described every word, every lie, Brian Draper told about my son, but at least his testimony answered one question for me. I always wondered why the detectives forced Torey's interview on the 27th, instead of allowing us to wait until Aaron was available the next day. Now I knew.

From the time Brian entered the police station, the detectives knew they were going to arrest Torey that night; they just needed to make sure they got an interview with him before they did so. Ganske called Sean while we were in our consultation with the attorneys probably seconds after his interview with Brian concluded. Thomas would have been on his way to Blackrock Canyon by then. When we got to the police station later that night, Thomas hadn't returned yet. That was why Marchand met us in the hall. Thomas and Ganske joined us after Thomas returned.

Torey was actually in custody when he took his first step through the police station door. The detectives had no intention of letting him go. They wouldn't have gotten an interview with Torey had we known that. They had to interview him *before* we found out.

Next Detective Thomas testified concerning Brian's fourth interview, which took place the day after his arrest, in a recorded room inside of the jail. Ganske was present. Thomas asked Brian if he would be willing to answer a few more questions and Brian; looking tired and resigned, agreed.

This time the detectives were after Brian's confession. Ganske told him he was still in a good position. "The first one through the door has the benefit," he said, lying.

Thomas added a psychological element. "We're going to be performing forensic testing on the evidence we've recovered. If it's going to reveal that you stabbed Cassie, we need to know about it now."

Ganske said, "I know you didn't want to stab Cassie. You're not that kind of kid. But you were so afraid of Torey; you felt you didn't have a choice."

Thomas asked Brian, "Is that correct? Were you so frightened of Torey that you stabbed Cassie? Is that what happened?"

It was a spoon-fed confession. Brian, being one to take

charge and act, did so on what he was given. Brian said, "Yes. It's true…I didn't want to stab Cassie, but…"

Thomas asked, "Where did you stab Cassie, Brian?"

"In…In…the l-l-e-g." Brian gestured with his hands to his chest area.

Thomas asked, "How many times did you stab Cassie in the chest?"

And Brian gestured four times with an up and down movement of his hand, as if he were holding a knife.

It was a successful interview.

During the preliminary hearing Pearson asked Thomas, "Did Brian confess to stabbing Cassie, when you interviewed him at the Bannock County Jail?"

"Yes, he did," Thomas said. "He admitted to stabbing her in the leg, and four times to the chest area."

On the following day, Friday, September 29, the two detectives questioned Brian again. This was their final interview with him. While questioning Brian in the same recorded interview room they'd questioned him in the day before, Randy Schulthies showed up from the public defender's office. Randy said that he was Brian's court appointed counsel, and that Brian was not going to be answering any more questions.

Before Brian was appointed counsel, he made grievous mistakes. He did not realize that as he talked to the detectives, trying to blame Torey, he was actually digging his own grave. Every word Brian spoke was used against him. I know that Brian killed Cassie. It was a meaningless, shocking, horrendous crime, which he deserves to pay for. But I am still amazed that no one stood up to tell Brian what was in his best interest. Not the detectives, not his parents, no one. Until Randy Schulthies arrived, Brian was effectively on his own.

During the final interview with Brian, the detectives had been going over pictures with him. Now Vic Pearson wanted to enter those pictures into evidence. He attempted to do so through Detective Thomas's testimony, but Dave Martinez objected. He had never seen the photographs Pearson was attempting to submit.

Judge Naftz overruled the objection.

Dave Martinez reminded Judge Naftz of the promise that he had made the day before. That he would limit the evidence to evidence in which defense counsel had been provided. So far that had not been the case.

Vic Pearson countered that it was "only a preliminary hearing," implying that the standard procedures were not as high as during a trial.

Martinez said, "This is not 'only' a preliminary hearing. It's my client's *fundamental right* to cross-examine the evidence used against him, which he's unable to do if he's never seen the evidence in the first place."

Judge Naftz finally agreed. He sustained the objection and even went so far as to say that Detective Thomas's testimony should be stricken.

But Vic Pearson objected, "Everything that we've discussed here today came from the detective's reports," he said, holding up a folder, "I haven't seen these items either. The defense had just as much opportunity as the State to get prepared for what we've done here today."

Dave Martinez accused Vic Pearson of being disingenuous. "They are in control of the State. Whether or not Mr. Pearson puts forth the effort to get the reports into his file does not exempt him from turning the reports over to us," he said.

Judge Naftz agreed. He asked Thomas if he had the information defense counsel was asking for. Thomas said that he did, but that some of the information was incomplete.

Judge Naftz asked, "What does that mean?"

"We're still working on the photographs and the photograph logs, putting them into a packet to give, not only to the prosecution, but to the defense," Thomas said.

Judge Naftz asked Detective Thomas about the other items that he had testified to that day. Thomas said, "Everything's available, except the photographs."

"Okay. Why would it take so long to download the photographs?" Judge Naftz asked.

"Just the sheer amount of them has been the problem," Thomas said.

Judge Naftz made a decision: "Gentlemen, what I am going to do is recess for lunch. I am going to allow Mr. Thomas to provide you with the information that is in his possession. Any discussion with regards to photographs, or knives, has been stricken and there will be no further inquiry with regard to that."

Dave Martinez stood. "Your Honor, is it the court's position that we are to reconvene at 1:30, and start questioning on documents that we've had for five minutes?"

"Well, you won't have them for five minutes. We will give you an opportunity to review them, but the preliminary hearing will go on today," Judge Naftz answered. He asked Detective Thomas, "How long will it take you to gather the information?"

Thomas said, "They're here at the courthouse right now. They've been turned over to the prosecuting attorney's office, so…ten minutes."

"Ten minutes? You want to reconvene at two?"

Martinez said, "That's fine, Your Honor."

"Okay. We will reconvene at two o'clock then."

During the break we went to my brother David's house and waited for the hearing to resume. I sat in the kitchen and listened to the talk around me. My brothers were unhappy with our attorney's performance, and Mary wanted to dissect Brian's statements piece by piece, but all I could think was that this was my son's *life* we were discussing. My son's *life*. And I was scared to death.

Back at the courthouse we lined up in front of the courtroom doors. I saw Adam was with his parents at the top of the stairwell. They were standing in a little recessed area to the side of the stairs huddled together. Adam was leaning over, crying. I wanted to help him, but there was nothing I could do. Lori put her arms around her son and David put his hand on his shoulder. After a few minutes, Adam stood up and wiped his eyes. I thought they were leaving, but they joined us in line. The testimony was obviously painful for Adam and his family to hear, but they wanted to support Torey.

At two o'clock, Judge Naftz pronounced us back on record. He asked Vic Pearson if the materials had been delivered to the defense. Pearson confirmed that they had been. Bron and Martinez agreed, but stated that the material was so voluminous, over sixty pages, that it was impossible to read and absorb in the short time allowed.

Dave Martinez renewed his motion to continue. "At this point I think due process has clearly been jeopardized on behalf of Mr. Draper," he said. "It's not just a matter of whether we have an opportunity to briefly read through the material provided, it's whether we have an opportunity to digest it and have some conversation with our sixteen-year-old client, who needs to be able to assist us in his defense, and at this point that's not possible. We haven't had time to digest the information, and we certainly haven't had time to walk a sixteen-year-old through it."

Judge Naftz didn't care. He thanked Mr. Martinez, noted his request, and asked Detective Thomas to resume the stand.

Thomas had testified regarding his five interviews with Brian. Vic Pearson now began questioning the detective about his interviews with Torey.

CHAPTER TWENTY

Torey's Interviews

Vic Pearson began by questioning Detective Thomas about the interview that had been conducted in our home on Sunday evening. As he testified to the events of that night, I could see that Detective Thomas's memory and mine were almost identical. But when Vic Pearson asked Detective Thomas about the interview that took place at the Pocatello Police Department, the detective failed to mention the meeting that Sean and I had in Marchand's office before the interview began.

In spite of the intentional omission, Detective Thomas's recollection of the actual interview itself was again similar to mine. But what I heard for the first time was the events that took place after I left the interview to pick up Jamie.

I did not realize that the interview had continued without me. I thought that Torey had been immediately arrested. That's what Sean told me. Sean always described the events after I left, as an arrest. Torey's arrest was the biggest, most traumatic event of our lives and it happened mere minutes after I left the room. But there was a short conversation that took place first.

As soon as I was gone, Detective Ganske told Torey that they knew a crime had been committed, and that he was involved. He said they were placing him under arrest for First Degree Murder. Torey asked for an attorney, which was the advice we had been given earlier, and Sean--visibly shaken, asked if he could speak to Torey in private.

The detectives said yes and Sean and Torey were taken into a second interview room. Sean could tell that it was an interview room where they could possibly be recorded. He asked if they could use a room that was not recorded. The detective said they could make sure the recorder was turned off, but Sean pointed to an office across the hall and asked if he could speak with Torey alone in there. The detectives said that he could.

While Sean and Torey were in the office, two detectives waited outside the door. When Sean and Torey came out they were ushered back into the interrogation room with Thomas and Ganske. Unbeknownst to Sean, when they returned, the video was still recording and the "interview" was still in progress.

Before I left it had been a very straightforward interview of questions and answers. Ganske asked Torey a question, Torey answered and Thomas took notes. After Torey asked for an attorney, Sean thought the interview ended, but it hadn't ended, it just changed gears. Only someone schooled in the legal process would know that Torey was still in the interrogation process. Neither Sean, nor Torey, had that kind of legal knowledge.

Once Torey asked for an attorney, the detectives could no longer question him, but they could still *talk* to him. Sean and I knew nothing about the law, but since then we have learned. Miranda only applies to questioning. Once you have asserted your rights to an attorney detectives can no longer question you, but they *can* continue to make statements directed at you. The law states that those statements must be innocuous and not designed to appeal to the defendant's sense of vulnerability, nor that an objective observer sitting in the room would consider likely to illicit a response. However, if you do respond to the statements made by the detectives, it reinitiates the questioning process all over again, at which time if you want the interview to stop, you have to *reassert* your rights per Miranda.

Detectives Thomas and Ganske either misunderstood what types of statements they were allowed to make, or they became so carried away in the emotion of the situation that they lost sight of what they were doing. Either that, or they simply and deliberately manipulated Sean and Torey by making illegal, coercive statements designed to illicit a response.

Thomas and Ganske told Torey why he was being arrested. Thomas testified that they did so out of concern for Sean, and a desire to tell Torey why he was being charged. But the manner in which they did so deliberately played on Sean and Torey's ignorance of the law, and they got away with about ninety-nine percent of it.

Detective Thomas told Torey that another individual had come in earlier and disclosed everything. He said that they had a full confession, but not only that; they had some overwhelming trace evidence that would prove that Torey was involved. The detectives informed Torey that Brian was already in custody.

Detective Ganske told Torey that he knew what he had done, that he (Torey) knew the right thing to do, and that his full cooperation could do nothing but help him. He said, "This is one of those things…it will only get worse, my friend. It'll eat you up. It will start right here, (he touched his heart) and it will eat its way up all the way until it destroys you. I can tell you, (pointing upward) there is only one person watching right now. Okay? Cassie's here, she's watching…she knows. And you know she knows."

Ganske said, "I just want you to hear before your dad, that it's not the end of the world, okay? Things can only go up from here. But it's up to you. You can either make it really spiral down, or you can make it go up. And by going up you have to come clean."

The detectives were doing more than telling Torey why he was being arrested. They were playing on Torey's vulnerability and applying relationship building tactics to make him believe that confessing to a murder might be a better idea than talking to an attorney. That confessing to murder would somehow give Torey a brighter future than speaking with an attorney would do. It was a highly deceptive approach, designed to illicit a response and coerce Torey into admitting that he had killed Cassie. But Torey did not kill Cassie and he denied it.

Sean kept saying, "I think you need an attorney, Torey." He mentioned an attorney at least seven different times, but the detectives just kept going.

Detective Thomas told Torey that they knew he had gone to Blackrock Canyon, and disposed of the evidence with Brian.

Sean looked at Torey and said, "If this is true, and what they are saying is right, then it sounds like you need an attorney." Torey looked at Sean, who was nodding his head at him, and nodded his head back--the way you do when you are actively listening to somebody, and softly said, "yes," agreeing that he needed an attorney.

But the detectives used that one response from Torey as a confession to everything, to make it sound as if Torey confessed to murder, as well as disposing of evidence, which was untrue. Torey has always denied any part in Cassie death. He has never denied going to Blackrock Canyon with Brian.

Sean was attempting to get Torey to reiterate his request for an attorney because he did not think that he could make the request for him. We had already tried that in Marchand's office, to no avail. That is what Sean thought happened; he thought that his statement prompted Torey to agree that he needed an attorney. He did not realize that he was involved in something that the detectives could actually use against Torey as a confession.

Aaron told us before the hearing that there was a portion of the interview that the State might try to misrepresent. This was it. Aaron believed the State's claim was a long shot, but he was going to try to get it removed before it became an issue anyway. He was fairly optimistic that he would be successful because it was in violation of Torey's Miranda Rights.

When Pearson had directed Detective Thomas through the interview, to the point where Torey admitted that he left Cassie's house with Brian, Vic Pearson asked, "Did you question him regarding what happened after they left the address on Whispering Cliffs?"

Thomas said, "Detective Ganske did, yes."

"Were you present?"

"Yes I was."

"Did you overhear what Mr. Adamcik stated?"

"Yes I did."

"What was his response?"

But Aaron objected before Detective Thomas could answer. "Your Honor, I need to vior dire slightly in aid of my objection," he said.

I watched nervously.

Judge Naftz said, "Okay."

Aaron asked, "Detective, isn't it true that at some point during this interview my client asked for counsel?"

Detective Thomas said, "Yes, he did."

Aaron asked him, "Isn't it true that there was some communication that took place after he indicated the right to counsel?"

"Yes there was."

"Isn't it true that for a period of time, Mr. Adamcik and his father left the room and went into another room for discussion?"

"That's correct," Thomas answered.

Aaron asked, "Isn't it true that after the indication of counsel, they came back into the interview room that we were referring to earlier and the camera was still rolling. Isn't that true?"

"That's correct."

"Isn't it true that Detective Ganske and yourself made some statements with regard to your belief as to my client's guilt?"

Thomas said, "I am not sure of your question."

Aaron rephrased it: "Well, there was continuing discussion with regard to whether or not you believed my client was guilty of the offense. Correct?"

Thomas said, "We told your client that he was being placed under arrest for First Degree Murder."

"And he was placed under arrest when they came back into the room. Correct?" Aaron asked.

"That's correct."

"And did you subsequently read his Miranda rights to him after that point?"

Detective Thomas shook his head. "No."

Aaron said, "Your Honor, we think that based on Miranda, anything after the indication of my client's right to counsel, should be excluded from being presented here today based on the existing case law of Miranda v. Arizona."

Judge Naftz said, "I don't think Mr. Pearson is there yet, are you?" he asked, referring to the point in the interview where Torey asked for an attorney.

Vic Pearson said, "We're not there yet."

Judge Naftz asked Pearson, "And when you get there, do you know when to stop?"

Pearson had no intention of stopping. "Your Honor, I think at that point, what Mr. Thompson is referring to are statements made by the defendant, Torey Adamcik, in response to his father's questions. There was no further interview by our detectives at that point. So I think, you know, we can cross that bridge when we get there."

Judge Naftz said, "Yeah, why don't you have that argument when it occurs Mr. Thompson."

"I thought it would be appropriate to address it now before we even went down that road," Aaron said.

"Well, why don't we address it at that point?" the judge said. "Mr. Pearson, when you reach that point, if you would indicate that to the court, and then Mr. Thompson can renew his objection."

Pearson said, "Yes, Your Honor."

The prosecutor readdressed Detective Thomas. He again asked what Torey said happened after he and Brian left the house on Whispering Cliffs. Thomas said that Torey admitted that he and Brian had in fact not gone to a movie, but had instead been burglarizing cars in the Whispering Cliffs neighborhood.

Pearson asked Thomas if Torey had made any phone calls from his cell phone while in the Whispering Cliffs area.

Thomas said that Torey had called Matt Beckham three times and that Matt had called Torey's cell phone a couple of times as well. Each call had been meticulously examined during the interview.

Torey said that he and Brian had burglarized a few cars and then gone home, to our house, where he and Brian spent the night. Torey said that after they had been home for awhile, he and Brian went to the convenience store to buy a drink for Brian, who did not like the soda we had in the fridge.

Detective Thomas described the interview as I remembered it, except that he testified that Torey indicated the reason they went to the convenience store was to buy matches. It was during this part of the interview that I left to pick up Jamie.

Next Detective Thomas started to describe events that I was previously unaware of. Thomas testified that Torey claimed he tried to take Brian home after they left the convenience store, but that he got lost and ended up on South 5th, over by Century High School.

Pearson asked, "Did you question Mr. Adamcik specifically where they ended up?"

Thomas said, "Mr. Adamcik indicated that they ended up in the Blackrock Canyon area."

Thomas had testified earlier that Brian took detectives to Blackrock Canyon, and to the location of the buried evidence. Now he was placing Torey there too. For some reason, Sean had kept this from me, never telling me exactly what happened when I left the interview.

Pearson asked, "What did Torey say happened in Blackrock Canyon?"

"Torey indicated that Brian got out of the car and smoked two cigarettes, and that he, Torey, urinated on the ground."

Detective Thomas said that Torey was asked if he had used a shovel while they were in Blackrock Canyon, and Torey said he remembered one being in his car, but he did not know if they had used it or not.

Pearson asked Thomas, "What happened next?"

"At this point, Detective Ganske proceeded further by telling Mr. Adamcik that we knew that a crime had been committed and that he was involved with the murders, or the murder of Cassie Stoddart."

Pearson turned to the judge. "Your Honor, at this point in time, we are going to be proceeding into some different areas including the fact that the defendant asserted his Fifth Amendment Right, at this point in time."

Judge Naftz said, "Okay."

Pearson said, "So I want to make the court aware, because the court requested to make that."

Judge Naftz said, "Okay. Mr. Thompson, how do you want to proceed? Do you want to renew your objection and inquire further?"

Aaron said, "Your Honor, I would like to ask a few additional questions in aid of the objection."

"Okay."

Aaron asked Detective Thomas, "Detective, when Mr. Adamcik and his father returned to the room, wasn't it true that either yourself, or Detective Ganske, said to Torey, 'You know what you need to do.'"

Thomas said, "I'm not sure."

Aaron asked, "Isn't it true that either yourself, or Detective Ganske said, 'You know exactly what happened.'"

Thomas answered, "That's possible."

"Isn't it true that you said something to the effect, 'Torey's full cooperation could do nothing but help him.'"

Thomas said, "Again, I'm not sure. It is very possible that those statements were made."

Aaron asked, "Isn't it true that after my client had indicated his right to counsel, the question was asked, 'You know what I am talking about?' Isn't it true that question was posed to Mr. Adamcik?"

Thomas said, "I don't believe that was a question. I believe it was a statement."

Aaron asked, "This interview was taped was it not Detective Thomas?"

"Yes."

"So, if we had access to the tape we could replay it and see exactly what occurred."

"Yes."

Aaron turned to the judge. "Your Honor, simply put, my client indicated his right to counsel. We think that the case law including Miranda v. Arizona, State v. Pearson, which is an Idaho case, and Edwards v. Arizona, which is the United States Supreme Court case from 1981 where it said in Edwards that if a suspect requests counsel at anytime during the interview he is not subject to further questioning until a lawyer has been made available, or the suspect himself reinitiates conversation. Torey indicated his right to counsel. They left the room. They came back in. There are additional comments being made by the interrogators. There may have been some responses to those questions, and we would ask that everything beyond the time that my client invoked his right to counsel be suppressed."

Judge Naftz said, "Well, I guess my question to you Mr. Thompson is, I'm getting the impression that Mr. Adamcik and his father left the room, they came back, that was after he invoked his rights to counsel, and when he came back, there were some statements made, but not necessarily questions of the investigators."

Aaron said, "It's not entirely so. There were some questions, like for example the last statement that I cross-examined Detective Thomas, 'You know, you know what I am talking about?' That was phrased in the form of a question."

Judge Naftz asked, "And did Mr. Adamcik respond?"

Aaron could not remember who responded to that particular question, but he asserted that there was an element of questioning at that point that should have been shut down, and was not.

Judge Naftz asked Aaron what the situation would be if there weren't *any* statements made by the detectives to either Sean or Torey, and Torey had been asked questions by his father that he had responded to? What would the situation be then?

Aaron was momentarily thrown by the hypothetical. It was not what happened. The detectives *had* made statements to elicit a response. Aaron asked Judge Naftz, "In this hypothetical are we presuming that the detectives are sitting in the room?"

Judge Naftz said, "Yes. In the hypothetical, Torey and Sean momentarily leave the room, and when they return the detectives are still there, and Sean asks Torey a question in front of the detectives, and Torey responds. Where would that leave them?"

Judge Naftz was asking for Aaron's interpretation of the law. He wanted to know if Aaron understood what constituted a custodial interview. If Sean, who was not an agent of the court, asked Torey a question, unsolicited by the detectives, and Torey responded, it would be admissible, even if it was in front of the detectives, because Miranda would not apply. Aaron knew that. But that was not what happened.

The detectives manipulated Sean and Torey. They made comments specifically with the intention of drawing out a response. Since they were trying to elicit a response, Torey was still in the equivalent of an interrogation, which was illegal under Miranda and suppressible.

Judge Naftz asked Aaron, "Were those questions from Mr. Adamcik to his son encouraged or drawn out by the investigators? Is that what you're saying?"

"Yes, Your Honor."

Judge Naftz asked, "How is that? Explain it to me?"

"Because these statements were elements of coercion. It was interrogating coercion," Aaron said.

Judge Naftz asked Mr. Pearson if the interrogation video was available.

Pearson said that it was. "But," he argued, "Miranda does not apply. Mr. Adamcik, (Torey) made a voluntary 'utterance' in response to a question his father asked him, not an agent of the court."

Judge Naftz said, "We haven't heard that yet. So I guess what I would ask is for now, Mr. Thompson, at least, baseline, I'm going to sustain the objection subject to you further questioning the witness. Alright?" He turned to Pearson.

Pearson nodded. He asked Detective Thomas, "What happened after the defendant terminated, or invoked his right to an attorney?"

"We stopped questioning him," Thomas said.

Pearson asked, "What did you do specifically?"

"I remember that Mr. Adamcik, Sean Adamcik, which would be Torey's father, was in the room and he asked to speak with his son. He made an indication, Mr. Sean Adamcik, that he wanted to speak with his son out of the ears and eyeshot of a camera, which we tried to provide that for them."

"How did you try to provide that for them?" Pearson asked.

"We took them to a separate room that was not a recorded room."

Person asked, "What happened next?"

"They came back. I don't know what conversations took place. Torey and his father went back into the room that was being recorded. At this point we explained that we were waiting for a transport vehicle to pick Mr. Adamcik up. We had arrested him, and told him he was under arrest for First Degree Murder."

Pearson asked, "What happened when you told him he was under arrest for First Degree Murder?"

"At this point I explained to Mr. Adamcik what the charges were about. I felt that he needed to know why he was being arrested. Therefore I went into several of the incidents of the case with him--some of the evidence that we found. The fact that there was a videotape and that somebody had already talked to law enforcement and given a full confession implicating him."

Pearson asked Thomas if he was questioning Torey at this point.

Thomas said, "No."

Pearson asked, "What happened when you finished telling him these things?"

"At some point during this, his father asked him if what we were saying was true."

The exact moment was when the detectives told Torey that they knew he had been to Blackrock Canyon with Brian. That is what Torey admitted to. But Detective Thomas was obviously rehearsed to misrepresent Sean's statement and imply that Torey confessed to something that he did not. Aaron had tried unsuccessfully to prevent it. Now Bron stood up.

"Your Honor, we renew the objection at this point particular," he said. "There is something I think for the record we need to clarify. And that is one of the real dilemmas with this. There is an inference that the statement that's being made is about certain things, and that's not accurate."

Judge Naftz said, "I'm sorry you've lost me. What do you mean?"

Thomas had just testified that Sean asked Torey if what the detectives were saying was true. Bron knew the prosecutor was going to imply Sean's question referenced *everything* the detectives had said, which was incorrect. The question was asked during a specific exchange.

Bron knew a verbal debate was not going to satisfy the argument. The best chance to shed light on what actually occurred was to watch the interrogation video. Bron attempted to get Judge Naftz to do that. "I think before it goes any further, we better have an in camera review (of the video)."

Judge Naftz said, "But the video has not been offered as evidence."

"I understand," Bron replied. "But Mr. Pearson has indicated that such a recording exists. In that case we have best evidence objection that Mr. Thomas is not the best authority to describe what happened, and, in fact, if we go much further he's going to taint the record, and make an inference once again. Something was said or something was done that isn't what actually happened. The best way to look at this is by looking at that document."

Judge Naftz asked, "Mr. Pearson, are you intending to make an exhibit and offer it?"

Pearson said, "No, Your Honor. The State does not intend to mark the interrogation video as an exhibit. I think Detective Thomas is perfectly capable of testifying regarding his memory."

Pearson knew if he marked the interrogation tape as an exhibit, and the court viewed it, he wouldn't be able to make the inference he was making through Detective Thomas's testimony.

Judge Naftz said, "The objection says best evidence rule. Under this objection, Mr. Rammell is saying that the best evidence is the tape recording of what happened in that room, and not Mr. Thomas's testimony."

Pearson said, "I think there's plenty of case law that contradicts that, and says that Detective Thomas's testimony is just as reliable. He was there. He was present."

The truth is detectives are agents of the State. They are *not* unbiased witnesses. They have a personal stake in the convictions they recommend, and judges know it. How could a judge use the biased testimony of a detective, over the actual tape of the events?

But Judge Naftz ruled. "Mr. Rammell, I'm going to overrule your objection," But he gave Aaron a chance. "Mr. Thompson, are you going to be heard further with regard to your objection? We're at that point. I want to know what you wanted to tell me."

Aaron stood up, "Your Honor, we believe that we were in a custodial situation. Torey was under arrest. They were making comment as regard to that. We've already covered those. It was custodial. It was coercive and we do believe that it is still suppressible, pursuant to Miranda."

Aaron did not have the skill to argue it further at that point, but he did draft a motion afterwards that was partially granted in trial and continues to be an issue in Torey's appeal.

If Bron could have convinced Judge Naftz to watch the interrogation tape, instead of relying on the biased testimony of Detective Thomas, Judge Naftz could have seen things differently, and may even have suppressed the interview after the invocation of Miranda.

Judge Naftz said, "All right. Based on the testimony I've heard with regard to the situation, Mr. Thomas was explaining to young Mr. Adamcik the charges and what the basis of those charges were, and that during that period, the senior Adamcik interjected a question with regard to, 'Is this true?' and I don't believe that comes within the confines of a custodial interview, or is coercive, or that there would be a need for the court to sustain that objection. So I'm going to overrule your objection, Mr. Thompson. Of course it will be a continuing objection and subject to review. So Mr. Pearson go ahead and ask your next question."

Pearson said, "I want to back up just a hair. What was it that Adamcik's father said to him?"

Thomas said, "Sean Adamcik looked at Torey Adamcik and said, 'Is this true? Is what they are saying true,' or something to that effect."

Pearson asked, "What was Torey's response?"

"He indicated yes, he nodded his head yes."

I looked over at Sean who was pale and stunned and looked like he was going to be sick.

Pearson asked Thomas, "What happened next?"

Thomas said, "At that time, myself and John Ganske told Mr. Adamcik not to ask his son any further questions."

"What happened at that point?"

"He was not asked any further questions by his father."

Pearson asked, "Was that the conclusion of the interview?"

Thomas said, "Yes, it was."

Pearson asked, "Did his father make any further statements to him?"

"His father makes a statement that if that's true, then I think you need an attorney, or something to that effect."

Pearson asked, "Did Torey Adamcik make any further responses to his father's questions or statements?"

"No."

Pearson said, "I have no further questions for this witness, Your Honor."

Judge Naftz said, "Mr. Thomas, I need some clarification for purposes of this hearing. You indicated you explained to the Adamciks about the charges. Can you explain to me what you told them?"

Thomas said, "Yes. I was telling Torey that he was being charged with First Degree Murder and that we had found some evidence that corroborated the fact that he and Mr. Draper had killed Cassie Stoddart, and that we had a confession from another individual, meaning Mr. Draper, and that we were placing him under arrest for First Degree Murder."

Detective Thomas did not tell the judge that Torey was told that his confession could do nothing but help him, that Cassie was watching, and that he knew the right thing to do.

Judge Naftz said, "Thank you, sir. All right. Mr. Martinez and Mr. Schulthies, I will allow you to begin your cross examination of this witness first."

CHAPTER TWENTY-ONE

Cross-Examinations
& The Judge's Decision

I entered the courtroom believing that there was little Brian's attorneys could do for him, and I was right. He was guilty of murder, he admitted it on tape, but Brian was a child, and his attorneys wanted to give him the hope of a future someday. They mustered a defense from the scraps they had--and fought hard.

Brian's interviews, as well as the video, proved that he stabbed Cassie. But Brian blamed Torey for Cassie's death in his third interview, and in doing so--he provided his attorneys with his own defense. They attempted to argue that even if Brian had, as he admitted, stabbed Cassie, there was not enough evidence to prove that he *killed* her.

When Dave Martinez questioned Detective Thomas, he set up his scenario as picturesquely as Vic Pearson had done when questioning the detective himself. And Martinez's scenario was that Brian could have stabbed Cassie after she was already dead.

But he got off to a shaky start. Dave Martinez tried to imply that the first interview the detective conducted with Brian Draper was inappropriate, because it was conducted after midnight, in the home of a sixteen-year-old child.

"Was there really some reason you felt you needed to interview Brian right that second?" he asked.

Thomas looked Martinez directly in the eye and said, "Because a female had been killed."

Cassie's family erupted in cheers. They were there to see justice done. Sympathy for a murderer was not an option. The judge had to call the courtroom back to order. Martinez quickly skimmed over the first two interviews, and settled on the third.

Martinez asked Detective Thomas, "What was Brian's demeanor during that interview?"

"Brian was very distraught," Thomas said.

"Very distraught?" Martinez asked.

"Uh-huh. Yes."

"Did he cry?"

"Yes."

"Did he wail at points?"

"Yes, he did," Thomas answered.

Martinez asked, "And he was explaining to you what happened in a tearful manner?"

"Yes, sir."

"And he explained to you that he thought this was a joke, correct?"

"That's correct."

"And that he did not go there to kill anyone?"

"That's correct."

"And that he did not have any idea that that's actually what was going to happen."

"Correct."

"And he was afraid when he saw Torey begin to stab Cassie. Correct?"

"Yes."

"At one point, he did not even think it was real. He thought maybe Torey and Cassie were playing a joke on him. Correct?"

"Yes."

"But he was honest with you as far as you can tell?"

Brian had given the detectives a detailed account of what occurred the night Cassie was killed. He placed himself in the center of the action, taking credit for every single thing that happened--except stabbing Cassie.

"He (Brian) was walking up the stairs first?" Martinez asked.

"That's what he said."

"And then Torey rushed passed him and stabbed Cassie."

"That's what he said," Thomas answered.

Martinez said, "The difference, I guess, when we get to the fourth interview, as you said, at some point, Brian admitted that he had stabbed as well."

"That's right."

"And it would be accurate wouldn't it, to say that at some time that would have occurred, based on the conversations and your understanding of Brian's statement, that Torey had just rushed passed him and begun to kill Cassie."

"That's what he indicated in the previous…"

Martinez interrupted, "Right. So he is seeing another human being killed by someone he thought was his friend."

Bron stood up and objected on mischaracterization of the evidence. "You're saying that something happened that this man does not have personal knowledge of. You have to at least talk about where he got the information, so that it's understood that it's Brian

Draper's *testimony*, not this is actually what's happening. The inference is, of course, that this is what happened and asking Detective Thomas to corroborate that."

Judge Naftz overruled the objection, stating that Thomas could testify to his understanding of the conversation with Brian. He implied that everyone knew that Detective Thomas was not testifying to the truthfulness, or the validity, of Brian's statements, but just to the statements themselves.

But it did not matter if everyone knew the detective's testimony was not about the truthfulness of Brian's statements. The statements themselves seriously compromised Torey. Allegations were being reported in the news that Torey had no opportunity to defend himself against. A bell was rung in the mind of the public that could not be un-rung.

Martinez continued his questioning. "So, it would be your understanding that Mr. Draper would have been in a situation where he had just watched Mr. Adamcik kill Cassie Stoddart."

Thomas said, "True."

Martinez asked, "That would be a stressful situation, obviously. Right?"

Thomas nodded, "I would think so."

Martinez asked, "Have you ever been in a situation like that, seen something like that?"

Thomas shook his head, "No, sir."

"Well, I ask you this. You weren't there when it happened. You came afterward and saw the condition of Cassie's body. It had an effect on you, didn't it?"

Thomas said, "Yes, sir."

Martinez said, "And it was very emotional."

"Yes."

"You didn't even know Cassie before this."

"No."

"And it broke your heart."

"Yes."

Martinez illustrated how traumatizing it would be for the person who saw Cassie murdered. He let that sink in for a moment, and then asked, "So, Brian tells you at that point he maybe stabbed someone in the leg. He stabbed Cassie in the leg?"

Thomas said, "That's correct."

"But at that point, Torey had suggested to him that he better do something as well. Correct?" Martinez asked.

"That's correct."

"And Torey's standing there with a knife. We can only assume it's still dripping with blood after he's killed Cassie. Correct?"

"Correct."

"Do we have any reason to believe that Cassie was alive at the time Brian stabbed her?"

This time Vic Pearson objected. "It calls for speculation, Your Honor," he said.

Judge Naftz asked Thomas, "I don't know, can you answer the question?"

Thomas said, "I don't know that answer."

Judge Naftz told Martinez, "I don't think he has the scientific background to be able to answer that question."

"Well, I didn't ask for a scientific opinion," Martinez said. "He's been qualified as an officer and I wanted to know if this officer, as part of his investigation, had any reason to believe that Cassie was alive when that occurred."

"I am going to overrule the objection and allow you to answer if you can," Judge Naftz told Thomas.

Thomas said, "I don't know that answer."

"So, she may have been dead already?"

"She certainly could."

"And she would have been dead at Torey's hands," Martinez said.

"She could have been," Thomas answered.

I knew that Detective Thomas had watched the tape. He knew that Brian admitted to Torey that *he* killed Cassie. But Thomas answered the question the way he did, because he still believed that both boys had stabbed Cassie, and he did not really care which one inflicted the fatal wound.

I knew that months down the road people would hear Brian, on his own homemade videotape, tell Torey that he'd just killed Cassie, and Dave Martinez's argument would pass into thin air, like the wind that it was. But that was no comfort to me that day. What mattered to me was what was said--that day--in that courtroom--and how badly it hurt.

There was no way to prove, through the detective's testimony, that Torey did not stab Cassie, but we could, with the information Thomas possessed, dispute Martinez's argument clearly and effectively. I wanted Bron to do that. To prove that Brian was lying. And that's all I wanted from him. Nothing more.

Thankfully he was able to score some valid points.

Bron demonstrated that Detective Thomas's testimony was based on hearsay. There were no eyewitnesses to collaborate Brian's story, and it was possible that Brian was lying to protect himself. Thomas agreed all that was true. He also agreed that Brian's statements were inconsistent with each other.

Bron started by asking, "Detective Thomas, everything that you've testified to today came through hearsay. Would you agree with that statement?"

Dave Martinez objected, "It calls for a legal conclusion, Your Honor."

"Objection sustained," Judge Naftz said.

Bron rephrased, "Would you agree with me, you have no personal knowledge of the events that you've just described?"

Thomas asked, "What do you mean by personal knowledge?"

"Well, the only way that you've acquired any of the information that you have been here testifying about is essentially through what you're saying other people told you."

Pearson spoke for the State, "Your Honor, I am going to object also. It misstates testimony. He has testified to being at the scene, seeing certain stuff. That is not stuff he's heard from other people, so I think this question misstates testimony."

Judge Naftz asked Bron, "Do you want to make an argument?"

"Sure," Bron answered. "I don't agree that that's accurate. I think what he has testified about has all been hearsay. I don't think frankly that it is a situation where it calls for a legal conclusion. I think laymen know what hearsay is. Additionally, I think that what we have here is a gentleman who is testifying about things that Mr. Draper told him, or Mr. Beckham told him, those types of things, so I don't think that's a valid objection."

Judge Naftz agreed, "I'll overrule the objection," he said. "If you can answer the question, sir. Do you need it restated?"

Thomas said, "No. I think I can do this. I think what you're trying to say is, in my interview, did I get anything other than hearsay?"

"No," Bron said.

"Then I guess I need the question restated."

Bron said, "Okay. Sorry. The things you're testifying about

here today--about what happened to Cassie, you've obtained that information, not through personal knowledge, but through information coming from other parties. Would you agree with that?"

"That and evidence."

"Well, let's talk about that for just a second. Identify each item of evidence that you believe tends to prove that Cassie Stoddart was murdered."

"Objection!" Pearson yelled. " That's overbroad, Your Honor."

I wanted to object myself. I didn't know what Bron was doing. Of course Cassie was murdered.

Judge Naftz said, "I'll allow it Mr. Pearson." He looked at Bron. " It would be helpful if you could narrow that a little bit and go through it with him Mr. Rammell, but I will allow the question."

Bron said, "I will do that, Your Honor. I will narrow it over time. Thank you. But if you don't mind, let's start here."

Detective Thomas asked Bron, "Would you restate the question?"

"Sure. Would you identify each item of evidence that you contend shows that Cassie Stoddart was murdered in this case?"

Pearson renewed his objection, "Your Honor, just for the record, if the State could have a continuing objection."

Judge Naftz answered, "Absolutely."

Thomas began to list the crime scene photos, the knives, and the videotape.

Bron asked Detective Thomas, "Did you take the crime scene photographs personally?"

"No."

"Did you ever see the defendants with the knives?"

"No."

"Did you ever see the defendants at the crime scene?"

"No."

"What evidence did you, personally, collect?"

"I did not collect evidence."

"Is there any evidence that you observed, that you were asked to render your opinion on?"

"No."

Bron said, "So again, getting back to my original question, isn't it fair to say that everything that you know about this case comes from some third party other than what you saw when you went to the crime scene some two or three days after the alleged event?"

"Yes. That's fair."

And I realized that Bron hadn't been trying to minimize what happened to Cassie, but simply demonstrate the detective's limited knowledge of the actual event.

Bron asked the detective what items of evidence he'd reviewed prior to the hearing.

"Police reports, as well as a videotape," Thomas answered.

Bron commented on Detective Thomas's recollection. Certain events seemed to be perfectly clear to him, while other events were lost. Thomas had recalled Brian's interviews very specifically, but he could not recall certain statements that he and Detective Ganske had directed at Torey during their second interview with him. Bron asked Thomas to explain why he could not recall that information.

"It's a large case. I'm just trying to do my best to remember everything," Thomas said.

Bron asked Detective Thomas how many people he interviewed.

"Three. I interviewed Matt Beckham, Torey Adamcik and Brian Draper."

"Now you did a number of interviews with Brian Draper?"

"That's correct."

Bron asked, "Did you find him to be a truthful person? You interviewed him five different times. Was there any time, any interview, where there weren't differences between the interview he had originally given, and the last interview?"

Martinez stood up. "I'm going to object, Your Honor. He cannot possibly testify as to whether someone is being truthful or not."

Judge Naftz said, "I agree with you Mr. Martinez, but I am not sure that's what he's asking." He turned to Bron, "Maybe you could restate the question?"

Bron said, "Sorry. Thank you. Yes, Detective, based on the information you obtained from Mr. Draper, did you find his version of events to be consistent?"

"No."

Bron asked, "Would you agree with me that Mr. Draper has a motive for blaming the events on Mr. Adamcik?"

Martinez objected again, "He cannot possibly speculate to someone else's motives for speaking."

Judge Naftz said, "I understand. I am going to overrule the objection and allow you to answer the question, if you can."

Thomas said, "I did not fully understand the question. Would you please restate it?"

"Sure," Bron said. "Would you agree with me that Mr. Draper has a reason to blame this on Mr. Adamcik?"

Detective Thomas nodded, "Yes."

Bron asked, "Based on the evidence that you have reviewed, do you find that Mr. Draper's version of events, even at the last event--to be consistent with your investigation?"

"No."

Bron asked Detective Thomas if he knew anything about Torey's character. "Prior to this investigation, did you know of Torey Adamcik in any way?"

"No."

"Had he ever been in trouble with the law, as far as you know?"

"Not that I am aware of."

"Are you familiar with anything about Torey, with his mannerisms?"

"No." Thomas shook his head.

"Are you familiar with his voice?"

"No."

"Is he a quiet person, or a talkative person?"

"That I do not know."

"Are you familiar with how he would act if he were excited?"

"No."

"How about if he were sad?"

"I don't know."

"How about if he were happy?"

"I don't know."

"How about if he were depressed?"

"No."

"How about if he was scared?"

"I don't know."

"How about if he were intimidated?"

"I do not know."

"Do you know how long Mr. Draper and Mr. Adamcik have been associated together?"

"No, I don't."

"Do you know anything about Torey Adamcik's goals for the

future, for example with respects to education?"

"No."

Bron asked, "Is it fair to say that you do not know what his long term plans were prior to September 22, 2006, with respects to school, travel, or family?"

"No."

Bron asked Thomas, "How many times have you been to the homicide scene?"

"At least three."

"Do you have any idea whether or not Torey Adamcik may have been threatened by Brian Draper?"

"I have no idea."

Bron asked, "Would you agree with me that it is just as plausible that Brian Draper did the things that he accuses Torey Adamcik of doing?"

A reasonable question, but before Detective Thomas could answer, Martinez objected, "That's speculation, Your Honor. He doesn't have any testimony to that effect."

Judge Naftz said, "I'm going to sustain that objection, Mr. Rammell."

Bron must have felt that airing the question was adequate. He did not rephrase. "I have no more questions for this witness," he said.

Judge Naftz asked, "Mr. Pearson, Mr. Martinez, any redirect?"

They each answered no.

Judge Naftz said, "Okay. Officer Thomas, thank you very much, you can step down."

Mr. Pearson stood and turned the time over to Mr. Hiedeman.

Judge Naftz asked the prosecutor whom he planned to call next. There were only two witnesses left, Dr. Steve Skoumal, and Detective Alex Hamilton. Mark Hiedeman stated that he wanted to call Dr. Skoumal first. He was the pathologist who autopsied Cassie, but the doctor had taken a medical call early that morning and was currently unavailable.

Judge Naftz agreed to give the doctor an opportunity to arrive. He ordered a fifteen-minute recess, but at the end of the recess, when Dr. Skoumal was still unavailable, Mark Hiedeman had no choice but to call Detective Alex Hamilton to the stand.

Detective Hamilton approached the bench and was sworn in.

He was younger than Detective Thomas, probably in his mid-thirties, and he had the thick, muscular build of a football player. His demeanor was serious, and he exhibited the unmistakable characteristics of a law enforcement officer, or a military man.

Detective Hamilton's testimony was meticulous in its detail. You could tell, as he spoke, that he lacked imagination, but he did not seem devious, although in the end, it was he who was responsible for misrepresenting one of the most vital pieces of evidence in Torey's case. And I am convinced he did so purposely.

Mark Hiedeman wanted to call Detective Hamilton last, because he planned to introduce the videotape though the detective's testimony. Detective Hamilton had been present when the videotape was uncovered in Blackrock Canyon, and it was he who was given custodial responsibility over it. Playing the videotape at the end of the hearing would have been Mark Hiedeman's grand finale.

Now, Mark Hiedeman laid the foundation for the admission of the videotape, through the detective's testimony, and motioned for the tape to be played in court. Immediately the defense attorneys objected. They argued that the tape was prejudicial, and asked Judge Naftz to review the tape in chambers, and out of the presence of the press so that the defendants' rights to a fair, unbiased trial would remain intact.

Of course they meant the appearance of a fair and unbiased trial, because by then, both boys were already presumed guilty.

Judge Naftz stated that he would view the video in chambers before deciding if he would allow it to be played in court. We sat in the courtroom and waited for the half an hour that he spent viewing the tape. When he returned you could see his reaction to the video on his face.

Judge Naftz denied the prosecutor's motion to play the videotape in court. "The tape is certainly prejudicial," he said. "Playing it in front of the press would undoubtedly damage the two defendants' rights to a fair trial."

The ruling angered Mark Hiedeman. He had continually threatened to play the tape during the preliminary hearing, and now he knew that he would not be able to do so until the trial. He visibly seethed with frustration, but there was nothing he could do about it.

Detective Hamilton was released from the stand and Dr. Steve Skoumal called.

Dr. Skoumal began his professional career as an attorney,

practicing law for eight years before going to medical school. Currently, he was a Board Eligible Forensic Pathologist, and owner of Western Pathology. He contracted with the county, who contacted him after Cassie was discovered on Sunday afternoon. He autopsied her the following Monday morning.

Present at the autopsy were Dr. Steve Skoumal and his assistant Steve Williams, Detectives Mark Ballard and Alex Hamilton, Deputy Karen Hatch, Idaho State Police Investigator Tom Sellers, Idaho State Lab Technician Shannon Larson, and Vic Pearson from the Bannock County Prosecutor's Office.

The autopsy began at approximately 9:30 a.m. Shannon Larson clipped Cassie's fingernails and collected them for DNA testing. She also collected some hairs that were found in Cassie's left hand.

Detective Hamilton photographed the autopsy, while Deputy Hatch kept a photo log and numbered the wounds found on Cassie's body for the pathologist.

As Dr. Skoumal located and identified each wound, Karen Hatch placed a numbered placard over it. The wounds were numbered in numerical order. The locations of the wounds were noted. At approximately 10:30 a.m., Dr. Skoumal and Steve Williams began taking measurements of the wounds, carefully measuring the outside opening and depth of each. Cassie's internal organs were removed, and the damage they suffered documented. As he completed his examination of each wound, Dr. Skoumal sealed it off and taped it shut.

During the course of the autopsy, Dr. Skoumal advised that there were approximately seven fatal stab wounds. He stated the cause of death was stab wounds to the chest and trunk, but he was unable to tell the length or size of the weapon used.

It was through Dr. Skoumal's testimony that we learned what happened to Cassie. She had been attacked and stabbed *twenty-nine* times. *Seven* of her wounds were potentially fatal. I knew that Cassie had been stabbed, but I never dreamt that she had suffered an attack as brutal as this. I wondered how, *how* could this have happened?

This was an intentional act. You do not stab someone twenty-nine times accidentally.

I was also confused about the time frame. Torey had indicated that everything happened so fast, that he did not even have time to drive away before Brian was running out to the car. How could that be? I thought it would take a long time to stab somebody twenty-nine times. What in the world had Torey been doing during that time, and why hadn't he left?

Later I talked to Aaron about it. He said that nothing in Dr. Skoumal's testimony contradicted Torey. Aaron told me that an attack like the one Cassie suffered, only takes a matter of minutes. It's fast, and Brian was probably pumped up on adrenaline when it happened.

Aaron said the fact that Torey did not have blood on him was important. If two people with two different knives were stabbing Cassie, as the State alleged, they would have splattered each other with blood. Even if Torey was merely in the room with Cassie, while she was being stabbed, he should have had some of her blood on him. There was blood all over the living room and even splatters of it down the hall and stairs.

When Torey came home that night, literally minutes after Cassie had been stabbed, he did not stop to wash. I heard the garage door open, and Torey came directly upstairs to my room. He had no trace of blood on him. Brian, on the other hand, spent a considerable amount of time in the downstairs bathroom cleaning up. Aaron told me, had the police checked the trap in that bathroom, they probably would have found Cassie's blood in it. A thought that made me sick.

Dr. Skoumal described each of Cassie's wounds individually. Which wounds were potentially fatal, which were defensive, and which were probably inflicted post mortem. He testified that he could not determine if the knives in evidence, which were recovered from Blackrock Canyon, were the weapons used to attack Cassie.

Dr. Skoumal testified that he could not tell if Cassie had been attacked with one knife, or with multiple knives, and in fact, he stated that it was impossible to determine if she'd even been attacked with a knife at all. All that he could say, with medical certainty, was that Cassie had been stabbed with a sharp object.

Like everyone involved in the case, Dr. Skoumal was touched by the tragedy of Cassie's death. But he was an ethical witness. He performed a thorough autopsy and based his findings--not on speculation, or opinion, or what the prosecutor wanted, but strictly on the physical evidence found during the autopsy.

After he was excused from the stand closing arguments began.

Closing arguments should have been a simple rendition of the day's testimony. The defense attorneys knew their clients were going to be bound over; there was really nothing they could say. But in spite of his win, Mark Hiedeman was still fuming over the judge's refusal to play the videotape in the courtroom. He wasn't about to let the matter drop.

After recapping the day's events, Mark Hiedeman began blurting out his version of the videotape, knowing full well that at any moment he was going to be ordered to stop. All four defense attorneys leapt to their feet, screaming objections, but Mark Hiedeman's voice rose above them. He told the courtroom that both Torey and Brian were on the videotape joyously celebrating their successful murder of Cassie. He quoted Brian saying he has just stabbed her in the throat.

Judge Naftz rapped his gavel, desperately calling the courtroom back to order, while Mark Hiedeman, ignoring Aaron who was yelling that he was misstating the contents of the video, and Dave Martinez, who was begging Judge Naftz to do something, went on and on.

Finally Judge Naftz prevailed. He angrily informed Mark Hiedeman that he'd heard enough. The prosecutor sat down, claiming he had done nothing wrong, while the defense counsels seethed in shock and disbelief.

Judge Naftz rendered his verdict. "Based on the evidence that is before the Court at this time, the Court finds that a public offense has been committed, that of First Degree Murder and Conspiracy to Commit First Degree Murder. The Court finds further that there is probable and sufficient cause to believe that Brian Draper committed those crimes. So I am going to bind defendant Brian Draper over to District Court to answer those charges."

Next he addressed Torey. "In determining the admissible evidence against Mr. Adamcik, the Court did not consider the testimony of Detective Andy Thomas. This was the confession of another person, implicating Mr. Adamcik in the commission of a crime. It certainly violates the defendant's rights of confrontation under the Sixth Amendment. What the court did consider was the statement he made to his father during the interrogation and after he had requested counsel. That he indicated, 'Yes,' he did commit the crimes that Detective Thomas had explained to him."

Torey's life could very well be determined by the rendering of his police interrogation. In his own words, Judge Naft stated that Torey's statements during the interrogation were a determining factor in binding Torey over to District Court. Given its significance,

I'll never understand why the judge chose to rely solely on Detective Thomas's testimony, rather than watch the actual interrogation video itself.

After the hearing I went home, and straight to my room, where I lay in the dark. Sean came in and lay down with me, but our family came over to check on us and he got up to speak with them. I stayed in bed, unable to face anyone.

Torey called that night. It was all I could do to talk to him. He was depressed. The day had affected him more than any of us, but I simply could not muster the energy to talk him through it. Lacey came in the room when she heard the phone ringing, she knew that I was in no position to talk to anyone, including Torey. She took the phone away from me and I was grateful that she did.

Lacey comforted Torey. She told him that it was okay.

Torey asked, "How can you say that? Everyone in Pocatello is going to think that I killed Cassie."

"Not everyone," Lacey said. "Not those that matter." She reminded Torey of the many people who loved him, and believed in him, and she told him that every single person who supported him before the hearing supported him still. We'd already had a houseful of people stop by to check on us. Nothing had changed. It was going to be all right. Lacey told Torey that it had been a bad day, but it was over, and we wouldn't have to go through it again.

That became one of the methods Torey used to cope. When he got through one bad experience he'd say, "That's over. I don't have to do that again." And he would try to put it behind him. I was grateful it helped, but what a way to live a life. One bad experience put behind another. Nothing to look forward to, nothing to hope for, just days and time to get past.

I fell in my bed like it was a life raft. That's what it was to me. I could relate with Tom Hank's character in *Castaway*. He made a life raft and sailed toward his only hope. While he was in the ocean he clung to a raft that broke apart piece-by-piece, and all he could do was hang on and hope that it would be enough to get him through. I felt like that. Every day that I had to go out in the world, talk to people, go to work, was like swimming in the ocean, tossed and turned by deadly waves, and all I wanted to do was climb back onto my life raft and lay there and wait for someone to come along and save me from the nightmare I was in.

Torey,
Age
five.

Torey, fourteen, reacts to a playful kiss from Lacey.

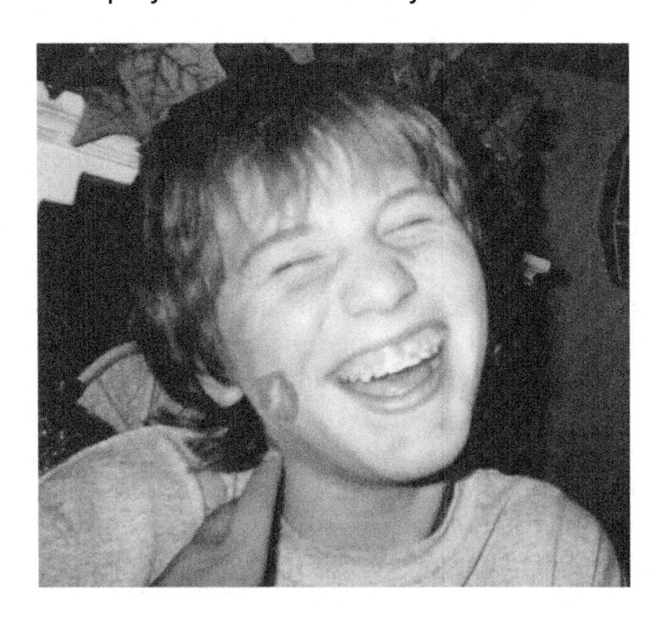

Lacey, Torey and Jamie,
Christmas 2004.

Torey in his backyard with friends, 2004.

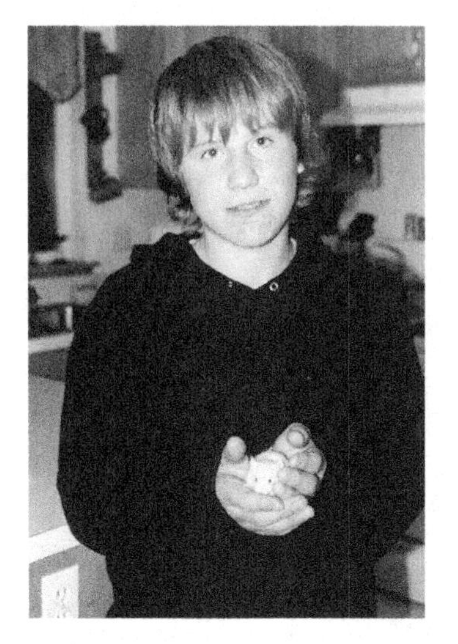

Painting Easter eggs.

Torey, 2003.

Playing ping-pong on a cruise, 2004.

Building with Knex.

Our house on Pointe View Drive, 2005.

Lacey and Jeff, 2006.

Torey, two weeks before his arrest.

Torey and Jamie Camping. Summer, 2006.

Torey's sixteenth Birthday. Three months before his arrest. One year before he was sentenced to die in prison.

Cassie, in front of Pocatello High school.

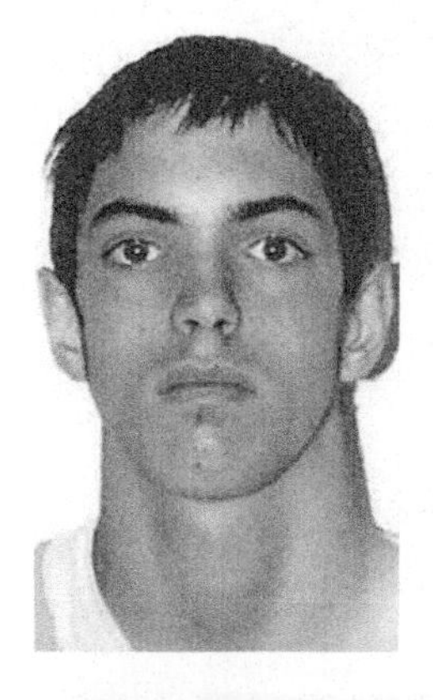

Brian Draper, 2006.

The house on Whispering cliffs Drive.

Entering the courtroom for the Preliminary Hearing. November, 2006.

Bron and Torey, 2007

Aaron , Torey and Greg

Greg and Aaron after the sentencing hearing.

Sheriff Nelson and Mark Hiedeman.

Lacey, Shannon and Sean react to the verdict.

Torey is led out of the courtroom following the verdict, June 8th, 2007.

CHAPTER TWENTY-TWO

Surprising Information Revealed

The preliminary hearing momentarily bolstered Brian's case. For days afterwards the news reported his version of the events, while his friends gave interviews affirming their belief in his innocence. When I complained to Aaron, he told me that I just needed to be patient. It didn't matter how many people professed Brian's innocence, or if Brian blamed Torey or not, because it was just a matter of time before the truth came out. Let Brian have his moment in the sun. It wasn't going to last.

But Aaron didn't understand. This *hurt.* And every day that we remained silent, was a day too long.

Unbelievably, Bron was satisfied with the outcome of the hearing. He told us that Aaron was going to concentrate on vigorously fighting for the suppression of the interview. The firm recommended we hire an expert in interrogations and Youth Miranda Warnings. Mom wanted a Board Certified Forensic Psychologist, who specialized in children. They began searching for one.

With Torey and Brian now bound over to District Court, they were scheduled for a new arraignment. There were four district judges possible. It fell to Judge Peter D. McDermott. I didn't know any of the judges and had to rely on our attorneys' advice. They, along with Brian's attorneys, elected to keep Judge McDermott instead of exercising their right to excuse him. I took that as a good sign, but it was a grave mistake.

Judge McDermott was in his seventies, well past retirement age. He had silver hair and a ruddy complexion. Underneath his robes, he wore cowboy boots and tan wranglers. His rulings were some of the harshest in the county, if not the state. But his "good ol' boy" methods appealed to the community, who respected him.

Judge McDermott started his career as a defense attorney. Rumor had it that he and his sister worked together in the public defender's office years ago. Ours was a sensitive case, not easily entrust to anyone, and our attorneys struggled with the choice, but they believed Judge McDermott had the most experience, and that is what they based their decision on. It certainly wasn't his sentencing record.

Once in possession of the case, Judge McDermott moved

quickly. He arraigned Torey and Brian on November 15th, 2006, and scheduled their trial date for March 20, 2007.

Adam Dykman was almost as upset as Sean and I were with the news coverage of Torey and Brian after the preliminary hearing, and the fact that Brian was coming off so well. He had some information about Brian that he thought we should know.

Adam came to our house and told us that Brian was obsessed with the Columbine High School Massacre, and its two killers, Dylan Klebold and Eric Harris. He asked if we were aware that Brian had been suspended from school in the eighth grade for planning a school shooting.

We were not aware. This was something I'd never heard before, and if Adam had not come forward, I don't think it would have ever been reported. Brian's family knew about his suspension from school, his supporters knew about it, and even Mark Hiedeman knew, but none of them were going to bring it up for obvious reasons.

Mark Hiedeman was not going to disclose the information because he did not want to paint Brian differently than Torey. If it was discovered that Brian had a long-standing preoccupation with violence, while Torey did not, and that Brian was deeply disturbed and had manipulated Torey, Brian might receive one sentence and Torey another. Mark Hiedeman had no intention of allowing that to happen.

On November 6th, Mark Hiedeman signed a notice seeking the harshest sentence under the law for both boys. Life Without Parole. As juveniles, Torey and Brian were ineligible for the death penalty. But had it been an option, Bron assured me, Mark Hiedeman would have sought that sentence instead.

Adam told us that Brian talked about school shootings and killing people nearly every day. Everyone acquainted with Brian knew it, but no one took him seriously. Brian was a joker, a clown, and it was difficult to take anything he said seriously. Brian claimed the incident in middle school was the result of a joke that was blown out of proportion, and it was easy to believe him.

But now that Cassie was dead, Brian's words came back to haunt Adam (and perhaps some of the other kids that went to school with him as well).

I could not believe what I was hearing. I had been struggling to understand how this had happened ever since Torey's arrest.

There was nothing in Torey's background that could have led to this. I knew Brian was responsible, but I had been unable to find out why.

The newspapers reported that Brian listened to the band Slipknot. I'd never heard of them, but it seemed unlikely that his choice of music could have influenced him enough to commit a murder. The only thing I had been able to find was a *Myspace* account Brian created. On his *Myspace* Brian admitted that he loved horror movies, which he also included as some of his favorite books to read. He wrote that he loved horror books, mountaineer books and reading *books that he had written.*

Books that he had written escaped me. It did not occur to me that Brian might be writing things down that would be relevant to what happened to Cassie.

But there was a section titled "Finish the Line" on Brian's *Myspace* account that caught my attention. It started a sentence for the person filling out the profile to finish. A couple of Brian's answers were troubling.

For the line, "So many people don't know that…"

Brian filled in, "that I am insane, no really, I'm sick in the head."

Of course the fact that he killed somebody made his answer all the more relevant.

Under the line, "who I'd like to meet…"

Brian wrote, "anyone that survived Columbine." He had also written the names Dylan Klebold and Eric Harris, but at the time I did not know who they were.

Under the line, "I am…"

Brian wrote, "an atheist, anarchist, anti-Christ."

That was the only information I had about Brian before Adam came to us. But as soon as I heard it, I knew how important Adam's information was. It could answer *why this happened.* Maybe this happened because Brian had spent years fantasizing about violence and was basically a ticking time bomb by the time he met Torey.

I scheduled an appointment with Aaron. I told him everything Adam told me about Brian Draper. Aaron promised to look into it. Eventually he recovered a police report that verified that Brian had indeed been involved in an investigation into an alleged plan to commit a school shooting. The incident was more serious than just a joke that had been blown out of proportion though. It had been taken seriously enough that someone was removed from the school. It took some research, but Aaron found out what had happened.

Aaron discovered that Brian's family moved to Pocatello when Brian was in the seventh grade. Prior to that, they had been living in Utah. Kerry and Pam Draper had both been raised in Pocatello, and after returning they enrolled Brian at Irving Middle School where he seemed to quickly settle in and make friends.

First Brian met Joey Lacey, a small, shaggy headed kid he quickly befriended. Joey and Brian shared many interests; they skateboarded, loved music and learned how to play the drums together. They were best friends through middle school and high school.

Another friendship Brian developed was with Chris Nix. Chris was a nice boy, but he was going through a difficult period in his life. His parents had divorced a few years earlier and he recently lost his father to cancer. Chris was vulnerable. He did not have many friends and his friendship with Brian was extremely important to him.

Brian's family was well to do. His father worked out of state, flying back and forth to work, but his mother stayed at home with Brian and his younger sister, Brittany. By all accounts Brian had everything he wanted. A wonderful life. But something happened in his middle-school years that changed him. After reading Brian's journals, Bron told me that you could see Brian growing from a typical kid, into someone with deep psychological problems.

I thought there must have been some event in Brian's life that brought the change on, but it could have been biological, or perhaps even self-induced. Whatever it was, Brian became obsessed with violence. By the time Chris met him in the seventh grade, Brian was already obsessed with the Columbine High School Massacre. Brian had even created a website devoted to the school on his computer.

Brian's fascination with Columbine truly was an obsession. He read everything written on the subject, memorizing the FBI reports. He knew every detail of the shooting, what the killers wore, how many people they injured, how many people they killed, what kinds of wounds they inflicted, what weapons they carried. Everything that could be known about the shooting, Brian knew.

Until Brian met Chris, he'd kept his obsession with Columbine somewhat of a secret. It was too powerful to keep hidden, Brian could not stop himself from talking about it, but he had learned how to mask it. He did so by becoming the class clown, the jokester. Using that persona, Brian was able to talk about things that otherwise would have been unacceptable.

But there was nothing funny about Brian's obsession with Columbine.

With Chris, Brian did not need to hide behind a persona. Chris's friendship offered Brian an opportunity to talk about anything he wanted to without fear of rejection or criticism, and it may have been one of the major contributing factors to just how deeply rooted Brian's fascination with Columbine was allowed to grow; because, with Chris, Brian was never checked, never questioned, never forced to hold back due to social norms.

For over a year, on almost a daily basis, Brian talked about how cool it would be to commit a school shooting and kill the kids he went to school with. And Chris was more than happy to follow along, participate in the conversation, and encourage Brian as much as Brian needed him to, *as long as Brian remained his friend.*

That was what mattered to Chris. Not the talk, not the planning. That was not real. What was real to Chris was that he wasn't alone anymore. That he had a friend who needed him, who sought him out and made him feel important, at a time when Chris desperately needed to feel that way. The loss of his father had left a gaping hole in Chris's life. Brian came along and filled it.

Chris's mother, Tanya, said that Chris was almost immediately affected by his friendship with Brian. She noticed a change in his behavior right away. He became morose and withdrawn. But as soon as Chris was removed from Brian's influence, the effects wore off just as quickly. He became the Christopher she had always known. Brian's influence over her son was a brief and painful time that Tanya would like to forget, and who could blame her? It was during his friendship with Brian that Chris was accused of planning a school shooting and expelled from school.

Chris and Brian talked about a school shooting long before anyone paid attention to them. Their conversations began in the seventh grade. It was not until the eighth grade that they were investigated. What led to the investigations? Chris. Chris told other students that he and Brian were planning a school shooting, and those students turned him in…*twice.*

The first investigation seemed harmless enough. It was February 2004. Chris was at Brian's house, and they were talking with a girl they knew from school on Brian's speakerphone. She had a friend over to her house as well and the four of them were chatting over the phone line. During the course of the conversation the subject of a school shooting came up. Chris told the girls that he and Brian were planning a school shooting for the next school dance. Chris even went so far as to give them a date for the shooting. March 12th. The girls questioned Brian and Chris about their plans and recorded the conversation on their answering machine. Later, the girl's parents took the recording to the school and the police were notified.

Every school in Pocatello has a resource officer assigned to it from the Pocatello Police Department. Kristen Oaks was the officer assigned to Irving Middle School. It was her responsibility to perform an investigation into the reported incident. She, along with Irving Principal Jim Harrell, questioned Chris and Brian about the phone call.

Chris told Officer Oaks that he and Brian were talking with the girls when the subject of a school shooting came up; the girls egged him on during the conversation and that was why he made the comments that he did. Brian backed Chris up.

The girls may have egged Chris on because they had ulterior motives. Many students were aware of Brian and Chris's fascination with Columbine. Perhaps the girls were concerned about it, and were attempting to get proof that they could take to the authorities. But it didn't matter. Nothing came of it.

According to Officer Oak's report, the incident was cleared up after Brian and Chris assured her that they were teasing the girls about the shooting. There was an hour-long discussion in which both boys agreed they had behaved inappropriately and promised not to toy with anyone like that again.

But what Officer Oaks did not realize was that even if Chris and Brian were not seriously planning a school shooting, they were not joking. Their talk was a symptom of a deep psychological problem that at least one of the boys was either developing, or already suffered from.

The second investigation was not so easily dismissed.

The dance that Chris had been referring to in the phone call with the two girls arrived. Chris and Brian did not commit a school shooting, but they reenacted one on the bleachers across from the dance floor.

During the dance, Brian and Chris stalked the bleachers pretending they were carrying weapons and shooting people. Sometimes Brian's friend Joey Lacey joined them. Brian and Chris practiced their positions. They discussed how they would set up for the next dance, what their disguises would be, and which rooms in the school they would hide their ammunition in. They even planned out their best strategies for escape.

No one paid much attention to them and the dance ended uneventfully.

But Chris was about to change that.

The dance was the last event before spring break, which ran from the thirteenth of March through the twenty-first. School was out until Monday, March twenty-second.

Every year over spring break, the middle schools offer a class trip to Washington DC for students who can afford to attend. Thirty-six Irving students and their chaperones spent a week in Washington DC, New York City, and Gettysburg and Arlington National Cemetery. Chris was one of them. At the end of the week, on Sunday March 21, the students returned to Pocatello. They flew into the Salt Lake City airport and boarded a bus for the three-hour drive back home. Chris sat next to Andrew Witcher, a friend of Brian Draper's, on the bus. Katie Moore sat in the seat in front of them. At some point during the trip, Chris asked Katie if she would go out with him, but Katie turned him down, saying she was not interested in having a relationship with a boy at that time. She wanted to concentrate on her schoolwork and her grades.

Afterwards Katie turned to Chris. She knew that he and Brian talked obsessively about Columbine. She did not want him to hurt himself, or commit a shooting, because she'd turned him down. She asked Chris to promise her that he wouldn't.

Chris told Katie and Andrew that during the last dance he and his friends Brian Draper and Joey Lacey had planned out a school shooting--a dance would be the perfect opportunity, with the large number of students in a small confined space. Chris said the three of them had made up positions at the dance as to who would stand where, and who would use what weapon. Chris would bring the guns to school because he and his father had collected guns, and Brian was unable to get any.

Katie asked Chris why he would want to do such a thing.

Chris said, "I want to kill myself, so that I can be with my father."

Katie knew that Chris's father had died of cancer. She said that she understood: "I've had those kinds of feelings myself."

Later, when the bus arrived in Pocatello, Katie and Andrew

approached Officer Kristen Oaks, who had been one of the chaperones on the trip. Katie and Andrew told her what Chris had said on the bus ride home.

Andrew also informed Officer Oaks that Chris had a friend who was obsessed with the Columbine High School shooting. He was referring to Brian Draper. Officer Oaks noted the statement in her report, but she did not specify who that friend was, nor did she question Andrew about his identity.

Officer Oaks stated in her report that Andrew informed her that Chris had gone so far as to describe the disguise he and his friends were planning to wear during the shooting: ski masks, leather gloves, thick shoes, hoods, overcoats and dark sunglasses. Chris had said he would transport the guns to the school in a large bag with a large amount of M-80s.

Chris was already on Officer Oaks radar because of the previous incident with the phone call. This was the same subject coming up yet again with him. She had to take it seriously. The officer informed Principal Jim Harrell of the situation, and they immediately began setting up meetings with the three boys involved: Chris Nix, Brian Draper, Joey Lacey, and their parents.

That Monday morning, Brian Draper found himself in the principal's office for the second time facing questions regarding his actions and a "planned" school shooting. Officer Oaks questioned Brian about the dance, asking if he'd been pretending to hold a gun and shoot people. Brian, thinking someone had seen him, and probably turned him in, came up with a quick story.

Brian said that he had been with Chris Nix at the dance, and they had been walking around acting as though they were holding paint ball guns and shooting students with paint balls. This story seemed to satisfy Officer Oaks because she did not pursue the line of questioning further. Nor did she remark upon the coincidence of her previous investigation and the fact that Brian and Chris were found mimicking a shooting during the very dance that they had once claimed, on tape, they were going to use to commit a school shooting.

It was a testimony to Brian's power of manipulation. He knew enough to mix fact with fiction to make his story more believable. Brian told Officer Oaks that while he and Chris were walking around the dance, Chris accidentally bumped into another student, Wyatt Calvin. Wyatt was angry with Chris for bumping into him, and they argued. Chris tried to walk away, but Wyatt wouldn't let him go. Finally Chris became angry and accused Wyatt of trying to start a problem with him. By the time Chris was able to break contact with Wyatt, he was upset. He began walking around the dance still pretending that he was holding some sort of a gun, but now Chris was acting as though he were actually killing people.

It was an easy story to verify. Chris had bumped into Wyatt, and there had been an altercation. It gave Brian added credibility. It did not hurt Brian that his mother was present for the interview either.

Pamela Draper would never give the impression that her family was anything less than perfect. She had no problem convincing the officer that there was no way Brian could be involved in the kinds of problems Chris obviously had.

Officer Oaks asked Brian, "Do you know if Chris has access to guns?"

Brian said that Chris claimed there was a large safe in his father's house that was full of guns, but Brian admitted he had never seen the safe because he had never been in the house.

"What about Joey Lacey?" Officer Oaks asked.

Brian said that Joey had spent his time going back and forth between the boys and the dance floor, and had no real involvement in what happened.

Officer Oaks asked Brian if he believed Chris would commit a school shooting. Brian said that he wasn't certain, but he believed Chris was all talk. When Officer Oaks asked Brian to explain what he meant, Brian said that Chris had once told him that he had an X-box and a trampoline, but when he visited Chris at home, he learned that Chris did not have either one.

Brian stated that he was under the impression that Chris would say things in the hopes of having friends.

Officer Oaks next spoke with Joey Lacey about the incident. His mother was present also during the meeting. It is clear from the police report that by the time Officer Oaks met with Joey, she'd already minimized Brian's involvement in the incident. Her questions focused primarily on Chris.

Officer Oaks asked Joey if he had been with Chris Nix during the dance. Joey admitted that he had been with Chris at the beginning of the dance, but left to dance with his girlfriend. During this time, Joey said that he saw Chris and Brian together on the bleachers, and they were both acting as though they were holding some sort of a long gun. Officer Oaks asked Joey what he thought the two boys were doing. Joey said he didn't know. He hadn't asked them, or participated in the activity.

Officer Oaks asked if Joey had heard Chris planning a school shooting. Joey recalled an incident in which Chris had been talking on the phone, and had been recorded saying there was going to be a school shooting during a dance. But that had already been reported.

Officer Oaks asked Joey if he felt that Chris was capable of committing a school shooting. Joey said he wasn't certain, but that Chris said a lot of things in order to get attention, and what he said was not always necessarily the truth.

Chris was questioned last. He was brought into Principal Harrell's office, along with his mother, and told that he was being questioned about comments he had made. In spite of the fact that Chris had spent a year discussing school shootings with Brian, he immediately denied that he'd ever taken part in such a conversation, other than the previously reported phone call that had been made in February.

Officer Oaks calmly told Chris that Andrew Witcher and Katie Moore had informed her of the conversation that took place on the bus ride home from the American Heritage Tour. Chris was caught, but he tried to explain his actions.

Katie and Andrew must have misunderstood him, Chris claimed. He never said that *he* was planning a school shooting--his friends Brian Draper and Joey Lacey were. Chris said he was with Brian and Joey as they walked up and down the bleachers during the last dance, pointing out places where they could stand, planning a shooting. Chris also stated that Brian and Joey were seeking out people at the dance that they specifically wanted to kill, and he named Wyatt Calvin as one of those individuals.

When Officer Oaks asked Chris if he thought that Brian and Joey were serious, Chris said that he did not think so. They didn't have the guns. Officer Oaks asked what kind of guns Brian and Joey would use if they had them. Chris said Joey would probably be holding a shotgun and Brian was probably holding an M-16. He based his belief on the way he saw the two boys holding their pretend weapons.

During the meeting with Officer Oaks, Chris flatly denied that he had any personal involvement in the talk, or planning, of a school shooting, which undoubtedly hurt his credibility. But he repeatedly told the officer that Brian was obsessed with the Columbine High School massacre and that Brian wanted to see another Columbine occur at Irving Middle School. Chris claimed that Brian had violent posters hanging on the walls of his bedroom, as well as letters about the Columbine shooting on his computer. If Officer Oaks really believed someone was dangerous; she needed to look at Brian.

Chris was allowed to leave the office, but Officer Oaks wasn't finished with him yet. In her report Officer Oaks stated that she questioned Pamela Draper about the items Chris claimed were in Brian's bedroom. Pamela Draper denied there were posters depicting weapons or violence on her son's walls, and said that she did not allow those types of items in her home.

But Officer Oaks did not take the time to drive over to the Draper home and verify the information for herself, and she never questioned any of Brian's other friends either. She could have asked them to confirm, or deny, Chris's story, but she didn't. And as a result, Brian's obsession with Columbine was left unobserved by those in authority who should have caught it.

One week later, Tanya Nix was called back to the school. She was met by Officer Oaks and Principal Harrell. They told her that they'd finished questioning everyone involved in the incident, and they had some concerns about Chris, whom they felt had been talking to Katie and Andrew about the school shooting in the first person, and that when he was confronted, he had put Brian and Joey into the scenario without their knowledge.

Officer Oaks leaned forward and looked directly at Tanya. "Does Chris have access to any types of weapons, especially guns?"

Tanya is a tiny woman with long dark hair. Chris is her only child. She had lost her husband through divorce and then to cancer. She knew what her son was going through, but she never saw this coming.

Tanya said that Chris's father had actually collected guns, and had allowed Christopher to shoot them starting at a very young age. She described a green gun safe, installed in a wall in her ex-husbands house, where she believed he had kept his guns while he was alive, but since he had passed away approximately two years earlier she did not know if someone had taken possession of the guns, or where they were located. She was unaware of the combination to the safe in his home.

Tanya said that she did not own any guns herself, and that there weren't any weapons inside her residence where Christopher resided with her.

Officer Oaks asked Tanya about Christopher's bedroom. What was in it?

Tanya said Christopher's bedroom was decorated in a sailboat theme with the main colors being red and white. There were several nautical type pictures around the room, as well as a couple of posters that Christopher had hung up, displaying fancy cars. There was nothing of a violent nature, depicting weapons, or having anything to do with the Columbine shooting in Christopher's room. When Officer Oaks asked her how she could be certain, Tanya said that she regularly went into her son's bedroom where she straightened up and put away his clothes.

Mr. Harrell asked Tanya for permission to have the school psychologist evaluate Christopher. Tanya agreed. She also agreed to allow Christopher to attend Kinport Academy, also known as New Horizons, when Mr. Harrell explained to her that it would be a smaller classroom environment with more one-on-one contact from the teacher, but Tanya knew the truth.

The school district could not afford the risk of allowing Chris to remain in school. He was being expelled. They considered him dangerous, they wanted a psychological examination, and for now they were putting him in the school for troubled youth, where they could closely monitor him.

Chris wasn't present for the meeting, but Officer Oaks and Principal Harrell needed him to clear up some things that he'd told them earlier. They asked Tanya to remain in the office while they talked to her son once more.

When Chris arrived, Officer Oaks said that there were several inconsistencies in his story. She told Chris that Brian's mother denied there were violent posters in Brian's bedroom.

Chris said that the posters were definitely there, placed between the bunk beds and the wall. When Officer Oaks asked Chris why Mrs. Draper would lie, Chris said that he didn't know, but he was the one that was there. He knew what he saw. He insisted he was not making it up.

Next, Officer Oaks asked what exactly happened at the school dance. Chris said all he remembered was leaving the gym to go to the bathroom, and that when he returned, Brian and Joey were acting out a shooting. But when Officer Oaks asked Chris specifically what they were doing, Chris was vague and said he couldn't remember.

Officer Oaks and Principal Harrell believed that Chris was

the one obsessed with Columbine, and Chris's absolute refusal to admit his own involvement made it impossible for them to believe anything he said. The more Chris pointed his finger at Brian, the less they listened to him. Officer Oaks told Chris she believed he was trying to involve Brian and Joey in something they were not involved in.

Chris vehemently denied it. He said that Brian was the one who instigated everything. Chris admitted that he did not have many friends at school, but he had no intention of hurting anyone. It was Brian they needed to talk to…

But they would not listen.

Officer Oaks told Chris that people will sometimes do things that anger or hurt us. She said that it would not be normal to actually kill a person because of this, and if he were experiencing those kinds of feelings, of actually wanting to take another person's life, he needed to talk to someone he could trust about it, so that they could put him in touch with the appropriate person to help him handle those feelings.

Christopher said that he would do that. He had a close relationship with his mother, and he could talk to her. But he again insisted that it was Brian she needed to talk to.

That was the end of Officer Oaks report.

Instead of looking at Brian, Officer Oaks looked the other way. She labeled Chris the troubled one, and removed him from the school. The problem was solved and the issue closed.

And it probably would have remained closed except that Brian truly was the troubled one. Brian desperately needed help, but he never received any help at all. And he ended up killing his classmate, Cassie Jo Stoddart, in the eleventh grade.

After that horrible tragedy Brian's computer was seized, opened and searched. There sat the proof that Chris Nix had warned them about two years earlier.

Brian had created a website dedicated to the Columbine killers. There were hundreds of pictures of the school downloaded on his computer, some taken as the shooting was actually taking place. But more troubling still were the stories Brian had written. The ones he'd been referring to on his *Myspace* account when he said that some of his favorite things to read were the stories *he had written.*

Brian clearly lived out his fantasies in his writings, and some of them were deeply disturbing. One of the stories was called *Black River*, which Brian originally wrote when he was in the eighth grade, but he updated it as he grew older.

Black River is the story of Brian Draper and Chris Nix performing a school shooting in all of its gory and gruesome detail. Brian describes his thoughts and feelings; and the sights, smells and taste he experiences as he kills his fellow classmates. He gives a body count, a detailed description of what types of wounds he inflicted, and ends with his own obituary and memorial testimonies. It is a very graphic and horrific piece of writing.

Chris Nix was unaware of the story. Brian wrote it alone in his room unbeknownst to anyone. After Cassie's death, when *Black River* was found on Brian's computer, and Chris's name was identified, Chris was questioned by the police.

Detectives told Chris that his name was linked to a story they'd found on Brian Draper's computer, and revealed the subject matter. They may have even let Chris read it. Chris swore to the detectives investigating Cassie's homicide that he'd never heard of *Black River.* He explained that he lost all contact with Brian in the eighth grade. He knew nothing about the story and could not explain why his name was in it.

I don't know if the detectives were aware of the history behind Chris Nix and Brian Draper or not. Maybe Chris told them about Brian's fascination with Columbine. If he did he wasn't the only one. As detectives questioned Brian's friends, Brian's obsession with Columbine came up again and again.

After having spent years fantasizing about his heroes, Dylan Klebold and Eric Harris, when he was arrested for murder, Brian found he did like the comparison after all. From his jail cell Brian proclaimed his innocence to everyone he could reach, either by phone or letter, including friends from his past. Chris Nix was one of them.

Chris hadn't spoken with Brian since the day he was expelled from Irving Middle School. That event had been dramatic enough to separate the two boys completely. When Brian called Chris, after his arrest, it was from the recorded phone at the jail. Brian called collect and Tanya Nix answered. She accepted the charges and called Chris to the phone.

Brian began by telling Chris that he was calling to apologize for the way their friendship ended "on such a sour note." Chris told Brian it was all right.

Brian said, "I guess you heard what happened?"

Chris said, "Everyone has. So are you…calling from the

jail?"

Brian said, "Yeah, Dude. I can't believe it. I'm, I'm locked in a cell for like twenty-three hours a day. It's *un*-real."

"Jeez"

"Yeah. But I didn't do it. Ya know, ya know I didn't do it," Brian said.

"Yeah, I didn't think so." Chris responded, even though he did.

It was while talking to Chris that Brian found out that the detectives had a copy of *Black River*.

Chris said, "You know, the police questioned me about a story they found on your computer."

"What?"

"Yeah. A story with my name in it, about a shooting."

At first Brian acted as if he didn't know what Chris was talking about, but as Chris provided more details, Brian suddenly said, "O-h-h…God! *That* story. Oh man…I wrote that a long time ago, I…forgot all about it." There was panic in his voice. "Ohh man…that's really going to hurt me!" And he meant it. It was. "I just wrote that story to vent my emotions. I didn't mean anything by it. You believe me don't you?"

Chris said, "Sure."

"I just used your name in the story, it didn't mean anything."

"It's alright."

They talked about the jail and what it was like for Brian to be there. Brian told Chris he was a Christian now; and Chris, who is a Christian, replied, "I'm glad to hear that. I'm proud of you for that."

Brian's time ran out and the call ended. I believe that was the last time Chris Nix ever spoke to Brian Draper. It was kind of strange. The last time Chris had contact with Brian was the day he'd been removed from the school. Chris had sat in the principal's office and told the principal and Officer Oaks that Brian was dangerous. They didn't believe him, but he'd been right. The very next time Chris spoke with Brian, Brian was sitting in a jail cell awaiting trial for murder.

Four years after his involvement with Brian Draper, Chris Nix is doing well. His mother removed him from Kinport Academy almost immediately after he was placed there and sent him to live with friends in California, where he attended a Christian prep school.

Chris returned to Pocatello the following year as a sophomore and attended Century High School where he graduated in May of 2008. Chris is now a student at the University of California in Santa Barbara, majoring in psychology.

I believe Chris Nix had a relationship with Brian Draper similar to the one my son Torey had. Both boys briefly talked about things with Brian that they never meant. And neither boy took Brian seriously until it was too late. Thankfully, Chris made it out okay. Torey did not.

CHAPTER TWENTY-THREE

Recorded Conversations

The prosecution was recording and listening to every phone call that Torey and Brian made, as well as every visit that they received. It was easy for them. They had available personnel at the jail that they assigned to listen to the tapes during their regular shifts at work. But if we wanted our attorneys to listen to the tapes, we had to pay them an hourly fee to do so.

Our attorneys charged a hundred and sixty-five dollars an hour. For them to listen to the tapes would have cost us approximately fifteen hundred dollars a week. We couldn't afford that on top of the legal defense. The best solution was for me to listen to the tapes, and log any important information that I found.

I went to the attorneys' office and picked up a disc of the available recordings. They ran in chronological order starting from the day of the boys' arrests on September 27th, 2006, and ran through December 3rd. I started listening to the tapes in mid-December. I finished them at the end of January.

Because the tapes were chronologically recorded, I was able to follow the emotional journey of both families from the arrests through the preliminary hearing. As I listened to Brian's tapes, I felt more empathy for his family, an *understanding* of what they were experiencing, rather than a reliving of the events themselves.

But as I listened to Torey's tapes, my heart actually remembered what it felt at the time the words were spoken, and the feelings of horror, pain and loss overwhelmingly came back to me. The tapes only covered an eight-week period, but it felt like a lifetime.

I started with Brian's tapes.

The first recording was of Brian and his father, Kerry. It was the night of Brian's arrest, and Brian was asking Kerry how long he thought it was going to be before he, (Brian) was allowed to go home. He had cooperated with the police. Blamed Torey. He was ready to go.

Kerry told Brian that he didn't know how long this was going to take, but he tried to reassure his son that it was going to be okay. Brian said he had a cell by himself and he was going to be kept separate from the rest of the inmates. He was not scared; he just wanted to go home.

Kerry told Brian that their house was being searched. Kerry was standing on the front lawn of his residence, watching detectives and sheriff personnel swarm his house. You could tell by Kerry's voice that he was in shock, but his concern was for Brian. Brittany and Pam were not there, it was just Kerry, alone, watching what was happening in disbelief, and trying to reassure his son.

I could picture Kerry. I hadn't watched our home being searched, but I'd driven by it. I knew what Kerry was seeing. The sheriff's department would have sent out a task force of vehicles and people to surround and search his house. I imagined Kerry watching as every window in his house was lit up, and he could see the people inside rummaging through every nook and corner of what had been, just a few short hours earlier, his life.

Kerry had already been through a gamut of emotions that day. He'd learned that Brian had been present when Cassie was killed. He had sat through an extremely emotional police interrogation with his son. He had accompanied Brian and several sheriffs' personnel to Blackrock Canyon where Brian located the evidence. He had watched as his son was taken into custody and charged with First Degree Murder. Watching the detectives search his house was a continuation of the day's nightmare.

I don't know if Kerry believed his son's story that day or not. Deep down I doubt it. But Kerry was hoping and praying with every fiber of his being that what Brian said was true, and his son was not a murderer.

The next call was Pam and Kerry Draper. They were at home, speaking with Brian on separate phone extensions so that they could talk with him simultaneously. That was how they conducted most of their telephone conversations, and I soon observed that Kerry was available for most of Brian's calls.

At first I wondered how Brian was able to catch Kerry so often while he was at home from work. But as I listened I realized that Kerry actually worked out of state. His job flew him back and forth periodically, but most of his work was done from home, which enabled him to be available for Brian when he called during the day.

The majority of the conversations recorded were between Brian and his parents. I noticed that Brian had little interaction with his sister during the period of time I listened to. I found that odd. Each had lost essentially their only sibling. I thought they would have fought harder to stay together. Especially when I considered

Lacey and Jamie's reactions. They never missed a visit with their brother. But Brian's sister seemed to be shielded from what was happening.

Our family's goal from the beginning was to get through this together. Families function better as a whole, and when one part of the family component is missing, or in trouble, it throws everything off balance and the family relationships suffer. Our goal was not to allow that to happen. Torey may not have been *physically* with us, but he was still a very important part of our family and we would do whatever it took to keep him an active part in each of our lives.

When I first started listening to the Draper tapes, I expected them to reveal a dysfunctional family, or at least a family dealing with the repercussions of what their son had done. That is what I truly believed I was going to hear. But there was no hint of that. There were no breakdowns, no acknowledgements of guilt. Just love and support for a son, who was lost and in trouble.

It caught me off guard.

Pam and Kerry called Brian, "Their Little Bry-Bry" and themselves "Mommy and Daddy." Brian's mother told him over and over again that she loved him more than any other mother ever loved her son. She was so convincing that as I listened to her, I started to have an insane thought. *Perhaps Pam loved Brian more than I loved Torey! Perhaps this happened because I did not love Torey enough!*

I began to question everything I believed. I'd always thought that Sean and I were good parents. Sometimes we argued and fought, and money was tight, but we loved our children and each other. But suddenly I could see that Sean and I were not the parents that we thought we were. That we had not done the job of raising our children that we thought we had; and that we had, in fact, failed our children in several ways.

Kerry seemed so smart. So successful. And Pam was patient and nurturing. Their family life sounded so perfect. Our family life, which I had been so proud of, so grateful for, paled in comparison to theirs. Every family that I knew paled in comparison to theirs, and I wondered, how could this be? It did not make sense. Brian was sitting in prison for murder for Christ Sake!

I went to Sean. I told him about my feelings and how deeply the contents of the tapes were affecting me. Sean hadn't listened to the tapes, but he told me that the Drapers had an agenda. They were purposely portraying themselves in a particular manner for the prosecutors and detectives whom they knew were listening to the tapes. Sean said that my emotional reaction was proof of their manipulative abilities.

It was my guilt over losing Torey that made me feel that I hadn't loved him enough. I thought that if I'd loved Torey more, watched him closer, listened harder, this never would have happened. I blamed myself, and that is what I never heard in the Draper tapes. The Drapers never blamed themselves. Not once.

Sean told me that if I was going to effectively listen to the tapes, I needed to put my emotions aside and listen to them objectively. That was ridiculous. I'm a mother. I knew I would never be able to do that. But finally Sean came up with a technique I could use. Before I let my emotions take over, I needed to stop and compare every statement that the Drapers made to what we already knew about them. That helped; that and the information that I had gotten from Adam about the school shooting.

Deep down I knew that Brian's family was not as perfect as they pretended to be. But I could not understand how they could act as if Brian were innocent, when they had to know that he was not.

The reality was, the tapes were disingenuous. These were not conversations that were being secretly recorded. These were conversations where everyone was mindful of whom they were speaking to, as well as to who was listening. Everyone was careful of what they said, and everything said had a purpose.

In our attempt to comfort our sons, the Draper's conversations and ours were very similar. We proclaimed our love for our children, our belief in their innocence, and a hope for their future. We tried desperately to give them a purpose and a reason to go on. Both families used everything from the spiritual promise of God's plan, to a decent book, as a way to make sense out of the senseless, and take our children's minds off their circumstances long enough to fill a few of the long, lonely hours of nothingness.

But how we dealt with the detectives listening to the tapes was where we differed.

Sean and I were instructed not to talk about the case with Torey. That was very difficult for me especially, but we tried our best to follow the guidelines the attorneys laid out for us. But the Drapers must not have been given the same advice. They must have been told to use every opportunity they had on the recorded phone to blame Torey for Cassie death and proclaim Brian's innocence, because that is exactly what they did.

Within days of Brian's arrest Pamela Draper started talking to him about Nori Jones.

Nori was a young woman who had lived around the corner from us, when we lived in the house on Nixon Street. I did not know Nori personally, but she attended the church I grew up in, and was engaged to the son of a friend of mine. Nori had been brutally murdered in her home two years earlier. The crime was unsolved.

An early newspaper report following Brian and Torey's arrest commented on how closely Torey lived to the Nori Jones homicide scene and insinuated that Torey could have been responsible for her death. Brian's defense attorneys leapt at the possibility, but the prosecution admitted that there was no evidence linking Torey to the crime.

After the story ran, Sean and I were contacted and told not to worry about the allegations. We were told that the case was solved, but that there was not enough evidence as yet to charge the person responsible, who was currently in prison on unrelated charges.

But, Brian's attorneys kept trying to link Torey's name with Nori's, until finally Judge McDermott had enough. He told them they could no longer waste the court's time with smoke screens and ordered them to stop.

I thought that would be the end of it--but it wasn't. Pam Draper continued to talk about Nori Jones when she was alone on the phone with Brian. Even though Kerry did not seem to support her point of view, Pam continued to insist that Torey could have killed her.

At the time of Nori's death, Torey was just fourteen years old. For him to kill Nori, he would have had to sneak out of the house on a school night, even though his bedroom was directly across from Sean's and mine. Torey would have had to break into a house that he was unfamiliar with, alone, in the pitch-dark, and kill someone that he had never met before, with a weapon that he did not own. He would have had to leave behind DNA evidence that belonged to someone else, and dispose of everything that linked him to the crime in a location that would never be found, and still manage to attend school the next morning.

It was ludicrous.

Pam's allegations made me so angry that I wanted to confront her. The truth is, Nori Jones and her family deserve to have her killer brought to justice, and hopefully someday that will happen. But Pam's self serving agenda did not seem to care about that. In my opinion, Pam acted as if she would have been just as happy to see Torey blamed for Nori's death, and Nori's killer go free, as to see the real killer caught, and that is extremely sad and selfish. Perhaps someday Pam will realize that.

As I listened to the tapes I noticed that, while our lives clearly ended, the Drapers seemed to go on. Sometimes when Brian called, his parents would be in a restaurant. Once they were at a sporting event with friends. Even at this early date, after their son's arrest, there seemed to be a life in the background. While Kerry and Pam were clearly concerned about Brian, he wasn't all they talked about.

I couldn't understand it. I couldn't understand how they could love Brian and leave him, because that is what it felt like to me. To move on would be to leave behind, and that, to me, was unthinkable.

We didn't go to restaurants. We tried, but we couldn't. One Sunday, Jeff offered to take us out to breakfast, but it wasn't the same without Torey, who always ordered a German pancake and buttered it so particularly that most of us would finish eating before he even started.

I appreciated Jeff's offer, but it was the last time I went out for a long, long time.

I used every bit of energy I had to go to work, and the rest of the time I lay in bed or on the couch. Lacey and Jamie were with me, but I was consumed with Torey. I did not want to let go of Torey. I was hanging on to him, his fear, his loneliness, his hopelessness. I did not know what Torey had to live for, and if Torey had nothing to live for, then I had nothing to live for either.

Before Torey's arrest the kids and I would watch the sitcom *Friends* together. Jamie, knowing that we needed a diversion in our lives, continued the practice. He recorded the program on the DVR and each day after school and work, while I was lying on the couch and he was doing his homework, he would play an episode. Lacey would come downstairs and watch it with us. It was good to be together and it became our routine.

One day we were downstairs watching an episode of *Friends*, and before I knew what was happening I laughed. It caught me off guard and I clasped my hands over my mouth and burst into tears. How could I laugh while my son was in prison? Both Lacey and Jamie told me it was okay, I hadn't done anything wrong, but I knew that Torey would never laugh again, and I hated myself for forgetting that for one single second.

I was incapable of letting go, and it confused me when the Drapers could, and it made me angry when Sean tried. If Sean tried to have a good day, crack a smile, or enjoy a meal--I saw it as a betrayal. A physical betrayal of our son and I told him so. If he truly loved Torey, he would not want anything that Torey could not have. It was different for Lacey and Jamie. Their lives were still ahead of them. But for Sean and me, life was over.

Sean told me that Lacey and Jamie deserved a normal life and that would only be possible if they had two parents who shared a normal life with them. If we sacrificed everything for Torey, we'd have nothing left to give them, and that wouldn't be fair to anyone.

I knew that what Sean was saying was true. I loved my children so much, but everything hurt so bad, and felt so wrong. All I wanted was my baby back. I could not see a way to go on without him.

It took me a long time before I understood that adjusting was not moving on, that adjusting was not accepting what was happening. That adjusting is just what we do when we have no choice. It does not mean our love is diminishing. Surviving does not mean we've forgotten. But it is a hard lesson to learn and it's a lesson that I still struggling with every single day.

I believe it *seemed* easier for Kerry and Pam because they knew that their son had problems. They were not negligent parents. And as unbelievable as it must have been for them, they had to face the fact that Brian stabbed Cassie, and they had to deal with the host of emotions that that knowledge brought.

It didn't mean they stopped loving Brian. They didn't. But they dealt with the situation differently. Brian was not an innocent child. It wasn't easy to let Brian go, but it was possible. It was not an injustice. It was just a devastating loss.

Brian never admitted on any of the tapes that I listened to that he stabbed Cassie alone, but he might have come close.

In one hysterical call, Brian told his parents that he needed to speak with Dave Martinez right away. He'd just received a letter from Matt's father telling him that he needed to man up and tell the truth. Brian said he wanted to do that. He was tired of lying. Brian kept threatening to tell his parents what he'd done, while they kept cutting him off, begging him to stop and remember what he had to lose.

At the end of the call, Brian had not confessed, but only because of the efforts of Kerry and Pam to prevent him from doing so.

When I finished with Brian's tapes, I began listening to Torey's. His began with the first visit we had with him at the jail. I recognized it right away when I heard it. Torey had been arrested three days earlier, but we had not been separated from him by mere days. It had been an eternity.

It was Sunday morning, October 1, 2006. Sean and I rose early and waited for Lacey and Jamie to wake up. When they did, we headed to the jail. It was dawn and the sun was rising.

We did not know what to expect when we got there. The jail sat on the outskirts of town. We passed it every time we went snowboarding at Pebble Creek in the winter, or dirt bike riding in Blackrock Canyon during the summer. (Ironically, Blackrock Canyon was right around the bend from the jail). But we'd never paid any attention to the building. It was so nondescript. Just a long, low, mud colored facility with a flagpole, and a tidy strip of narrow lawn that separated a row of parking spaces from the highway.

Sean pulled into the parking lot. There weren't any windows in the front of the building, but there was a sidewalk that led to two double doors. When we tried the doors they were locked. We looked around to see if we were in the right place, but there was nowhere else to go.

I asked Sean if this was where he had dropped the commissary money off on Thursday night. Sean said it was. We noticed an intercom system outside the doors and pressed the button. We were told that we needed to wait outside. They would unlock the doors a half an hour or so before visiting began. While we stood outside other people started to arrive and soon we were part of a group waiting to get in. It was cold and there were complaints about the weather.

I looked at the faces around me. There were a few men, but mostly women, and young mothers with small children. There was a mother with her teenaged daughters, hard-faced and tightly clothed; and an elderly grandmother, ancient and shaking with the cold. Almost everyone smoked. I tried to imagine the other prisoners who were inside with Torey by the looks of the people who were outside with us.

Finally the doors opened and everyone rushed to get inside.

Before Sean and I knew what we were supposed to do, they immediately formed a line and we found ourselves at the end of it. In front of the line was an old desk with a computer monitor. A single officer sat behind the desk and checked each visitor in one at a time on the computer. He performed some sort of ID check, verifying driver's licenses, and I was grateful Sean had thought to bring Lacey's driver's license and Jamie's school activity card with us.

There were a few chairs scattered along the two facing walls of the waiting room, and as each person finished checking in they sat in one of the available chairs until all were taken. We had Lacey and Jamie sit down while Sean and I waited in line, so they got a seat, but a lot of people did not. Those of us left had to sit on the floor or stand as we waited to visit our loved one.

Even after everyone was finally checked in, it took a long time for the visits to begin. An officer had to gather the requested inmates, transfer them to the visiting booths, and secure them inside before they could go and get Torey, who wasn't even allowed to intermingle in the halls with the other inmates.

The last time I saw Torey was when he was taken into custody. It had been such a surreal experience. I'd simply watched as officers led my baby right out of my life. Sitting in the waiting room, waiting to see Torey--was almost as unreal. It was hard to believe that we were really at the jail, and that Torey was somewhere deep inside.

Finally our names were called and we were directed to a door through which we could visit our son and brother. They let us in together: Sean, Jamie, Lacey and I, though they let us know that generally only two people were allowed to visit at a time.

We entered a small room. The door locked as it closed behind us. There were three booths. The first was empty, the second was empty, Torey sat alone in the third.

I think I smiled when I saw Torey. I wanted to give him that small gesture of hope and I believe I was able to. He looked so frightened, but it was good just to see him. Of course he was separated from us by a glass partition, but he was *there.* He was real and he was alive.

There was a metal stool on each side of the glass and a phone secured to the wall. Torey sat alone on his side of the glass and I sat directly across from him on ours. Sean and the kids gathered close behind me. I looked intently at Torey. I longed to reach through the glass and hold him, but my eyes were the only part of me that could reach him.

Lacey was quietly crying, but Torey could not hear her. The glass was soundproof. Torey picked up his phone and Sean picked up ours. There was a pre-recorded message on the phone, but as soon as it ended, Sean began to gush excitedly. He told Torey how much we loved him. But Torey cut him off.

Torey had been through hell. After being arrested, he was taken to the jail, booked into custody, given a handbook, taken to a cell, and placed in isolation. Aside from the one phone call he had been allowed the day after his arrest, Torey had sat for three long days, alone in his cell, completely cut off from human contact, with no idea what was going on and when he would see his family again. One guard said that Torey had sat on his bunk, staring at one spot on the wall, hour after endless hour.

He was alone and terrified. When we saw Torey on Sunday we had a mere half an hour with him before he was again taken back into isolation, where he would ultimately remain for the next ten months.

Torey told Sean, "I need to be able to contact you. I'm let out of my cell for an hour each day, but I can't call you on the cell phone."

We did not know that we could set up a calling account through our cell phone. Sean said, "We're getting a landline installed Torey. It should be up in a few days. Can you hold on until then?"

Torey shook his head emphatically, "No."

Sean said, "Could you write to us?"

It was the wrong thing to say. Torey was frustrated. He knew the time was ticking on this visit and he wanted us to know that he needed us. *Now!* We had to think of a solution.

"I don't have an envelope. I don't have a stamp. I don't know how to send a letter from here!" he snapped.

Sean knocked on the door and asked the visiting guard who answered how Torey could get the supplies he needed to send a letter, and explained the procedure to Torey. But writing a letter and speaking with someone were two very different things, and Torey needed to be able to *speak* with us. We were all frustrated. But the only thing we could do, was wait for the phone line.

We quickly told Torey that we loved him, that we supported him, and that he had attorneys who were going to fight for him. The visit ended before we were ready, and as I listened to our goodbyes, promising to be back, begging Torey to hold on, I could feel myself being torn from my son all over again. I could see Torey standing, the guard entering the room, shackling Torey's wrists behind his back and leading him away. Torey walking down the corridor with his head hung so low he could see nothing but his shoes. It was a scene I witnessed week after week.

When the tape ended I felt the same as I had when I first started listening to Brian's tapes. That I was attempting to do something that was too difficult for me to do. I did not think that I was physically strong enough to relive what I was still struggling hard to deal with everyday. But this time I could not even talk to Sean about it. My feelings for Torey were too private and too personal.

But I had to continue listening. And I did.

During one of our early visits with Torey, Sean and I noticed how chapped his lips were. Torey kept licking his lips, and he had deep, dark circles under his eyes. Torey said he was so thirsty; he was only given a cup of milk at breakfast and dinner to drink.

Sean asked, "What about water?"

"They don't give me any."

We asked the visiting guard why Torey was being denied water, and he said that Torey had a sink in his cell to drink from. When we told Torey he was supposed to be drinking out of his sink he couldn't believe it. He never considered drinking from the sink a possibility.

It was a startling revelation. Torey had been raised on the water from the fridge dispenser. Drinking from a dirty sink next to a toilet hadn't even crossed his mind, as he lay dehydrating from thirst.

We wanted Torey to see a counselor. He had been through an incomprehensible experience and instead of getting help, as he could have had he been charged as a juvenile, Torey was thrown into an adult jail and placed in isolation.

The attorneys kept assuring us they would find a counselor for Torey, but it wasn't the priority for them that the legal case was and they procrastinated the chore. I was frustrated, but I didn't know what to do. Then I listened to a tape between Adam and Torey that forced me to act.

It was shortly before Halloween. Torey called Adam. His voice was low, barely audible, shaky and monotone, unlike anything I had previously heard. Torey told Adam that he'd been placed on suicide watch, where he was stripped naked and put in a smock (straightjacket), and thrown into a room off booking where he could be watched 24-7 by the guards, as well as anyone being booked into the facility.

Torey had a pillow and a blanket, and nothing else. He was fully exposed and restrained in a cold, concrete room where he was alone and scared and uncared for. That is how they prevent a suicide at the Bannock County jail.

I'm not sure how many days Torey spent on suicide watch. He never told us about it. Many of the details I received were from other families of inmates who had been placed there. But as I listened to the call between Torey and Adam, I realized that things were happening to Torey that he wasn't telling me about.

After Torey was released from suicide watch, he was put back into his cell. He called Adam at the first available opportunity. His voice was weak, as if he didn't want to talk about the experience, but had to. And as I listened I knew that Torey had called the right person. Had he called me, I would have lost it.

But Adam said and did all the right things. He listened. He was empathetic and upset by what his friend had endured, but he remained calm and supportive. Adam pointed out that Torey was safely back in his cell, which now did not seem as bad as it once had. By the end of the call Torey and Adam were actually talking about movies, and Halloween, which was right around the corner, and writing poetry. Torey had his voice back and he was ready to move forward. Adam took Torey through the crisis and came out on the other side with him. Something I do not believe I could have done.

But after that call, I got a counselor to see Torey myself. I did not concern myself with doctor-patient privilege, which does not exist in Idaho. Torey needed a doctor and I made sure he got one. There were three doctors who saw Torey while he was at Bannock County Jail. One counseled him weekly; one monitored his mental health, making sure he was not suicidal, and one conducted his psychological evaluations for the trial. Nothing they had to say hurt him.

Torey called Adam at least as often as he called home. Torey could be open and honest with Adam, but he could also just relax and be himself. They talked about movies and music and life. Adam gave Torey some normalcy, some laughter, and an opportunity to forget, at least temporarily, what was happening.

It was uncomfortable for me to listen to Torey and Adam's

private conversations. I felt like I was eavesdropping, but I learned some things about Torey that I never would have known if I hadn't.

Torey had never been separated from me. I believed he was dependent on me. I never saw Torey as an independent individual capable of taking care of himself, especially through something like this. In my mind, he was still my baby. But I found that Torey had an inborn ability to cope that *was* completely independent of me. Something I had never considered before.

If he were having a bad day, Torey would tell himself Calvin and Hobbs jokes to cheer himself up. He started an exercise routine in his room. He wrote poetry. He studied the Bible, read a large collection of books, and copied page after page of song lyrics and movies he hoped to own. He found ways to carry on. It was not easy, but Torey did it, and he did it by himself.

Torey's tapes were completely different from Brian's. All Brian did, in every conversation I listened to, was talk about his case. Listening to Brian going on and on about it every day made me sick. His voice got stuck in my head and I would wake up in the middle of the night in a cold sweat, with Brian's voice from the videotape ringing in my ears, saying, "I just killed Cassie, I just killed Cassie," over and over again. My heart would be racing a million miles an hour and I would have to lie in the dark and wait for it to slow down before I could roll over and try to go back to sleep again.

But Torey was exactly the opposite. He could not bring himself to talk about the case at all. If we asked Torey anything about life in the jail, or what happened to Cassie--we'd lose him. Torey did not want to talk about the jail, and he was not yet ready to face what had happened to Cassie.

Torey's refusal to talk about the situation was difficult for me. I worried about what was happening to him constantly. Sometimes, Torey would give us small tidbits of information, but it was hard to drag it out of him and frustrating for both of us. Torey told me not to worry about him, and I told him that was not possible.

Torey struggled with the emotions of losing his friend, Cassie, and watching his own life disappear right in front of his eyes. There was the denial, the grief, the loss, and the pain. Everything was gone so fast, all the potential. The life. Over.

Torey dealt with it the only way that he could. Instead of looking at the loss of his entire life, a future with a wife and children, he focused on the immediate loss of his friends at school and his family at home.

Torey dreamt about high school. He thought everyone there had turned against him. He had awful nightmares. It is hard for me to look back at the pictures from those days. In the first few news clippings Torey looked like a child, so young and scared, a deer caught in the headlights. In no time at all he looked like an old man, haggard. He lost weight and dark circles grew under his eyes and spread down his cheeks. He could not sleep and he refused to take anything to help, scared of what dreams might come.

Torey needed constant reassurance that he was still loved, because being in isolation, he could not directly see or feel that. He needed daily reminders, letters and cards, just to keep him going. Thankfully our family and friends were faithful in providing that support.

Torey spent long hours alone, waiting for someone to talk to. When he was finally allowed out of his cell, and the use of the telephone, he would talk so fast, trying to say everything he needed to say, but there was never enough *time*. The call would end and Torey would be cut off, taken back to his cell, and locked down for another twenty-three hours of solitude, before he would be let out again and given another half an hour usage of the phone, and a chance to speak with another living soul.

It was hard, and sometimes Torey gave up and turned inward. Sometimes he had nothing to say for days and we would have to draw him out. During our visits, Torey would sit and trace the lines in the wall with his finger, lost in his own thoughts, and ignoring everything around him. Torey once told me how many days he had gone without physical contact from another person. He counted the days where there was nothing, no brush or touch of human compassion.

Torey couldn't understand how this happened. In the beginning he could not even seem to believe that it *had* happened. It took a long time for the denial to pass. And even then, Torey couldn't believe that Brian actually planned to do it. That Brian, his friend, had been serious when he talked about killing Cassie. Torey believed it was an accident. That Brian was as impulsive as hell, and had probably surprised even himself by his own actions.

It is something I believe Torey questions to this day.

Once Torey told me he didn't think he could be friends with Brian again, after what he'd done. I wanted to shake Torey and scream at him, "Are you kidding me!! Of course you can't be friends with Brian! He's a murderer. He ruined your life and he killed

Cassie!" But I held my tongue. Torey had to work through the details of what happened in his own mind. I could not help him with that.

Torey's attorneys told him that Brian blamed him for Cassie's death. But until the preliminary hearing, Torey couldn't believe it. He thought that Brian was going to tell the truth and that the whole story would come out. After the preliminary hearing he was devastated. That night he called and talked to Lacey, who soothed him.

Torey was too young to help in his own legal defense. He trusted his attorneys. He put his whole future into their hands without a word or a question. In spite of what happened with Brian, it was difficult for Torey to lose his faith in people. He had spent his whole life with no reason not to trust them. Torey had experienced the greatest shock imaginable, but he was still the same person that he'd always been. He was still a loving, trusting child. Torey would not talk about his case. He left it up to his attorneys, and shut his eyes to what was happening around him.

After attending Brian's trial, I realized his whole defense was laid out in the telephone conversations he had with his parents. His defense had been laid out since the preliminary hearing. We should have laid out Torey's too. We should have been proclaiming Torey's innocence from the beginning. Instead we followed our attorney's advice. We waited until Torey's trial to say anything. We talked to Torey for nine long months about nothing but the books he could read, how he could fill his time, and all the different ways we loved and missed him.

As I was busy searching for my own answers, our attorneys were testing the physical evidence. They wanted to know exactly what we were up against. They hired an expert in crime scenes investigations to test the blood-splatter evidence and determine how exactly the attack on Cassie took place. They also hired a forensic pathologist to examine the autopsy procedure, the wounds Cassie had suffered, and identify if there had been one knife, or two, used in the attack.

They sent the items recovered from Blackrock Canyon to a lab in California for DNA testing, and we hired a forensic psychologist to evaluate Torey's psychological makeup. There was a lot of work to do and a lot of evidence to collect. Things we needed done, because we knew that what Torey was saying was true, and with the physical evidence we could prove it.

But everyone knew the videotape was going to be the most difficult challenge to overcome, and our attorneys simply did not know how to do it.

PART FIVE

The Videotape

CHAPTER TWENTY-FOUR

A Dangerous Acquaintance

The prosecution's case was built on the evidence collected from Blackrock Canyon. Quite literally without Brian Draper's cooperation, Mark Hiedeman would not have had a case. The items recovered were: two long sleeve black shirts, two masks, two pairs of gloves, a pair of heavy work boots, a sheet of paper, wooden matches, an empty bottle of hydrogen peroxide, four knives, and the videotape.

According to Mark Hiedeman the videotape was an obvious plan to commit premeditated murder, and the clothing was the disguise to carry it out. Plain and simple. He backtracked the purchase of the knives to a date in August, and placed that date as the beginning of the conspiracy. It was a hypothesis that made sense. But it was wrong. The real events did not quite fit together that easily.

Torey and Brian's friendship began with a plan to make a *movie* together. Some of the items recovered from Blackrock Canyon were fruit of that plan, specifically the two dagger knives and the masks. But something happened between the planning of the movie, and the murder of Cassie, that changed the original intent of the items. And to understand how that happened, you have to understand the mind of Brian Draper.

Brian had been talking about murder for years. He never talked about it seriously. It was always a joke to him. But murder was a "joke" Brian obsessed about. And his friends knew it. Torey got caught on tape, and Chris Nix got caught at school, unwittingly indulging Brian's relentless fixation with killing--but they weren't the only ones who did so. All of Brian's friends did. Just the week before, Brian sat with a group of friends in the Wal-Mart parking lot acting as if they were shooting people. Brian used the phrase, "It's just that easy," as he "picked-off" one unsuspecting shopper after another.

But no one came forward after Brian was arrested and said that they weren't surprised by his arrest. Everyone who came forward and told the police that Brian had been talking about killing people for years *also* told the police that they *were* surprised that he'd been involved.

It did not matter if Brian's friends indulged him or not. *No one* was taking him seriously. But unfortunately Cassie was killed because Brian *was* serious. Not just that weekend. He'd crossed the line a long time ago. By the time Brian found himself actually alone with Cassie, an unbelievably, perfectly vulnerable victim, he simply did not have the impulse control to stop himself.

And Torey, like Brian's other friends, was unaware of the danger.

Torey actually met Brian in his tenth grade science class. (I've always found it ironic that such a dangerous acquaintance could be made in such a presumably safe setting.) Their teacher, Mrs. Wilcox, allowed her students to sit together at tables set up throughout the room. Torey usually sat next to his friends, Cassie and Jade, but Jade moved near the end of the school year, and Brian would occasionally fill her vacant seat.

For most of the year, Torey and Brian were simply classmates. It was not until after they discovered that they shared a mutual love of movies that they became friends. Everyone who knew Torey knew that he wanted to be a director, and Brian was enthralled by the idea. Soon they were planning to make a movie together.

Torey and Brian talked about their plans at school, intending to get together over the summer and write a script. Cassie, who sat next to them, planned to be in their movie, along with her boyfriend Matt.

When the school year ended, Brian took a job for the city of Pocatello, and Torey enrolled in summer school classes. They seemed to lose touch. But then, in mid-July Brian knocked on our door. He didn't stay long that day, but that is when he and Torey resumed their plans to make a movie. A few weeks later, Brian came over to our house and he and Torey sat down and outlined their ideas together.

Torey used a black and white composition notebook to take notes. On the inside cover of the notebook Torey wrote IDEAS FOR THE MOVIE in bold letters. On the top line of the first page he wrote the word NAME, underneath which he listed two titles, *Black River* and *Dead Hills*. *Dead Hills* was Torey's suggestion; *Black River* was Brian's.

On the following page Torey wrote the word MASK on the top line. Under the heading are two descriptions. *Latex White* is first, and underneath that, *White Solid Pull Over.* On the following page the word WEAPONS is written. Underneath that category eleven different types of weapons are listed. *Hunting Knife, Survival Knife, Cutting Knife, Throwing Knife, Switch Blade, Pocket Knife, Sythe (sic) (Hand Held), Hatchet, Axe, Handgun, Chain Saw.*

The next page is the last page that's written on; it's headed KILLS. There are two brief movie plots outlined, each approximately a paragraph long. The first is of a girl who hits a deer while driving through the woods and is chased by two killers. The second is a description of a man running from a killer who gets stabbed.

When Torey and Brian finished discussing their movie ideas, Torey placed the notebook on his bedroom shelf where it sat for the next several weeks. Even though the notebook sat in plain sight, I never opened it. If I had, I would have been upset by the graphic outline and I would have spoken to Torey about it.

But Torey did tell me that he and Brian were planning to make a horror movie together. It was never a secret. And while I disapproved of the genre, truthfully I was not as concerned as I should have been. I knew that Torey was more interested in humor than violence, and even if Brian did intend to make a real "horror" movie--I didn't see how that would be possible. They were just a couple of kids. They wouldn't have the resources.

But thanks to Brian's summer job, he did have some money, and the plan moved forward. As specified in the outline, Brian purchased two masks, but they weren't latex; they were ceramic. I found one of the masks in Torey's bedroom closet. It was white with yellow and gold geometrical shapes painted on it. When I asked Torey what it was, he told me it was a prop Brian bought for the movie, but Brian was going to replace it because it wasn't right. They needed masks they could wear. This mask you had to hold in front of your face. The ceramic mask sat on Torey's shelf for a few days and then Brian took it home. Later, Brian purchased two white latex Halloween-style masks that slipped on over the head, with holes for the eyes and nose.

Next Brian purchased knives. Torey told me that he and Brian wanted to use realistic looking weapons, not the cheap plastic Halloween knives that he and his friends had used when they filmed scenes from the comedy *Scary Movie.* I told Torey that I didn't think we could find realistic looking weapons that were *safe*. I did not even consider looking. So, unbeknownst to me, Torey and Brian went looking for themselves. Only they did not go to a toy store, they went to a pawnshop and looked through a case of real knives.

They found two cheap, dagger-style knives that they thought would work. But while they were there, Brian also found two large hunting knives he decided to buy.

I am not sure why Brian wanted the hunting knives. In his final interview, Detective Thomas asked Brian about the four knives recovered from Blackrock Canyon. Brian told the detective that the two dagger knives were movie props that he and Torey had purchased, but he did not have a chance to explain why he bought the other two knives because his attorney, Randy Schulthies, arrived during the interview and put a stop to the questioning.

It turned out that Torey and Brian couldn't purchase the knives from the pawnshop because the store had a policy prohibiting anyone under the age of eighteen from buying weapons. Brian asked Torey if he knew anyone old enough to buy the knives for them. Torey called his friend Joe Lucero.

Joe testified about his involvement in the purchasing of the knives, stating that Torey called and asked if he would buy some knives for him and his friend Brian Draper. Joe had agreed. Torey and Brian picked Joe up in Torey's car. They went to Bank of America where Brian withdrew forty dollars from his account and headed to the pawnshop.

Once at the pawnshop, Joe said, Torey and Brian went directly to the knives that they wanted him to purchase. Brian gave Joe the forty dollars that he had withdrawn from his account and Torey contributed five dollars. With this, Joe paid for all four knives.

While driving Joe home, Joe stated that Torey had asked Brian if he could look at one of the knives. Brian told him no, it was his knife; he'd paid for it. When Joe got out of the car Brian was holding the knives.

That is how the purchasing of the knives and the masks occurred. At least the two dagger knives and the masks were originally intended as movie props. What intent they held later is open to interpretation. But the actual planning at the time of the purchase is not. I cannot say what Brian was thinking, but the only planning that was taking place at that time, in Torey's mind, was the planning of a movie.

I used to wonder if Torey and Cassie had been doomed from the very first day that Brian Draper entered our lives, but I no longer do. I believe it was a series of events, impulsive actions, and negligence that led to Cassie's death. But one of the major contributing factors was the videotape filmed by Brian Draper. Brian may have begun filming it as a game, but that is certainly not how it ended.

It is important to know that the videotape that Brian Draper filmed is *NOT* the movie that Torey and Brian were planning. That movie was never made, although an outline of it was written, and was read by various friends, including Amber Phillips.

I am not sure what the videotape is that Brian Draper made. Whatever it is, it meant nothing to Torey. He had no intentions when it was filmed, and he will not speculate about Brian's intentions because, he says, Brian never shared any intentions with him.

But I *will* speculate. I believe Brian began by once again mimicking his heroes, Dylan Klebold and Eric Harris. Emulating them on videotape only added a new dimension to what he'd already been doing for years. But the timing was terrible, because when Brian picked up the camera, he opened Pandora's box. For the first time in his life, Brian was not only talking about murder, he was actually going to be presented with the perfect opportunity for murder.

And he took it.

Brian's video actually began on Wednesday night, September 20, 2006. That night a short piece of film was taped that I only know about because Torey noticed that it was missing when he was shown the tape after his arrest. Unbeknownst to Torey, Brian had recorded over it.

According to Torey, on Wednesday night he and Brian were alone in Brian's truck. Brian had his video camera with him and while he was playing with the camera he began making "dark jokes" about killing people. Brian turned the camera on and filmed himself.

Torey said that Brian's comments did not concern him because he believed that Brian was joking. Torey said that he joined Brian in the conversation, and Brian filmed them both. After a few minutes, Brian put the camera down and laughed. He said that was really good. He wanted to film some more. He repositioned the camera and told Torey, "This time let's take the humor out." But Torey said no, it was time he went home.

That was the end of that night's filming, but the start of what would eventually become the videotape.

The next night, Thursday, September 21, Torey picked up Brian at his house. They had no plans; they were just going to hang out. But Brian brought his camera with him and the filming continued, this time in Torey's car.

CHAPTER TWENTY-FIVE

The Video

There is no question as you watch the videotape that Brian controlled both the camera and the conversation. While Torey participated in much of the video, there are scenes that Brian filmed alone. An example you will see a little later, was when Brian filmed Cassie on the morning of the day that she was killed--a very disturbing piece of film that Torey was completely unaware off.

During Torey's trial, Mark Hiedeman accused him of encouraging what he called "Brian's relentless talk on tape." In actuality Torey was just following Brian's lead. That's apparent when you watch the video, but it also helps if you know the two boys.

The videotape is approximately thirty minutes of film comprised of what appears to be a random mix of recordings. That is because Brian ran out of film before he was finished filming, and he was forced to rewind the tape in order to continue. For this reason the tape does not play in sequential order. I am going to briefly describe each section, not in the order that it appears on tape, but in the order in which it was recorded. I am also going to give a description of the context during each section, and how events transpired during the filming of the video. By piecing the video together this way you can actually see what Brian was thinking and doing as he was filming. Before each segment was filmed Brian directed the subject matter. There was no "script", but there was plot.

There is nothing pleasant about Brian's videotape. The whole thing is awful. I wish my son had never even heard the name of Brian Draper. Torey's life was ruined and Cassie's lost because of that opportunistic, manipulative kid, who joke or no joke, destroyed three lives, and adversely affected countless others, as quickly as most people take an afternoon lunch break.

Segment # 1

September 21, 2006, 8:05 p.m. Torey and Brian are driving in Torey's car. It is dark outside and the road is visible in front of them as Torey's headlights reveal it. Both boys are speaking simultaneously. The film begins mid sentence.

Brian: "We're going for a high death count…"

Torey: "We're not going not to get caught Brian. If we are

going for guns we're just gonna end it..."

Brian: "...Oh yeah."

Torey: "...grab the guns and get out of there...Kill everyone and leave..."

Brian: "We're gonna make history. We're gonna make history."

Torey: "For all of you FBI agents watching this..."

Brian laughs.

Torey: "You, uh, weren't quick enough."

Brian (laughs): "You weren't quick enough and you weren't smart enough.

Brian says they are going to go over to Danielle Morrison's house, a girl he is madly infatuated with, and check out of she is home alone or not. If she is, Brian says, "Splat...She's dead." He turns the camera off.

This is a continuation of the film that Brian had begun the night before. At this point the situation is still relatively harmless. Brian's psychological evaluation will later reveal that he is indeed a deeply disturbed young man, but there is no evidence that he is actually planning to inflict harm on anyone--yet. He does threaten Danielle Morrison, but that is just talk. Brian was infatuated with Danielle. He even wrote about her in his Black River story: "I had my eye on a couple of girls," he wrote, "but they didn't even know I existed. The first one's name is Danielle Morrison. She is one of the most beautiful girls that I have ever seen, and I wanted her. I wanted her to be a part of my life, and I was willing to give up anything for her. She is in my first hour and she sits across the room from me. All hour, when she isn't looking, I just stare at her. I stare into her short blond hair and her beautiful face. I almost have orgasms just thinking about her, but in three months, I have yet to speak a word to her." Page 2. Even in a fictional piece of writing, Brian could not bring himself to harm Danielle. Hers is the only life he spares in Black River.

This part of the film is all talk. Nothing in the segment is real. There were no guns, no place to run into, nobody to shoot. The FBI speech was meant to be funny. It was just two teenaged boys being young and stupid.

Segment # 2

8:08 pm. Three minutes after the last segment began. Torey and Brian are still in Torey's moving car. Brian obviously turned

off the camera for just a moment. Now it's back on.

Brian states that they have driven past Danielle's house and are now on their way to a church where they are going to call their friends Cassie and Matt. Here the talk gets more serious. Brian says, "I feel really weird that--you know--inside my stomach and stuff. And I feel like…I…wanna kill somebody. (pauses). Uhmm, I know that's not n-*normal* but, what-the-hell?"

This is not just a boy trying to impress his friend. This is a serious statement entrenched in the middle of a "game" between two boys, and Torey missed it. He did not realize that Brian just might mean what he was saying.

The vehicle enters a parking lot and Torey parks the car. From the driver's seat, Torey says, "I feel we need to break away from normal life…"

Brian aims the camera at Torey and Torey squints in the light.

Brian asks, "How bright is this light?" referring to the camera's light shining in Torey's face. Torey turns off the ignition to the car, and Beethoven's Midnight Sonata, which had been playing in the background, ceases.

Torey engages Brian in a conversation about God, debating if he is real or not. Torey states that God is used to get people to do good under the threat of going to hell. He mimics quotation marks with his fingers.

Brian, still acting like a serial killer, says, "And we're obviously going to hell if it's real, but you know what? Who gives a shit?"

Brian points to the ignition and tells Torey he is ready to go. Torey attempts to continue the debate but Brian is ready to travel. He is not interested in sitting in a parking lot philosophizing about the nature of God; his impatience is visible. Finally Torey gives up, leaves behind the topic that bores Brian, and picks up the one that does not.

"…we are also taught that things like killing people…" he begins.

"…is wrong." Brian finishes. Brian puts the video camera on the dashboard of the car and films himself. "Natural selection, dude. That's all I gotta say. N-natural selection."

Brian shakes his head at the camera and adjusts his seat.

Torey's lost his train of thought. He pauses for a second, trying to regain it.

Torey: "There should be no law against killing people. I know it's a wrong thing but..." he looks over at Brian, sits up straight, and reaches for the ignition. "Hell...You restrict somebody from it, they're gonna want it more."

Torey starts the car.

Brian: "Exactly. Goodbye Camera."

Segment # *3*

The Camera comes on and Torey and Brian are once again driving in Torey's car. They've already left the parking and they're on the road. The camera reads September 21, 2006, 8:15 p.m. Classical music plays in the background.

Brian: "Okay. And we're gonna go over to Cassie and Matt's house. If they're home alone, we're gonna see..."

Torey (interrupts): "It's Cassie's house. Matt is there." *This is the only time on the entire tape that Torey uses a person's name.*

Brian (corrects himself): "Matt is there. *Sorry.* We're gonna go there. We're gonna knock on the door. We'll s-see who's there. We'll, we'll s-see...if their parents are home or not. If they're home alone we'll leave right away. And then we'll come back in about...ten minutes. We'll s-sneak in...through the door. Because, chances are, they're probably in Cassie's room. *S-soo* we'll sneak in the front door...we'll make a noise outside. And... Matt will come to investigate. Kill him. A-And it'll scare the shit out of Cassie. Okay?"

Brian is basically describing a scene from the movie *Scream.*

Torey says, "Sounds like fun."

Brian turns the camera off.

Segment # 4

September 21st, 2006, 8:36 p.m. Torey and Brian are in Torey's car. It is dark and raining outside. The camera picks up Torey's darkened profile as he drives; the road illuminated by his headlights, and the windshield wipers scraping across the windshield. Beethoven's Moonlight Sonata is playing on the CD player.

Between this segment and the last, Torey and Brian had driven over to Cassie's house and spoken with her. Matt was there when they arrived. While Torey and Brian were at her house, Cassie told the two boys of her plans to house sit over the weekend, and invited them to her aunt's house on Friday night. It was unbelievable timing. As soon as Torey and Brian returned

to Torey's car, Brian turned on the camera and began speaking.

The entire situation had changed.

Brian (hyper, gleeful): "We found our victim and…s-sad as it may be…she's our friend. But you know what? We all…have to make…s-s-sacrifices. Our first victim is going to be Cassie Stoddart and…"

Torey (interrupts): "God!"

Brian: "…her…friends."

A car passed, briefly bathing the interior of Torey's car in yellow light. "Turn off your brights asshole," Torey said rudely.

Brian (laughs): "We'll…find out if s-she has f-friends over. She's gonna be alone in a big…dark…house…out in the middle of (laughs out loud) nowhere. How perfect…can you get? I-I mean, like *holy sh-hit* dude!"

Torey still believed that he and Brian were just "acting" for the videotape. But this was actually the first time that Torey really could have taken Brian seriously. Brian's threats earlier that night were unrealistic. He did not have any weapons with him, and he was not about to attack anyone in their own home just because their parents happened to be gone for the moment. But here, Brian was talking about attacking Cassie, and she was going to be alone. Torey should have been worried, but he wasn't.

Torey said, "I'm horny just thinking about it."

Brian yelled, "Hell-Yeah! So we're gonna f---ing kill her *and* her friends and we're gonna keep moving on! I heard some news about Kirsten. She's gonna be alone from six to seven. So we might…kill her, then drive over to Cassie's thing and scare the *shit* out of them and kill them *ONE…BY…F---ING…ONE!*"

Brian's voice is loud and excited. His stutter is gone.

In 'Black River' Brian wrote about killing people one by one and two by two. (Chapter 11. Page 7.) He likes this theme. But his theme was so insane that it was impossible for Torey to take him seriously.

Torey asked sarcastically, "Why one-by-one? Why can't it be a slaughter house?"

Brian gleeful replied, "Two-by-two and three-by-three? 'Cause, we gotta keep it…classy. So…yeah."

Torey: "Keep it classy?"

Brian: "It's gonna be…*e-extra* fun."

Torey: "You're *e-evil*!"

This was actually an interesting change of topic. Torey does not discourage Brian from saying what he does, but Torey does not partake in the conversation. Torey doesn't say that he is going to kill anyone, but he continues to indulge Brian.

Brian says that they are sick psychopaths that get pleasure off killing other people. He says they are going to go down in history like Scream, like Ted Bundy and the Hillside Strangler.

Torey says those people are armatures compared to them.

He asks Brian if he knew what Ed Gein's words were.

Brian: "What?"

Torey: "Saw a girl walking down the street, right?"

Brian: "Yeah."

Torey: "Two questions came to his head. Hmm, I could take her out. Have a nice time with her."

Brian: "Then kill her?"

Torey: "A-And show her a good time."

Brian (laughs): "*S-skin* her alive?"

Torey: "Charm the pants off her. *Or*...I wonder what her head would look like (Brian laughs) on a stick."

Brian: "Holy shit!"

Torey (laughs, voice cracks): "That's *creepy* huh?"

Brian (laughs): "Yeah."

This was a quote from the movie, "American Psycho," with Christian Bale. During Torey's trial, Detective Alex Hamilton testified that he watched the movie and identified where the quote was taken from. In his police report, Detective Hamilton wrote: "In the movie 'American Psycho' a character, who is a serial killer, goes by the name of Patrick Bateman. In the movie, Patrick Bateman is sitting around with three other individuals and they have the following discussion:

Patrick Bateman: "Do you know what Ed Gein said about women?"

David Van Patten: "The Maitre d at Canal Bar?"

Patrick Bateman: "No, serial killer, Wisconsin, the 50's."

Craig McDermott: "So what did he say?"

Patrick Bateman: "When I see a pretty girl walking down the street, I think two things. One part wants me to take her out, talk to her, be real nice and sweet and treat her right."

David Van Patten: "And what did the other part think?"

Patrick Bateman: "What her head would look like on a stick."

Brian looks directly at the camera. "Murder is power. Murder is freedom," he says. This too is a quote, taken from the movie *Murder By Numbers.*

Brian turns the camera off.

The last four segments were filmed in chronological order. All together they do not comprise much film, mere minutes actually, but they do depict what was happening *on camera* the night before Cassie was killed. What they do not reveal is what was happening off camera, and what Torey was really thinking.

When Torey picked Brian up that Thursday night, the 21st of September, he had no plans. Brian brought his video camera with him and Torey went along with Brian in what he considered to be the same stupid, but harmless behavior that they had engaged in the night before. Torey knew that what he was doing was wrong, but he never suspected that what he was doing was dangerous. He never suspected Brian could be serious about murder. And maybe Brian wasn't serious--in the beginning.

Torey said that Brian only spoke to him about killing when the camera was on. The video camera, the film, and the role he was playing, gave Brian a vehicle in which he could safely voice his secret fantasies. But Brian did not conspire with Torey, nor voice a desire to actually carry out a murder, with the video camera off, when he had no role to hide behind. When he was just himself.

I believe things changed for Brian when he realized that Cassie was truly going to be left alone for the weekend. Everything that he said up until that point was the same sort of twisted fantasy that he's always engaged in. But suddenly Brian realized it did not have to be a fantasy. It could be a reality. And he could not let the thought go.

The video camera allowed Brian to express an extremely frightening piece of himself. He did so that very night. But Brian kept that piece of himself hidden behind a role that he was playing. He did not share his innermost thoughts with Torey; and when Torey came home that night, he had no idea that Brian was contemplating murder.

But he was. And the next scene, which Brian filmed alone, and Torey was completely unaware of, proves it.

Segment # 5

It is September 22nd, 2006, 8:28 a.m. Brian Draper is circling the hallways of Pocatello High School. He is holding his

video camera next to his hip, filming. An unidentified male is with him. The camera picks up a cacophony of voices engaged in numerous conversations, none discernible. For a moment, Brian follows two young girls. Their jean clad bottoms fill the camera screen until they turn off the hallway. Suddenly, the camera picks up a girl with long black hair standing in front of her locker. She is the reason Brian is filming.

Brian: "Hey look, it's Cassie. Hello Cassie."

Cassie is placing items inside her locker and does not respond.

Brian (laughs): "I'm getting you on tape…okay?"

He circles around her, moving the camera up to his eye. Cassie glances over her shoulder at him.

"Say hi, please," Brian coaxes.

"Hi," Cassie responds.

Brian (starts to leave): "K-see ya. (pauses) Wait, have you seen Torey?"

Cassie (shakes her head): "Huh-uh."

Brian: "He's supposed to meet me here at s-seven…*thirty*. And it's-s eight nineteen… (pauses) He's an hour late."

Cassie doesn't respond.

Brian: "You…You don't even care, do you?"

Cassie: "Not really."

Brian (laughs): "Okay. See ya."

Cassie (smiles at the camera): "Bye."

Brian walks down the hall to the boys' restroom. He films himself holding the camera in front of a mirror. His hair is short and black and he's wearing a long-sleeved black shirt with a yellow logo and black pants. He sweeps the camera around the room in a panoramic view of urinals, stalls, floor and drain and then goes back out into the hallway.

Brian tells the person walking alongside him to watch the cord and keep up. The sound is muffled, the students in the hall loud.

Brian: "Let's go back up to the library. See if Torey's there."

Boy: "All right."

The camera records as they turn down the hall, and then shuts off.

This is a difficult section of the video to watch, and one that is played on almost every program made concerning this crime. It is hard for me to watch Cassie, and hard for me to reconcile my feelings for Brian. I know that Brian was just sixteen years old when this happened, and I don't believe he realizes even now what he took from Cassie. But Brian knew what he was doing. He knowingly filmed Cassie on the day that he killed her. Torey was not with him. Torey did not know what Brian was doing. But inside Brian's mind he was thinking that Cassie Stoddart might die that night, and he filmed her that morning knowing it.

Brian Draper made the choice to live out a fantasy that he had been thinking about for a very long time; and every minute of the day he made decisions that brought him closer to his goal. And I will *never* understand why.

Segment #6

Friday September 22, 2006, 12:11 p.m. Torey is sitting at a round table in the library of Pocatello High School. He has a textbook and notepad in front of him. The camera sits directly across from Torey on the table, and Torey is looking into it. He makes clicking-type noises with his tongue.

Brian, on the other side of the camera, focuses on Torey and then zooms out so that the video captures Torey and an empty chair on his left. There's a book and an open can of Coke on the table in front of the empty chair. Brian moves from behind the camera and sits down next to Torey. "Alright. Cool," he says.

This section is by far the longest recorded and comprises almost half of the tape. It is actually broken into two sections. Brian stops the recording when a classmate comes over to say hi, and resumes it when the student leaves. It begins with Brian announcing the date, and explaining that he and Torey are skipping their fourth hour class. A teacher almost catches them. They spend the first few minutes on tape hiding behind their textbooks, but the teacher leaves and the dialog begins. While Brian talks, Torey takes notes.

Brian (apologizes to the camera): "There's not much going on, I know. I'm sorry. He looks over at Torey, who is writing in his notebook. He tells him to hurry up.

Brian takes a drink of his coke. "Yeah--if you're watching this, we're probably…deceased. S-so that's pretty creepy. I just thought of that."

Torey (looks at Brian, shakes his head): "You're an idiot."

Brian (defensive): "Whatever."

He leans across the table stretching his left hand out to the camera, palm upward.

Brian: "Life's life. That's what happens. You die."

Torey taps his pencil on the table. He looks bored. He sounds bored when he asks Brian, "This documentary should last about twenty minutes?"

Brian (nods): "Roughly about that time."

Torey: "Twenty maybe…thirty minutes?"

Brian tells Torey the tape was already used half way through. He does not know for sure how much time is left. Brain says if they need more time they will just buy more tapes. Torey says he wants to keep it on one cassette.

This is a section of the video the prosecutor never talked about. Torey called Brian's film a documentary and asked how long it was going to last. Twenty minutes, maybe thirty. Even though Torey was a willing participant in Brian's video, he was ready for it to end.

Torey yawns and goes back to dictating in his notebook: "*Cassie…and…Matt…Brian…*"

Brian: "Our plan is suppose to-to happen tonight. So, hopefully nothing will go wrong. Everything will go…*s-smoothly.* And we can get our *f-first* kill done. Get started. And we can go on." He taps the table.

Torey sets his pencil down. He rests his elbows on the table and interlocks his fingers as if he is saying a prayer. For a moment Torey sits still, clicking his tongue, searching for something to say. Then he joins his two index fingers together and points them at the camera.

Torey: "For you…future serial killers watching this tape…(Brian laughs, Torey looks at him, shakes his head) I don't know what to say. Uhmm…"

Brian: "*I-it's*…(gestures the OK sign) really fun."

Torey: "Good luck with that."

Brian: "Yeah. Good luck."

Torey tells the camera they have tried eight or nine times to find a victim, but they had never been successful. This is an exaggeration of the previous night's escapades. But Brian next statement reveals his true intentions.

Brian: "As long as you're patient, you know…and we were patient. Now we're getting paid off 'cause our victim's home alone. So we got our…our plan all worked out…now. So. I'm sorry. I…I'm sorry, Cassie's family but…she had to be the one. We have to stick with the plan, and s-she's perfect. So…s-she's gonna die."

Brian laughs as he finishes "apologizing" to Cassie's family.

Brian has now voiced a plan, twice on tape, to kill Cassie. He was thinking about it. Now he says he has a new victim.

Brian: "Miranda Erickson. She told me to be quiet and to…sh-shut up. So now she's…*dead*."

Torey (glances at Brian, shakes his head, laughs): "That may be f---ed up, but hell, its funny."

Brian looks pleased with his wit. He explains his motivation. "I've always wanted to make my mark on the world. And this is a good way to do it…"

Torey (interrupts): "We ought to kill those f---ing Wangsters and Mormons out there."

Brian (nods, laughs): "I know."

Brian (continues): "Combined with my love of horror movies, with my love…wanting to be-- you know, popular. Famous."

Torey (surprised): "You wanna be popular?"

Brian: "No…You know, like…"

Torey: "O-Ohh." He knew where the conversation was headed.

Brian: "They talk about me. Everybody knows my name. Like Erik--Erik Harris and Dylan Klebold."

This is important. Brian's desire to be like Eric Harris and Dylan Klebold not only reveal his state of mind, but also give us the closest thing we have to a motive. Brian said the same thing in 'Black River' when he wrote, "I am going to be known by everyone. Just like Eric and Dylan. They were just like me and know (sic) people fear their name." (Page 2.)

But Torey never said that he wanted to be famous. He did not even know who Dylan Klebold or Eric Harris were until he met Brian, and he never mentioned them on this tape once. Throughout his trial the prosecutor and Cassie's family accused Torey of killing Cassie for notoriety, but they were mistaken. It was Brian alone who wanted to be famous. It was Brian alone who had the motivation to murder.

The conversation takes a predictable turn after Brian mentions his heroes. Torey and Brian discuss entering a party, killing eight, ten, twenty people with guns they do not own and then committing suicide.

Torey looks bored and pricks Brian's arm lightly with the tip of his pencil until Brian notices what he is doing, looks down at his arm, and asks Torey what the hell he's doing. The boys fall silent for a moment.

Torey (resumes writing and dictating): "*...me...chasing her...through the...house. And...Torey...cuts...*"

Brian (looks down at Torey's notebook): "Well...it could be me."

Torey (looks up at Brian, nods) "That makes more sense. It wouldn't look right, a short person like me...chasing her."

He acts as if he is writing a script.

Torey (puts down his pencil, stretches, rubs his stomach): "My abs are so sore."

Torey and Brian discuss the home coming game at the University that Saturday. Brian says he plans to go with his grandfather. A student approaches the table. He asks Brian what he is doing out of class. Brian tells him he is filming for a school project. They talk about sports. The student plays football, he asks Brian, who was a goalie in soccer, why he wasn't playing this year. Brian tells him he has more important things to do, and shuts the camera off. When it comes back on the student is gone and there is a pile of candy on the table.

Brian (to the camera): "Okay. We're back. Sorry for that little thing. That's not...planned, but uh, you know...shit happens."

Torey: "You sounded kind of gay there."

Brian: "Really?"

Torey: *"Sorry for that...little thing..."*

Brian (laughs): "*O*-kay."

Brian unwraps a piece of candy and puts the wrapper with the other wrappers in front of him.

Torey: "At least he bought us candy."

Torey reaches over and attempts to take a piece of candy from Brian, but Brian pulls it away.

Brian: "That's my candy dude!"

Torey (raises his eyebrows): "*Well*...now you know what kind of a person *Brian* is." Brian: "Hey...come on."

Brian leans to the right, momentarily out of sight of the camera.

Torey (talking as he writes): "I like the way scenario 'B'ends. *And...we...kill...her...*"

Brian (points to the camera for emphasis): "That's a good way to...end it."

Torey: "Mm-hm."
Torey picks his teeth while Brian chews his candy.
Brian: "Okay, lets…scenario "C."
The segment ends.

Segment # 7

September 22, 2006, 12:54 p.m. Torey and Brian are in front of Brian's locker. It's the lunch recess and students line the halls. There's a Coke can sitting in a wall-mounted drinking fountain to the right. Torey is standing in view of the camera on the left. Brian is filming, so though you can hear him, you cannot see him.

Brian: "…locker…assigned…to…me…Got my Halloween stuff…"

The camera zooms in on some DVD covers of *Halloween* and *Friday the Thirteenth* taped to the inside of the locker door.

Torey: "Pretty f---ing sweet isn't it?"

Brian zooms in on a long black coat hanging in the locker: "*M-My* trench coat…Got my smokes…here."

He lifts a pack of cigarettes from the pocket of his trench coat.

Torey (turns away from the camera): "Well, I'm going to lunch."

Brian shuts the locker door. The hallway fills with sounds. Lockers closing, people talking. The video focuses on a boy wearing a red t-shirt, white shorts and black leggings, walking by. Brian zooms in on him. "Look at those little legs," he laughs.

"What a fag," Torey says rudely. "Let's go."

Segment # 8

September 22, 2006, 5:27 p.m. This is another segment that Brian filmed alone without Torey's knowledge. Brian is alone in his bedroom manically playing the drums. His shirt is off and he's wearing "happy dog" boxer shorts that hang over the top of his baggy pants. Brian is extremely dark and skinny. In the background there are shelves lining his bedroom wall. They are filled with the empty energy drink bottles that Brian collected. On a television screen in front of him, Brian is watching, as he drums, the movie *Scream*.

In less than six hours, Brian will kill Cassie. I do not know the song Brian was playing, but I believe he was

drumming a death song--and psyching himself up with the movie he was watching.

Directly after school that day, Brian packed a kit that he took with him later that night. Into his soccer bag, Brian stashed knives, shirts, gloves, boots and masks. Everything that was later recovered from Blackrock Canyon came from Brian Draper's house. Brian carried the bag outside and placed it in the bed of his truck. When he finished he went into his bedroom and watched his videotape. Brian rewound the tape to where he wanted it, set up his camera, and filmed himself drumming.

While watching Brian drum on the tape you can easily visualize him angrily stabbing Cassie twenty-nine times in just a few seconds--just as he manically played the drums as he fantasized about what he might do that night.

At the same time that Brian was drumming his death song, Torey was asking me for permission to go to Cassie's house, giving me her address and telling me about Matt, asking if Matt could spend the night that night.

Torey and Brian are clearly two very different boys, and they each had very different expectations about what was going to happen that night, and how they wanted the night to end.

Segment # 9

September 22, 2006, 9:53 p.m. The video is dark. Torey and Brian are in Torey's car, which is parked. Torey is in the driver's seat and Brian is in the passenger seat. There are streetlights in the background. This scene was filmed after Torey and Brian had been to Cassie's aunt's house and left.

Brian: "We're here…in his car. The time is nine…fifty p.m. September 22, 2006. Um…unfortunately we have the grueling task of killing our two friends. And they are right in--in that house…just down the street."

Torey: "We just talked to them. We were there for an hour…but..."

Brian: "We checked out the whole house. We know there are lots of doors. There--there's lots of places to hide. Um…I unlocked…the back doors. That's all unlocked. Now we just got to wait and umm…yep. We're--we're really nervous right now, but, you know? We're ready."

In his third interview Brian admitted to the detectives that he unlocked the doors. He admitted it here, too.

Torey: "We're listening to the greatest rock band..."

Brian interrupts him: "We've been…"

Torey: "…ever."

Brian: "…waiting for this for a long time."

Torey finishing: "Pink Floyd. Before we commit…the ultimate crime of *muurder*."

Of all the comments Torey made on the videotape, this was undoubtedly the most damning. Cassie was killed less than an hour and a half after this segment was filmed, so it's reasonable to say that a real threat was made. But before turning the camera on, Brian told Torey that he had concocted a plan to reenter the house where Cassie and Matt were staying--to "scare" them. Scaring Cassie and Matt was all that was supposed to happen. This segment was staged. Torey was acting for the camera, imitating Brian, following his lead. Even Torey's enunciation of the word Muurder was purposeful. He was mimicking Mike Myers and the way he pronounced the word in his movie, "The Cat in the Hat."

Torey never expected anyone to actually get killed. And that is clear if you look at his behavior. Torey told me where he was going that night. To Cassie's house. He gave me her address. I called him while he was there, about a half an hour earlier. Torey told me he was still at Cassie's house with Matt and Brian. If Torey was actually planning to commit a murder, he would have hid his whereabouts.

At this point it was just a joke to Torey. He was not taking Brian seriously. Brian said it was a joke, and Torey believed him.

Brian repeats: "We've been waiting for this for a long time."

Torey echoes: "A long time."

Brian: "We'll--stay tuned," He turns the camera off.

Segment # 10

September 22, 2006, 11:31 p.m. Minutes after Cassie was killed. It is dark outside and Torey and Brian are in Torey's car. Torey is driving.

Brian (breathless voice): "…Just killed Cassie. We just left her house. This is not a F---ing joke."

Torey: "I-I'm shaking."

Brian: "I stabbed her in--in the throat a-and I saw her lifeless body…just ah…disappear. Dude, I…just killed Cassie."

This is a clear confession. There is no reason for Brian to lie. He is holding the video camera. He is confessing on tape, to the world, and to Torey who is sitting next to him, what he did. Brian did not say 'we' just killed Cassie. He did not say 'you' just killed Cassie. It would have been easy for Brian to say either one of those things. But he said truthfully, "I just killed Cassie." It is a clear confession. Brian stabbed Cassie in the throat and he saw her lifeless body drop to the floor.

Torey: "Oh my God!"

Brian (exhales loudly): "Oh! Oh f---! That felt like it wasn't even real. O-Oh…I mean…it went by soo fast."

Torey: "Shut the f--- up! We got to get our act straight."

This was another statement Torey made that the prosecutor used against him. Mark Hiedeman said that if Torey was innocent, he wouldn't have helped Brian cover up the crime. In reality Torey was scared. He knew that he and Brian were both in serious trouble and he panicked.

Brian (takes a breath): "It's okay. Okay…We…We'll…Let's go buy movie tickets now."

Torey (pauses): "*Nooo.*"

Brian: "Wh-? (pauses) Goodbye."

He turns the camera off.

Torey did not know until after his arrest, when he watched the video for the first time, that Brian turned on the camera when he returned to the car after stabbing Cassie. It shocked Torey. Cassie lay upstairs in her aunt's home stabbed to death, and it is hard to tell if Brian was shocked or surprised or excited by what he had just done. But one thing is clear. However Brian was feeling, he had the presence of mind to turn on the camera and talk about it.

On the surface, the whole crux of the video is Torey and Brian planning and executing a murder. But, contrary to what the prosecutor would have one believe, it is not that simple. It is true that Brian talked about killing Cassie on the tape, and that Torey heard him. It is also true that Torey seemed to support Brian. But the question is: Did Torey really believe that Brian was going to kill Cassie? And the answer is no, he did not.

The video is the strongest evidence the prosecutor had against Torey, and it is the evidence that he focused the heart of his case on. But the video contains multiple layers, and you have to peel it like an onion to see the thoughts, feelings, and motivations of the two boys involved.

The reason that's important is because the *intent* of the boys is a major portion of what they are convicted of, and if there was a mistake made about Torey's intentions, then Torey is serving an unjust sentence.

Mark Hiedeman claimed that Torey *intended* to kill Cassie. He said that Torey and Brian purchased the knives a month earlier with the *intent to kill*. He told the jury that Torey drove to Cassie's Aunt's house intending to stab her to death. He submitted the videotape as proof. But if you separate out the words spoken by each boy on the videotape--you can see there is a real difference in what they were thinking.

That's what I did. I made multiple copies of the transcript of the video and I separated the words spoken by Torey from those of Brian. And I found that every single comment made about murdering Cassie, or planning her death, came from Brian.

I found that if you take the comments Brian made about Cassie, and run them together chronologically, over the two-day period of tape that exists, Brian tells you exactly what he's planning. Even if you remove all the superfluous talk on the video that has nothing to do with Cassie, and even if you remove every single word spoken by Torey on the videotape entirely, you can still see exactly what Brian planned to do.

Brian did not need a single collaborating comment from Torey. Brian said it all. Brian made *every single comment* that pertained to Cassie's death. And for a hyper, impulsive kid, he stayed amazingly on task.

On the first night, Brian said that he felt really weird, like he wanted to kill somebody. He said he knew that wasn't normal, but what the hell? That night Brian found out that he might get his chance. Cassie was going to be left alone for the weekend. Brian was visibly excited by the news. He said, "We'll find out if she has friends over, (or) if she's going to be alone in a big, dark house out in the middle of nowhere." He laughed. "How perfect can you get?" He said, "Holy shit!" He tells the camera, "We found our first victim, and sad as it may be, she's our friend, but you know, we all have to make sacrifices. Our first victim is going to be Cassie Stoddart and her friends." Before he turned off the camera for the night Brian said, "Murder is power. Murder is freedom."

The next day, Brian continued. He filmed Cassie on the morning of the day that he planned to kill her. A sick thrill. When he recorded next, he said, "Our plan is suppose to happen tonight. So hopefully nothing will go wrong so we can get our first kill done and started, and we can keep going." Brian apologized to Cassie's family before he killed her, saying, "I'm sorry Cassie's family. But we have to stick with the plan. And she's perfect. So she's gonna die."

Brian explained himself, "I've always wanted to make my mark on the world and this is a good way to do it. Combined with my love of horror movies with my love (of) wanting to be popular. Famous. Everybody knows my name like Eric Harris and Dylan Klebold."

Brian carried through with his plan. When he got to Cassie's house that night he checked out the house, found places to hide, got everything ready. He said, "We have the grueling task of killing our two friends. I unlocked the backdoors--it's all unlocked. Now we just have to wait."

Brian said, "We've waited for this a long time." And we know that *he* has. Brian has written about this, talked about this, thought about this, for a long, long time. And no matter what Brian thought, or said he thought, going back into that house, that night--there was a possibility that was present with Brian all along--and every word he spoke up until that point verifies it, because less than an hour and a half later, Brian ran out of the house, to the car, and breathlessly, remarkably said, "Just killed Cassie. I stabbed her in the throat and saw her lifeless body just disappear. Dude, I just killed Cassie."

Brian's statements leave no doubt about what he was thinking. He said he wanted to kill someone. He found someone vulnerable. He knew what he was doing was wrong. He apologized. He waited for the right opportunity and then…he tells us, he took it.

Torey's statements on the tape are different. He philosophized about God and the origin of evil. He talked about Ed Gein in the movie American Psycho and quoted movie lines. But Torey *never* said that he wanted to kill anyone, Torey *never* said that he planned to kill anyone, and Torey did not say that he did kill someone.

Neither Torey nor Brian expected anyone to watch this video. Not their parents, not the police. Brian said what he was thinking. Torey followed along, not knowing that Brian was serious.

There were three statements on the tape that the prosecutor used against Torey. The first was after Brian voiced his plan to attack Cassie. Torey responded, "I'm horny just thinking about it." The second was after Torey and Brian left the house where Cassie and Matt were staying. Before reentering the house, Torey said they were going to commit the "ultimate crime of murder." And the last statement the prosecutor used against Torey was made after Cassie was killed. Brian told Torey that he'd just killed Cassie, and Torey told him to "Shut the f- up. We have to get our act straight."

Those statements appear to prove that Torey conspired with Brian to kill Cassie; that he willingly followed Brian into the house to carry out the plan, and that after Brian killed Cassie, Torey helped him cover it up.

But if you look at each of the statements in the context in which they were made, the claim is disputable. I am going to back up to Wednesday night, when the video was first started, and tell the whole story. That is the only way to understand what really happened.

CHAPTER TWENTY-SIX

The Untold Story

On Wednesday night, September 20, Brian and Torey were alone in Brian's truck. Brian had Joey Lacey's video camera with him. Brian had been driving Joey to school every day, and charging him ten dollars a week for the gas. Joey offered to give Brian the video camera in exchange for the gas money and Brian agreed. That is how Brian came to posses the camera.

While parked in his truck, Brian brings up his usual subject: school shootings and killing people. The video camera is on the floor of the truck. Brian reaches over by Torey and picks it up. He turns the camera on and makes some "dark jokes." Torey thinks that Brian is just trying to be being funny. He joins in the talk and Brian films them both.

It did not last long. Brian wants to film some more, but Torey has to go home. As Brian drives Torey home, neither boy speaks about what they said on camera and by the time Torey's in bed that night, Brian's video is far from his mind.

But the recording made a large impression on Brian. It started as a joke, but he quickly saw the potential. He'd recently watched the movie *Elephant*, which documented two teenagers discussing on tape their plans to commit a school shooting. Brian could do something similar.

Mark Hiedeman claimed the videotape was the result of months of planning. But he was wrong. It was actually the result of a recently acquired video camera and a stupid, childish prank.

The next day, Torey and Brian made arrangements to get together. Torey didn't have any specific plans and when Brian said he wanted to continue the tape he'd started the night before, Torey agreed. By then Brian had a theme in mind. Instead of just randomly taping, he wanted to portray two teen-aged killers.

At first the talk is general, but as Brian warms to his subject, (and Torey allows him to) Brian infuses it with a dose of reality. He begins listing names of real people. Brian suggests they drive by first Danielle Morrison's house and then Cassie Stoddart's.

Brian's selection of Cassie and Danielle is another layer in the psychological onion that has to be examined. Brian selected not only people he cared about, but people whose lives intertwined in one way or another with his own. Suggesting to drive by Danielle's house or Cassie's was not suspicious behavior. Torey could understand why Brian selected both.

Torey knew that Brian was infatuated with Danielle Morrison. Driving by her house would be a thrill for Brian, and Cassie Stoddart was a mutual friend. Their selection as Brian's intended "victims" made Brian's talk seem all the more unreal. At least to Torey who could not understand the mind of a sociopath.

The fact that Brian said that he wanted to kill Danielle was simply, in Torey's eyes, Brian acting for the videotape. Torey saw nothing to be concerned about. As he drove to Danielle's house, Torey knew that neither he, nor Brian, would ever approach her door. He didn't know her well enough, and Brian was too intimidated by her to even speak to her.

Torey parks in the church parking lot across from Danielle's house. It's one of the scenes in the movie where you can see the difference in the two boys. Torey turns off the car and settles himself comfortably into his seat, satisfied to just sit and talk, which is all that he has been doing since the video was turned on. It makes no difference to Torey where he's at. But Brian remains upright in his seat, fidgety and ready for action.

Brian makes a clear statement. He says he feels like he wants to kill someone. He says he knows that isn't normal. Torey doesn't say he feels the same way, but he uses Brian's statement to open a dialog about why people believe in God. Brian is thinking about murder, and Torey justifies him with philosophy. Their behavior provides an insight into their personalities. Torey is relaxed in the car, content to just sit and *B.S.* But Brian is a man of action. He's hyper, ready to *go*.

And the more Torey talks, the more impatient Brian grows, until finally Torey turns on the car, and at Brian's urging, heads to Cassie's house.

When they arrived, Torey parked his car in front of the house, and Brian knocked on the door. Cassie's stepfather, Victor Price, let them in.

While they were at Cassie's house, Cassie told Torey and Brian that she was going to be house-sitting for her aunt that weekend and invited them over. Matt was with Cassie when she told them. Torey and Brian stayed at Cassie's house for about fifteen minutes, judging by the time stamp on the video, and left.

Up until that point the situation was harmless. Brian was videotaping, but there was no thought involved with it. It was a school night. Both Torey and Brian had to be home by nine pm. They did not have any weapons with them. They were not truthfully conspiring to commit a crime. The videotape that Brian was filming was simply an impulsive act by an impulsive kid and Torey was along for the ride.

Unfortunately, Brian realized at this very moment that Cassie was truly going to be left alone for the weekend, and everything that he had been so recklessly talking about, both on tape and in the years prior, could actually come true. Brian's previously self-indulged fantasy suddenly took an incredible turn toward reality.

Torey and Brian left Cassie's house and got back in the car. It was now approximately eight thirty-six p.m. Torey started the drive to Brian's house, where he dropped him off for the night. Brian was excited, but Brian was frequently hyper and his elevated mood was not a red flag to Torey, who did not realize that anything had changed.

Brian grabs his camera. In a voice filled with pleasure, and a mocking semblance of regret, Brian Draper tells the camera, "We found our first victim and sad as it may be, she's our friend, but you know what, we all have to make sacrifices. Our first victim is going to be Cassie Stoddart and her friends."

Torey yells at a passing driver to turn off their brights.

Brian continues, working himself up as he speaks, "We'll find out if she has friends over, if she is going to be alone in a big, dark house out in the middle of nowhere." He laughs gleefully and asks Torey, "How perfect can you get? I mean like *holy shit* dude!"

And Torey says in response, "I'm horny just thinking about it."

That one sentence is the *only* statement Torey makes in response to Brian's excited rantings. If Torey truly meant to kill Cassie, and if he was, "horny just thinking about it," as he said, (and as the prosecutor insisted) Torey would have been equally as excited as Brian was. He would have joined Brian in describing what they were going to do to Cassie. But Torey did not do that. Instead he gave a cliché one-line response to Brian's statements, and Brian alone goes on to continue talking about Cassie.

Brian says, "Hell yeah! So we are gonna f---ing kill her and her friends and keep moving on." Brian says he's heard some news about another girl, Kirsten, who is going to be alone for an hour. He says they might kill her first and then drive over to Cassie's thing…scare the shit out of them and kill them one by f---ing one.

Brian has now mentioned killing two people, maybe more. What he is saying is not very realistic, but it shows that Brian is thinking about killing *people.* The actual person is not the important factor for him. The opportunity is. The practical application of how he could do it is running through Brian's mind. What is running through his mind is coming out of his mouth. Whether he was planning or fantasizing, who knows? It is a thin, thin line.

Torey was not thinking about killing anyone. The idea of murder was so far out of the realm of reality, it did not even exist. He was a high school student with plans and a future. His whole life lay ahead of him. He assumed Brian's did too.

It was impossible for Torey to take Brian seriously. Especially when Brian talked about murdering first one person and then another. It was completely implausible. As far as Torey was concerned, Brian could never be a murderer.

For Torey, his part in this movie was *role-playing.* He was *acting*, doing his *interpretation* of what a killer would say, and how a killer would act.

Torey asks Brian, "Why one by one? Why can't it be a slaughter house?"

Brian tells him, "Two by two and three by three. 'Cause we got to keep it classy."

Torey asks, "Keep it classy?"

Brian says, "It's gonna be extra fun."

Torey tells Brian, "You're *evil.*" And that comment changes the direction of the subject, but not the subject itself.

Torey did not talk about *murder* with Brian, but he engaged Brian in a debate over how they should define themselves on the tape, as evil or bad.

But Brian's definition of self was not going to be as simple as evil or bad. It was not going to be listen to me talk--I'm bad, or listen to me talk--I'm evil. No. Brian would not be stopped there. That would not satisfy him.

Brian carries on until he gets the definition that he wants, that he craves. He says, "We're sick psychopaths that get pleasure off killing other people," (because that's what he was.) And, "We're gonna be just like Scream. Except real life terms," (because that's what he wanted to be.) And, like a parrot, Torey says, "sounds good baby," to whatever Brian says.

Brian says, "We're gonna be murderers…like Ted Bundy, like the Hillside Strangler…" He's veering off. He is too grandiose.

Torey tells him, "Nooo. Those guys are amateurs compared to us." Torey tells Brian the story of Ed Gein from American Psycho. And Brian, almost home and finished recording for the night, makes his last statement of the day: "Murder is power. Murder is freedom." He tells the camera, "Goodbye," and turns it off.

Brian started filming with one thing in mind. Maybe it was nothing more than his idea of having fun. After all, he had been talking like this for years and nothing had ever come of it. But now the seeds of murder were planted in his head. He went home and let them grow.

Torey drove home after dropping Brian off and went to bed. He knew that what he was doing was wrong, but he didn't see the danger.

By Friday, Brian is obsessed with his video. He takes his camera to school and purposely films Cassie at her locker. Later that morning Brian meets Torey during a school assembly and arranges to film with him in the library during fourth hour.

Torey is already showing signs of boredom with the video. He is ready for it to end. But to please Brian, he goes along.

Torey felt that Brian was more important to him than he was to Brian. This gave Brian an advantage in the relationship that he recognized and exploited, just as he had with Chris Nix. Brian could use it to get Torey to do things that Torey otherwise wouldn't have done. But Brian was still careful.

Though his comments on tape were troubling, Brian immediately retracted them off camera to Torey. Brian never said anything to Torey that gave Torey a reason to believe that what he was saying on camera was serious, and Torey equated the possibility of something happening to Cassie as about as real as a school shooting, something that Brian may talk about, but was never going to happen.

But no matter what Torey thought, Brian was definitely planning something. When Brian returned home from school that day he packed a kit. He placed two long sleeved black shirts and two sets of gloves into his soccer bag. He took the four knives purchased from the pawnshop and the two masks that he and Torey had intended to use as movie props and placed them in the bag as well. The last thing Brian added was a pair of heavy work boots that he'd swiped from his welding class the year before. Brian zipped the bag shut and carried it outside where he placed it in the bed of his truck.

Brian then returned to the house and filmed himself

drumming while he waited for Torey.

There were actual plans that had been made for the night. Brian was going to spend the night at our house, and he and Torey were going to go to Cassie's aunt's house and visit Cassie and Matt while Cassie house-sat. In Torey's mind, the videotape that Brian was filming--was separate from that plan. While in Brian's mind the two events were clearly linked.

Brian told his mother that Torey was going to pick him up, and they were going to a movie. She gave him permission to spend the night at our house afterwards. Brian lied to his mother, failing to tell her that he was going to Cassie's house, either because he was scared that if he told her the truth she wouldn't let him go-- or because he was covering his whereabouts. I don't know which, but Brian was certainly being careful.

Before Torey left to pick up Brian, he told me where he was going. We had the discussion that I described at the beginning of the book. I agreed to let Torey go, and he left. When Torey arrived at Brian's house, Pam let him in. It was one of the few times that Torey ever set foot inside the Draper home.

When Torey and Brian left, Brian stopped by his truck. He took the soccer bag out of the bed of his truck and placed it in the trunk of Torey's car. Torey did not know what was inside the bag. He thought it was extra clothes, something like that. He asked Brian what he had in the bag, and Brian told him that he'd have to wait and see.

Brian did not share his plans with Torey. He did not film on the way to Cassie's house, and he did not tell Torey what he had in his soccer bag.

Brian wanted to check out the situation at Cassie's aunt's house before he said anything. He did not know if she had invited anyone else over or not, but he knew that Torey had. (Torey had told Adam and Amber where they were going.) If they arrived at the house, and it was full of people, there'd be no reason to tell Torey anything.

At approximately eight-thirty p.m., Brian and Torey arrived at the house on Whispering Cliffs. They had some difficulty finding it, but Torey called Cassie on his cell phone and Matt gave him directions. When they arrived, Cassie and Matt were standing on the front deck waiting for them.

According to Matt, Torey and Brian looked through the

house while he and Cassie followed them. The four kids ended up downstairs in the garage where there was a universal gym. After playing on the weights, they found a box of Popsicles in the freezer, which they carried upstairs to eat. Afterwards they decided to watch a movie. Torey selected *Kill Bill Volume Two*. He sat in a banana chair next to the TV in the living room with Cassie and Matt, who were seated together on the couch, and watched half the movie. And had it not been for Brian, Torey would have been happy to watch the entire movie with his friends. In fact, Torey would have been content to watch movies until he had to be home.

But Brian did not go to Cassie's house to simply hang out with his friends and watch movies. Brian went to Cassie's house with an agenda. He just needed to check out the situation once he got there and see how things developed.

While the movie played, and the other three watched, Brian went into the upstairs bathroom. There he found something that sent him into a rage--a used condom in the trashcan. The sight of the condom affected Brian like a sharp slap in the face.

Brian is a jealous person. After Brian's arrest, his friend, Joey Lacey, told him that he had a girlfriend. Brian told Joey that he was happy for him, but detectives searching Brian's cell shortly afterwards found a story Brian had written about the murder of a young girl. Likely a fictional character based on the girl Joey had told him about.

In *Black River* Brian wrote about his love for Danielle Morrison, and his inability to speak to her. He wrote about his hatred and jealously of the "guys" who could talk to girls, and his desire to kill those who had what he did not.

The condom was a reminder to Brian that Matt had something with Cassie that he did not have. And for Brian, seeing someone with something that he did not have--was very difficult.

Brian carried the condom out to the living room. He wanted to know where it came from, and asked Matt if they could all, "tag-team" Cassie together. Matt said that Brian made obscene thrusting motions with his hips and acted, "like a two year old."

Brian may have tried to hide his anger by pretending that he was joking, but inside he seethed. Brian went downstairs alone. He unlocked the back door leading from the garage to the house. In case someone followed him, he went to the universal gym and pretended to work out. That is where Cassie found him when she went downstairs looking for him minutes later. Matt came down after

Cassie and all three, Cassie, Matt and Brian, walked back up the stairs together where they rejoined Torey, who was still in the living room watching the movie.

By then, Brian knew that Cassie and Matt were truly alone. No one else was going to show up. He'd unlocked a door, and was ready to go. He invented a story so that he could leave, but the details of the story are sketchy. Brian told detectives that he was bored, so he told Cassie and Matt that he had to be home by 9:30. But Matt told the same detectives that Brian and Torey left to see a movie, and that he talked to Torey on his cell phone while they were at the movie.

Whatever the excuse, Torey and Brian left. But before doing so, Matt asked Torey if he could spend the night at our house that night. Torey said he thought that would be okay. Torey offered to come back later and pick Matt up if he needed a ride. Matt said he'd ask his mom.

Torey and Brian left. They headed to Torey's car, where they had a discussion.

CHAPTER TWENTY-SEVEN

Brian's Plan

I can understand why Torey was unable to believe that Brian actually planned to murder Cassie. It is even difficult for *me* to believe it. From the evidence of Brian's behavior, I know he thought about it, but some part of me still wants to believe that Brian surprised even himself with his actions.

Torey did not know what Brian had in mind when they left Cassie's house. He was just along for the ride. If Brian wanted to stay, they could stay; and if Brian wanted to leave, they could leave.

After they returned to the car, Brian told Torey that he wanted to play a joke on Cassie and Matt. Brian said that he had two shirts and the masks in his soccer bag. They could put on costumes and sneak back into the house and really scare the shit out of both of them. (Maybe Brian even thought that would be enough to punish Matt for the condom.) Brian described to Torey how funny it would be after they revealed themselves.

But how could Torey go back into the house with Brian, especially after everything that Brian had said on the tape? Precisely because everything that had been said--*was* said on tape. Knowing Brian, the subject matter was not out of the ordinary. Placing it on the tape made it even more unbelievable. And Brian was notorious for his childish pranks. It was completely plausible that Brian originally intended only to scare Cassie and Matt.

Still, Torey felt a tinge of nervousness. Brian was always doing something crazy (just as he had earlier that night when he'd discovered the condom), and Torey worried that Brian would do something that would get them both into trouble. There had been a couple of instances before with Brian, where Torey saw him pull off some crazy stunt that he couldn't believe. But Brian always seemed to know where to draw the line, and he never went *too* far.

This wasn't the first time that Torey went along with Brian against his better judgment. Almost every one of Brian's friends found themselves in some kind of trouble with him at one time or another. There had been just such an incident the past week during the lunch recess. That day Torey, Brian, and Joey Lacey left the school grounds, as they did every day, to go to lunch. Torey was driving his car and they had entered a line of cars at a local dive through restaurant. Brian jumped out of the car, and using hand signals, directed Torey. Brian motioned with his fingers to move forward and then held his hand up to stop. He motioned again with his fingers and held his hand up to stop, all the while his face the picture of utter seriousness, until finally, Torey was bumper to bumper with the car ahead of him, which was full of teenaged girls, watching with wide eyes and shocked faces as Brian directed Torey right into their bumper. And Torey did it. He parked his car and jumped out and saw that he was less than a paper width away. No one was hurt, and the cars were okay, but it had been a stupid, childish prank.

Torey felt the nervousness, but it was a tinge of emotion, just a tickle under the bigger, broader knowledge that the world was safe. That nothing could ever really happen to him or his friends in the world that they occupied.

Torey thought that Brian would play his little prank and everything would be okay. He backed up out of the driveway and parked his car around the corner, out of sight of the house.

Inside the dark car, Brian turned on the video camera and filmed. The scene was well planned, the dialog perfect. Brian couldn't have been happier.

CHAPTER TWENTY-EIGHT

Entering the House

(This is my account of what happened. It is based on my conversations with our attorneys, crime scene analysis, and police reports.)

Brian put the camera down and he and Torey walked to the back of the car. Brian reached into the trunk and opened the soccer bag. His costume was going to be a black, long-sleeved shirt, gloves and one of the masks that he had purchased earlier. It was not a disguise, he was completely recognizable, and the only part of him that was covered was his head. But Brian called it his costume and he was satisfied with it.

Brian took the work boots out of the bag and put them on instead of his tennis shoes, because he thought they made him look cooler.

Brian brought another long-sleeved, black shirt for Torey. It was smaller than the one that he'd brought for himself. It was one that he'd worn in middle school that he'd outgrown, but Torey was smaller than he was, and Brian told Torey that he could wear it if he wanted to. Brian handed Torey one of the masks and the other pair of gloves. Spread out in the bottom of the bag, were four knives. Brian retrieved one, and handed another to Torey.

Once they got back to the house, Brian went in through the garage. Torey waited outside for what felt like a long time, but was probably only minutes, before Brian returned. Torey hoped they were leaving, but Brian motioned for him to come inside. Torey gently, quietly stepped into the garage and closed the door.

Because of the unique layout of the house, the garage felt like part of the home. The interior rooms wrapped around the garage and two of them, a bedroom and a bathroom, were accessible directly from the garage.

There were four interior doors inside the garage: one on the left, and three along the back wall. The door on the left opened directly onto the landing at the foot of the stairs. This was the door the detectives had entered when they followed Kelsey Contreras's path into the home on the afternoon that Cassie was discovered.

Around the corner from the landing was an open family room that was being used as a master bedroom. Directly behind it was another room. It was small and decorated as a young boy's bedroom. Through that room there was a bathroom accessed on the right. There was also a door leading from the bathroom to the garage so that the bathroom could be entered either through the garage, or the child's bedroom.

Allison had entered the bathroom through the garage entrance when she carried Cyrus inside after they returned from Jackpot. The interior garage door that led to the bathroom was on the back wall of the garage. On the other side of the bathroom was a utility closet only accessible from the garage, and in it was stored the furnace and water heater. On the other side of the utility closet, in the right hand corner of the garage, was a small storage room that the family referred to as the "clubhouse."

Brian motioned for Torey to follow him into the house, but Torey slowly shook his head no. He already felt like he was in the house, and in actuality he was. Brian passed through the door at the foot of the stairs and shut the door. Torey entered the "clubhouse" and waited for Brian to come out. It was approximately ten-thirty p.m.

Torey tried to listen to what was going on inside the house, but from his location he couldn't hear anything. Brian joined Torey in the clubhouse a few minutes later and told him that he's made some noise trying to lure Cassie and Matt down the stairs, but it hadn't worked. While he was in the clubhouse with Torey, Brian noticed that there was a circuit breaker in the room.

Brian turned off the lights to the house. (He later told detectives he got the idea from the movie *Valentine.*)

Matt described what happened. He said that he and Cassie were upstairs in the living room when the power went out. It was pitch dark. He and Cassie went through the upstairs and turned every light switch to the "on" position so that they would know when the power came back on. When they finished, they returned to the living room and sat on the couch. Eventually the hall light came back on and the outlet in the kitchen that powered the cordless phone, but nothing else.

Matt called Torey on his cell phone and told him the power was off. While Matt was talking to Torey (who was hiding downstairs in the garage), he noticed that Torey was whispering. Matt asked him why. Torey told Matt that he was whispering because he was at the movie theater with Brian. Matt seemed to accept the explanation. He did not question Torey further.

While Torey was on the phone with Matt, he could hear Matt teasing Cassie, trying to scare her. Matt did not seem concerned that the power was out. At first, he and Cassie sat on the couch making out. But later, Matt noticed the dogs acting funny. That's when he began to get scared. After waiting for the power to come back on, and realizing that it wasn't going to, Matt called his mother and told her the lights were out. His mother told him that she was coming to pick him up soon.

Meanwhile, Brian was going back and forth from the downstairs bedroom to the garage. He wanted Torey to come into the house with him, but Torey wouldn't go past the hallway. Brian was at a standstill. He was unable to lure Cassie and Matt down the stairs and he was too scared to go up. Finally, in desperation, Brian threw a glass ashtray down at the foot of the stairs hoping to create enough noise that Cassie and Matt would have to investigate, but they didn't hear it.

Torey was upset when he found out about the ashtray. Brian had gone too far. Now something was broken and they were going to get into trouble. Torey was ready to go, but Brian had no intention of leaving. Not yet. He was determined to either scare Cassie and Matt--or worse.

How I wish Torey would have left Brian then and there. Got in his car and drove away. But he didn't…

As long as Matt was in the house, everyone was safe. Brian probably wouldn't have had the courage to try to attack both Cassie and Matt simultaneously. If Brian had been successful at luring Cassie and Matt down the stairs, as he attempted to when he first entered the house, he would have had no choice but to play his little "joke" and leave. During that part of the night, that may have been enough for Brian. It may have even been, as he said, the reason he entered the house in the first place.

But as the night wore on, the situation changed. Matt told Torey, during one of their telephone conversations, that his mother was picking him up. When Torey relayed the information to Brian, Brian realized that Cassie was going to be left alone. His imagination probably ran wild. Still, Brian was working under the constraints of a time element, during which Matt's presence was, quite literally, saving Cassie's life.

Torey had an eleven p.m. curfew. Because we thought that Torey and Brian might have gone to the movies there was a little leeway with that, but not much. If Matt wasn't picked up soon, Brian was going to miss his opportunity. It was already close to eleven.

I believe there are a number of possibilities that could have saved Cassie's life. Had Matt's mother, Sherry Beckham, arrived just a half an hour later, Cassie would still be with us today. Ironically Sherri Beckham picked up her son, and left his sixteen-year-old girlfriend alone in the dark, at just the right moment to leave Brian barely enough time to attack and kill Cassie and still get home before anyone noticed something amiss.

Unfortunately, Sherry Beckham and her husband stood the greatest chance of preventing this from happening. They arrived at the house on Whispering Cliffs knowing full well that the power was out and that Cassie would be left alone. The power was not off in any of the neighboring houses. That should have been a red flag, if not to Cassie and Matt, at least to the Beckhams.

Had the Beckhams refused to leave a sixteen-year-old girl alone in the dark, in a house with no power; if they had taken her with them, or at least investigated the situation, entered the house to look at the circuit breaker--this nightmare could have been prevented. I will never understand how they were able to ignore such a precarious situation, and drive off with their son as if it were no big deal.

If Matt had stayed the night, as he had in the past, Brian wouldn't have climbed the stairs with his heart beating and his adrenaline pumping, knowing full well that he was alone with a victim at last. But once Matt left, it was over. When Matt walked out the door, the stopwatch on Cassie's life began to count down. She had minutes; perhaps even just seconds, before Brian, pent up from his years of longing, flew up the stairs and straight toward her.

Brian gave the police a very detailed description of Cassie's death. He lied when he told them that he watched Torey kill her from the hall. Matt told the detectives that when he left it was so dark inside the house that you could not even see your hand in front of your face. But Brian "saw" everything. He gave the detectives a clear eyewitness account of Cassie's death, down to the sights and the sounds she made as she lie on the floor dying.

Brian described the sound of the knife piercing her flesh, and the sound of her breathing as she struggled to take her last breath. As Cassie's lungs filled with blood, Brian said she "gurgled and snored." Brian "saw" it all because he was there inflicting every wound, and he heard it all because he was so transfixed in the moment.

Torey did not see what happened. He did not want to scare Cassie, especially now that she was alone, but he felt too intimidated by Brian to stop him. When Brian went up the stairs to "scare" Cassie, Torey refused to follow. He stayed behind, in the stairwell, hoping that Brian would hurry up and play his prank and they would be on their way home soon.

Above him, Torey heard a door slam. Seconds later, he heard the blood-curdling scream that Brian described to the detectives. Torey's car keys were in his pocket, his key chain held a penlight. He fished the keys out of his pocket and ran to the top of the stairs. As he flicked the small beam of light into the living room, he could not believe what he saw. Brian appeared to be hovering over Cassie, stabbing her, as she was lying on the living room floor.

Torey ran down the stairs to the breaker box. What was he thinking? That he was going to turn on the lights and go see what was really happening? He turned the lights on, but instead of going to Cassie, Torey ran to the car. Ran to the car and jumped in.

Torey fumbled with his keys, trying to start the ignition. Brian came running out of the house, almost right behind him. Brian threw everything in the car and Torey tried to back up, but he couldn't drive. He could not work the clutch and the brake. Rocks were spinning under his wheels as he killed the ignition time and again. It took a super human effort for Torey to get himself under control and able to drive. At this point, Torey did not know if Cassie was alive or dead. The scream had gone through his ears to his heart and stopped it like a lightning bolt. His mind and body were in shock.

Brian sat next to Torey and somehow managed to grab the camera, which he'd left in the car when he entered the house. Torey did not even realize that Brian was filming. Brian spoke the most important words on the videotape: words that were more than just words. Words that could not be dismissed as the immature talk of a child playing serial killer. But words that said, *I am a killer.*

Brian said, "*I* Just killed Cassie. We just left her house. This is not a f---ing joke."

Torey said, "I'm *shaking*."

Brian said, "I stabbed her in the throat and I saw her lifeless body. It just disappeared. Dude, I just killed Cassie. Oh, oh f---. That felt like it wasn't even real. I mean it went by so fast."

These *are* the most important words spoken on the tape.

Torey did not say that he killed Cassie, nor did Brian say that

Torey killed Cassie. Those words are not on the tape, and they never existed--because Torey did not stab Cassie. Not once. Not ever. Brian Draper did, and he admits to it.

Brian's words exist on the videotape he created and nothing will ever take them away. Detective Hamilton and Mark Hiedeman tried to slant them to include Torey, but the lone confession exists exactly as it was recorded. What is said on the tape is indisputable, and can be heard by anyone who cares to listen.

Brian Draper confesses: "…*I* stabbed her in the throat and *I* saw her lifeless body just disappear. Dude, *I* just killed Cassie..."

There is not one single "you", meaning Torey, in the entire statement, or confession, that Brian Draper makes. Early in the video, Brian is seriously (or honestly) contemplating murder. And now again, in his final recorded statement, he is speaking honestly when he says to Torey, "Dude, I (not "you", not "we"…I Brian Draper) just killed Cassie." And still the prosecution put Torey on equal footing, as if Torey and Brian were one and the same: thought alike and acted alike.

Torey did not go to Cassie's house with the intention of throwing his life away. He was completely shocked by what happened. But he knew enough to know that he was in serious trouble. He panicked. Torey knew that he had to get himself and Brian under control. Torey told Brian: "Shut the f--- up. We have to get our act straight." And there is no denying that is exactly what they had to do.

When Brian attacked Cassie--he trapped Torey. Right up to the moment Brian plunged his knife into Cassie's body, Torey never saw it coming. Cassie's scream signaled the end of her life and Torey's. From that moment on, Torey was trapped in a nightmare worse than anything his own imagination could have ever produced. And he did not know how to get out of it.

Cover it up. That was all that Torey could think to do. He knew that he was going to *look* as guilty as Brian, and he *felt* guilty for having allowed himself to be suckered into a *game* that turned deadly, because Brian lost control. Torey's first response was logical for a six-teen-year old child. He tried to avoid, or at least prolong, the punishment. Later, denial set in.

One of my brothers once asked me why Torey didn't tell us what happened. If he had, it could have saved him. I did not know the answer to that question for a long time. It took a doctor's explanation for me to understand. Torey could not talk about what happened. He was physically and psychologically incapable of it.

After the crime, Torey and Brian came back to our house where Brian spent the night. After everyone in the house was asleep, they collected a half empty bottle of hydrogen peroxide from under the bathroom sink and a blue garbage bag out of the pantry. They took one of the shovels from the garage and left to dispose of the evidence. They stopped at the Common Cents down the road from our house and Brian went into the convenience store and bought a box of wooden matches.

They drove to Blackrock Canyon, one of the many recreational sites surrounding Pocatello. Brian got out of the car and smoked a cigarette, a habit he'd just recently acquired. Torey stepped out of the car and urinated on the ground. He opened the trunk and Brian scooped everything from the car into the garbage bag.

Brian later told detectives that it did not look right: the bloody knife in the trunk.

While Torey waited in the car, Brian took the shovel and the bag and hiked into the bush off the trail. He walked far into the sagebrush and selected a spot that was unlikely to be discovered even by someone on foot adventurous enough to explore the rough terrain. He dug a shallow hole and placed the bag inside it. But before he buried it, Brian opened the bag and tried to catch the contents inside on fire.

Brian poured what was left of the near-empty bottle of hydrogen peroxide into the bag and lit a match. It burned, but not well, and soon went out. Brian lit another match and another. None of it burned. He threw the whole box of matches into the bag hoping to ignite it, but it didn't work. Brian gave up and covered the hole with dirt. It was dark and late. He threw some branches and pieces of brush over the dirt, disguising its recent disturbance, and headed back to the car.

Back at our house, Torey and Brian waited for the sun to come up. Neither of them slept. They did not talk. They did not discuss what happened. When it was safe enough to leave, when Brian could go home without arousing suspicion, Torey drove him.

Torey sat at Brian's house. A movie played on the television set, but Torey wasn't watching it. He was staring at Brian, wondering exactly what he had done, wondering if all this was real, and knowing deep down that it was.

It was almost as if Torey was waiting for Brian to do or say something that could take what happened away. Place it in the realm of a close call. What *almost* happened. But Brian did not have the power to do that. There was nothing to be said, nothing to be done. Torey came back home.

The prosecutor claimed that covering up the evidence was proof of Torey's guilt. But it was actually proof of Torey's fear. Fear of Brian, and fear of going to prison *with* Brian if Brian was caught.

I have no doubt that Brian's videotape was the catalyst in a chain of events that fell perfectly, effortlessly, into a path that led straight to Cassie's death. And that the things that could have prevented it...well...those things just fell along the way.

There was the unbelievable coincidence that Cassie was allowed to be left alone and unsupervised on the very weekend that Brian began his tape.

That Brian, deeply disturbed and preoccupied with horror films and murder, found out that she was going to be alone. And his mind would not let this perfect opportunity go.

That Cassie's boyfriend, who had been dropped off with her, and may have even stayed with her, had he wanted to, left her, because his father had unexpectedly returned to his family, on the very night and hour that Cassie was in peril.

There are lingering, troubling questions, and certainly enough blame to go around and around. I could have called Cassie, or talked to her mom; found out there was no adult supervision and kept Torey home. That would have put an end to it right there, at least as far as Torey was concerned. And for failing him in this respect, I can place the blame right at my own two feet.

PART SIX

The Trials

CHAPTER TWENTY-NINE

Brian's Trial

In January 2007, Judge McDermott finally severed Torey and Brian's cases and set two separate trial dates. Brian's trial was scheduled first. It would be held in April; Torey's the end of May.

Brian's attorneys knew their client was going to prison. Their only hope was to focus their efforts on a defense that could possibly limit the amount of time he spent there. They used the same strategy they'd developed during the preliminary hearing. They argued reasonable doubt for the murder charge by trying to convince the jury that Cassie could have been dead by the time Brian stabbed her. But it was a useless defense. No matter how hard they tried to blame Torey, they could not escape the hard evidence that Brian had, in fact, killed Cassie.

But Dave Martinez and Randy Schulthies used a two-pronged strategy. They also claimed that since Brian helped solve the case--he deserved special treatment. There is no doubt that Brian's role was pivotal. The detectives deny it and they will continue to deny it, but they really have no leg to stand on. Every bit of evidence used in the trials to convict both Torey and Brian came from the evidence that Brian Draper gave them when he took them to Blackrock Canyon.

But Brian's cooperation did not make up for the fact that he murdered Cassie, and his attorneys' claim that it did was absurd. Brian hadn't cooperated because he felt remorseful: he was trying to point the finger at Torey.

In spite of the saturation of pretrial news coverage, Judge McDermott refused to allow Brian a change of venue. With a frankly disturbing amount of ease, a jury was selected from the local County, and Brian's trial began on April 11, 2007.

Mark Hiedeman gave the State's opening argument. He told the jury about a beautiful young woman whose whole life lay in front of her. Cassie's picture was displayed on an easel in front of the jury. Gesturing toward the photograph, Mark Hiedeman informed the jurors that the young woman's name was Cassie Jo Stoddart and on Friday, September 22, 2006, Brian Draper, the defendant who sat in front of them, brutally and viciously murdered her.

Mark Hiedeman went on to say that over the next several days he would be calling witnesses and presenting evidence that would prove beyond a reasonable doubt that Brian Draper was guilty. He described the events that began with Anna Stoddart dropping her daughter off on Friday afternoon, the 22nd of September 2006, and concluded with Brian Draper's interviews and the discovery of the videotape.

Mark Hiedeman held up a highlighted copy of the videotape's transcript. He told the jury that what he was about to read, came straight from the mouth of Brian Draper. He quoted Brian apologizing to Cassie's family before he killed her, saying that because she was perfect, she was going to die. He flipped the pages and read some more, quoting Brian's words that murder was power and murder was freedom; that he had the grueling task of murdering his two friends. He concluded with Draper's confession: Brian saying that he'd just killed Cassie, that he'd stabbed her in the throat and watched her lifeless body disappear.

When he finished reading from the transcript Mark Hiedeman removed his glasses. He looked directly into the eyes of the jurors and solemnly told them, "That, ladies and gentlemen, is proof beyond a reasonable doubt that this defendant conspired to commit murder and then murdered Cassie Jo Stoddart. And when you deliberate, we'll be asking you for a guilty verdict on both those counts."

Mark Hiedeman did not lie. By the time he concluded his case against Brian Draper, he'd not only proved beyond a reasonable doubt that Brian was guilty; he'd proved it beyond *any* doubt.

Anna Stoddart was one of the first witnesses to take the stand. She described dropping her daughter off at the house on Whispering Cliffs alone with her boyfriend Matt on Friday afternoon. Anna said that she spoke to Cassie on the phone Friday evening, but that she had been unable to reach her after that. Anna did not see, nor hear, from Cassie again until Sunday afternoon, when she was found dead.

Mark Hiedeman performed the direct examination: "How many times did you attempt to call your daughter over the weekend?"

Anna said, "I can't recall specifically. Numerous times."

"Why? Why did you attempt so many calls?"

Anna looked defensive. "I don't know. I guess I was just being…I'm just an overprotective mother."

On the bench behind me, Brian's aunt scoffed. "Over protective mother my *ass*," she hissed.

It was not lost on anyone in the courtroom, including Anna, that she could have driven over and checked on her daughter at any time during the weekend, and did not.

Allison Contreras was called to the stand next. Through her, the discovery of Cassie's body and the 911 call was introduced to the jury. Within minutes of the call, sheriff personnel and paramedics began to arrive at the scene.

Deputy Karen Hatch, as first responding officer, testified next. She confirmed that Cassie was deceased when she arrived at the scene. Deputy Hatch described how she secured the home and interviewed the family. Through her interviews it was discovered that Matt Beckham had been dropped off on Friday afternoon with Cassie. Detectives Thomas and Ganske were sent to interview him.

Detective Thomas was called to the stand. He testified regarding his interview of Matt Beckham. Through Matt, Detectives Thomas and Ganske learned that Torey and Brian had been to the house on Whispering Cliffs on Friday night. Detective Thomas briefly described his interview with Torey, and then Mark Hiedeman began the long process of questioning the detective regarding his five separate interviews with Brian Draper.

Detective Tomas quickly went over Brian's first interview, which was conducted in Brian's home. When he finished, Mark Hiedeman played the DVD recording of Brian's second interview recorded at the Pocatello Police Station.

Brian was dressed in jeans and a black, long-sleeved shirt, and he initially appeared relaxed. The detectives left him alone in the interrogation room for a few minutes and he nonchalantly pulled out his wallet and counted his money as he was recorded. When the interview began, Brian Draper told the detectives that he and Torey had nothing to do with Cassie's murder. He stuck to his original story--claiming that he and Torey were at a movie when Cassie was killed. But when confronted by the detectives, Brian admitted that they hadn't been to the movies. He claimed that he and Torey had actually been burglarizing cars during that time. The interview concluded when Brian promised to come back the next day and take a polygraph examination. His relaxed manner was gone. Brian knew that he was under suspicion and he was showing obvious signs of stress.

After the recording was played, Judge McDermott recessed for the day.

On day two of the trial, Detective Thomas was back on the

stand and Brian's third interview was played for the jury. This was the interview where Brian, accompanied by his parents, arrived at the sheriff's office and implicated Torey. It had been referred to during the preliminary hearing, but the actual interrogation video itself had not been shown.

Without question, Brian's third interview was an extremely emotional event, and it was difficult for many people in the courtroom to watch it. It was especially difficult for me because I knew that Brian was lying. I had to listen to him blame Torey while there was nothing I could do about it. It was hard for Cassie's family because for them it provided details of their daughter's death, and it was hard for Brian's family because they had to relive the anguish of that excruciating day.

The recording showed a boy on the verge of an emotional breakdown. Brian's emotions ran extreme throughout the entire duration of the tape. He cried and shook, gestured and pled. That too was very difficult to watch, and when the tape finally concluded, Judge McDermott called a break. I went outside alone, surprised to see the blue sky above me. Just minutes earlier it seemed the whole world had been a dark, hopeless place.

Jimmy Hancock, the reporter from the Idaho State Journal, was standing on the front steps of the courthouse, smoking a cigarette. I had briefly spoken with him a few times since Torey's arrest. Now, he was reacting to the testimony he'd just witnessed. "That was too much emotion for me," he told me, shaking his head. "It just makes me sick. If I were on the jury, I'd have a hard time convicting Brian, after watching that interview. It looks bad for Torey."

"Torey's innocent," I said. "Wait until Mark Hiedeman plays the video Brian made, and I think you'll change your mind."

I had no idea at the time, but that was the pinnacle of Brian's defense.

During opening arguments, Brian's attorney, Dave Martinez, had truthfully stated that only one boy went into the house on Whispering Cliffs to commit murder. But he never told the jury that that boy was Brian Draper.

At this point in the prosecution's case, no evidence had as yet been presented that linked Brian to the killing. The interview we'd just watched was the first evidence submitted that proved that Brian was even present during the crime, and Jimmy's reaction to it seemed reasonable. It was hard *not* to feel sorry for Brian. He was such an emotional wreck during the interview.

Jimmy Hancock honestly stated his reaction to watching the unraveling of a human being. A child. And at the time the interview was actually taking place, I am sure the detectives sitting with Brian felt the same way. Brian came across as *real, raw* emotion.

But Brian was lying about who had done what. And it was not long before his entire defense quickly, irreparably, fell to pieces.

Back in the courtroom the interrogation tapes continued. The fourth interview was played and the jury heard Brian admit that he had stabbed Cassie a little bit in the leg and the chest. After Brian's fifth interview concluded, Mark Hiedeman played Torey's interview for the jury. Then he began his direct examination of Detective Thomas, who was by this time well prepared to testify.

During the detective's testimony, Brian's attorneys attempted damage control. But it was a vain endeavor to get the detective to admit, as he had in the preliminary hearing, that Cassie may have been dead when Brian stabbed her, because it was just as likely that she was not. This time Thomas avoided the trap.

On the fourth day of the trial, Mark Hiedeman introduced most of the physical evidence. Cassie's blood stained pajamas were submitted and hung next to the witness stand, a few feet from the jury box, where they remained throughout the trial.

Everything recovered from Blackrock Canyon was submitted, including the matchsticks and an old sock that had been found lying nearby when the evidence was gathered. Mark Hiedeman told the jury that blood had been found on one of the shirts, one knife, and one glove. It was the first time that it was publicly admitted that physical evidence existed that pointed to a lone killer. But the prosecution did not forensically test the blood stained items to see which boy was wearing them. They fully intended to use the same items to convict both boys.

When Mark Hiedeman submitted the masks, he handed them to the jurors so that they could examine them in detail. I tried to see what I could from where I sat. Though I knew what evidence the prosecutor had, I'd never actually seen it.

The videotape was the last item entered. As soon as the proper legal foundation was laid, Mark Hiedeman requested and received permission to play it. The press had been anxiously awaiting this moment. The bench behind us, where they sat, fairly buzzed with activity.

A technician was called to set up the television. There was a discussion about where to position it. The video was going to be played for the jury, but the press needed to be able to record it from where they stood as well. When everything was settled, the lights were turned off and the video played.

By then, I had already viewed the tape a handful of times. Instead of watching it, I watched the jury. Of course they realized within moments that Brian was guilty, but I wanted to read their emotions. I wanted to know if they were mad or sad or a combination of both. But they were stoic and composed and impossible to read in the dark.

I found myself wondering what Brian was thinking as he watched the video. He had not merely alluded to killing Cassie. He said that he was going to kill her, and that he did kill her. I wondered how he was rationalizing his statements in his mind. But of course I could not read his thoughts, and I just waited for the video to end, and hoped they wouldn't play it again.

When it was over, the lights were turned back on. Some of Cassie's family members were sobbing, and I believe Anna was escorted from the courtroom. The Judge said that concluded the day's proceedings and we left. Silently. I do not remember anyone saying a word.

Later, Jimmy Hancock wrote in his newspaper blog that much hype had already been made about the videotape's inflammatory nature, but, as he put it, "Little could be done to prepare one for just how incriminating the tape was for Brian Draper."

After that there was nothing that Brian's attorneys could do to proclaim his innocence and remain credible.

The next day Dr. Steve Skoumal was called to the stand. Mark Hiedeman began his direct examination by laying the foundation for his testimony. Dr Skoumal's professional history, education, and accreditations were relayed to the jury.

During his testimony, Dr. Skoumal explained how he performed Cassie's autopsy. First he examined her body for wounds, marking each wound individually as he located it. Once all of the wounds were located, he carefully went back and inspected them. When he'd finished, each wound was logged, marked with a numbered placard, photographed, and taped shut.

Next, the photographs that were taken during the autopsy were entered into evidence. It was a long and grueling process. Each photograph had to be entered individually, and there were dozens submitted. First, Mark Hiedeman would ask the court's permission to introduce a photograph. The court would then instruct Mr. Hiedeman to show it to the defense attorneys, who were then given the opportunity to examine it.

From where I sat, I saw Brian looking at each photograph as it was shown to his defense counsel. The pictures were large eight by tens. Again and again, Brian's eyes turned to see what he had done to Cassie, as he sat nestled between his attorneys. But his face displayed nothing more than the usual miserable countenance he wore throughout his trial.

After the defense attorneys examined the photograph, Judge McDermott asked them if they had any objection to its being submitted as evidence. That seemed to be a formality. When the defense objected, for whatever reason, they were overruled. But they were asked before each submission anyway.

Once a photograph was admitted, Mark Hiedeman carried it to the witness stand where Dr. Skoumal sat waiting. Dr. Skoumal would look at the photo; identify the wound it portrayed, and relate the damage to the jury. Mark Hiedeman would then carry the photograph to the first juror, who examined it and passed it on to the next, until each juror had an opportunity to see it.

The lengthy, arduous process was performed over and over again. Everyone was silent as we watched the well-orchestrated movements of the legal system in action. We knew what the jury was seeing, and we were sad. The only sound from the gallery was an occasional cough.

During cross-examination, Randy Schulthies asked Dr. Skoumal if he was able to conclude if it was a knife that made the wounds to Cassie Stoddart's body or not.

"Only in category. Based on my inspection of the wounds, I can only conclude that it was a sharp instrument."

Dr. Skoumal explained that stab wounds could be caused by anything sharp enough to pierce the body: a pair of scissors, a tool, or a sharp piece of glass, for example. The only thing a pathologist can determine is the depth of the wound, which he measures with a probe, and the width of the opening. Using those measurements, he can determine the *minimum* width and length of the object used, but there is no way to be certain of the exact nature of the object itself.

Not only was Dr. Skoumal unable to say what weapon Cassie Stoddart had been stabbed with, he certainly could not say for certain that it was one, or both, of the knives the prosecutor had in evidence. In fact, during cross-examination, Dr. Skoumal testified that it was impossible to tell if more than one weapon was used to inflict the wounds on Cassie's body or not.

Mark Hiedeman knew the problem he was going to face when his pathologist testified. Detectives from the Sheriff's Department were present during Cassie's autopsy. Detective Hamilton stated in his report that, "Early in the autopsy procedure, Dr. Skoumal advised that he was unable to determine if there had been multiple weapons used in the homicide."

At first, that was not a major problem. Initially the detectives thought, (or so I believe) that they were more than likely searching for a sole assailant. But by Wednesday afternoon, the situation had changed. Brian went into the Bannock County Sheriff's Department and gave them *two* assailants. The detectives needed a forensic pathologist who would testify that *two* weapons were used to commit the crime. When Dr. Skoumal was asked to do so, he refused.

The prosecutor was left with no choice. If he relied on the testimony of his pathologist, the jury could conclude that only one knife was used to stab Cassie. And if the jury concluded that only one knife was used, then they could easily conclude there was only one killer.

Mark Hiedeman was not going to allow that to happen. He sought a second opinion from a retired forensic pathologist. Dr. Charles Garrison was contacted by the State and asked to "re-examine" Cassie. He agreed to do so, which he did on September 28th, 2006. The day *after* Torey and Brian were arrested. Cassie had been dead for six days, and autopsied three days earlier.

When he finished his examination, Dr. Garrison was remarkably able to say that in his professional opinion two knives were used to attack Cassie, and that both of those knives were consistent with the knives the prosecutor had in evidence. What's remarkable is not only that Dr. Garrison was able to reach such a definite conclusion in the first place, but that he was able to reach that conclusion under the circumstances in which he examined Cassie.

By the time Dr. Garrison examined her, Cassie's autopsy had been completed, her organs removed, her wounds taped shut, and her physical condition deteriorated. What happened to Cassie was horrible, but she was violated a second time to get a testimony that I believe in all probability was inaccurate. And it was only done because Mark Hiedeman *needed* credible evidence that he could take to the jury that two boys stabbed Cassie instead of one. Because he did not have any evidence without Garrison that that was the case.

Therefore, after Dr Skoumal was excused from the stand, Dr. Garrison was immediately called.

Dr. Garrison was a Board Certified Forensic Pathologist in his mid-seventies. He had been retired for a number of years, but still contracted on the side. He reminded me of a stern old man, more like a retired judge than a doctor. His hair was silver, his face square, and his eyes a pale, pale blue. He wore a black suit.

Dr. Garrison based his opinions on what he perceived as hilt marks left on the body in at least one wound, and wounds that he claimed were consistent with serrated and non-serrated blades. Dr. Garrison testified that most of Cassie's wounds were consistent with each other, and caused by a serrated knife, but he thought that at least one wound was inflicted with a non-serrated blade. Dr. Garrison also differed in opinion with Dr. Skoumal over the total number of injuries Cassie suffered. Some wounds that Dr. Skoumal identified as two, Dr. Garrison identified as one.

Brian's attorneys did not cross-examine Dr. Garrison thoroughly regarding his two-knife theory; they knew that Brian had stabbed Cassie--it only benefited them to have Torey stabbing her as well. What they did question Dr. Garrison about were just two of the wounds Cassie had suffered, specifically two wounds that were found on her back.

Randy Schulthies asked, "Dr. Garrison, do you believe the wounds to Cassie's back were inflicted first?"

Garrison replied in the affirmative. "Not only is that plausible, but it is my opinion that they were inflicted first."

"Were those wounds sufficient to kill Cassie? Could one of those wounds have fatally injured her, and could she have passed away quickly from that wound while the other wounds were being inflicted?"

Dr. Garrison admitted that was possible, which was all that Randy Schulthies wanted from him. He excused the witness, hoping and praying that the jury would somehow believe that Torey stabbed Cassie in the back, and that Brian only stabbed her after she was already dead, or lay dying. As if that mattered.

Next, Cynthia Hall from the Idaho State Police Lab took the stand. She was the technician who performed the DNA testing in the case, and she could have shed valuable light on what happened to

Cassie, but her testimony was purposely, woefully, lacking.

Cynthia Hall explained to the jury how the items recovered from Blackrock Canyon were searched for blood evidence. Blood was found on only one shirt, one knife and one glove. Those items were turned over to her lab where they were checked for Cassie's DNA. Unsurprisingly, she confirmed the blood found on those items belonged to Cassie.

Because the prosecutor only had one shirt and glove with Cassie's blood on them, and because he planned to use the same shirt and glove to convict both boys, he did not forensically test the items to determine who was wearing them.

Mark Hiedeman did not need to prove that Brian was wearing the blood stained clothes to put a knife in his hands; and he could not afford to prove that Torey *wasn't* wearing them. The lack of forensic testing was a strategic decision.

When Cynthia Hall was excused from the stand, the prosecution rested its case.

The jury had the videotape, the items recovered from Blackrock Canyon, the pathology reports, the doctors' testimonies, and Brian Draper's police interrogations. I wondered how in the world Brian's attorneys could weave all that evidence into anything other than a clear conspiracy to commit murder. And apparently, so did they.

There was really nothing that Brian's attorneys *could* do. They did a reasonable job cross-examining the witnesses during the prosecution's case. They tried, whenever possible, to shift the blame off their client and onto Torey. But that was the brunt of their defense. Because once the prosecution rested its case, it was clear Brian had very little defense to present, and certainly nothing that could in any way clear him.

Brian's defense lasted approximately half an hour and relied on one witness. A forensic pathologist from San Diego named Dr. Harry Bonnell. Dr. Bonnell was a heavy, balding man who carried a briefcase and referred to notes that he had taken for his testimony. He presented no photographs or collaborating evidence to substantiate his beliefs, but his findings were probably accurate. Unfortunately he was so nondescript, he is barely memorable.

Dr. Bonnell confirmed parts of Dr Skoumal and Dr. Garrison's testimonies. Like Dr. Skoumal, he told the jury that he did not believe a conclusion that a knife was used to inflict the wounds on Cassie could be drawn from the autopsy photos or report. He explained that, unlike guns and bullets, it is impossible to link a knife to a particular crime. But, Dr. Bonnell agreed with Dr.Garrison that the two wounds to Cassie's back were likely inflicted first, as evidenced by the amount of bleeding those wounds had produced. He testified that in his professional opinion, Cassie had suffered one primarily fatal wound, which caused her death.

This is what he had been brought in to testify to.

All three of the forensic pathologists could probably agree, and Doctors Bonnell and Garrison *did* agree, that Cassie was stabbed in the back first. Dr. Skoumal testified that one of the stab wounds to Cassie's back was the only wound he could identify directionally, meaning he could accurately determine what angle the knife went in. Downward.

Dr. Bonnell described how Cassie was probably standing, turning to flee her assailant, when the knife pierced her back in a downward thrust, once, twice. The attack immediately disabled her. Cassie dropped to the floor where she lay while the rest of her wounds were likely inflicted. But her struggles would have been brief. The wound in her back was lethal, and she was dead within minutes.

The pathologist described the grizzly details. He did not testify regarding Dr. Garrison's assumption that two knives were used. But Dave Martinez told the jury that Torey could have stabbed Cassie in the back, and that she was already dead, or dying, before Brian's knife ever touched her. It was a defense Brian's attorneys tried desperately to present.

But, if both boys were stabbing Cassie, as Brian's attorneys' claimed, would it matter to parents, aunts, uncles, cousins or friends, to anyone who had ever loved a sixteen-year-old girl, and could not imagine her meeting an end like the one that had just been described, who exactly inflicted the fatal wound?

Still, it was the best defense Brian had. And I am sure he and his attorneys put quite a bit of hope into it.

Mark Hiedeman's cross-examination of the pathologist revealed that there was no way to determine who held the knife and inflicted the wounds to Cassie's back--or anywhere else. The pathologist admitted that even if there were multiple weapons involved, there was no way to prove that Brian Draper hadn't used them all.

As Dr. Bonnell was released from the stand, Randy

Schulthies stood and announced that the defense rested. For a moment there was a stunned silence in the courtroom. The defense was resting after only one witness? It did not make sense. Even if Brian were guilty, he deserved a fair trial. But before what was happening could even register, Judge McDermott was ordering closing arguments, and Mark Hiedeman was addressing the jury once again.

In closing, Mark Hiedeman simply restated the facts.

Brian's attorneys countered that their client was a frightened kid, who stabbed Cassie because he feared Torey. But the videotape worked against them. It showed Brian, not the least bit fearful of Torey, bragging about what he not only intended to do, but had done.

To be fair, Brian's attorneys had an insurmountable mountain to climb. They did the best they could with the time, money and resources they had. And now it was over. Shortly after 4 p.m. on April 17, 2007, the jury was instructed and entered deliberations.

I had an irrational and overwhelming fear that the jury would acquit Brian. I was scared that Torey would really and truly end up taking the blame for Brian, just like Brian wanted him to. And I couldn't have lived with that. Not with such a crushing injustice as that.

But the jury had everything they needed to convict Brian. Throughout the trial there was always that large, framed photograph of Cassie, alive and smiling, in one corner of the courtroom, and her bloodstained clothing in another. A stark reminder of what had been lost. Across the aisle, Brian sat with his attorneys, in an olive green suit and tie. Still a child, but dressed like the man he was becoming. Brian did not need a jury to condemn him. The evidence of what he had done was in front of him every day.

The jury, a group of twelve ordinary men and women, professionals and homemakers, had the picture of Cassie and the person of Brian sitting in front of them. Two children who lost their lives in two very different ways; an unbelievable, tragic waste staring them in the face. All they could do in an effort to salvage something was to give one family some justice and hope that it brought them some peace.

Five hours after they entered deliberations, the jury returned with a verdict. Guilty on both counts. Some jurors cried as the verdict was read, knowing exactly what this meant. But it was not an empty victory for everyone involved. The Stoddart family wept with relief.

During the trial, Mark Hiedeman had countered Brian's attorneys' claim of Torey's guilt with proof of Brian's. I desperately hoped that the prosecutor had reached the conclusion that there was only one assailant. Brian.

Now, my thoughts went to his family. What had this done to them? How were they going to make it through the night, and the days that lay ahead? That was what I wondered, as I still would not, could not, let myself believe that maybe, just maybe, we were next. That we might actually hear that same dreadful word spoken against our son: *Guilty.*

I saw Brian's parents during the next visit at the jail. I studied them, wondering how they were sitting there, carrying on, looking the same as they looked before. I thought it was over for them. *Over.* That's what my mind said.

I did not yet realize that there was a series of adjustments to move through. Sentencing and appeal notices. The shock of a son being moved to the other end of the state, the problem of how to see him, an adjustment to conditions revealing themselves one after another in a long series of steps meant to move the "justice" system forward, but in actuality is really nothing more than a treadmill that keeps the family going one small step at a time into eternity, forcing survival the only way it can. One foreseeable step at a time, never looking down the road farther than you have to.

CHAPTER THIRTY

A Chance To Help

For one hour each week, for the three weeks prior to his trial, Judge McDermott allowed Torey to be transported to his attorney's office. (Sometimes his escorting officer allowed Torey to stay a little longer.) The judge made it clear that these visits were for the sole purpose of allowing Torey and his attorneys the proper environment they needed to work on his case. Because of the security issues involved, the visits were to be conducted with absolute secrecy. No one could know about them.

I believe Judge McDermott made the same arrangements for Brian before his trial.

Our attorneys felt that Sean, his mother, and I could provide valuable assistance, and they motioned for us to be allowed to attend the visits. Because of the nature of the motion, the hearing was held in the judge's chambers away from the press.

Mark Hiedeman fiercely objected. He stated it was nothing more than a ploy by Sean and me to get more visits with Torey than we were entitled to. But Judge McDermott disagreed. He knew that Torey, as a minor child, could use all the guidance he could get. But he stated that the visits to the attorney's office were not for Sean, Barbara, or my benefit. We could attend if we wished, but first we would have to submit to a security check. If any contraband was found, the visits would come, in his words, "to a screeching halt."

For us, the opportunity was priceless. We could finally talk to our son, unrecorded, not behind glass, but in person. We could actually participate in the decisions concerning his defense.

Sean and I were never given the opportunity to ask Torey about what happened on the night that Cassie was killed. During our initial visit in the attorney's office we questioned Torey about it. Torey told us about going to Cassie's house and hanging out with Cassie and Matt. One of the attorneys, or maybe it was Sean, asked Torey if he thought that Brian was going to attack Cassie. Torey shook his head no. He said, "Brian never said anything about, about…"

Someone in the room asked, "killing?"

Torey nodded his head. "Yeah. He never said that, that he was going to…"

One of us asked about the video. Brian certainly said it on the video. But Torey said that was different. All Brian talked about when the video was off was what he wanted to film on the video. He never spoke about killing Cassie.

Someone questioned Torey further about that and Torey was adamant. It was obvious that Torey did not see the correlation between what happened to Cassie and the videotape. To Torey, they were two separate events.

The attorneys had been through that night with Torey forward and backwards. They knew exactly what happened, but we did not. One of us asked quietly, "What happened to Cassie, Torey?"

Torey tried to tell us. He started strong, but almost immediately broke down. He couldn't even say Cassie's name. His face went purple and he gasped, "Cass…Cass…" The veins on his head and neck stood out. He broke out in a sweat. His face was such an unnatural color. His eyes shut tight and it was evident he could not go on. Aaron and Bron and Sean told him it was okay, he didn't have to.

Later, Torey's psychological expert explained to me that Torey had physiological responses whenever he tried to talk about what happened to Cassie. I had seen that myself--in the attorney's office and at home on the night the detectives questioned him. The same expert thought the jury should see it too. He favored Torey testifying.

As Torey tried to gather himself back together, I reached for him. He was cold, and I knew from what I'd already been told that even though Torey did not see Cassie murdered--he'd heard it. And if that is not awful enough for somebody to have to live through, I don't know what is.

Torey's testimony was one of the issues we discussed. We did not know if Torey should testify or not. The biggest consideration was his age. Torey was very young, and Mark Hiedeman, a skilled attorney, could easily outmaneuver him. It was something we had to consider. But the fact was Torey needed to explain the videotape, and though I was scared, Sean and I both believed that Torey had to testify if we were going to win the case.

The attorneys were split. Bron believed as we did--that Torey needed to testify. Greg felt it was too risky, and Aaron wavered back and forth. Ultimately, Greg took it upon himself to adequately prepare Torey for the possibility, while Bron decided that he would perform the direct examination.

Everyone knew, except Bron, and perhaps Torey, that Bron was not the right person for the job. Bron's too wordy and cumbersome to understand. Why Bron's two partners did not tell him so, I don't know. But what I do know is that the hours we spent watching Bron question Torey were awful.

Torey sat in a chair in the middle of the room trying desperately to follow what Bron was saying as Bron questioned him as if he were both a defense attorney *and* a prosecutor. Depending on how Torey answered a question, Bron would switch back and forth between the two roles--until Torey was so confused he didn't know what to say.

Finally, Aaron told Bron that what he was doing was unfair. There was a big red flag in the room screaming that this was not going to work, and for a second it looked like Aaron was actually going to acknowledge it and confront Bron. But then he didn't. There was a collective sigh in the room, everyone ignored the warning signs, stood up, walked around, shook it off and prepared to start again. Torey was sat back down. Bron resumed his spot. Pain filled my heart. The firm was locked in a bureaucracy of hierarchy and ego, and I knew that Torey was going to pay the price.

To make matters worse, as Bron was questioning Torey, it became clear that Bron did not know the facts of the case. He was attributing comments to Torey that Brian made on the videotape. I was flabbergasted that Bron could be so ill prepared this close to the trial.

Noticing my anxiety Greg came over and sat down next to me. He told me not to worry. He'd go to the jail later and continue practicing Torey's testimony with him every night until Torey was ready. But it wasn't Torey I was worried about. It was Bron.

Later that night, I called Aaron at home. He knew I didn't want Bron to question Torey and he wasn't surprised when I asked him to do it instead. Aaron told me that Bron would never allow him to question Torey. It was not even an issue that we could discuss. He wasn't prepared to do it anyway.

Cutting to the heart of the matter, I asked Aaron if he felt comfortable putting Torey's life in Bron's hands. After a long pause, Aaron said that Torey would do just fine. But it sounded to me like he was lying.

We never did decide if Torey should testify or not. It was something we discussed every day, all the way through the trial. If Aaron had agreed to do the direct examination, I would have insisted. As it was, I just didn't know...

Another issue we discussed was what Torey should wear to trial. Torey wanted to wear a suit and tie and Bron agreed. Bron wanted to dress Torey like a deacon at church serving the sacrament. But I thought we should dress Torey in a manner that accentuated his age. I had visions of sweaters and hush puppies.

But an attorney visiting the firm weighed in on the decision. She said that Torey needed to dress as himself: a sixteen-year-old boy. She offered to accompany Aaron on a shopping trip. They went to JC Pennys and Dillards where they purchased cotton button-up shirts and khaki pants. They brought the clothes back to the law firm where they were available for Torey to try on during one of his visits.

The visits took place in the law library, and because we were all locked in the room together, for security purposes, we were with Torey when he tried on his clothes. The attorneys and Mom and Sean were respectful. They turned their backs as Torey slipped out of the baggy prison scrubs that he had been wearing for months and stood in his boxers. But I gasped when I held his pants out to him.

For a moment I stood suspended in time. I knew that Torey had lost weight, but I was unprepared for the severity of how much. Torey was literally skin and bones. His legs looked like they had when he was a knobby-kneed kid of about ten or eleven.

The others in the room, understanding what we were seeing and sensing Torey's discomfort, once again shifted their eyes and looked away. For a moment we talked about the practicality of the situation. Torey stood in pants that should have fit, but hung so loose upon his shrunken frame that it was obvious that they were going to need serious alterations. We had to find someone who could do the job quickly.

The talk diverted attention away from the situation, perhaps so that we could focus on something that we could do something about, as opposed to something that we could not. But I questioned myself. How could I have missed my child practically starving himself to death?

Later, I told myself that I couldn't have seen it. Torey wasn't with me. I only saw him in a baggy, shapeless outfit through a small glass window. I never got to touch him. But it didn't work. I could not appease my guilt so easily. I knew that I should have tried harder to reach Torey in his pain, instead of wallowing in my own. But how

I was supposed to do that, I do not know.

I am thankful that Judge McDermott allowed us the opportunity to assist Torey in his defense. He did not have to, and the time that he allowed us to spend with Torey was priceless. Torey was grateful too. He repeatedly thanked Sean and I, Grandma and the attorneys, for being there for him. He was very earnest in his desire to help, and he wanted to come home so badly.

But Torey never put up a fuss when it was time to leave. He obediently allowed Detective Fonsbeck, who was his guard throughout the trial, to handcuff him, and with his head hung low, submissively followed the detective to the car.

I followed Torey and Officer Fonsbeck down the hall as far as I was allowed. When they turned down the stairs, I went to the window overlooking the parking lot and watched them exit the building. Torey climbed in the back seat of the car, and Detective Fonsbeck shut the door behind him. The detective circled the car, climbed in the driver's seat, and drove Torey away.

And I wished, with all my heart, that there was some way, some way that I could go with him.

CHAPTER THIRTY-ONE

Mark Hiedeman's Opening Argument

Because of the news coverage during Brian's trial, Judge McDermott granted a change of venue for Torey's. He found a jury from Twin Falls County, about one hundred and eighteen miles west of Pocatello. Lacey and I traveled to Twin Falls and watched as Torey's jury was selected from the two hundred and forty citizens that Judge McDermott summoned for jury duty.

It was May 30th, 2007. The first day of Torey's trial.

In some ways, I actually looked forward to the trial. I knew it would be our only opportunity to get the truth out, and I trusted our attorneys to do that.

During our first meeting with Bron and Greg, I told them that they would never have to tell me that Torey stabbed Cassie, because he didn't. But they took the case believing that Torey was guilty. That was a hurdle they had to overcome, but I had faith that they would, and over time they did.

Our attorneys needed to prove to the jury, in the same way that they proved to themselves, that Torey was innocent.

In trial, the prosecutor always gets the first and last word. Testimony began with Mark Hiedeman's opening argument. He crossed the courtroom and addressed the jury with the same words he'd used in Brian's trial. "Cassie Jo Stoddart, a sixteen-year-old high school student with her whole life in front of her, died on September 22nd, 2006," he told the jury. "But she didn't just die on September 22nd, she was brutally and viciously murdered by that defendant, (he pointed at Torey) and his friend, Brian Draper."

It was mere weeks since Brian's trial. The prosecutor was determined to get justice for Cassie and her family, and he knew that he would. But he possessed physical evidence that pointed to one killer. I hope Mark Hiedeman questions the morality of the price he asked Torey to pay.

When Brian was sixteen-years-old he made an immature, possibly impulsive decision that he will never be able to rectify. No amount of pain, or sorrow, or regret, will change what he did. But Mark Hiedeman's decision was different. He knew exactly what he was doing to Torey, and the ramifications. He had nine months to decide if he was going to leave the door open for hope and redemption, and chose not to.

The prosecutor stood in front of the jury and methodically laid out his case. It was a story the jury may or may not have heard before. Cassie was house-sitting at the time of her death. Her friends, Torey and Brian, visited her and her boyfriend Matt while they were alone in the house she was tending. The two boys stayed for a while and left. After they left, strange things began to happen; the power went out. Eventually Matt's mother picked him up. And when Cassie was alone, Torey and Brian, who had reentered the house, murdered her. She was discovered two days later when the Contreras family arrived home.

After the murder, Torey and Brian headed to Torey's house where they spent the night. But sometime during the night the two boys left the house and drove to Blackrock Canyon, where they disposed of the evidence from their crime.

Mark Hiedeman told the jury that they would see the evidence recovered from Blackrock Canyon. They would see the shirts, the knives and the gloves, but the most damaging piece of evidence they would see was a videotape.

"The videotape," Mark Hiedeman said to the jury, "is a pretty compelling piece of evidence. On the videotape are the defendant and his friend, Brian Draper, conspiring and planning to murder Cassie Stoddart. The tape itself is chronologically in disarray--meaning that it jumps from day to day, time to time, so the planning and conspiracy--you'll see all during the tape, different places where they have planned, and they have conspired, to murder Cassie.

"One portion of the tape I would like to quote is toward the beginning of the tape itself and the following conversation takes place between Brian Draper and this defendant," he gestured toward Torey.

"Brian Draper: 'We're here in his car. The time is 9:50, September 22nd, 2006. Unfortunately we have the grueling task of killing our two friends, and they are right in that house just down the street.'

"Torey Adamcik: 'We just talked to them. We were there for an hour.'

"Brian Draper: 'We checked out the whole house. We know there are lots of doors; there's lots of places to hide. I unlocked the back door. It's all unlocked. Now we've just got to wait and, yep, we're really nervous right now. But, you know, we're ready.'

"Torey Adamcik: 'We're listening to the greatest rock band

ever, Pink Floyd, before we commit the ultimate crime of murder.'"

Mark Hiedeman looked at the jury. "The tape then jumps to 11:31 p.m., approximately an hour and a half after that was recorded, and the murder just occurred."

Again, reading from the transcript, Mark Hiedeman intentionally misquoted Brian. "Brian draper, '*We* just killed Cassie. We just left her house. This is not a f------ joke.'

"Torey Adamcik: 'I'm shaking.'"

Mark Hiedeman told the jury that the video, "goes on," but he laid the transcript down and read no further, intentionally ignoring the next few statements, Brian's excited exclamation that *he'd* just killed Cassie, stabbed her in the throat, and watched her die.

But Mark Hiedeman claimed the videotape wasn't the only proof of Torey's guilt. He faced the jury and said that Torey actually confessed to the murder during an interview with detectives. Mark Hiedeman relayed his interpretation of the events. He stated that during Torey's interview, the detectives were going over the evidence they had against him--and while they were doing so, Sean Adamcik, Torey's father, who was in the interrogation room with Torey, asked, "This is right, Torey?" and Torey responded, "Yeah."

Mark Hiedeman said, "Torey's father then asked him, 'What they're saying is true?' and Torey shook his head affirmatively."

"That, ladies and gentleman," Mark Hiedeman said, "and the videotape, are proof beyond a reasonable doubt that this defendant murdered Cassie Jo Stoddart. And this defendant conspired with Brian Draper in the days and weeks before the murder. And when you deliberate we will be asking you for a guilty verdict on both those counts. Thank you."

CHAPTER THIRTY-TWO

Aaron's Opening Argument

I had been waiting nine months to hear somebody publicly proclaim Torey's innocence, but it was not until Aaron gave his opening argument that I got to hear those words. To me, these were the first real words spoken in Torey's defense.

Aaron did not veer from the truth when he addressed the jury; he embraced it, and I felt certain that if he and Bron presented our case to the jury as he promised them he would--we stood a chance of walking out of the courtroom with Torey in our arms. And after listening to Aaron, Mark Hiedeman may have thought the same thing. This case wasn't the same as Brian's. It was not a clear-cut case of guilt. Torey was claiming innocence.

Aaron addressed the jury. "I know I introduced myself to you yesterday. *(During jury selection.)* My name is Aaron Thompson. This is my law partner, Bron Rammell, and this is my other law partner, Greg May," Aaron indicated each attorney in turn, "and we will be representing Mr. Torey Adamcik during this case.

"Folks, we face a lot of difficult challenges in our lives. We see loved ones and friends pass away. We watch our children grow and move on. We struggle in our financial situations to make ends meet. We make decisions that affect the rest of our lives, and these are the moments that make up who we are.

"The journey that you are about to embark on is going to be one of the most difficult tasks that you have ever been given. You're going to be away from your family. You're going to be away from your friends. You're going to have a lot of time to think. And you're probably going to be depressed over a lot of the issues, and the evidence that you're going to see. But our justice system does not work without you, and I want to offer my and Torey's sincere thank you for the sacrifice that each and every one of you are making.

"Over the next two weeks you're going to hear things that are going to change your life, and that's true of every person who has been involved in this case. And I can tell you from personal experience, that everyone sitting at that table," he looked over at Greg, Bron and Torey, "has shed tears, and my guess is, each one of you is going to shed tears in this case as well. And that's okay. There's no shame in that."

Aaron told the jury that this case was a tragedy from every

single angle. It dealt with teenagers. A beautiful young lady was killed due to stupidity, a young man was drawn into a myriad of darkness, and another young man was the source of that darkness.

"Folks, you're going to see a videotape," Aaron said, shaking his head, "and I'm not going to pull any punches. This video is awful, and you are going to hear and see things that quite frankly you do not want to hear, and you do not want to see. You are going to hear curse words, words of disregard for human life, talk of killing, and a lot of ignorance.

"And when you're finished watching this video, you're going to be angry, and you're not going to like Torey Adamcik very much. But that's okay. You just need to understand that the video is not a representation of Torey's life. It's simply a thirty-minute video that Brian Draper filmed and Torey participated in. It is not the real Torey Adamcik."

Aaron assured the jury that they were going to get to know the real Torey Adamcik. They were going to hear from his family, his parents, his older sister and younger brother. Torey's friends were going to testify, as were his teachers. Torey's teachers were going to tell them that Torey was quiet, hard working, obedient and respectful. That he had never been in any trouble.

Aaron explained that Torey wanted to be a film producer, and that he loved movies of every genre. "The State is going to infer that Torey only likes horror movies, but that's not true. Torey loves action films, cartoons, comedies, and, yes, even scary movies. Torey made movies with his friends. He wrote scripts."

Aaron described Torey's physical makeup. "Torey is five foot eight. He weighs a hundred and twenty pounds. He's not athletic. He's shy around girls, and just plain timid.

"But unfortunately, some time in 2006, Torey met a bad influence. Let me introduce you to that influence. His name is Brian Lee Draper. The Brian Lee Draper that exists when he shuts off the camera, is identical to the Brian that is on it.

"First of all, Brian Draper is more physically equipped for this. He is six feet tall, four inches taller than Torey. He's heavier, muscular and athletic. Brian played soccer in high school."

Aaron said that Brian Draper was infatuated with killing and death. He loved horror films and created a website dedicated to the band *Slipknot* and death metal music. When the police searched his computer, they found a story Brian had written where he fantasized about committing a school shooting.

"You will see that Brian was obsessed with the Columbine Massacre. And he wanted to be famous, just like those kids were famous. He even admitted it on the videotape.

"On the video that Brian made, you'll see him playing the drums. And this scene will absolutely haunt you. He is alone in his bedroom--he is shirtless--he is angry, he is beating on his drums. You'll see an angry prelude to a murder."

Aaron apologized for the language that he was about to use, but he told the jury that he was going to make a direct quote from the video. "You're going to hear a sixteen-year-old boy say, "This is not a f---ing joke. I stabbed her in the throat, and I saw her lifeless body just disappear. Dude, I just killed Cassie. Oh, oh f---. That felt like it wasn't even real. I mean it went by so fast.

"A sixteen-year-old boy admits on this tape that he killed Cassie Stoddart. Cold, callous admissions of a murder--enjoyment of a murder; exhilaration of committing a murder. He stabbed her in the throat. He watched her lifeless body disappear. He says it--her life--went by so fast. This boy takes ownership. He does not say 'we' he says '*I*.'

"That sixteen-year-old boy speaking was not Torey Adamcik. That individual was Brian Lee Draper. There is no dispute as to who makes the statement I just read to you. Ladies and gentleman, point blank, Brian Lee Draper murdered Cassie Stoddart. Brian Draper stabbed her in the throat. Brian Draper saw her lifeless body disappear.

"The State has to prove that Torey killed Cassie. It has to prove that he stabbed her, and it must be proven beyond a reasonable doubt. They also have a duty to prove beyond a reasonable doubt that Brian Draper did not act alone. But the evidence will be clear. The evidence will show that Brian Lee Draper killed Cassie Stoddart.

"Now, you heard Mr. Hiedeman speak about how there was a taped interview, and how Torey nodded his head and how he acknowledged. But Torey was not acknowledging that he killed Cassie--he was acknowledging that the evidence was found. And when you watch the interview, you will see that that is true."

Aaron continued with the evidence recovered from Blackrock Canyon. "Besides the videotape, the State found two shirts, two masks, two gloves, a pair of boots, and four knives. The State tested this evidence for DNA and blood, and you will see that the State's evidence falls woefully short.

"One shirt, which we will call the Calvin Klein shirt, has blood on it and the other shirt does not. One glove, a right-handed Puma soccer glove, has Cassie's blood on it. The other gloves do not. The State could have tested these items to see who was wearing them, but it didn't. We did. We did do the testing, and you'll never guess what we discovered. Brian Draper is wearing the bloody glove. Torey Adamcik is excluded from wearing the bloody glove. Brian Draper was wearing the bloody shirt. Torey Adamcik is excluded from wearing the bloody shirt. We will prove this to you through scientific DNA testing.

"The State relies on when Brian Draper had the camera on. The real world requires us to explore what happened when Brian Draper had the camera off.

"Let's talk about the boots that were found up in Blackrock Canyon. They're Draper's boots. No one contests the fact that they're Drapers. No footwear of Mr. Adamcik was found in Blackrock Canyon.

Let's talk about the knives. Cassie's blood was found on one knife and one knife only--a folding knife with a black handle. Now you're going to hear from several pathologists-- pathologists are doctors who look at wounds and try to recreate what happened.

"The State's doctor can't say which knife was used. In fact, he can't even say that it was a knife that was used to cause the wounds. But you're going to hear additional medical testimony that only one knife was used and we'll show that that was Mr. Draper's knife.

"Ladies and gentleman, the police shut off their investigation when this video was found. We'll provide you expert testimony that will take you through the mistakes that were made. We'll show you that the investigation of the crime scene was incomplete. We'll show you that the autopsy was incomplete, and the subsequent reexamination of the body was incomplete.

"We will show you that the State collected evidence from the crime scene that they did very little with. They did not investigate what happened. They did not test the blood splatter. You're going to see that there are experts available who can reconstruct the crime by looking at where the blood droplets are on the walls, the size and the angles. None of that was done.... Wasn't done. And they did nothing with the information it obtained.

"The State assumes that you will watch the video and you will convict. Ladies and gentlemen, the video does not prove that

Torey killed Cassie. It proves that Brian Draper did. He admits it.

"You're going to see some horrific things that you should not have to see. You're going to see Cassie's body. You're going to see wounds on her body. You're going to see blood. We do not dispute the fact that Cassie is gone. And we do not dispute the fact that she died by stab wounds. The State wants to inflame you with these pictures, and it will work. You're going to be mad and you're going to want to blame someone.

"The correct person to blame is Brian Draper. Torey did not know Draper's true intentions. He did not know that Draper was going to kill Cassie. He thought they were making a movie. He talks about making a movie on this video. You will hear him discuss that. He talks about scripts. He writes out a script.

"You're going to hear Torey say a lot of things on this video. Listen to the inflection of his voice. Is he serious? Imagine what you would think about Torey's words if Cassie weren't gone. And imagine when you watch the video that Mr. Draper had a different motive. Imagine that Draper wanted to be famous just like the Columbine shooters. Well, he got his wish.

"Like I said, you're going to hear Torey say some bad things. You aren't going to like him very much, but that doesn't mean he murdered Cassie. All the proof is consistent with one murderer. They caught him. His name is Brian Lee Draper.

"The State must prove beyond a reasonable doubt that Torey killed Cassie, and that's a very high standard. You must be so sure that Torey did this that you don't wake up months or years later wondering if you did the wrong thing.

"Torey did not murder Cassie. The State will fail to prove this.

"Now, I'm going to leave you with this last quote, again from Brian Draper. 'I stabbed her in the throat, and I saw her lifeless body just disappear. Dude, I just killed Cassie.'"

Aaron looked solemnly at the jury. "And then, just as he shut off Cassie's life, Brian Draper shut off the video."

Aaron gathered his papers and returned to his seat.

As we left the courtroom, reporter Jimmy Hancock met me in the stairwell. "I can see why you said you have hope," he said. "Aaron Thompson needs to give Dave Martinez a lesson in the law."

"Dave Martinez didn't have the same client to work with," I told him.

CHAPTER THIRTY-THREE

Testimonies

Mark Hiedeman began his case against Torey in the same way he began his case against Brian. He had set up the photograph of Cassie during his opening argument. Now, Allison Contreras, the 911 dispatcher, Anna Stoddart, Deputy Hatch, and Matt and Sherry Beckham were called to testify. They quickly laid down the chain of events that led to the discovery of Cassie's body. It was familiar, but emotional, testimony.

The detectives were scheduled to testify next. I knew what to expect from them and it was not good. Before Torey's trial, we motioned to exclude Torey's second interview with the detectives. Sean and I had asked for an attorney in Marchand's office before the interview took place, effectively asserting Torey's rights per Miranda, and because Torey was a minor child we had the right to do so. But the detectives denied our request and insisted the interview take place.

During the pre-trial hearing, Marchand, Thomas, and Ganske denied on the stand that Sean and I had requested counsel. They stated we willingly allowed Torey's interview to take place. At the time, I could not believe it. I never thought a police officer, or a detective, would deny the truth on the stand. Now I know better. I personally saw three of them do it in one day.

So when the same detectives took the stand during Torey's trial, I was terrified they would purposely misstate the facts again.

The first detective to testify was Ganske. It was through his testimony that the two interviews conducted with Torey were introduced to the jury. Mark Hiedeman began by asking the detective to describe the events that led him to Torey's house on Sunday night, the 24th of September. Ganske relayed the story, and the interview that took place.

Next, Mark Hiedeman asked permission to play Torey's second interview for the jury. When the tape concluded, Mark Hiedeman asked Detective Ganske if Torey had lied to him during his interview.

"Yes," Ganske said. "Everything that Torey told us during his interview was a lie."

Mark Hiedeman asked Detective Ganske why he disclosed the evidence he had against Torey, to Torey and his father during the interview.

Ganske claimed that at the time of the disclosure, Torey was being arrested, and that he was simply explaining to Torey the reasons for his arrest.

Mark Hiedeman asked Ganske, "Did Torey make any admissions during his arrest?"

"Yes," Ganske said, "as I was telling Torey why he was being arrested, Torey's father asked the question, 'This is right Torey, what they're saying is true?' and Torey responded, 'Yeah,' and nodded his head."

Bron began his cross-examination of Ganske by trying to get the detective to admit that Torey could have lied about what happened on the night of Cassie's murder because he was scared of getting into trouble. It was not a huge leap to make. Other teens, as well as adults, have lied to the police for similar reasons.

But Detective Ganske refused to admit that may have been the reason. Torey was not simply frightened of getting into trouble; he was concealing his guilt.

For some reason, Bron fixated on the issue. Instead of moving on, he badgered the detective until everyone in the courtroom was frustrated with him. To the jury, the spectators-- why did it matter? Everyone knew Torey lied. The question was "Why?" Bron was not going to get Detective Ganske to admit that it was because Torey had been surprised and horrified by Brian's actions; that he'd been terrified of both Brian and getting into trouble with Brian; and that he was young and inexperienced and simply did not know what to do.

Ganske would never admit that. Bron's best hope was to imply it, and hope the jury listened.

But, by refusing to drop the matter, Bron angered everyone in the courtroom. He lost respect with the jurors, and most importantly, he forgot to address the vital issue of what Torey was actually admitting to when he admitted to Sean that he had been to Blackrock Canyon.

I was angry. When we left the courtroom for the lunch break, I followed Aaron outside. I wanted to know what Bron thought he was doing. Aaron said he didn't know. It was Bron's cross-examination. He couldn't talk about it. Aaron crossed the street and got into his car.

I headed to the parking lot and climbed into my own car. I drove to the attorney's office so that I could talk to Bron. When I got there, Bron was standing in the hallway asking Greg and Aaron what the hell he could have done with a witness like Ganske? He stormed into his office and slammed the door.

I didn't know if Bron had noticed me or not, but Aaron and Greg did. Greg shook his head, and walked down the hall to where I was standing. "Bron's a tenacious bulldog," he said. "Once he gets a hold of something, he refuses to let it go. At least now you know what kind of a determined defense you're going to get." He insinuated this was a good thing.

Before I could respond, Bron came out of his office. Obviously he had noticed me in the hallway; and by the look on his face, he was irate. I immediately felt I had no business to be there questioning *him.* Bron pointed at me:

Note: Two days earlier, during jury selection, Judge McDermott had talked to our attorneys. The items they'd sent off for DNA testing: the clothing, knifes, fingernail clippings, etc...hadn't been returned to the evidence locker. He wanted to know where they were. Aaron and Bron told the judge the items were in the mail.

Now Bron told me, "You know the situation. The lab mailed the package back to us and it hasn't arrived. It's lost. That's the whole DNA case. That's what you *should* be worrying about. If I were you, I'd be on the phone to FedEx right now." He stormed off.

I couldn't believe it. I asked Aaron if it was true, the DNA evidence was lost?

"It appears so," Aaron said.

"It has to be found! Torey's life depends on it!" I cried. But Aaron didn't respond.

"Oh my God," I said, sick to my stomach. I felt like I was going to pass out.

"You could drive to Salt Lake, look through the warehouse. It's probably somewhere in their lost packages," Aaron said.

I looked at Aaron in disbelief. For one second I wished I was someone else, someone with some power and a backbone.

Greg said to Aaron, "We need to prepare for this afternoon's testimonies."

The attorneys entered the conference room at the end of the hall and closed the door. I stood for a moment trying to collect myself. When I felt that I could drive, I left.

Every lunch hour during Torey's trial we went to Quiznos and ordered Torey a sandwich, which we took to the jail across the parking lot from the courthouse where Torey was held. Though we could not see Torey, we could leave the food with a guard and hope they allowed him to have it.

That's what Sean was doing when I learned the DNA evidence was lost. I'd been so upset after Ganske's testimony that I'd followed Aaron outside without telling Sean where I was going. I did not see Sean again until we met back in the courtroom after the lunch break. I tried to tell Sean then about the missing evidence, but there wasn't time. Court was back in session.

The next detective called to testify was Thomas. He was the opposite of Ganske. Detective Ganske wore his emotions on his face. Detective Thomas was a stone-cold professional. He knew this was a career defining case, and everything he said was calculated. He came to the stand incredibly well prepared.

The first thing I noticed about Detective Thomas was his physical appearance. He looked exactly the same as he had when I first saw him sitting at our dining room table. As I sat in the courtroom, I found it difficult to believe that was only nine months ago. It felt like a lifetime.

Detective Thomas wore a suit and tie, but you could still see his massive forearms and thick build underneath; and when he spoke it was in the same deep, lisping voice that I remembered coming down the hall to where I was lying in my bedroom, trying to figure out who it was that was in our kitchen.

I believe that when Torey and Brian were first arrested, and the videotape viewed, Mark Hiedeman and Detective Thomas were certain that Torey and Brian were both killers, equally guilty. But they are both intelligent men. When the physical evidence started to come in, they could not deny that what it revealed was true. That Brian alone stabbed Cassie.

But I also believe, that neither man will ever be capable of admitting that.

Before Torey's trial, the blood evidence was not analyzed. But after we had the clothing tested, and it was determined that there was irrefutable evidence that Brian was wearing the blood-splattered clothing, and that Torey was not, the prosecution was forced to come up with an explanation--how had Torey stabbed Cassie without getting her blood on him?

For the first time since Cassie was found murdered, the prosecution "noticed" a lack of blood in the homicide investigation.

In Allison Contreras's 911 call she said that Cassie was covered in blood, and she was right. There was blood pooled under

Cassie's neck and knee and splattered throughout the living room. Blood was found in the hall leading from the living room, down the stairs, and on the doorframe leading out of the house. Cassie did not drop her blood there, her killer did.

Cassie put up a struggle. She may have been incapacitated early, but she reached out and grabbed at her assailant as he attacked her. Brian's DNA was found underneath Cassie's fingernails on both her left and right hands. When she was stabbed, Cassie bled profusely. Her blood splattered across the room and hit the wall under the window, across the couch and over and behind the television set. Her blood splattered on the person standing next to her and over her as he plunged his knife into her body again and again. Cassie marked both her killer and his knife with her blood.

Detective Thomas told a newspaper reporter after the two trials were over that Cassie's homicide was the most horrific crime scene that he had ever seen. "I honestly felt as if we were walking in a house where a monster had been," he said. "I thought we had a psychopathic killer on our hands."

He was not the only detective who felt that way. Detective Alex Hamilton, who had previous experience with murder scenes, and who personally took over *nine hundred photographs* of the crime scene in which Cassie was discovered; much of which was blood splatter evidence, told the same reporter that he had never seen such a brutal crime scene.

No one ever said there was a lack of blood, or that they were surprised by the lack of blood on or around Cassie, until Torey's trial. But suddenly, after the DNA tests were conducted, there was a *surprising* lack of blood involved in the case.

During his direct examination, Vic Pearson asked Detective Thomas, "How much blood did you observe during your time inside the house?"

"I noticed small amounts of blood on and around Cassie's body," Thomas said. "I was actually surprised at the lack of blood."

Pearson asked, "What about cast-off blood, which might come off a knife as it is pulled out of a body. Did you notice any of that?"

"I didn't see any of that," Thomas said. "I remember thinking it was weird. I didn't see the magnitude I would have expected."

During his cross-examination, Bron pointed to the magnitude of blood that actually existed, while Detective Thomas repeatedly, shamelessly, tried to minimize it. Most of Bron's questions centered on where the blood splatter was located, and how that location might have helped determine if it was Brian, who was taller, or Torey, who was shorter, who committed the murder. But Bron's questions were frequently met with Thomas telling him that he was not in charge of the crime scene investigation, and could not speak of issues relating to that.

Examining the blood splatter evidence would have aided the prosecution in its quest to determine if there was one killer or two. But they did not perform that testing. It was better for them to leave the question unanswered, than risk revealing what the test might prove.

Detective Thomas would never admit that the investigation was essentially completed when the videotape was found; that forensic evidence ceased to matter, as did the question of who stabbed Cassie. All that mattered after the video was found, was that there would be two convictions, and any investigating that could have jeopardized that--*was not done*.

Detective Thomas's testimony concluded late Friday afternoon. Judge McDermott did not want to see the jury sequestered for the weekend. He ordered us back Saturday morning. I could not imagine what was going to happen when the prosecution learned the DNA evidence had been lost, and I was so sick with worry that I could not imagine making it to the next day.

On Saturday morning, Detective Alex Hamilton was called to the stand. As photographer and custodian of the evidence, he played a large role in the prosecution's case, and it was through his testimony that Mark Hiedeman introduced the autopsy photographs and the videotape to the jury. He started with the autopsy photographs.

While Detective Hamilton sat on the stand, thirty-eight photographs that were taken during Cassie's autopsy were entered into evidence and passed to the jury. The procedure was the same as it had been in Brian's trial. Each photograph was entered individually. The only difference was--when the photographs were taken to our attorneys to examine, Torey didn't look at them as Brian had. He turned away.

While those of us in the courtroom could not see the photographs, we knew what they depicted. The mood in the room was somber. As one photograph after another was admitted into evidence, a member of Cassie's family began to cry. Soon he was sobbing hysterically and had to be escorted from the courtroom. Someone whispered it was a ploy, a plan to manipulate the jury's emotions.

At this point, no clear testimony had been heard as to who inflicted the wounds. Of course it was implied that Torey had; he was the accused, but I hoped the jury would listen to all of the evidence before reaching a conclusion.

I glanced at Sean's mother, Barbara, to see what she was thinking. She took notes throughout the trial, and during the admission of the autopsy photographs her mouth was set in a grim line; her pencil flew and her eyes were glued to the paper in front of her.

After Mark Hiedeman finished admitting the autopsy photographs into evidence, he questioned Detective Alex Hamilton about his trip to Blackrock Canyon. Seven more photographs, taken from the location where the evidence was found buried, were entered into evidence. Afterward, Detective Hamilton was excused from the stand, but he was told that he would be recalled for additional testimony later. He exited the courtroom.

Detective Brennan was then called to the stand. It was he who had excavated the evidence from the hole in Blackrock Canyon in which it was buried. During his testimony, Detective Brennan admitted that the evidence was not buried very deep. It only took him one and a half scoops with his shovel to reach it. After giving a description of the evidence recovered, Detective Brennan was excused from the stand.

Another quick witness was called: Detective Walker was the technical expert who had cleaned the videotape after its discovery. The videotape had been placed, along with all of the other evidence, inside the blue plastic garbage bag before it was buried, so it was protected from the elements. But a small piece of film, perhaps an inch, was pulled out of the case when it was first located. Detective Walker manually replaced the tape into the casing, and cleaned the case. He then played the video to see if it worked. Detective Hamilton, who had custodial responsibility over the videotape, was also present.

Now the stage was set for the admittance of the videotape. That had been the decisive moment in Brian's trial. Once the video was played--it was over for him. But Torey wasn't Brian; and, I thought, our attorneys had better damn well make that clear.

It had been a long day of emotional testimony. Now it looked like it was going to end with the video. But Judge McDermott recessed until Monday. We would not have to face the videotape until then.

We were exhausted. When Judge McDermott announced that the trial wouldn't resume until one p.m. on Monday afternoon, Mom said that she wanted to take the kids and go to the cabin.

Barbara always dreamed of owning a vacation home. She finally had one built near Yellowstone Park in 2005. It was a beautiful getaway, and one she needed. Barbara wanted to take Lacey and Jamie and leave Pocatello. The kids needed a break, and so did she. Sean agreed. He took the kids, and his brother Chris, who had flown in from California for the trial, and headed to the cabin.

Alone at home, I began a calling campaign. I talked to everyone I could get a hold of at FedEx. Aaron called them as well. We both explained the situation; a package containing evidence from a homicide investigation was lost in their system, and we had to locate it. Someone's life depended on it.

I was given the names of supervisors all the way up the company, but no one could help me on the weekend. Everyone I spoke with asked me to call back on Monday morning, as if that were an option. In the meantime, they assured me that they were doing everything they could to locate the package, which did not amount to much. Essentially a trace.

I couldn't understand how such a vitally important package could simply vanish, and no one seemed to care.

I called Aaron at home every few hours to find out if he'd heard anything. Finally, he snapped in exasperation. "You know, I'm not relishing the idea of telling the judge the package is lost. *I'll* be facing some sort of reprimand."

But I'd reached my breaking point as well. No matter what reprimand Aaron faced, it was nothing compared to the damage that Torey would suffer. But Aaron already understood that.

In actuality, everyone in the firm was working diligently to locate the package. Finally on Sunday afternoon, Tyler Bair, a law intern with the firm, had an idea. He suggested that maybe the shipping label was the problem, and the package was actually on its way back to Crime Scene Technologies, the firm that had conducted the research.

That was it. When Crime Scene Technologies shipped the package back to us, they failed to remove the original shipping label, causing the package to be lost in transit, unsure of where to go. Aaron called me early Monday morning to tell me that the package had been located and was on its way.

I had carried the phone outside. After we hung up, I sat on the back patio, with the phone still in my hand, and began to sob. Great wrenching heaves wracked my body. I needed to call Sean and tell him the good news, but I couldn't. It took forever before I could get myself back under control and by then I was drained. I sat looking at the sky and the ground and everything around me, too tired to move. Suddenly I realized the phone was ringing. I pushed the button to answer it, thinking it must be Sean, but it was Bron.

Mark Hiedeman had contacted him that morning with an offer we needed to discuss. Bron asked how soon we could be in the office. I told Bron that Sean and Barbara were at the cabin, and would be back in time for the trial that afternoon. Bron couldn't believe they'd left town. He told me to get a hold of them and tell them that we needed to meet as soon as possible. I told Bron that I could be in the office in ten minutes, but he refused to speak with me alone.

I called Sean and told him the prosecution had presented an offer. We needed to meet with the attorneys before the proceedings began. Sean said they'd leave right away. I asked him what he thought the offer could be. Sean said he didn't know, but he'd hurry home and we'd find out.

My mind raced. I wasn't tired anymore. I was frenetic. My hopes soared and so did my fear. I actually, seriously, considered the possibility that Mark Hiedeman was going to admit that Torey hadn't stabbed Cassie; that Brian had acted alone. But I knew the prosecutor would ask Torey to plead guilty to accessory and that we'd be discussing a prison term, and I wondered how many years of incarceration I could agree to let my son serve. Ten, fifteen?

I wanted Sean home *now*. I showered and dressed, convinced that everything was about to change.

I called Sean on his cell phone trying to determine when he'd arrive. While we were on the phone, I remembered to tell him that the DNA package had been located. Sean had been just as worried as I was over the lost package, and he was upset with me for not telling him earlier that it had been found. We were both at the end of our ropes emotionally and it was difficult not to argue.

Sean and Barbara finally arrived in Pocatello around twelve p.m. By the time we met with the attorneys there wasn't much time left before the trial was scheduled to resume. I was thinking (very *Law and Order* like) about plea deals. I could picture a meeting between Mark Hiedeman and us trying to talk about what happened.

But in reality we met alone with our attorneys. In the conference room at the end of the hall they presented us an offer from the prosecution that was unlike anything I could have imagined. It *wasn't* an offer. It was a threat. And in that brief thirty-minute window, before the trial resumed for the day, our attorneys made a decision that I believe may have cost Torey his freedom.

Aaron shut the conference room door. If Torey was about to be offered a deal worth considering--there was no hint of it in the air, not in the faces of the attorneys, not in their manner. As soon as we were seated, Bron told us that the prosecution had discovered additional evidence against Torey. They threatened to use it if we refused to cooperate with their demands.

I had no idea what Bron was talking about.

Bron said that the prosecution had just discovered pornographic material under Torey's user name on our computer. If we put on any character witnesses, Mark Hiedeman was going to show it to the jury.

Character witnessing would be information about Torey's home and school life, testimony from friends, family, teachers and psychiatrists, anyone who could shed light on what type of child Torey was.

From the beginning Sean and I had a defense in mind. We made it clear. Bron was the lead attorney in the case. The medical testimonies and homicide investigation we trusted to him. But we wanted the jury to *Know Our Son.*

We wanted to give the jury every single piece of information about Torey that we could, because if anything was going to save Torey, it was his character. Torey was incapable of killing Cassie, and unless the jury knew him, they would never understand that.

To give the jury an adequate understanding of who Torey was, we would need the testimonies of everyone involved in his life: our family, friends, neighbors, clergy, Torey's teachers, classmates, his bowling coach, his best friends and their parents, everyone who knew Torey had to be heard.

And Torey's psychologist needed to testify. Dr. Mark Corgiat was a Board Certified Forensic Psychologist. After examining Torey, he confirmed what we already knew. That Torey shouldn't have been involved in this crime, and that he had been completely taken aback by Brian's actions.

Torey was a normal, happy child. He wasn't obsessive, depressed or suicidal. He had no history or inclination toward violent behaviors, thoughts or tendencies. Dr. Corgiat found that Torey was trusting, and he had been manipulated.

The jury *had* to know Torey. As far as I was concerned the prosecution was asking for the impossible. To give up our character witnesses would be to give up our defense.

Sean felt the same way, but he wanted to know exactly what we were talking about. Bron gave him a disk and the two of them, Bron and Sean, carried it down to the computer at the end of the conference table. Sean loaded the disc into the computer and searched the file record. The State hadn't just found it. The disk was created almost six weeks earlier. Mark Hiedeman knew the material existed before he ever went to trial, he just intended to use it as a weapon.

Sean pointed out that the material was *not* late discovery. The prosecution should have admitted it into evidence before the trial began. Sean wanted Bron to file a motion asking to suppress it, but Bron refused, stating that it would be a losing battle.

I did not believe anything on the disk could be damaging enough to justify the loss of our character witnesses. But the attorneys disagreed. They told us the disk contained six pictures of a nude teen-aged male. It was homosexual pornography, and extremely prejudicial.

I couldn't understand why Torey would have something like that on the computer. I asked if anyone had questioned Torey about it. Aaron said that he met with Torey right after receiving the disk, and Torey denied any knowledge of it.

Sean said we could fight it. Our computers weren't password protected. Anyone could access any profile. The fact that the file was located on Torey's profile proved nothing. There was no telling who put it there.

Sean also pointed out that this was a murder trial. Pornography had nothing to do with the charges Torey was facing. Even if the jury believed Torey downloaded the pictures on the computer, what did it matter? It was irrelevant to what happened to Cassie.

Greg shook his head, "It is relevant. It goes to character. Pornography speaks so negatively against a person's character, jurors simply can't get past it."

That may have been true, but Sean and I didn't care. We wanted to put everything we had into Torey's defense. Let the prosecutor do what he had to, we could still give the jury the facts. All of the facts. But the attorneys refused. The decision was made, and we did not have a voice in the matter.

I asked about Brian. Were we still going to tell the jury about him? His character had nothing to do with Torey's. But Bron shook his head no.

"At this point, if we paint Brian black--it will just rub off on Torey," he said. "It's better not to have any character witnesses at all."

And to give up the entire defense we'd been promised.

I couldn't believe it. We had planned and paid for a defense that was suddenly over. Our attorneys did not see it that way. They pointed out the physical and forensic side of the case. But I knew that if the jury did not see Torey and Brian for who they were, two separate-minded individuals, they would lump them together. Torey and Brian would be just like Eric Harris and Dylan Klebold. Synonymous in everyone's eyes.

Brian had deep psychological problems that the jury needed to know about. The jury also needed to know that Torey did not share those problems. Not everyone is capable of plunging a knife into another person's body. Brian was that sick. Torey wasn't. And now the jury would never know it.

The day wasn't over, and it wasn't going to get any better. When the trial resumed, Detective Hamilton was called back to the stand. Through his testimony the knives, masks, shirts, videotape and other items collected from Blackrock Canyon were entered into evidence.

I realized that Mark Hiedeman couldn't have played the videotape on Saturday. He hadn't finished laying the proper foundation for its admittance. But this worked out better for him anyway, because by playing the video directly after submitting the evidence that was found with it, he tied his case together perfectly.

Presented so, it appeared that the knives and masks were intended for the purpose in which they were used. It would be up to our attorneys to prove that that wasn't the case.

After admitting the videotape into evidence, a television set was brought in, the lights were turned out, and the video played. I'd always known this moment was going to come, and I was well prepared for it. In fact, by now, I was quite desensitized. My main concern was for my family. They, like the jury, were the only ones in the courtroom who hadn't previously watched the video. Of course, portions of it had been released after Brian's trial, so they knew what to expect. But, quite honestly, I was worried about the language they were about to hear.

After the video was played, Mark Hiedeman turned the time over to our attorneys so that they could cross-examination Detective Hamilton, the detective responsible for the transcript of the video prepared by the State.

When Brian turned the video camera on, after jumping into Torey's car, he said, "Just killed Cassie, we just left her house. This is not a f------ joke."

The State's transcript reads, "*We* just killed Cassie, we just left her house. This is not a f------ joke."

The word "We" was inserted where it does not exist.

Instead of filing a motion and asking that the transcript be corrected, our attorneys waited until the trial to point out the mistake. That was *our* mistake. Because for months, Mark Hiedeman was allowed to claim that Brian said that he *and* Torey killed Cassie, when in fact Brian never did.

Now Aaron rewound the tape and played the misquoted section for the detective. When it was over, he turned the tape off and asked Detective Hamilton what he'd heard.

Hamilton said, "I heard Brian Draper saying, 'We just killed Cassie.'"

Aaron asked the court's permission to replay the section once again, and when he was finished, he once again asked the detective what he'd heard.

Hamilton said, "Brian Draper saying, 'We just killed Cassie.'"

Aaron said, "That's quite remarkable. Because what the video actually depicts, as anyone watching it and listening to it can hear, is Brian Draper saying, 'Just killed Cassie.'"

Of course Hamilton knew that, but there was no way he would admit it. The State's transcript, which he'd provided, was the only evidence linking Torey directly to the murder. Because right after saying, "Just killed Cassie," Brian *clearly* took ownership of the murder himself. "I stabbed her in the throat, I watched her lifeless body just disappear, dude I just killed Cassie," he'd said.

Hamilton was fully aware of the position he was forced into

taking. But it wasn't easy for him. He looked sick, and for a large man, he looked small, as he misquoted the transcript on the stand.

Still he managed.

And Aaron, (unlike Bron) knew a losing battle when he saw one. He also knew he'd made his point. He let it go.

Aaron next questioned the detective about some of the statements Torey made during the video. "Would you agree with me that some of the things Torey said came straight from the movie American Psycho?" he asked.

"Yes," Detective Hamilton said, "when Torey and Brian were in the car, and Torey asked Brian if he'd heard Ed Gein's words, that conversation was a direct quote from a scene in the move *American Psycho* with Christian Bale."

Aaron asked Detective Hamilton, "Have you ever heard of the *Blair Witch Project*?"

Hamilton shook his head, "I'm not familiar enough with that movie to comment."

"What about a form of movie genre called mocumentaries, are you familiar with them?"

"No."

With no more useful information to obtain from Detective Hamilton's testimony, Aaron excused him.

The next day Dr. Skoumal was called to the stand. This was the third time I'd heard him testify, and his testimony was the same as it had been from the beginning. Dr. Skoumal did not seem to be personally invested in the guilt or innocence of either defendant in whose trials he testified. He was simply giving the jury the information that he possessed that pertained to the case.

Once again, Dr. Skoumal described his autopsy procedure and the results. He pointed out the damage that had been done to a young girl in a brutal attack, but he was still unable to attribute any wound to any weapon, and could only say with medical certainty that Cassie had been attacked with a sharp object.

After Dr. Skoumal was excused, Dr.Garrison was called to the stand. He too had previously testified during Brian's trial. But this time his testimony was a lot more detailed. There were a couple of reasons for that.

During Brian's trial, Mark Hiedeman did not need to prove that Brian stabbed Cassie. Brian admitted it himself. But Torey's situation was different. Torey claimed that he was innocent, and there was no forensic evidence linking him to the stabbing. If Mark Hiedeman was going to claim that Torey stabbed Cassie, which he had to do in order to justify a first-degree murder charge, he needed something to substantiate his claim. The only evidence he had that would do so, was Dr. Garrison's testimony.

Mark Hiedeman also needed something to substantiate the first-degree murder conviction, if one was attained. Public opinion was strongly in his favor, and it would take a miracle for the jury to acquit Torey. But Mark Hiedeman knew his problem lay beyond the trial. If years down the road an appellate court looked into the case and noted the lack of forensic evidence tying Torey to the stabbing, it might create an appellate issue. Mark Hiedeman was determined not to allow that to happen.

He *needed* testimony that two knives were used in Torey's trial record.

Dr. Garrison put together a power-point demonstration that the whole courtroom could see. For the first time since Cassie's death her wounds were openly shown in court. In large, color slides, Dr. Garrison showed the slit marks in Cassie's skin where a sharp object, presumably a knife, had stabbed her.

Using a pointer, Dr. Garrison outlined some of Cassie's wounds, telling the jury that a flap of skin, or jagged opening, indicated a serration mark. He found serration marks on most of the wounds Cassie suffered, and determined that the majority of her wounds were inflicted with a serrated blade. But there were a couple of wounds where he was unable to find serration marks. He concluded a straight-edged knife caused those wounds. And while Dr. Garrison found a serrated knife had inflicted the majority of the fatal wounds, he believed a non-serrated knife inflicted at least one fatal wound as well.

During cross-examination, Dr. Garrison admitted that even if there were two knives used to kill Cassie, he could not say who used which knife. He could not even say that more than one person used both knives. All that he could say was that it was his opinion that two knives were used, and that those two knives were consistent with the knives found in Blackrock Canyon.

When asked to offer an explanation on why DNA evidence was found on only one knife, Dr. Garrison said that he believed degradation could have been responsible for the findings.

When he left the stand the doctor had given Mark Hiedeman exactly what he needed.

Next, Mark Hiedeman's forensic expert was called to testify. He knew that she was going to have to tell the jury that Cassie's blood was found on only one of the shirts, gloves and knives that were recovered from Blackrock Canyon. Since our expert was going to reveal that Brian was the one wearing the blood stained items, the prosecutor needed testimony that could explain how Torey could have stabbed Cassie and removed the evidence. He used his expert to show how that could have happened.

Shannon Larson, of the Idaho State Forensic Laboratory, explained to the jury the forensic testing that she had performed, and what the results revealed. When she was finished, Mark Hiedeman asked if it was possible to remove blood evidence from an item by having hydrogen peroxide poured on it, burning it, and burying it.

Miss Larson answered, "Yes, that's possible."

And it sounded reasonable.

But what Mark Hiedeman did not reveal was that Brian had used a near empty bottle of hydrogen peroxide that was taken from underneath our bathroom sink, and that when Brian poured the small amount of liquid he had inside the bag--where all the evidence from the crime was placed together--and tried to catch it on fire, it did not burn. It burned so unsuccessfully that it could not even ignite a single sheet of paper that was inside of the bag. And it had not been buried deeply, or for long.

If one set of DNA, (Torey's) had deteriorated to the point of non-existence inside the bag, as Mr. Hiedeman insinuated, Brian's (and Cassie's) DNA would have too, and to suggest otherwise was ludicrous. Truly the evidence was well protected inside the blue plastic bag it was buried in. And the DNA evidence inside the bag was preserved, discovered, and revealed to belong to Brian Draper.

During cross-examination Bron tried to point that out. He also asked about the findings under Cassie's fingernails. Evidence, which the prosecution could not claim, was compromised.

"Did you check Cassie's fingernails that you clipped during the autopsy?" Bron asked Miss Larson.

"No," she answered. "The fingernail clippings were not tested because they rarely come back with usable data."

It was more evidence of what the State had not done. Cassie wasn't shot. She wasn't killed from across a room. She'd been stabbed. There was every likelihood that she reached out at her attacker. And for the State to refuse to test for evidence under her fingernails and on her body, evidence from the scene and collected at Blackrock Canyon, was more than simply negligent. I believe it was criminal.

But the State's job was not to find the truth. And it was obvious that that was not what they were seeking.

When the detectives searched our home during the second police search, they took Torey's school notebooks out of his room. Inside one of the notebooks was a page that had the same categories written on it, as did the notebook entitled *Ideas for the Movie*, which was also taken during the same police search.

There was a partial "script" found buried with the evidence in Blackrock Canyon. It was written on a single sheet of paper, less than half a page long. The police called it a "murder script" but it too resembled the kind of short movie outline that the scripts on the last page of the notebook, *Ideas for the Movie*, contained.

It was obvious the same person wrote all three articles. The prosecution brought in a handwriting expert to prove that the writings were Torey's. When they were finished, the prosecution entered the script found at Blackrock Canyon and the page taken from the school notebook into evidence.

We never denied that Torey wrote the two items entered into evidence that day. He did. But as everyone that has watched the video knows--Torey was taking notes as Brian was filming in the library. It's only logical to deduce that's what Torey was writing. And even the detectives called it a "script."

Later, during the defense, Aaron entered the notebook the prosecution failed to submit into evidence. The notebook entitled *Ideas for the Movie*, which truly was the template for the other two writings.

Bron was unsure if he wanted Aaron to enter the notebook or not. But what the notebook contained was identical to what the prosecution had submitted into evidence, with the only difference being that it was written in a notebook that was clearly labeled for what it was--ideas for a movie. Aaron thought the jury needed to see that, and so did I.

Aaron had warned me earlier that the prosecution's case was wrapping up. I was the first scheduled to testify for the defense, and Aaron told me that I could be asked to take the stand as early as that afternoon.

He was right. After the handwriting expert was dismissed, the prosecution rested its case.

It was June 6, 2007. Eight days after the trial began.

CHAPTER THIRTY-FOUR

The Defense's Turn

I am not sure if the attorneys felt that my testimony was considered "character witnessing" or not. But I had pertinent information and I had to testify. It was probably one of the hardest things I've ever had to do. I felt that Torey's life rested right in my hands.

I've never considered myself smart, articulate, or even competent; and I was sick to my stomach with worry. It did not help that the only preparation I was given was for a brief hour the night before I actually took the stand. That was when I was called to the attorney's office and told that I needed to prepare. Aaron presented me with a list of questions and we sat down and reviewed them.

Most of the questions were straightforward. The only ones that concerned me were the questions dealing with the videotape Brian made. We had not yet reached a decision about Torey testifying. I knew that if he did not, it would be up to me to explain his role in the video. Something I was not, at the time, prepared to do.

As we reviewed the questions in his office, Aaron could tell that I was nervous and he gave me some advice. He suggested that when I testify, I put everyone in the courtroom out of my mind except for him. Just concentrate on him, watch his face, and pretend that he and I were alone in a room conversing.

That's what I did. The next day when I was called to the stand I focused on Aaron. I did not look at Torey, or the jury, or at anyone else that could have distracted me.

Aaron asked me one question after another. Who was Torey? How is he related to you? What kind of a child has he been? How did he do in school? What were his interests and hobbies?

I told Aaron that Torey loved movies and that he wanted to be a film director.

Aaron asked, "Has Torey ever made movies with his friends or family?"

"Yes. Lots of movies. When Torey was eleven years old we bought a new video camera. We always had an old VHS camera, but when we replaced it with the camcorder, Torey started using it to film short commercials and interviews. He recorded his brother and sister until he finally progressed to filming short movies, using them as characters. The kids had fun. They loved seeing themselves on film. Eventually Torey's friends started participating."

Aaron asked, "Do you have access to any of the movies Torey created?"

This was a moment we'd prepared for.

"Yes," I answered.

Sean and I wanted to show the jury, not just tell them, that Torey made movies. So before the trial began we compiled the movies Torey made onto one disk and took it to the attorney's office and asked them to watch it. Only Bron did.

When we told Bron we wanted the DVD submitted as evidence, he told us that it was too long. We needed to shorten it to twenty to thirty minutes of tape. But when Sean asked Bron which recordings he wanted us to include, Bron did not offer his advice.

Sean and I did not know what to do. Sean felt we should compile a combination of everything Torey filmed. But I felt we needed to concentrate on films that would show the jury that even if Torey was planning a scary movie with Brian, he was not going to make a horror film.

We could show the jury that the scary movies Torey made were simply childish spoofs. And that's what we did. We compiled a thirty-minute video of multiple recordings that Torey filmed with his friends that ranged in subject matter from different scenes taken from the *Scary Movie Trilogies*, to a hamster that was fed nuclear waste.

When we finished the disk, we took it back to the attorney's office. When Sean handed it to Bron, Bron told him not to be hopeful. He doubted it would be admitted into evidence. Mark Hiedeman had already been given a copy of the original, longer version of the disk and he had objected to its admittance. Judge McDermott ruled in his favor. Bron doubted the shortened disc would fare any better.

Maybe that explains why Bron, Greg, and Aaron *failed to watch* the shortened disk that they motioned to have submitted and played during the trial.

But we argued, when the time came, to allow the disc into evidence because even if it was not evidence of the murder, it was still part of our defense. It went to frame of mind. And at the very least, we believed, it would show the jury that Torey was just a child.

I believed that's why the State objected in the first place. But what we did not understand was that the video was a double-edged sword. It would either humanize Torey or condemn him. One way or the other it was going to have an impact on the trial and the prosecutor knew it. It was a risk the prosecutor did not want to take, and one we never saw.

Now, while I sat on the stand, Aaron held up the DVD. "Do you recognize this?" he asked me.

I told him, "Yes. It's a compilation of some of Torey's movies."

Aaron faced the Judge and asked to submit it.

When Aaron turned from me to the judge, I turned to the judge as well. From where I sat on the witness stand, he was on my left, high above me. Suddenly I felt very, very small. The whole courtroom came into focus, and I lost my connection with Aaron.

Judge McDermott grumbled sounds of irritation. Looking displeased, he told the jury that he did not see the relevance in what they were about to see, and he told Aaron that what he was attempting to show was a stretch, but if we wanted the DVD submitted, he'd allow it.

And almost immediately I wished he hadn't.

The judge set the tone, and Cassie's family cemented it. As the television set was wheeled in, Cassie's mother, with loud words and angry tears, left the courtroom. Her boyfriend, Victor, followed her.

Now that I'd lost my center of concentration, I could not get it back. As the movie was played, I watched the jury, the judge, Torey, everyone around me. The movies themselves were amateur affairs. There was nothing incriminating in them and anyone watching them could see them for exactly what they were. Neighborhood children with a video camera acting out scenes from movies, at once loud and obnoxious and funny as kids are. But since I had chosen to show movies with a common theme, it implied a common thread of interest that did not exist.

It wasn't good. The atmosphere in the room was cold and I could tell that the jury was not just seeing what was on the screen. They were viewing what they were seeing through the eyes of those who did not know Torey, but were viewing him as a potential murderer.

I suddenly realized that everything that Torey had been was stripped away from him as effectively as Cassie's life had been stripped from her. When Brian killed Cassie he not only rewrote the future, he altered the past. Eyes that would have never viewed Torey as anything other than a typical child, now searched for signs in his behavior.

And no matter how innocent Torey was, everything he had ever said, or done, or thought, or felt, could now be viewed as a portent to murder. An incredible leap, made possible only by the murder itself.

When the lights came back on, I tried to regain my composure, but I didn't have a chance. Aaron went straight from the DVD compilation to questions about the movie Brian Draper made.

Aaron asked, "How did you feel when you found out there was a video involved?"

I tried to cast my mind back to the first time I was told of the existence of the video.

"I knew that Torey was planning to make a movie with Brian, so I wasn't surprised."

Aaron questioned me about the damaging comments Torey made on the video, why he said them. I tried to concentrate on Aaron as I answered, but I felt hostility all around me. I was scared we'd made a mistake with the DVD and I wanted to start my testimony over. But I couldn't.

The comments Aaron asked me to explain were understandable in their context. But suddenly, sitting on the stand, I realized it was a matter of simplicity. You simply got it or you didn't. I knew that if the jury could not understand what Torey was thinking, there was nothing I could say that would make them understand. It was not an explainable truth--it just *was*.

Brian was talking about murder in a sarcastic, playful voice, with a video camera running. How could Torey take him seriously? How could anyone take someone serious who is never serious? Especially when the subject matter, so unfathomable to begin with, is taken so lightly?

Aaron asked, "Is Torey an atheist?"

I shook my head no. I told him, "We may not have gone to church every week, but we prayed together every night."

Finally, Aaron asked me about the night Cassie was killed. "Okay," he said, "Now I want to walk you through the night of September 22, 2006. Take us through that day from the best of your memory."

That was easier. September 22nd is permanently burned into

my memory.

I told Aaron about the discussion Torey and I had that night, when he asked if he could go to Cassie's house. How I finally relented and let him go after he gave me Cassie's address and told me that Brian was going with him.

Aaron asked, "Had you heard of Matt Beckham, before the 22nd of September?"

"Only as a friend from school. I didn't know Matt, but Torey asked if Matt could spend the night at our house that night, or Saturday night, and I'd agreed."

"What was Torey wearing when he left the house?"

"A brand new pair of jeans and a t-shirt with a band logo on it."

Aaron questioned me specifically about the pants Torey had on. "Did anything happen to those jeans, Shannon?"

"Yes. I took the jeans back to Zumies and returned them Sunday morning, the 24th of September."

Aaron asked me to explain how the pants were returned.

"I took the pants back to Zumies, where they'd been purchased, along with the sales receipt. The sales clerk laid the jeans out on the counter and searched them front and back making sure that they were still in new and resalable condition."

"Did they ultimately take them back?" Aaron asked.

"Yes."

"Did you get your money back?"

"No. I exchanged them for a pair of shoes and another pair of jeans."

Aaron held up the exchange receipt that I'd been given. "Is this the copy of the receipt you received?"

"Yes."

Aaron moved for the receipt to be admitted.

Next Aaron asked what Sean and I were doing while Torey was at the house on Whispering Cliffs. It wasn't much, watching television and reading while we waited for our children to come home.

"What time did Torey return, and how can you be certain?"

"Torey came in close to eleven thirty, probably around eleven twenty. Sean left to pick Jamie up at eleven from the football game, and Torey arrived home just before Sean and Jamie returned."

Aaron asked me about Torey's physical appearance and

demeanor, and if I had seen Brian that night. I told Aaron that Torey was nervous when he came into my room to tell me goodnight, but that he looked normal. There was nothing wrong or out of place with his clothes, but he did forget to take his shoes off in the house, which was unusual. I did not see Brian that night, though I knew he was in the downstairs bathroom.

Aaron questioned me about Brian, how long he and Torey had been acquainted and if I had any concerns about him. I told Aaron that Torey and Brian had been friends for approximately two months before this happened, but that they had only begun hanging out together regularly after the school year began.

The only concern I had about Brian, before the arrest, was his preoccupation with horror films. I did not approve of the movies he brought to our home.

Aaron asked me about Saturday. I told him we'd attended the ISU football game with Brian and his grandfather. I described Torey and Brian's subdued behavior during the game. At the time I did not know what had caused it. I thought perhaps a lack of sleep. That night, Matt spent the night at our house as planned.

Aaron asked, "Was Torey still wearing the shoes he'd worn the night before?"

"Yes," I answered. "They're his only shoes, besides a pair of dress shoes that he wears when we attend church."

Aaron questioned me about Sunday night, the night the detectives knocked on our door. I am sure that each family involved in this case has a polarizing moment. Mine was the night that Torey was arrested. Anna Stoddart's life was split in two on Sunday, the day she went to pick up her daughter and found out that her daughter was never coming home again. Of course the real date our lives changed was Friday the 22nd.

But Sunday night, at the time, wasn't life altering for me. It was shocking, and tragic, and terrible, but it wasn't going to change our lives. The detectives questioned Torey, he knew nothing, and they left. When I shut the door behind them my biggest concern was how I was going to help Torey deal with his loss. It never crossed my mind that he could be involved.

I told Aaron about Torey's reaction after the detectives left. How he cried so hard that he scared me. How he asked me over and over again how someone could do that to Cassie.

When I finished reliving the night, Aaron thanked me and sat down. The direct examination was over. Now it was Mark

Hiedeman's turn to cross-examine me.

Aaron told me that Mark Hiedeman wouldn't beat me up on the stand. If Torey took the stand, that would be a different matter. But the prosecutor had nothing to gain by attacking me, and Aaron didn't think that he would do so.

Mark Hiedeman began his questions with Saturday. "So, you noticed something wrong with Torey and Brian on Saturday during the game."

"Yes, I did."

"But you thought they were just tired?"

"Yes."

"And they could have just been tired. After all, they had a pretty busy night the night before, right?"

I knew that Torey and Brian were more than just tired. I knew that anyone in their positions, Brian as murderer, and Torey as unsuspecting accomplice, would have been experiencing a host of frightful emotions and their behavior reflected it. But I was completely unprepared to argue with Mark Hiedeman, and he scored his point.

"But Torey wasn't too upset to have a friend spend the night Saturday night. Matt spent the night, and some cousins, I believe?"

"Yes."

"Humph," the prosecutor said, shaking his head. "Bizarre." He looked cold as steel. "For someone as upset as you say your son was, I'd say he sounds pretty callous."

I had no verbal skills. To tell Mark Hiedeman that we'd already planned for Matt to spend the night and that Torey didn't know how to get out of it, sounded lame. But that was all I could say.

What I could not convey to the prosecutor was that Torey was a child. He'd always had someone taking care of him. He did not know what to do, on his own, in this situation.

Of course Torey knew that he was on a one-way road to hell--and he wanted off. But he didn't know how to get off. Everything Torey did was reactionary.

Mark Hiedeman continued, "So, after the detectives left Sunday night, you say Torey broke down in his room?"

"Yes."

"And he cried?"

"Yes."

"But we haven't seen any tears in the courtroom," the prosecutor said, alleging that if Torey wasn't crying in public, he wasn't crying at all. It was an allegation the prosecutor threw at Torey again and again throughout the trial, because Torey didn't cry in public. But he didn't need to. Torey's *face* showed his grief. I cannot even look at the pictures of Torey during his trial. He was so haggard. The dark circles under his eyes reached clear down his checks.

Torey started the trial looking boyish. His thick blond hair was cut a little long. In his street clothes, he almost looked like himself. But every day you could see a difference. His face broke out, the light in his eyes dimmed. Halfway through the trial, Torey snapped. One night he asked to cut his hair. The guard brought him a shaver, and he buzzed his hair nearly off. The attorneys had been irate. But it was clear; Torey was struggling just to make it through the trial one day at a time.

I told Mr. Hiedeman that Torey was devastated over the loss of his friend, Cassie. "Really?" The prosecutor said dismissively, as if I were lying. "And you say he asked you over and over again, as you're lying on the bed with him and he's shaking, who could have done this to Cassie?"

But it was not *who*, it was *how*. *How* could someone have done this to Cassie? That is what Torey asked over and over again.

Mr. Hiedeman asked about the homemade movies, where we kept them, why I allowed them, and most importantly what I thought they showed Torey's interest to be. By the time the prosecutor finished questioning me, I felt beat up, as a mother. Why else had I lost my son?

I knew that Torey was being misrepresented, but I did not know what to do about it. Torey did say horrible things on the videotape--but did he believe Cassie was going to get hurt? No. Did he know that Brian was dangerous? No. I could not explain that to the prosecutor and I went back to my seat, sick and defeated.

Rudy Riet was called to the stand next. He was our expert in crime scene investigations. I tried desperately to focus as he walked across the courtroom, took the stand, and was sworn in. But while Bron was reviewing Rudy's qualifications, which were extensive, I broke down. I needed to go somewhere to pull myself together, get some air. I got up. Sean asked where I was going, and I told him to use the restroom. He whispered, "hurry," as I fled the courtroom.

Halfway down the hall I heard my name called. I turned

around and Aaron was there. He asked permission to give me a hug, something he'd never done before. Aaron told me that I'd done a good job testifying and I looked into his face to see if he meant it. He smiled reassuringly at me and led the way back into the courtroom.

During the prosecution's case, our attorneys tried to show that once the videotape was found, the detectives stopped their investigation. They ignored the forensic evidence that, without the videotape, would have had to have been collected and tested. And we had an expert who could prove it.

We hired Rudy Riet, a seasoned crime scene investigator currently retired from the Utah Medical Examiner's Office. Rudy wasn't a pleasant person; he was brash and smug, but he was good at what he did; and what he did was crime scenes.

Rudy attended the trial every day. He knew the proper investigative procedures that should have been followed, and weren't. As the detectives in the case testified, Rudy noted the mistakes they made and passed the notes to Bron, who cross-examined them. It was a line of defense that angered the prosecutor…and apparently the judge.

When Rudy Riet was called to the stand, Mark Hiedeman objected to his testimony on the grounds of a technicality. Much of Rudy's testimony dealt with the knives in the case. He had preformed tests using knives that were identical to the knives in evidence, but he had not used the *actual* knives that were in evidence. And because the actual knives in evidence were not used, Mark Hiedeman wanted the tests thrown out.

During the ensuing exchange, which took place in front of the jury, a fight broke out between Mark Hiedeman and Bron. Mark Hiedeman yelled that Rudy Riet had sat arrogantly throughout the trial taking notes and making accusations. If anyone should have known that tests required using the genuine article--it should have been him.

Bron told Judge McDermott that we tried to use the genuine articles. Brian Cheney, an attorney in the firm, had gone to the prosecutor's office asking for access to the knives, but Vic Pearson wouldn't let him have them.

Infuriated, Mark Hiedeman jumped up and called Bron a liar. According to the prosecutor, Vic Pearson denied Brian Cheney access to the knives at the time he requested them, but told him to come back later and he would get them for him.

Bron turned to the judge in disagreement. "Your Honor," he said, "We believe we did not have access to the knives. If there was a misunderstanding, I'm sorry. But the knives we purchased are identical to the knives in evidence..."

But it was obvious the judge felt the same about our defense as the prosecutor. In an abrupt ruling Judge McDermott stated that Rudy Riet would not be testifying. Period. He did not cite the knives in question as the reason. He stated that he simply did not find Mr. Riet qualified enough to take the stand.

It was an unbelievable move. Bron had spent twenty minutes going over Rudy Riet's qualifications. Besides his years of detective work, Rudy was employed by the FBI. He'd had extensive training. He'd worked hundreds of crime scenes, far more than the detectives in Cassie's case would ever see, and they were qualified enough to testify.

I was stunned. We'd lost a fight I did not even see coming. It was a huge blow to our case. Rudy was prepared to testify about the knife wounds and the DNA evidence. There was no way someone could have stabbed Cassie with the straight-edged knife and removed all traces of blood. Not with the handle the knife possessed. And the blood-splatter evidence. Rudy had analyzed that. Now all that testimony was gone.

But not only did we lose vital testimony: our attorneys looked like fools, Mark Hiedeman looked righteous, and the jury knew exactly which way the judge leaned.

After Rudy Riet was excused from the stand, Judge McDermott closed the day's proceedings. Aaron met us out in the hall. Another large portion of our case was gone and he was not sure what we were going to do about it. He left to consult with Bron and Greg, but promised to keep us posted.

There was no news until the next day. I waited for Aaron in the hall and caught him as he was entering the courtroom. Aaron told me that we couldn't replace Rudy Riet's testimony, but there was still reason to be optimistic. Our forensic pathologist, Dr. Edward Leis, was scheduled to testify next. And he had a strong case to present.

If Dr. Leis could prove to the jury that Torey did not stab Cassie, then a first-degree murder conviction would be unjustifiable. The physical evidence pointed to a lone killer--and Dr. Leis's medical findings supported it. But it would be up to the jury to decide which doctor they believed--Leis or Garrison.

Dr. Leis was the Deputy Chief Forensic Pathologist in Salt Lake City Utah, Board Certified. His credentials were impeccable. He had performed over 7900 forensic examinations, and 5300 of those were actual autopsies. Even Mark Hiedeman was impressed when he took the stand.

During his direct examination, Bron asked Dr. Leis to explain how he had become involved in this case. Dr. Leis explained how Bron's office had contacted him and asked him to review materials that would assist them in gaining an understanding of the case, and he had agreed to do so.

"Now, Doctor," Bron said, "based on all of the information that you have received and reviewed, are you able to give any opinions to a reasonable degree of forensic certainty, that you believe may assist this jury?"

"Yes," Leis asserted.

There were two knives that the prosecution had in evidence, recovered from Blackrock Canyon, that they maintained were used to stab Cassie. One was a large folding knife with a serrated blade. It was a survival, or hunting knife, simply referred to as the "serrated knife."

The other was a straight-edged knife, manufactured by Sloan, and called the "Sloan knife" throughout the trial. It had a curved lower edge. Both would have been somewhat distinctive in the wounds they produced.

Dr. Skoumal could not attribute any wound Cassie suffered to any specific weapon, let alone the two knives in evidence. Garrison found serration marks in most of the wounds Cassie had suffered that were consistent with the serrated blade. But there was a wound to Cassie's chest, (identified as wound number "1" in Dr. Skoumal's autopsy report, not because it was the first wound inflicted, but because it was the first wound he inspected) where he was unable to find any evidence of the serrated blade, and this he attributed to the Sloan, or straight-edged knife, in his written report.

Dr. Leis believed that by lining up wound number "22", a wound which pieced through Cassie's hand as it lay on her chest, the knife entered into her chest inflicting wound number "1" in the same stroke. There were serration marks clearly present on her hand, and therefore all of her wounds were consistent with a serrated blade.

Dr Garrison also found that wound number "22" was

inflicted in this manner; but his written report stated that wound number "2", a separate chest injury, was the result of that thrust.

Dr. Leis used a power point presentation to demonstrate that Garrison was mistaken in his written report, and that Garrison had in fact used wound number "1" in lining up the injury to Cassie's chest during his examination of her body. The distinguishing features of the wound proved it.

"What does that mean?" Bron asked.

"That any description he gives wound number "2" is inaccurate, because the wound path from the hand is really associated with wound number "1"," Leis said.

Dr. Leis used wounds to Cassie's upper arm to demonstrate the position of her arm, and hand, across her chest, which further proved that her hand was not lying in the path of wound number "2" when it was inflicted.

Bron asked, "Based upon a reasonable degree of medical certainty, Dr. Leis, do you believe that of the knives presented by the State of Idaho in this case, that only one of those knives was used?"

Leis nodded, "Given the features of the wounds, the features of the knives, and the DNA evidence, yes."

Next, Dr Leis described the inferior autopsy that had been performed on Cassie; the lack of the pathologist, for whatever reason, to meaningfully document the physical findings.

"What about measurements of the wounds?" Bron asked. "Did you notice anything about that in Dr. Skoumal's report?"

"Yes," Leis replied. "He did some general wound measurements, but there is no mention as to whether these measurements were taken just as the wound is, with a lot of them gaping. Nothing was mentioned specifically that these measurements were taken when the wounds were apposed, or put in close proximity with each other. That is important because the best way to get an accurate measurement of these wounds would be making an attempt to put those wound margins side by side."

"Are there other distinctive features that are lacking in the report?"

"Yes. One of the things the doctor would want to describe is which direction did these wounds go. For example, was it from the front to the back? From the back to the front? Was it from the victim's left to right, or right to left? Did it go up and down, or was it pretty much horizontal?

"These have features. And when you have multiple wounds,

you want to compare these various pathways. If there is a big difference in several of these wounds, that may mean that there has been a change in the relationship, in the positioning, of the assailant.

"If all of these pathways line up--all in the same direction, that would mean that there is very little movement between the attacker and the victim."

That would be important information to have in a case like this, where the State claims that two people attacked Cassie, perhaps simultaneously.

Now, using the information available, Dr. Leis demonstrated how he believed the attack likely took place. Dr. Leis used a knife, which all agreed was similar to the survival knife taken from Blackrock Canyon, and Bron portrayed the victim. Dr. Leis demonstrated how the wounds left on Cassie's body could have been made.

Together, Bron and Dr. Leis reenacted the attack. Dr. Leis provided commentary of the wounds inflicted during the demonstration. Cassie was first stabbed in the back causing her to crumple to the floor, twisting as she fell and landing on her back. Her attacker, bending over her, then inflicted one wound after another, in a mad, rapid succession. At first Cassie may have held out her hand, in an effort to protect herself. The blade pierced her hand, nearly severing her pinky finger, and entered her chest. It was the end of her fight. There was no more resistance as the blade entered her again and again, and each time it withdrew, the serrated edge scraped and marked her skin, leaving behind evidence that could one day tell the story of what happened to a young girl.

Crime Scene Technologies was the forensic laboratory in San Diego California where we sent the DNA evidence for testing. Kelly Brockhohn was the forensic scientist who performed the tests. We flew her in from California to testify.

We supplied samples of Brian and Torey's DNA to the laboratory along with instructions for them to test the items we submitted to determine which of the two boys was wearing them. Miss Brockhohn testified that Brian's DNA was found on both the shirt and glove that we'd submitted for testing and she concluded he had worn both. Torey's DNA was not found on either item.

Earlier in the trial, Idaho State Police Forensic Scientist, Shannon Larson, testified that Cassie's fingernails had not been tested because fingernail clippings rarely come back with usable data. But Kelly Brockhohn had no problem retrieving usable data. She found the nail clippings from Cassie's right hand tested positive for DNA profiles from four different males, and Cassie's left hand tested positive for two. Miss Brockhohn stated that Brian Draper could not be excluded as a contributor of the DNA found under Cassie's left and right fingernails. She stated conclusively that none of Torey's DNA was present.

During his cross-examination, Mr. Hiedeman asked Miss Brockhohn several questions related to the DNA test results. He asked her to explain the methods she used to test for DNA. It was a complicated, scientific explanation but the results were conclusive. He could not argue them. The best the prosecutor could do was ask if it was possible that Torey's DNA could have been present even though she didn't find it in her tests.

"Was it there and not detected?" Miss Brockhohn repeated his question. "Yes, it's possible."

But it was not likely. Only one person could wear the blood stained clothes, and that person was Brian Draper.

Aaron told me that it was possible the defense was going to rest that day. I tried to tell our family that during the lunch recess, but no one believed me. There were too many questions left unanswered. But it was true. Back in the courtroom, Bron stood and told the Judge that he was calling his final witness.

When Mark Klinger, a former Idaho State Police Investigator, took the stand, I knew the jury was only going to get a fraction of the case we could have presented to them. Torey had a psychological expert, character witnesses, and his own testimony to give. But the jury would never know it.

Before we were introduced to Mr. Klinger, the attorneys told us that he was an expert in police procedures. But during his cross-examination it was revealed that he had spent the last several years investigating lottery fraud. It was Mr. Hiedeman's attempt to discredit the witness, but no matter how Mr. Klinger was currently employed, he was still qualified to testify about the evidence found inside the house where Cassie was killed.

Mark Klinger testified about the blood found throughout the home. When the detectives first entered the house on September 24th, 2006, they marked the blood droplets they found in the hallways and up the stairs with individual placards leading up to (or away from) Cassie's body.

When Detective Alex Hamilton photographed the crime scene, it was clear the photos revealed a single blood trail leading through and out of the house. A single blood trail, Mark Klinger pointed out, that was left by a lone killer as he carried his dripping knife out of the living room, down the hall, down the stairs and out of the door, brushing the doorframe with his bloody hand as he opened it.

When Mark Hiedeman finished cross-examining the investigator, (which was simply an effort to discredit him, not a rebuttal to his claim) Bron stood and told the judge we rested our case. Torey's defense was over. It had lasted approximately a day and a half.

Our attorneys later told us that they felt the case was in a good position when they rested it. Every single one of them told us that the State had not put Torey in the house when Cassie was killed, nor placed a knife in Torey's hands. Reasonable doubt existed.

The attorneys felt that for the murder charge, the confession from Brian on the videotape carried weight, and when coupled with the DNA evidence, and the forensic evidence, it was enough to prove that Torey did not stab Cassie.

It was harder for them to justify abandoning the conspiracy charge. The only person who could explain the comments on the videotape was Torey himself. But Bron was the only attorney who thought that Torey should testify, and for some unknown reason he gave up that fight.

But the attorneys told us that even if the jury believed Torey had planned to kill Cassie, once they saw the evidence, they would have to think he changed his mind. Because there simply was no evidence that Torey killed Cassie, and there was evidence that proved Brian did.

But what our attorneys seemed to forget was that the State did not need to put Torey in the house when Cassie was killed. Brian Draper did. When Brian said, "*...Just killed Cassie. We just left her house. This is not a F---ing joke.*" *He* put Torey in the house!

When our attorneys ignored that fact, and refused to state what Torey was doing at the time Cassie was killed--they cost us the trial.

Our only hope lay with honesty. Torey was on a videotape. He was at the house on Whispering Cliffs. By all outward appearances he was guilty. But Torey was not guilty and proving that to the jury hinged on truthfully confronting every detail of the case.

That was not done.

Torey called me the night his defense rested. Closing arguments were scheduled for the next morning. The trial had been hell for him. He wanted to come home so badly. He could be home in time for his birthday, June 14th. It was only the seventh.

I did not know how to tell Torey that his attorneys had miscalculated. I couldn't even tell myself. We talked about the hope we had, and tried to believe.

CHAPTER THIRTY-FIVE

Closing Arguments

Jury instructions are complicated legal documents. There is no one set of instructions for a crime. They are specific to the case, drafted by the prosecution, and dictated by state law. Defense attorneys have the right to object to certain points; but it is up to the judge to determine if the instructions fall within the limits of the law or not.

Friday, June 8, 2007 began with Judge McDermott reading Torey's jury instructions.

One of the instructions stated that, "If the jury found that Torey engaged in conduct that led to the death of Cassie Stoddart, the jury must find him guilty of First Degree Murder."

We objected that the terminology "engaged in conduct" was too broad. The jury needed to know specifically what engaged in conduct meant.

In the State of Idaho, to be found guilty of First Degree Murder, a jury must find that the defendant performed the act of murder; inflicted a fatal wound that caused death. That is why, during Brian's trial, it was so important for his attorneys to attempt to prove that even though Brian stabbed Cassie, he did not kill her.

But Judge McDermott allowed the instruction to stand. The jury could find Torey guilty of First Degree Murder even if they believed his only role in Cassie's death was driving to the house on Whispering Cliffs.

It took Judge McDermott approximately a half hour to finish reading the jury instructions; and when he was finished, it was time for closing arguments.

Vic Pearson gave the State's closing argument. During the trial he played a significant role assisting Mark Hiedeman. He performed direct and cross-examinations, but my only recollection of him is on this final day. When he gave the State's closing argument, Vic Pearson used every verbal and emotional skill that he possessed, and his words are still burned in my memory.

Standing and facing the jury, Vic Pearson began, "Cassie Jo Stoddart was born December 21, 1989. On September 22, 2006, this defendant," he pointed at Torey, "brutally and viciously murdered her. She was sixteen years old, ladies and gentleman. Sixteen years old."

Vic Pearson pointed to the large, framed photograph of Cassie, "Pictures such as this; and fading memories are all that her family has left of her. They will never see her graduate. They will never see her get married. They will never see her have children. They will never see her grow old. They will never see her reach any of the great milestones that she may have achieved throughout her life.

"Why? Because this defendant and Brian Draper wanted to be famous. They wanted to be *famous*, ladies and gentleman," he paused, allowing his statement sink in.

What Vic Pearson said could have been said about Torey as well. He too was only sixteen years old. We will never see him graduate from high school, get married, or have children. We might have the opportunity, if we're lucky, to watch Torey grow old--but in prison, alone and miserable. The great milestones that awaited Torey were robbed from him as well by the very same person who killed Cassie.

Vic Pearson continued, "Now, Mr. Thompson, in his opening statement to you, stated that this case is an absolute tragedy. It is. He also stated that Cassie was a beautiful young woman. She was. And he also told you that each and every one of you would have to see and hear things that no one should have to endure in their life. You have.

"You've seen photos of Cassie, listened to the 911 call, looked at autopsy photographs, and you have seen the videotape that was found in Blackrock Canyon. The videotape made by Torey Adamcik and Brian Draper."

It was clear from the videotape, Vic Pearson said, that two people were supposed to die on the night that Cassie was killed. Not just Cassie, but her boyfriend Matt Beckham as well. Vic Pearson told the jury that Matt Beckham was spared only because his mother would not allow him to stay the night with Cassie.

"What happened after Matt left," Vic Pearson continued, "we don't exactly know. But we have a good idea. The videotape gives us many of the clues." He pulled a copy of the video transcript from his papers and showed it to the jury. This was his crowning moment. Vic Pearson flipped the pages open and read the entire transcript to the jury, commentating the events from his point of view as he did so.

It was a dramatic and impressive performance. Vic Pearson punctuated the dialog with the skill of a seasoned thespian. His anger and righteous indignation filled the room as he impersonated the careless manner in which Cassie's murder was discussed, and the exuberance of Brian's final words after he killed her. I felt oppressed and sick listening to him. The jury's faces remained neutral, but their eyes followed him and I could see there was no disagreement in them.

The videotape was the best evidence the prosecution could ever hope to find, and Vic Pearson maximized it to its fullest potential.

After reading the transcript, Vic Pearson reminded the jury of a statement Torey made. "I quoted the defendant saying that killing should not be against the law. I think you each remember that particular section from the video," he turned and stared contemptuously at Torey as Torey's words hung in the air.

"I am here to tell you that killing someone *is* against the law. And a guilty verdict on both counts will send this defendant that message. Thank you."

As Vic Pearson returned to his seat Judge McDermott thanked him, then turned toward Bron and inquired, "Mr. Rammell?"

Bron stood, thanked the judge and the jury, and crossed to the podium where he gave his closing statement.

Aaron once wrote that Bron's closing argument brought tears to his eyes, and it was a deeply heartfelt appeal. But it was not so much the words that Bron spoke, as it was the way that he spoke them. Bron did not address the jury in a voice that was loud or forceful. But he pled with all the emotions of a man who knew that his client was innocent, and that a great injustice was likely to occur.

Bron was aware of Torey's age, and the fact that his life had just begun. Bron knew the only chance he had of saving that life, was the case he himself had presented to the jury. This was the last opportunity he had to address them.

Bron began his statement by thanking the jury and apologizing if he had offended them in any way. "I worry that personalities, styles, things like that, will be offensive to someone. And I want you to know that I apologize if I have offended any of you. I would ask that you do not hold that against my client or his family. I want you to know that my client and his family thank you."

In a surprisingly concise statement Bron got directly to the point. "You have a monumental task ahead of you," he told the jury. "You've just heard a passionate story. I suggest that you need to look deeper."

Bron asked the jury to do something that he said the prosecutor's office was unwilling to do. To set aside their passions and prejudice when they look at the videotape--and look deeper.

"If you do," he promised, "you are going to see a few things. The story that the prosecutor tells does not work. It does not work. Because once you open your mind to the possibility that the evidence tracks exactly what happened, you will see the physical evidence ties it all together."

Bron reviewed the physical evidence one last time. He told the jury that a defensive struggle took place in the living room between Cassie and her attacker. During the struggle, the cord from the play station, which was plugged into the television set, was wrapped around Cassie leg and foot. As she was attacked Cassie reached out at her assailant. Brian's DNA was found underneath Cassie's fingernails.

Bron told the jury about the blood evidence. There was a single blood trail in the house leading from Cassie's body, down the hall, down the stairs and out of the door. That blood trail could only have been left by a single assailant, as he carried a knife dripping Cassie's blood out of the house.

All of the evidence from the crime was buried in Blackrock Canyon, and of that evidence only one shirt, knife and glove, was found to contain Cassie's blood, and those items were worn by Brian Draper.

When Brian jumped in the car after killing Cassie, he confessed. In an emotional outburst Brian said, "Dude I just killed Cassie. Oh-- Oh--F---, that felt like it wasn't even real." But unfortunately it was real and everyone in the courtroom knew it was real.

Bron asked the jury to look at Dr. Garrison's testimony. Why wasn't he called as a rebuttal witness after Dr. Leis testified? Dr. Garrison sat in the gallery and listened as Dr. Leis stated that, based on a reasonable degree of medical certainty, only one knife was used, and he did not come before the jury and disagree. "What does that tell you?" Bron asked the jury, "It tells you Dr. Garrison actually agreed with Dr. Leis. That there was only one knife used."

Bron asked the jury to think about the physical findings on both knives. One contained blood, one did not. "Is the prosecution really going to tell us that because someone pours a little hydrogen peroxide on a knife, it's going to destroy the DNA from the nooks and crannies of that knife? That's ridiculous." Bron reminded the jury that they had heard evidence that you cannot get rid of that kind of DNA.

"But, I suppose I can understand why the police failed to look for the details. You cannot find what you do not look for.

"But ladies and gentlemen, there is a reason the State has an obligation to prove every element of a crime beyond a reasonable doubt. It is because we do not want the State to have the awesome power to come in and assume something--that may or may not be true." Bron shook his head. "They do not have the right to do that. They *have* to prove it."

"So when Mr. Pearson stands up here and holds up pictures of Cassie it makes my heart sad, but Torey didn't do it." Bron spoke emphatically, "He *did not* do it. And you know he did not do it because of the evidence."

"Ask yourself, what evidence has the prosecution shown you besides the videotape? None."

The videotape was used to get the jury to miss the fact that there was no concrete evidence that put a knife in Torey's hand. It was more than just an argument; it was the truth.

Bron told the jury that he could understand why they would be, "madder than heck" at Torey after watching the video, but the video did not equate to the State meeting its burden of "beyond a reasonable doubt."

"And," Bron said, "anger does not excuse sending someone to prison (for the rest of their life)."

Bron told the jurors that Torey's words on the videotape were the words of a "stupid, simple-minded kid, who was led along by the person who committed this crime--who had been convicted of this crime-- and who said on the videotape, 'I killed Cassie. I stabbed her in the throat. I saw her lifeless body just disappear.'

When Bron finished presenting the evidence, he assured the jurors that he believed they had doubts. "I think you've questioned if this defendant did anything," Bron said. "That's reasonable doubt."

But to make certain that the jury understood the definition of reasonable doubt, Bron explained it to them. "The prosecution must leave you saying to an abiding conviction, to a moral certainty, that not only did Torey say stupid stuff, but that he stuck a knife in Cassie Stoddart. That he did it. That it wasn't just possible, that it wasn't even just likely, but that you are morally certain, you have to be able to say, yes, I can say to a moral certainty, that the charges are true."

Bron shook his head, "They cannot prove that, ladies and gentleman. They have not, and they cannot. And the reason why they have not and cannot is because this defendant," Bron held his arm out to Torey, "did not do what he has been accused of. He did not do it."

Bron asked the jurors to remember the words of Lieutenant Toni Vollmer, the detective in charge of the investigation. She sat on the stand and testified that, "Words don't prove a murder. Evidence is what a person has to look at."

With a final word of thanks, Bron resumed his seat next to Torey, who had just heard the last words spoken in his defense.

In a trial, the prosecution is given the last word. Vic Pearson gave the State's closing argument, but Mark Hiedeman had the final say. He began by attacking Bron's definition of reasonable doubt.

"Reasonable doubt is a standard that we, as prosecutors live with," Mark Hiedeman said. "Not only in Pocatello, but throughout our nation. This is America. It is the way the criminal justice system works. Every defendant in this country has the right to go to trial--has a right to be proven guilty beyond a reasonable doubt."

One of the juror instructions stated that there are two types of evidence, direct and circumstantial, and that both should be given the same weight. Mark Hiedeman explained the significance of that instruction to the jury. "If you look outside and see it snowing--that is direct evidence that it is snowing. But if you go to bed, and it snows throughout the night, and when you wake up in the morning, and there is snow on the ground, and you say it snowed, that is circumstantial evidence."

Mark Hiedeman told the jurors that they had the circumstantial evidence they needed to prove reasonable doubt. He asked them to think, as they went into deliberations, about Torey's behavior in the days and hours following Cassie's murder. That behavior, he told them, was the sign of guilt they were looking for.

"One of the signs is they buried the videotape," Mark Hiedeman said. "And Torey lied to the police during two separate interrogations. If Torey was innocent and scared of Brian as his defense attorneys claimed, why didn't he tell the officers the truth during those interrogations and seek their protection?"

That is one of the problems with Torey's defense. Those kinds of questions were never answered. And now it was left in the hands of the jury, who like Mr. Hiedeman, did not understand.

Torey *was* scared of Brian, but he was also scared of going to prison with Brian. It was a justifiable fear. Torey felt trapped, framed. He did not kill Cassie, but he knew that he was on the videotape. How could he explain to anyone, let alone a detective, that the tape was meaningless until Cassie was killed? That he never suspected Brian was going to hurt anyone until he did.

Torey simply did not know how to do that, and because he didn't, the questions kept coming.

Mark Hiedeman refused to admit that Torey was not in control of the video, and that he did not know what Brian's intentions were. He asserted that the video must have been the movie Torey and Brian were planning all along. "But it's not really a movie, because they didn't film the ultimate act. In most slasher films, it's building up to the ultimate act."

But Brian's video was not a movie. And Mark Hiedeman was the only one who ever said that it was.

Mark Hiedeman told the jurors that the video we submitted of Torey's homemade movies showed a disturbed young man. "The video that the defense presented is frightening," he said. "What they are trying to get you to believe is that, even as a young boy, Torey aspired to acting. But does that videotape show an aspiring actor or director? Or does it show a troubled young man who is obsessed with violence and the making of a murderer?"

Mark Hiedeman could read anything he wanted into the DVD we presented. But there were twelve other children in it besides Torey, and none of them have ever been in trouble with the law, or shown signs of disturbance.

Mark Hiedeman claimed that, contrary to our claim that Torey was merely following Brian; he was actually the smart one. Torey distanced himself from the crime, refusing to say anything incriminating on the videotape, and cleaning his DNA off the evidence, whereas Brian stupidly laid out his whole crime and bragged about it.

Mark Hiedeman said that Torey was always planning his defense. Even when he lay in bed crying after the detectives left our house on Sunday night, Torey was merely acting a role, knowing that, "He and Brian had murdered Cassie two nights before."

"Torey is smart," Mark Hiedeman said, "he thinks."

In closing, Mark Hiedeman used the words of his Deputy Prosecutor, Vic Pearson. "In our system, in our society, murder is wrong. It's ethically wrong, it's morally wrong, and it's against the law. Torey Adamcik may have been smart, and he was. He did a lot of things to cover up this crime and to try and prevent the police from finding out that it was he that did it. But he was not smart enough to remember one simple phrase. 'Thou shalt not kill.' A guilty verdict on both these counts for Torey Adamcik will tell him that, thou shalt not kill."

And with those final words the trial was over.

It was 11:30 a.m. June 8, 2007. The jury left the courtroom and entered the small room behind them to deliberate.

Hope is one of the strongest emotions people hold onto. It is certainly difficult to let go of. I cannot explain how we felt as we left the courtroom, but it may have been something like a parent would feel if their child were in a coma. Unwilling to surrender and give up, we'd wait forever with all the hope in the world and pray for a miracle.

Barbara worried about the timing. She told the attorneys she did not want the jury to get the case on the weekend, and now here it was--early Friday afternoon. The jury would be anxious to go home. They would not spend the time they needed to go over every detail. She fully expected a verdict within hours.

Torey had great faith in his attorneys. He believed he was coming home. He went back to his cell, threw away the small amount of food he'd saved from the commissary, and packed.

Lacey also believed that Torey was coming home. She had been to the trial every day and she'd heard the physical evidence. She thought it meant something. Lacey carefully dressed so that she would be ready when we were called to the courthouse and the verdict read. Her friend Shaina came to our house and waited with her.

As we left the courthouse that morning, Aaron was out in the hall with the rest of the attorneys. He told me that though he was tired, he'd thoroughly enjoyed the experience. And he looked as if he had. My mouth could have hit the floor. I knew he spoke without thinking, spoke in the emotion of the moment, but it was a comment hard to forget.

A few hours later, Aaron wasn't feeling so well. After only eight hours of deliberation the jury returned with a verdict. We were called to the courthouse. Bron met us in the hall when we arrived and directed us to our seats. Lacey sat on one side of me, Sean on the other. As they had been throughout the entire trial, our family was with us.

The jury entered the courtroom from the narrow deliberation chamber located next to the judge's desk. I was watching them so intently I did not even notice Torey come in, until he was already seated in front of us, only the back of his head visible. Bron looked back at us from the defense desk and nodded, indicating with a finger to his lips that we were to be silent.

Judge McDermott opened the proceedings by announcing the time. It was 7:15 p.m. He addressed seat three: "It is my understanding sir, that you are the foreperson?"

Seat three, a man named Rob Steinke, replied that he was.

"Okay. Has the jury reached a verdict?"

Mr. Steinke said, "Yes, they have."

"Have you signed the verdict as the presiding juror?"

"Yes, I have."

"And have you reached a verdict on Count I and Count II?"

"Yes, we have."

"All right. Is there anyone on the jury who disagrees with the verdict your foreperson, Mr. Steinke, has signed?"

There was a moment of silence.

"All of those who agree with the verdict, please raise your hand," the judge instructed the jurors.

"All right. Thank you. The record shows twelve hands raised."

Judge McDermott asked Mr. Steinke, "Would you like to read the verdict, sir, or would you like us to do it?"

Mr. Steinke declined the offer.

"Okay," Judge McDermott said. "Ladies and gentleman, let's don't have--I know this is emotional, but let's try and not have any expressions of--you know, this is a court of law. And so please try to keep your emotions under control, okay?"

My entire body was shaking like a freight train. Sean put his hand on my shoulder and my legs jumped. I felt like I was going to fly into pieces.

"In the District Court of the Sixth Judicial District, State of Idaho, in and for the County of Bannock.

"State of Idaho, plaintiff, versus Torey Michael Adamcik, defendant. Verdict form.

"We the jury, duly empanelled, and sworn to try the above entitled action for our verdict unanimously answer the questions submitted to us as follows: One, Count I, question one, is Torey

Michael Adamcik guilty or not guilty of murder in the First degree?

"Jury has answered--guilty."

I do not know if I heard question number two or not. There was a picture in the Idaho State Journal the next day, which showed Lacey crying hysterically, me slumped headfirst into Sean's lap, and Sean looking devastated.

I may have blacked out, because unlike everything moving in slow motion, I really have no memory of anything at all. The transcript shows that Judge McDermott continued reading.

"Question number two, is Torey Michael Adamcik guilty or not guilty of Conspiracy to Commit Murder in the First Degree? Jury has answered: Guilty."

Bron asked that the jury be polled, and one juror after another answered that--*yes*, this was their verdict.

But I cannot remember any of that. All I remember is a loud rushing sound in my ears that gradually turned into the wailing of my daughter sitting next to me. A loud rushing and wailing next to me, but far away. Lacey seemed to fly from her seat and run, and I followed her as fast as I could down a hall, down the stairs and outside, but she was too far ahead and I could not catch her. When I got outside, she was gone and I realized I had missed Torey as he was taken away.

Somehow that is what I remember, but I understand that is not what happened. After the verdict was read--Sean and Lacey, Mom and I, were led down the stairs, all of us leaning on the support of family members who held us up and shepherded us on.

But no matter. Lacey was gone. I was alone, and there was only darkness. I did not see Torey.

Upon leaving the courtroom, Mark Hiedeman released a press statement: "We've convicted them both. I am glad the family has at least this much closure," he said.

And the Stoddart family was happy. The news showed them in the hall outside the courtroom celebrating their victory.

Bron was also asked for a statement. "It's a tragic thing when we have the loss of such a young person," he said. "There are no winners in this." He offered his prayers to the families involved.

There are no words to describe the days and weeks following the guilty verdict. We had already lived through hell; had our lives stripped, shaken and destroyed once. And we'd still not recovered. To me it was like the second wave of a deadly attack. To Torey it was far worse.

Sean and I were driven home by family, escorted up the stairs, and sat down in our living room in a state of shock. In the back of my mind, behind the denial and disbelief, was a small voice whispering, "*Torey, Torey,*" over and over again. Our family was with us, either just sitting or speaking words of comfort that I do not remember. In waves the voice in my head grew louder and louder until it was fairly shouting, and I stood and shouted, "*Torey*!" I had to get to Torey.

Someone put their hand on my arm, but I had to get to my son. I told Sean to call the jail and tell them we were coming. No one thought they would let us in, but they did. Gathering Lacey and Jamie--Sean and I left. We left the rest of our family in our house and drove directly to the jail, Sean in the driver's seat, our children behind us, stilled and silent. We were going to see Torey.

We entered the jail alone. There was no one else in the usually crowded visiting room. A guard met us in the corridor and unlocked the door behind which we'd spent the last nine months visiting our son. We watched as Torey was dragged down the hall toward us. *He was dead!* I saw Torey and that is the first thought that flashed through my mind. They were dragging Torey's limp body down the hall where they sat him in his seat across from us.

Sean grabbed for the phone, and one of the guards picked the phone up on Torey's end and tried to hand it to him, but it fell to the table where it stayed. The guards left and Torey sat slumped, limp and dead-like on the other side of the glass, unresponsive to our cries.

I told Torey we would follow him anywhere. Anywhere. He was not going to be left alone, and Jamie and Lacey told Torey they were going with him too. But he did not hear us. We were sound proof behind our glass partition, and Torey could not have heard us anyway from where he was, in the depths of his shattered soul.

It was awful. Something I will never forget as long as I live, my two children crying, begging for their brother to just reach out and pick up the phone, knocking on the glass, wailing for him. And Torey, lying unconscious and unaware, out of reach, all alone.

Like we were not even there, like he was already gone.

The next day our family returned to the house. This time we sat in the living room and no one spoke. There was nothing left to say. Pocatello police cars drove by the house every hour. My brother-in-law Chris noticed them. It was not hard. We lived on a quiet street; our large front window faced it. Someone asked why the police were patrolling, but I couldn't have cared less. My son was alone and we had to wait until Sunday to see him, and by then who knew what condition he would be in.

Finally when I could wait no longer, I called the jail and asked how Torey was doing. The person I talked with said that Torey was fine. He was not eating but so what, he would come out of it when he got hungry enough. I asked the heartless bitch if perhaps maybe she could tell me if Torey was drinking water; and she said if he wasn't, he was going to get awfully thirsty. She said, "A lot of these people act this way when they realize what's going to happen to them. But he won't let himself starve to death, so why don't you just stop worrying, and let me get back to work?"

CHAPTER THIRTY-SIX

Looking for Answers

The attorneys called and asked us to come to their office on Monday morning. Torey was found guilty, but this was not the end. The next phase would be sentencing. We needed to discuss it. Also there was the issue of *Dateline*. They had filmed the trial and a producer wanted to meet with us. That too had to be discussed.

Mom, mad as hell, wanted to know what had happened. If the attorneys thought we were meeting with them to discuss sentencing, or *Dateline* they were wrong. The first thing Mom said when she sat down was, "I want to know what went wrong."

Immediately a wall went up, the three attorneys on one side, we on the other. The attorneys felt they had done their job. We knew they hadn't.

Aaron looked pained and sat silent through the whole meeting. Greg, the grandfather figure negotiated the minefield. Bron left.

Greg told us, with infinite patience, that they proved Torey did not kill Cassie. He said he understood how we felt. We were angry, we needed to blame someone, but they were not the correct people to blame. They'd done their job. It wasn't their fault.

"How had you proven Torey did not kill Cassie!" I wanted to know. They did not call Dr. Corgiat, Torey's psychologist, to testify. They did not explain the videotape. They did not call Torey's character witnesses, *they did not let the jury see Torey and who he really was*.

We had been promised a defense. We had been told that the jury would see Brian Draper, his writings, his thoughts, his love of Columbine and adulation for Eric Harris and Dylan Klebold. His planned school shooting, and his *Black River* story.

Torey hadn't spent years talking about killing people. Torey never wrote about killing people. Torey was happy and well adjusted and not the disturbed and depressed individual that Brian Draper was. We had been promised that Torey and Brian's differences would be shown to the jury, and that the jury would be given all of the information they needed to be able to make a just decision.

We felt we were lied to, and that the attorneys had failed us. They'd failed with the murder charge, and we couldn't even see where they'd fought the conspiracy charge at all.

We wanted answers.

Greg said, "You're missing the big picture. We proved through DNA, *indisputable* testing, that Torey did not stab Cassie. We proved there was a defensive struggle between Cassie and her attacker. We proved there was a single blood trail through the house. We proved there was only one knife used. The physical evidence is there."

"The jury instruction is what got us," he said, referring to the instruction that read, "Engaged in Conduct."

"I want the jury polled," I said. "I want to know why they found Torey guilty of first degree *murder*." It was the first time I asked. I've asked about five hundred times since.

"We can talk about that," Greg said.

But what we ended up discussing was the money. We still owed, they did not want to bankrupt us. We were already ruined, but they wanted more. Of a bill of over three hundred and thirty thousand dollars, they accepted approximately two hundred and fifty. Maybe they felt their eighty thousand dollar write off would help make up for the loss of our son. It didn't.

During this meeting Greg assured us, "We're not abandoning you; we're not leaving Torey. You've got our word on that. We will see you through sentencing. The appeal process, as far as you want us to go."

And Aaron has. Aaron faithfully stood by us, and behind the scenes, I am sure that Greg has been there as well.

But Bron did abandon us. He was the only attorney in the firm who billed us for this meeting after the verdict. When we flat out told him we were out of money, we never heard from him again. Bron dropped us like a hot potato. But that was just fine. Aaron did a better job during sentencing without Bron, than he could have with him.

Aaron poured his heart and soul into fighting for Torey during his sentencing hearings, and I could sleep at night, knowing that we did everything we could. Unlike the trial, which left us with a lifetime of wondering what if…

CHAPTER THIRTY-SEVEN

Sentencing

In some states, the verdicts mandate the sentence, but Idaho is not one of them. Judge McDermott was not bound by law to sentence either Torey or Brian to a fixed prison term beyond fifteen years for the crimes of which they were convicted. The prosecutor, Mark Hiedeman, recommended life without parole for both Torey and Brian, but it was not his decision to make.

I always knew that Torey was going to prison. Torey did not stab Cassie, nor did he know that Brian was going to, but he helped Brian cover up afterwards. Truth be told, Torey was traumatized by the experience, as anyone would have been, but I knew the judge would never see it that way. There was going to be a price to pay. The question was: *what* exactly was that price going to be?

Judge McDermott scheduled both Torey and Brian for a sentencing hearing. Brian's would go first on August 22nd and Torey's would be the 23rd. The hearings were like a trial. There were different strategies to consider, but the main point was that we could submit evidence to show the judge why Torey deserved mercy--and the prosecutor could submit evidence to show why he did not. The judge was supposed to review all of the evidence, and then make a decision based on that evidence.

But there was actually a good chance that the judge had already made up his mind. Still, we held on to the small measure of hope that he hadn't, and considered our different options. Greg recommended that Torey apologize for the crime, basically admit guilt, and beg for mercy. His reasoning was that Torey's fate hung in Judge McDermott's hands, and that maintaining his innocence was not going to do anything except anger the judge.

Admitting guilt in exchange for a reduced sentence was better than a guaranteed life without parole. But Greg was the only attorney who felt that strategy might help. We'd finally been given the name of an experienced criminal attorney, Andy Parnes. We hired him to oversee the sentencing with Aaron. Andy and Aaron both held hope for the appeal, and did not want to see it jeopardized in a futile effort to appease the trial judge.

But Greg's suggestion was never an option anyway. If Sean and I had learned anything from the trial, it was that we hadn't done enough to prove Torey's innocence. This was going to be our last opportunity to do so and we weren't going to throw it away. We decided it was worth angering the judge to finish presenting the evidence that should have been presented at the trial, and hope for the best.

Aaron agreed with the decision. Together we attacked the sentencing hearing with the same hope we had at the trial. Torey was going to prison, but we were going to fight like hell to limit the time he spent there.

Before the sentencing hearing, Torey was asked to fill out a pre-sentence report. It was the first time he was asked, or more accurately required, by the court to give his version of the events that happened on the night that Cassie was killed. Judge McDermott opened the proceedings by reading from the report and asking Torey if what he had written was an accurate account. Torey replied affirmatively. That established, Aaron began to present his witnesses.

Aaron began by submitting previously unheard evidence regarding Brian Draper. He called Sergeant Gary Bush to the stand. In the weeks following Torey and Brian's arrests, detectives had questioned some of their friends and classmates in an effort to obtain more evidence against the two boys. Sergeant Bush was one of the officers who conducted the interviews.

Sergeant Bush was asked to testify about an interview he had conducted with one of Brian's friends. The student told the sergeant that Brian spoke frequently about hurting people, and that he had been doing so ever since the seventh grade. "He talks about shooting people two or three times a week," Bush read from his report.

During his cross-examination, Mark Hiedeman asked the officer to read portions of the report in which the student spoke about Torey. Bush said that the student had seen a knife collection he believed belonged to Torey in the trunk of the Torey's car. But they were not the knives found in Blackrock Canyon. They were three Gerber Pocketknives Torey had that his father had given to him.

Aaron then called Officer Ellen Meyers, a records custodian for the Pocatello Police Department, to testify. She read the police report Officer Kristen Oaks had filed after her investigation into the incident at Irving Middle School. It was the first time that it was publicly revealed that Brian had been investigated for the alleged planning of a school shooting.

During Brian's sentencing hearing Mark Hiedeman submitted

Black River and other inflammatory writings Brian Draper had authored into evidence, but he failed to present evidence of the alleged planning of a school shooting, perhaps because he was unaware of it. Next Aaron called Dr. Mark Corgiat, Torey's psychological expert. Judge McDermott ordered psychological evaluations performed on both Torey and Brian, supposedly so that he could use the information at sentencing. But apparently the judge was just crossing his T's. He did not consider a word Dr. Corgiat spoke during sentencing.

I wanted Dr. Corgiat to testify during Torey's trial. I thought what he had to say was important, and that a jury should hear it. But at least now it would be part of the court record.

During the sentencing hearing, Dr. Corgiat had to testify by phone. He'd just undergone back surgery in Utah and could not travel. Over a speakerphone, which everyone in the courtroom could hear, Dr Corgiat explained to the judge the tests he'd performed on Torey and the results.

Dr. Corgiat said that the average adolescent does not have a fully developed frontal lobe, the part of the brain determined to control compulsion, and that Torey was even further behind others of his age. That made him manipulable.

Dr. Corgiat testified that there was no evidence that would suggest Torey had a pathological personality. He stated that Torey had been "blindsided" by his association with Brian, and could not even explain or understand how he ended up in the situation in which he found himself. Dr Corgiat stated that Torey would be a very low risk to ever reoffend. In closing, he asked Judge McDermott to salvage Torey by giving him the time and environment that he needed to mature.

Next, Aaron called two of Torey's former teachers. Rusty Adamson and Catherine Murray. Rusty supported Torey from the beginning and looked forward to testifying on his behalf. She described Torey as naive and trusting; and she knew from her personal association with him that he was incapable of the act of which he was found guilty.

Catherine Murray was Torey's English teacher and Special-Ed counselor. She worked closely with Torey during his years at Pocatello High School. Mrs. Murray testified about the kind-hearted student that she knew Torey to be. She told the court that Torey had expressed an interest in directing film and Aaron submitted an I.E.P. she had written the year earlier, which documented that interest.

Aaron then called our family and friends. One person after another, who personally knew Torey, took the stand and described him. I knew from personal experience that there are no words strong enough when arguing for the life of a loved one, and it was very emotional for everyone who testified. As Aaron finished presenting one tearful interview after another, Mark Hiedeman let them go without cross-examination.

The only ones Mark Hiedeman cross-examined were Sean and I. The prosecutor asked Sean if he really believed his son was innocent and Sean replied, "I can sit up here all day and tell you why I *know* he's innocent." But the prosecutor released him.

I tried to convey to the judge what a sheltered life Torey had led. I prayed he would see the differences between Torey and Brian. Stabbing somebody, and running in fear, were two very different things. I prayed Judge McDermott would understand that, and attempt to salvage something from this tragedy.

When the character witnessing concluded, Aaron rested his case and Mark Hiedeman began his. The prosecutor called only one witness, Pocatello Police Detective John Walker, the same specialist in computer forensics that had cleaned and played the videotape.

Detective Walker analyzed the computers taken from our home on the night of Torey's arrest. He created a slide show presentation of images and documents that were located under Torey's user name. Of the thousands of pictures that existed he selected, not a random mix, but an inflammatory selection of DVD covers from primarily violent, or horror movies.

As the movie covers were shown to the courtroom via laptop one of the local news reporters behind us remarked that it looked like Hollywood was on trial.

Detective Walker then read the documents he'd selected from Torey's computer. When he finished, Aaron asked the detective if he would be surprised to learn that what he was reading were lyrics to Pink Floyd songs? The Detective said that he would not be surprised, (though he *looked* surprised) and admitted that he was unaware that that was what they were.

Last Detective Walker came to the pornographic photographs that had cost Torey his character witnesses during the trial. Mark Hiedeman told Judge McDermott that the photographs were sexually explicit, and recommended he view them out of sight of the courtroom and the press.

I was extremely thankful for that. I do not know if the

prosecutor made the recommendation out of consideration for us, or the law, or what, but I *was* grateful.

As Detective Walker carried the laptop he had been using for his presentation to the judge, Brian's family, who were seated behind us, whispered audibly, for us to hear, what they thought of Torey, and our family. That we were sick, and that Torey was perverted.

Judge McDermott took the laptop and placed it on the desk in front of him. Detective Walker, Mark Hiedeman, and Aaron stood behind the judge, and the four of them together huddled around the laptop and viewed the images while those of us in the courtroom waited.

Sean's sister Ann, a computer programmer, leaned over and asked Sean if the profiles on our computers were password protected. Sean said no. Aaron asked Detective Walker the same question as soon as the slide show concluded and they had returned to their previous positions.

Detective Walker answered, "No. None of the user profiles on any of the computers taken from the Adamcik home were password protected."

Aaron asked the detective how he could be certain that Torey was responsible for downloading the images they had just seen.

Detective Walker said that he could not be certain. He admitted that he really had no idea who downloaded them.

During his cross-examination of Detective Walker, Aaron submitted a document. He asked the detective to look at the document and tell us if he was familiar with it. He was--it was a copy of *Black River*, taken from Brian Draper's computer.

I knew this was necessary, but my immediate thoughts went to Brian's family behind us. I turned to look at Pam. I did not want to hurt her. I knew she was just trying to protect her son and I was sorry--for her, for us, and for everyone involved.

I whispered, "Sorry," and Pam's face broke into a rage. Kerry Draper, seeing what was happening, grabbed her arm and shushed her. I turned around in my seat and did not look back again.

When Detective Walker exited the stand, Mark Hiedeman announced that he had no further witnesses. He turned the time over to the victim's family and the next phase of sentencing--the victim impact statements.

Sentencing had lasted a day and a half, and we had spent every minute of it proclaiming Torey's innocence. Many people who knew Torey testified in his behalf, describing him in glowing detail.

And as Greg had warned--we angered the judge, and we angered the prosecutor, but unfortunately, and understandably, we angered Cassie's family as well. But there was nothing we could do about it. Torey did not stab Cassie, and we had to tell the truth.

Paul Cisneros, Cassie's grandfather, spoke in behalf of the victims first. "All your witness say how good Torey is," he said, glaring at Torey. "And he may have been, but something went wrong. You, Torey, made this choice, and now you and your family have to live with the decision."

Kristi Stoddart, Cassie's sister, directed her comments to both Torey and us. Looking at our family she said, "You all sat and denied his role in my sister's murder, but he was there." She turned to Torey. "You chose to leave Cassie dead in that house. You made the choice willingly. I don't feel there were three victims here. There was only one victim, my sister."

Kristi Stoddart said she believed Judge McDermott would see through our denial and added that she would not feel safe unless both Torey and Brian were locked up for life.

Cassie's mother, livid and shaking, incoherently told us what an outrage we were to the community and ordered us to get out.

Torey sat stoic, absorbing every word. We told him this was coming, but we forgot to tell him to close his ears. For months afterward, Torey repeated their words and the words of Mark Hiedeman verbatim, over and over again. He hated himself as much as they did.

Brian's sentencing hearing was held a day and a half before Torey's. His family took the stand and did their best to paint Brian as an affectionate, fun loving, practical joker. But the bulk of their argument for a reduced sentence did not lie in Brian's character. It lay in the fact that "Brian solved the case" for the detectives.

In a lengthy, tear filled testimony, Pam Draper described the day her son came down the stairs and told her that God had spoken to him in a newspaper article. His breakdown was proof to her that Brian would rather confess than live with the guilt.

Kerry Draper agreed. He said that Brian had been promised something for his cooperation. He did not mention what that something was, but he asked the judge to make good on the promise.

But a family's love for their son, and the glimmer of hope that he would be recognized for coming forward, was small grounds on which to beg for mercy. Cassie's family loved their daughter as well. And it was Brian who stole her from them.

But there was more evidence to consider. Like Torey, Brian had been psychologically examined. His attorneys retained two separate psychologists and, unfortunately for Brian, his family and his attorneys, the reports from both were damning.

First to testify was Dr. Alan Brantley, a North Carolina Forensic Psychologist who apparently worked with or for the FBI. He began by describing the methods profilers use to determine characteristics of known serial killers. Brian showed evidence of at least one of those characteristics, which was a stuttering or communication problem. But Dr. Brantley described another characteristic I found interesting. He said that many serial killers begin by killing animals.

During her testimony, Pam Draper described Brian's love of animals. Whenever a beloved pet died, she told us that Brian had to hold elaborate ceremonies for them. It sounded as if their backyard was a virtual pet cemetery, and I wondered if Brian was responsible for more than his parents knew.

Dr Brantley continued. He described Brian as a person with a low frustration tolerance that craved the acceptance of his peers. He said that Brian suffered with deep depression, which stemmed from the taunting he had endured throughout his childhood because of his stuttering problem. While many associate depression with lethargy and a desire to kill oneself, Dr. Brantley said it often manifests itself as irritability, anger and acting out against others.

During his cross-examination, Mark Hiedeman asked Dr. Brantley if he'd read a story written by Brian in junior high titled *Black River*. Brantley said he had read the story, which chronicled a fictitious school shooting. Brantley said he spoke with Brian about school shootings in general, as well as Brian's obsession with the Columbine massacre. Dr. Brantley stated that as far as he could tell, Brian had been fascinated with violence since at least the seventh grade.

Linda Hatzenbuehler, Dean of Health Professions at Idaho State University was then called to testify. She had performed a court-ordered evaluation of Brian in an effort to determine his future risk factors.

Dr. Hatzenbuehler testified that because Brian was a minor, it was difficult to locate an appropriate test to determine his likelihood to reoffend. The existing tests dealt with adults whose brains were fully developed. Because Brian's brain was *not* fully developed, she could not be certain that the tests she performed were conclusive.

After giving the disclaimer, Dr. Hatzenbuehler revealed her results. The best that she could ascertain was that Brian would be a medium to moderate risk to reoffend if he were medicated and supervised. She did not say what his risk factor would be if he were not.

Dr. Hatzenbuehler explained that the three main criteria she considered in determining Brian's future risk of violent behavior were: internal factors to Brian himself, his history of violence, and environmental conditions. She stated that Brian had no history of violence; either of inflicting violence or of violence happening to him, however he was hypersensitive to criticism and ridicule.

"While Brian Draper appeared to be a happy-go-lucky teen, he was actually a very deeply disturbed young man," Dr. Hatzenbuehler said, leaving the defense to rest on an extremely damaging note.

Now it was Mark Hiedeman's turn to present his evidence. He called Detective John Walker, who was also the only witness called against Torey in his sentencing hearing. Detective Walker had analyzed the computers taken from the Draper home as he had ours. He submitted over 130 slides of images and documents taken from Brian's personal computer, but he made it clear, they were a mere sampling of what was found.

While most of the material on Brian's computer was inflammatory, Detective Walker did say there were a limited number of images and documents that were innocuous.

Most of the images included in the detective's presentation related to the 1999 Columbine High School shooting. There were numerous stills taken from video cameras inside the school as the massacre was taking place. Many of the other violent images showed people pointing guns at their heads or at other people.

Violence was also a common theme throughout the eleven documents submitted in the presentation, with one exception, a writing titled "Why," in which Brian conveyed his anguish over the way animals are abused by people.

The bulk of the stories ranged from works of fiction about school shootings to Brian's angst about issues including his stuttering problem and the teasing he'd endured by classmates. "Why do I have sick, sadistic thoughts? Why am I obsessed with school shootings?" Brian wrote in one piece titled, "*My Hatred*."

Brian wrote that his stuttering problem was a roadblock to his happiness, and that if he did a school shooting, he would forever be remembered.

After Detective Walker's presentation concluded, Cassie's family members addressed Brian and the court. "No matter what the future holds for our family, there will always be an empty spot," Cassie's grandfather said.

Anna was vengeful. "You put our family through hell," she said, glaring at Brian, "and now you will know what hell is."

With the evidentiary phase of sentencing complete, it was now time to hear the verdict. Judge McDermott ordered Torey and Brian to the courtroom on the following day, Friday, August 25, 2007. For the first time since he severed their cases, Torey and Brian would appear in court together.

Except for select press, only immediate family members were allowed into the courtroom during the sentencing verdict. Everyone else was led to a large room where they watched the proceeding on a television monitor. Brian's parents, grandparents, and sister sat in front of Barbara, Sean, Lacey, Jamie, and I. Cassie's family sat across the aisle.

We were told to limit our responses. Bailiffs stood guard, ready to escort us from the courtroom as soon as the sentence was read. Brian and Torey were brought into the courtroom together and stood in front of the Judge. They were wearing dirty, disheveled prison garb, and were shackled at the waist and feet. Aaron stood next to Torey, and Dave Martinez next to Brian.

Both boys were asked for final words. Dave Martinez handed Brian a piece of paper and Brian turned and read a statement that he had prepared for Cassie's family. He apologized for not stopping the murder of their beautiful daughter, and said that because he was not worthy of their forgiveness he would not ask for it, though forgiveness was all that he desired.

Aaron held the paper for Torey that contained his final words. But trying to speak was impossible for Torey. His hands shook and he cried too hard to get the words out. Before he could contain himself his opportunity was over.

Aaron took the paper from Torey and made his final appeal in Torey's behalf. Aaron implored the judge to look at the facts.

"Your Honor," he said, "I shudder every time I think of June 7, 2007. On that date a jury found that Torey Adamcik engaged in conduct that led to the death of Cassie Stoddart. And as we were sitting here in the courtroom, those guilty verdicts might as well have been bullets to my soul. I was in that spare room right over there, (Aaron pointed) while I watched my client sob in sorrow, and I asked if I had done enough.

"I believe so much in our system of justice. I believe in most cases juries are 100 percent correct. They usually see through the smoke, and they usually reach the right conclusion. So I worried that I did not do enough personally to present Torey's version of the events.

"Your Honor, I have gotten to know this young man that's standing beside me today, Torey Adamcik, very well over the past year. The boy that I know is not the one that is characterized in the newspaper. The boy that I know is not the one that is characterized on the television. And I can tell you--he sure as hell is not the one that is on that homemade video.

"Your Honor, I know that a life has been taken. I also know that Torey has been found culpable of engaging in conduct that led to that death. The jury has heard the evidence and the jury has spoken. But, Your Honor, the Court can still consider the what-ifs. What if the DNA evidence was accurate? What if Mr. Draper acted alone? What if Mr. Draper walked into that room and stabbed Cassie to death? What if Torey was guilty of just being there? What if Torey was guilty of just covering it up? Although the jury has spoken, the only ones that know what truly happened are Cassie, Brian and Torey.

"Your Honor, how in the world do I know what to recommend for punishment? I am truly sorry that our community, our world, lost Cassie Stoddart. I just don't want to lose another teenager to this ignorance. I just don't want to lose another teenager because Torey couldn't see the big picture.

"Your Honor, kids cannot see the big picture. We have to ask the question: Do we throw away the key, or do we seek redemption? Justice requires more than punishment. Justice requires multiple considerations. We have the opportunity for redemption here. The community can heal. The relative families can heal. But we have to be better than these boys. We are the adults. We can see the consequences. And unlike them we can see the big picture. We just need to make sure that we keep our eye on it. We have the opportunity to overcome evil with good. Let's take it.

"Thank you, Your Honor."

Dave Martinez stood next to Brian and spoke for his client. He cried as he begged for Brian's life, a disturbed young man who had, after all, repented in his soul and come forward. The attorney seemed to be crying for Cassie, and Brian, and the senselessness of it all. He could see the train on the tracks moving faster and faster and he knew there was no way to stop it or to set it on a different course.

There was a different course. But it was never considered.

When Dave Martinez finished speaking, Mark Hiedeman stood and addressed the court.

"I've struggled with being able to determine throughout this entire ordeal who is more culpable," the prosecutor said. "But I do not think that it matters in the long run because both these defendants should and must be treated similarly in their sentences."

I don't know if anything we could have done would have made a difference. I believe Mark Hiedeman pursued Torey with the same determination he did Brian, because he was angry. He knew that Brian was the sole killer, but he did not like the way we defended our son. Had Torey appeared more remorseful, and taken more responsibility then he saw him take, he might have been more forgiving. But then again he might not--he might have used Torey's remorse and accountability against him.

The prosecutor made his case against Brian first. "Your Honor," he stated, "there can be no doubt left at this point in the proceedings that Brian Draper is a cold blooded killer. We need only to look at a few pieces of evidence to make that determination. When Brian is in the library at Pocatello High School he gleefully and smilingly apologized in advance to Cassie's family for her murder, which is to occur later that night. Brian Draper is not happy and smiling today.

"Immediately following the murder, his first words on the videotape were, 'I just killed Cassie. I stabbed her in the throat and I watched the life leave her body.' He is excited that he has finally succeeded in his first kill. These two items found on the tape convict Brian Draper of conspiracy to commit first-degree murder and first-degree murder. Unless," the prosecutor added sarcastically, "it was all a movie script and both of the defendants were acting the entire time."

Mark Hiedeman continued, "Both expert witnesses called by Brian Draper agree on a couple of things. One, that he is a deeply disturbed young man--two, that he has an obsession with violence and killing--and three, that if released back into society, he would pose a medium or moderate risk to commit future violent acts."

Mark Hiedeman admitted that Dr. Hatzenbuehler warned that there was no standardized test to gauge teenagers, but it was obvious the risk was there, and it was real.

Mark Hiedeman said, "We know from Brian Draper's writing and history that he was not the innocent All American boy he has been portrayed. Brian Draper referred to himself as evil and that even his parents did not know the side of him that was determined to kill others. Brian Draper was a time bomb and he was going to kill people one way or the other.

"Unfortunately, or perhaps fortunately, Cassie was his first victim. In a twisted way she gave her life to save others. If she had not been murdered, other people, and perhaps many other people, would have died at his hands.

"I know that Brian Draper is a deeply disturbed young man. I know there is no way to ascertain for certain what risk he poses in the future. I know that he wanted to be famous and he wanted to be a mass murderer. I know that the only way to protect society from this possibility is to see that he never again is a part of society. I implore you, Judge, to consider a sentence of Life Without Parole in the Idaho State Correctional Facility for Brian Draper. It is a harsh and unusual sentence recommendation for a 17-year-old boy, but Brian Draper is a harsh and unusual 17-year-old boy.

"He had no pity on Cassie Jo--he deserves none. He gave no quarter to Cassie Jo, and he deserves none. He showed no mercy on September 22, 2006, to Cassie Jo, and he deserves none."

The prosecutor then addressed my son: "Torey Adamcik says he didn't do it. He wants to be treated differently than Brian Draper because he didn't do it. His family says he didn't do it. His friends say he didn't do it, and others have said he could not possibly have done it because he is a sweet and innocent kid. His attorneys say he didn't do it. They said that the videotape was a mocumentary.

"The problem is that the jury said he did it. They said he did it because they heard the evidence, and they saw the videotape where the murders were planned. They saw the burned paper in the hole at Blackrock Canyon, which was written by Torey Adamcik earlier that day on camera at the Pocatello High School library.

"Why would Torey Adamcik make sure that that note was burned and buried? Because it was evidence of his murderous conduct.

"Torey Adamcik was the planner. While Brian Draper constantly and repeatedly spoke of murder on the tape, Torey Adamcik was at times quiet and at times encouraging those antisocial ravings. Torey Adamcik was making the hit list--writing down what equipment was needed for their nefarious plans. He was smart. He called himself smart on the videotape.

"Torey Adamcik tried to distance himself. He did not give money directly to Joe Lucero to buy the knives. He tried to distance himself. Torey Adamcik is devious. He says nothing to anyone to inculpate himself.

"And again, I would recommend to the Court that the Court consider a sentence of Life Without the Possibility of Parole for Torey Adamcik in the Idaho Department of Correctional Facility. It is a harsh and unusual sentence for a 17-year-old boy, but Torey Adamcik is a harsh and unusual 17-year-old boy."

Mark Hiedeman knowingly and intentionally lumped Torey with Brian, whom he knew to be the true and sole murderer. He had no physical evidence linking Torey to the stabbing; and he had proof after the evidentiary hearing that Brian was disturbed and dangerous while Torey was not. But the prosecutor refused to salvage anything from the tragic situation. He held relentlessly to his position and begged the judge to throw Torey's life away with Brian's. And in so doing, he, like Brian, was responsible for the destruction of a life.

We did not ask that Torey go free. A sentence of ten, fifteen, twenty years would have been enough to serve justice for what Torey had done. But Life Without Parole is a death sentence, and unjust for a child guilty of fearfully covering up a crime.

When sentencing Torey and Brian Judge McDermott also refused to acknowledge the different evidence that existed against each boy. He used the same evidence against Torey that he used against Brian. It was the same trick Mark Hiedeman used, when he used the same bloody shirt, knife and glove to convict two people instead of one.

Before handing down his sentence, Judge McDermott addressed Torey and Brian. He told Brian that he was an articulate young man who somehow went wrong. He said that Brian's two psychological experts had both indicated that he had an obsession with violent thoughts and wanting revenge against others. "You authored the *Black River* article. *Black River* ended with your thoughts of going to Pocatello High School and killing students that you didn't like, and you seemed pretty serious in that."

Judge McDermott told Brian that there was a positive correlation between people who make threats and then carry them out. He told Brian that he was really a very different individual than portrayed by friends and family, and that he should never be released into society again.

When addressing Torey, Judge McDermott said, "You have been found guilty of these crimes by a jury, and so your innocence isn't even an issue with me. You've been found guilty. You are guilty."

The judge then listed his reasons for justifying his sentence against Torey. He claimed that Torey had knowledge of *Black River*, and that he even helped coauthor it. (But this was not the case. *Black River* was on Brian's computer, in his bedroom. The only time Torey was inside Brian's house was on the night he picked Brian up to go to Cassie's. And *Black River* had been written long before Torey ever met Brian.)

Judge McDermott stated that Torey had an abnormal interest in horror movies and acting out death scenes as indicated in the videos that were shown to the jury. (That too was erroneous.)

And last, Judge McDermott quoted Linda Hatzenbuehler, Brian's witness, instead of Dr. Corgiat--Torey's. When Brian's attorney asked Dr. Hatzenbuehler what she thought of Torey Adamcik, she stated that she did not know Torey, and that she had never examined him, but she did say that he and Brian *appeared* on the videotape to be like-minded individuals.

Judge McDermott stated that past behavior is the best indicator of future behavior. And he said that he believed Torey was an entirely different individual than portrayed by his family and friends.

And with no DNA evidence to support him, and clear evidence of doubt in front of him, Judge McDermott linked Torey to Brian; blurred Torey's intentions with Brian's intention. He looked at both defendants and said, "You've both been found guilty by the Sixth District Court of conspiracy to commit murder in the first degree, and it's the judgment of the Court that you are guilty. You both methodically and intelligently planned to murder Cassie Stoddart.

"I'm convinced neither one of you thought this was a joke. You put your masks on--you took your real knives, and went back to the house with the definite intention of killing her, which you did.

You both wanted to be famous killers."

For the conspiracy charge, Judge McDermott sentenced each boy to thirty years fixed, plus an indeterminate life sentence.

For the murder charge he told them, "You both have been convicted of Murder in the First Degree. It's clear to the Court that Cassie was savagely stabbed many times. The horror, fright, and pain she encountered before death was surely immense. The killing was a barbarous, cold-blooded, and horrific act.

You both unequivocally changed the lives of the Stoddart family and your own families forever. If Cassie were able to speak today, I doubt she would forgive either one of you. You both have forfeited your right to live in a free society, and I'm convinced beyond a reasonable doubt that if either one of you were released, that you would kill again. I'm going to remand you both to the custody of the Bannock County Sheriff, to be delivered by him to the authorities at the Idaho State Correctional Institution where you will each serve a life sentence that is fixed and *without the possibility of parole*."

Judge McDermott rapped his gavel.

We were quickly ushered from the room. Brian's family was instructed to exit first, and they were in the hall when we came out. Brian stood in the open elevator, a guard on each side. His family was gathered in front of him. Brian's grandmother was sobbing so violently she was hardly able to stand. His sister yelled, "I love you Brian," and Brian answered in a strong, clear voice, "I love you too," before the doors of the elevator closed and he disappeared from view.

Brian was there, but where was Torey? I looked around, but I could not find him. We were herded down the stairs and out of the building. Friends and family were everywhere. There was a mass of people gathered on the sidewalk, sobbing. Lacey's friends met her and took her in their arms. While we were trying to gather ourselves together, an officer from the court came out to where we were standing, and called Sean and I, Lacey, Grandma and Jamie, back into the courtroom. They had Torey in the spare room behind the juror box, and they allowed us to see him together.

Torey was sitting in a chair alone at a table. We gathered around him and loved and touched and held him. I lied to Torey and myself. I pretended we knew this was coming and that it was just another step in the process. I told Torey to hang on to the appeal, which was where our hope always lay. He looked at all of us around him, dazed, but trying to be strong. I told Torey we would see him at the next available visit.

But the next day the newspaper reported that he was gone. Torey and Brian had been taken directly from the courthouse and placed in a van. Their guard, Deputy Fonsbeck, drove them to the Idaho State Correctional Institution in Boise, with the clothes on their backs--and nothing else.

CHAPTER THIRTY-EIGHT

Aftermath

With Torey's removal from the Bannock County jail, our life in Pocatello came to an end. It was where I was born, where our family lived, and where Sean and I had met and raised our children. But it was over, and we were more than ready to move on.

But we did not know where we were going. Torey could remain in Boise, or more likely be transferred to the smaller prison in northern Idaho where his small size and young age would not be so great a liability.

Ultimately, Torey was sent to Orofino Idaho, and placed in protective custody. Sean and I listed our house for sale and prepared to move. Sean found a job, paying just a bit less than he currently earned, in Lewiston Idaho, an isolated community surrounded by beautiful rivers and forest only an hour from Orofino, where we could visit Torey twice a week--and that was all that mattered.

Lacey stayed in Pocatello where she attends the university. When she graduates she will move closer. But Jamie came with us. He was a junior in high school. He left behind friends that he had known all of his life to be with his brother, whom he loves.

In the year it took us to sell our house and find a job, we were only able to visit Torey once a month. The trip to Orofino was nine and a half hours away; six of it on winding mountainous roads that lead, literally, to the middle of nowhere.

While Torey was in Orofino, and we were still in Pocatello, we prepared for the last hearing we would have in front of Judge McDermott. A Rule 35 hearing, asking for a reduction of the sentence. We asked that the Life Without Parole status be amended, and that someday in the distant future Torey be allowed the opportunity to see a parole board.

A national organization appalled over the United States practice of imposing life sentences on children contacted us and offered their support. With our permission they started a petition. We received letters from people from across the nation and as far away as Germany, Australia, and Italy, begging the judge to give Torey a chance at parole sometime in the future. Not a get out of jail free card, but a chance to earn redemption.

Aaron returned for the fight with the same determination he'd always shown. Again he presented evidence of Torey's character, and challenged the three criteria's Judge McDermott used to impose the sentence. But it was a losing battle, and when he lost, Aaron took it personally.

But even if Judge McDermott did sentence Torey to Life Without Parole, I refuse to believe that Torey could die in prison for his role in what happened to Cassie. It simply isn't justice and our justice system simply cannot allow it to happen. There is an appeal pending, and until that is exhausted, I refuse to give up hope.

On the day that Cassie, Torey, and Brian were supposed to graduate from high school I was alone in the house with Jamie. Sean had already moved to Lewiston for his new job, and the kids and I were still waiting in Pocatello for our house to sell.

It was a difficult day. The first great milestone missed. To make matters worse, Judge McDermott was giving the commencement speech for the graduating class. It was a slap in the face to anyone who cared about Torey (or Brian), but that didn't matter.

That morning I had to pray long and hard just to get out of bed. I couldn't go to work, and when there was a knock on the door later that afternoon--and our bishop stood on the step, I thought he was the answer to my prayers.

But instead of coming to comfort us, he was there to tell me that the LDS church was excommunicating Torey. I was so hurt and confused. There was no doubt in my mind that we were making it through each day on the power of God's love. It did not make sense that He was turning from us now.

I was devastated. Jamie, my son, drove me to Calvary Chapel, where I asked to meet with a member of the clergy. The clergyman assured me that he had no idea why Torey was being excommunicated by the LDS church now, just because a verdict had been rendered.

I eventually wrote a letter to the Prophet of the LDS church, begging him to reconsider. I explained that God was giving us the will to go on, and how dependent Torey was in his belief in God's love. I talked about wrongful convictions, and other lost souls in prison. Of David and Joseph from the Bible. I received a visit from our local Stake President in response. The excommunication stood, but there was a road to return: Admittance of guilt, and repentance.

For months I did not know what to do. But eventually I gained an understanding. People are not perfect, but God is, and he loves His children. I know that my love for my children is just a mere mirror of His love for them as well. And now, whenever hurtful words are spoken--I find great comfort in knowing that.

Sometimes things happen in life that teach us a powerful lesson, that no matter how understanding we think we are, or how much empathy we believe we have, we simply cannot feel what we have not experienced. We can have an idea--but that idea is more like a glimpse, it's a view from an outside window. You have to open the door and go inside to know what is really happening.

I cannot truthfully say that I know how Cassie's family feels. I've never lost a daughter. But I think that I can truthfully say that we are both in a world of pain. That this has changed all of our lives forever. And as one day slips into the next and one year passes into another…it is still there. The pain. It never goes away.

I pray for Cassie and her family every day. And I pray for Torey and my other two children.

At the prison where my son is kept, there is a mother and father who visit their son. He killed his three children, their three grandchildren.

And I know, I know…some people have it worse.

I used to spend hours, literally every waking moment, trying to figure out how this happened. Did Brian plan the whole event, or simply get carried away in the moment? Both are literally possible.

I thought the answer would tell me how I'm supposed to feel about Brian, because honestly, my heartbreak is so great, so consuming, that I have not yet been able to get past that to really examine how I feel about Brian. Perhaps I never will. It is not him I think about anymore.

It is Cassie that stays with me. I think about her every day. And of course, Torey.

I am thankful for my children. Lacey is developing into a strong and caring woman, and Jamie has graduated from high school and is now attending college. I was determined to get them through this intact, and so far, with God's help, I feel that I've succeeded.

As for Torey, he is still with us. I visit him twice a week, every Friday by myself, and Sundays with Sean and Jamie. It is not easy to visit a son in prison, and saying goodbye never stops hurting.

For the most part, Torey is still the same sweet boy that left home four years ago. He loves movies and keeps up with the current releases through magazines and television. I wish everyone reading this could meet him.

As for his future--I strive to remain hopeful. We are in the appellate process. In September of 2010, we attended our first appellate hearing, held in front of the Idaho Supreme Court. Torey's attorney argued that the physical evidence not only failed to prove that Torey killed Cassie, but it failed to prove that he even stabbed her at all. In an ideal world, that would matter; and hopefully it does. We are still waiting to hear.

If we were successful in that hearing, Torey could be granted a new trial, or a reduced sentence. If we were not…we move up the judicial chain. The Ninth Circuit Court of Appeals…

But, there is another avenue of hope. If there are enough people who care about Torey, and are willing to advocate in his behalf, I believe that the legal system will step in and right this wrong. Torey's appellate attorney is working hard to do that, but letters of support help a great deal in cases like this. There are public institutions that advocate for human rights, but it is the public who makes a real difference.

The trial is over and as they say, "life goes on." Yes, life does go on, and you endure, but it does not necessarily get any easier. The problem is, living with this is very difficult. It honestly affects our family every hour of every day. I am constantly on a roller coaster ride of emotions. No matter how hard I try to remain positive, I cannot escape the true, raw, and horrible reality of seeing my son in prison. Our only daughter lives 500 miles away from us, and deep down, Sean and I cannot escape the fear that we have chosen one child over the others, and we wonder if we will ever be able to live next to our grandchildren (when we have them) because of the remote location we have been forced to move to.

This is a life we never could have imagined. Our fairly tale ended and we are left with nothing but the memories.

Now we fight a day-to-day struggle against despair.

But there is still hope…

How You Can Help Torey

If you would like to help Torey you can donate directly to him or to his legal defense at:

goo.gl/cv5tp

You can write letters of support that will be forwarded to him or send a **text** or a voicemail to: **(347) 559-5907**

toreyadamcik@gmail.com

You can advocate against juvenile life without parole to give deserving youth like Torey a chance to at least see a parole board someday.
Search: Torey Adamcik or Visit the website at:

goo.gl/xt23K

Printed in Great Britain
by Amazon